Courts, Liberalism, and Rights

In the series

*Queer Politics, Queer Theories*

*edited by* Craig A. Rimmerman

Gary L. Lehring, *Officially Gay: The Political Construction of Sexuality by the U.S. Military*

Craig A. Rimmerman, *From Identity to Politics: The Lesbian and Gay Movements in the United States*

Shane Phelan, *Sexual Strangers: Gays, Lesbians, and Dilemmas of Citizenship*

Gerald Hunt, ed., *Laboring for Rights: Unions and Sexual Diversity Across Nations*

Valerie Lehr, *Queer Family Values: Debunking the Myth of the Nuclear Family*

Carl F. Stychin, *A Nation by Rights: National Cultures, Sexual Identity Politics, and the Discourse of Rights*

# Courts, Liberalism, and Rights

*Gay Law and Politics in the United States and Canada*

JASON PIERCESON

TEMPLE UNIVERSITY PRESS
Philadelphia

*To my mother, Sandy*

**Temple University Press**
1601 North Broad Street
Philadelphia PA 19122
*www.temple.edu/tempress*

⊗ The paper used in this publication meets the requirements of the American National Standard for Information Sciences—Permanence of Paper for Printed Library Materials, ANSI Z39.48-1992

Library of Congress Cataloging-in-Publication Data

Pierceson, Jason, 1972–
    Courts, liberalism, and rights : gay law and politics in the United States and Canada / Jason Pierceson.
        p.   cm. — (Queer politics, queer theories)
    Includes bibliographical references and index.
        ISBN 1-59213-400-9 (cloth : alk. paper) — ISBN 1-59213-401-7 (pbk. : alk. paper)
        1. Homosexuality—Law and legislation—United States.
    2. Gay rights—United States.    3. Homosexuality—Law and legislation—Canada.    4. Gay rights—Canada.    5. Courts.    6. Liberalism.    I. Title.
    II. Series.

    KF4754.5.P54 2005
    342.7108′7—dc22

                                                            2005040046

2  4  6  8  9  7  5  3  1

# Contents

Acknowledgments                                                                    vii

1  Introduction                                                                      1

2  U.S. Federal Courts and Gay Rights: A History of Hesitancy         21

3  Liberalism and Gay Politics: Rights and Their Critics                  33

4  Toward a Better Liberalism                                                    49

5  Sodomy Laws, Courts, and Liberalism                                     62

6  Lessons from Continued Sodomy Adjudication                          77

7  Courts and Same-Sex Marriage in the United States:
   Hawaii and Alaska                                                              104

8  Courts and Same-Sex Marriage in the United States: Vermont    130

9  Developments after Vermont: An Evolving Jurisprudence
   and Its Backlash                                                               144

10 Canada: Rethinking Courts, Rights, and Liberalism                  165

11 Courts, Social Change, and the Power of Legal Liberalism        187

12 Conclusion                                                                       195

   Notes                                                                            199

   Index                                                                            247

# Acknowledgments

THIS BOOK IS the result of several years of support and assistance from numerous sources. Many people deserve thanks. At Brandeis University, Jeffrey Abramson trusted me and provided much-appreciated freedom but also invaluable feedback at critical times. Steven Teles provided a tremendous amount of formal and informal support, suggesting crucial new literature and often providing a needed critical perspective. Elizabeth Bussiere, in addition to being a kind and supportive colleague while I taught at University of Massachusetts–Boston, provided remarkably detailed and substantive feedback as an outside reader. Her assistance was crucial in turning the manuscript into a book. I am also grateful to Craig Rimmerman who took a strong interest in this project and to the Temple University Press reviewers who provided important and insightful comments that strengthened this book. Thank you as well to those who reviewed various chapters of the book that I presented at conferences, including Keith Bybee, Caren Dubnoff, Frederick Lewis, and Ronen Shamir. I also had useful discussions about the book with Ellen Andersen and Anna-Maria Marshall.

There were others who were crucial to the success of this project. Shep Melnick's seminar on courts at Boston College first sparked an interest to explore the questions in this book. His questions and feedback on a seminar paper led to the compilation of the manuscript for this book. At Brandeis, Sidney Milkis deserves credit for the focus in this book on new institutionalist approaches, and Mark Hulliung did much to shape my views on liberalism. I am particularly indebted to him for introducing me to the work of J. David Greenstone. Richard and Linda Hayes deserve much credit for encouraging me to place U.S. politics in a comparative context. Research for this book was facilitated by financial support from the Politics Department and Graduate School of Arts and Sciences at Brandeis. Thanks also to the Faculty Development Program at St. Norbert College and the Faculty Publication Fund. Finally, thank you to my partner, Dylan White, for supporting me and dealing kindly with me as I prepared this book and to my family and friends for their support and encouragement, especially Jason Phillip and Eiren Caffall for crucial editing.

JASON PIERCESON is Assistant Professor of Political and Legal Studies at the University of Illinois at Springfield.

# 1  Introduction

IN INCREASING NUMBERS of nations, courts are significantly involved in the making of public policy. Particularly given the rise in the status of rights in modern liberal discourse, courts have been able to apply legal reasoning and decision making to areas of public policy that have traditionally been the province of more "political" branches of government. Judicial review, while largely originating in the United States, has spread to other liberal democracies in recent decades. In fact, while the U.S. federal courts have withdrawn from a period of rights-based activism and have been applauded by scholars of both the political left and right, high courts in other countries have picked up where the American courts have left off, often surpassing the Americans in their level of aggressive judicial policy making.

This phenomenon can be clearly seen with the issue of the legal status of sexual minorities. Many of the most groundbreaking and aggressive decisions concerning gays and lesbians have come from courts outside the United States. In the case of *M. v. H.* the Canadian Supreme Court held that a statute defining a spouse as only a member of the opposite sex was impermissible under Section 15(1) of the Canadian Charter of Rights and Freedoms.[1] This resulted in direct policy changes. The federal and provincial governments have amended scores of statutes to include same-sex couples where benefits are given for common law marriages, which include many of the same rights given for solemnized marriages, and two provinces, Quebec and Nova Scotia, have adopted Vermont-style civil union laws.[2] Building on *M. v. H.*, courts in several provinces and one territory have recognized same-sex marriages, and the federal government is poised to extend this policy to the entire nation.[3]

It is difficult to envision the U.S. Supreme Court handing down such a ruling. As recently as 1986, the Court ruled in *Bowers v. Hardwick* that there is no right to privacy for same-sex sex acts in the Constitution.[4] Although some activists and commentators see the decision in *Lawrence v. Texas*, which overturned *Bowers*, as a step in the direction of court recognition of same-sex marriage, this appears unlikely in the short term. U.S. federal courts have been generally unresponsive to aggressive gay rights adjudication. In fact, state courts, rather than federal courts, have handed down the bulk of decisions favorable to lesbians and gay men. In the past decade, the high courts of several states have struck down sodomy laws, and three state supreme courts and several lower state courts have ruled that prohibition of the recognition of same-sex relationships is unconstitutional. Both developments will be examined in later chapters.

Ultimately, this book attempts to address the following questions: What accounts for the differences in the approaches of national courts systems in the

United States and Canada concerning gay rights? What do these differences tell us about the future of judicial policy making in this arena? This book argues that the greatest opportunity for aggressive judicial policy making in the realm of gay rights exists when a judiciary with activist potential meets a political culture that accepts a form of liberalism that conceives of rights broadly—not simply as a negative set of rights to be held against the state, but as a set of rights that recognizes the inherent dignity and worth of every individual. Indeed, the future success of the gay rights movement appears to be centered largely in the courts in these two nations. Courts, often relying on legal norms and arguments that emphasize the dignity of every individual and a more positive view of rights, can push states beyond where they might otherwise go on the subject of gay rights.

## COURTS AS POLICYMAKERS

Courts possess a unique capacity to make policy decisions, particularly when policy questions are framed in terms of individual rights. Abram Chayes has argued that the unique position of judges, insulated from political pressure, provides them with a certain distance from the normal political process. Judges, unlike legislators, do not need to take multiple interests and values into account. They make their decisions on the basis of the adversarial legal process—a process that limits the parties to two and often narrows the questions involved. Norms that dictate judicial behavior also play a crucial role in judicial policy making. Chayes argues that judges are "governed by a professional ideal of reflective and dispassionate analysis" of the questions before them.[5] Judges are generally concerned with what is the "right" decision, not simply the one that is politically expedient. A respect for precedent and tradition is important, but also as important is the novel argument. Lawyers are trained to win an argument by being innovative and creative. Particularly in the United States and even more so in Canada, law is not simply about narrow procedural questions but often concerns itself with large questions of substantive justice.[6] Legal education contributes to this substantive concern by not simply teaching what the law is or has been, but also, according to Patrick Atiyah and Robert Sommers, "how to construct, analyse, compare, evaluate, and criticize arguments and decisions . . . and to 'project' lines of judicial decisions and legislation. . . . Law is not seen as a body of authoritative doctrine, so much as an 'instrument of political, economic and social policy.'"[7] Tocqueville's declaration that, in America, all political questions become legal questions continues to hold immense validity and is increasingly becoming true in other national contexts. The nature of the legal process and legal reasoning, combined with the American, and increasingly global, emphasis on individual rights, has led courts in many states, as well as supranational courts, to become an immensely powerful force in public policy making.[8] Indeed, Charles Epp has described this as a "rights revolution." And Ran Hirschl has noted the rise of "jurisdocracy."[9]

Courts, of course, are not the only source of new rights. As R. Shep Melnick has argued, the U.S. Congress has created new statutory rights in a wide variety of policy areas. This development, however, was the legacy of mid-twentieth-century federal court activism. Melnick argues that the success of the civil rights movement emboldened federal judges to increase their role in policy making and encouraged interest groups to pursue rights-based strategies in the courts. Congress also got into the game with rights-based legislation. Melnick describes this as an explosion of rights consciousness, stemming from the fact that "[t]he call for equality and justice is not easily confined."[10]

Melnick notes that the use of the language of rights is a winning political strategy for legislators in a polity, like the United States, where rights rhetoric is prominent.[11] The difficulty for gay rights claims in the United States is, however, that not all rights claims fit with a polity's dominant political tradition. Melnick notes this as well when he argues that the use of rights in welfare programs varies, given the nature of the program. In particular, "the political appeal of rights is substantially weaker in means-tested programs, where questions of fault, responsibility, and incentives remain at center stage."[12] In other words, not all rights are created equally in a polity. The negative take on rights in the United States poses a similar challenge to gay rights claimants as does the claim of the poor for guaranteed welfare benefits. The poor ran up against the "work ethic" limit to rights, while sexual minorities have a difficult time convincing the American polity to view their relationships with equal dignity and respect.

Nor does liberalism in the hands of the judiciary always result in more progressive change than that driven by political liberalism. As Elizabeth Bussiere argues, New Deal political liberalism was a much more potent force for the poor than the conservative legal liberalism of the federal judiciary.[13] This book suggests the opposite when it comes to gay rights, but the real distinction may not be the branch of government involved but the version of liberalism behind reform efforts.

This expansion of the concept of rights has coincided with the "rights revolution," most notably in the United States. Since the New Deal, an increasing number of public policy questions have been framed in terms of rights. Many scholars, like Mary Ann Glendon, bemoan this obsession with "rights talk," or, like Stuart Scheingold, point to the "myth of rights."[14] However, the legal realism and positivism that began as a reaction to the legal absolutism of the Supreme Court at the turn of the century and sustained legal theory through the New Deal and well after began to fall out of favor by the 1970s with some academic lawyers and prominent political theorists who called for more of a rights-based politics. Legal realism and positivism had no use for rights. They simply got in the way of sound public policy. Legal realists subscribed to Bentham's view of rights as "nonsense on stilts." To the extent that rights were at all useful, they were legislatively, not judicially, defined. Realist scholars turned their attention away from a discussion of rights to the role that judges played as policymakers, and the main assumption of the school of thought was that judges and their reasoning are fairly inconsequential as an independent force.[15] In this political jurisprudence model, judicially defined rights divorced from the political process were of little concern—the judiciary was merely responding to domestic political pressure and seconding the sentiments of the political arena, not carving out a separate policy realm.

However, as David A. J. Richards explains, this view of rights gave way to their current more prominent and richer manifestation. According to Richards, "Rawls's book [*A Theory of Justice*] initiated a paradigm shift in political theory, replacing the long dominant utilitarian theory (with its skepticism, at least in its Benthamite foundation, about rights) with a rights-based or rights-sensitive political theory."[16] Courts are the natural beneficiaries of this rights revolution. As mentioned previously, the nature of the process of adjudication facilitates a focus on rights. The parties in a case are narrowly defined. Additionally, the process does not necessarily concern itself with questions of widely distributed costs and benefits, so a strong sense of individual entitlement is not unreasonable.

## COURTS, POLICY MAKING, AND SOCIAL CHANGE

This book challenges the assertions of scholars regarding the ineffectiveness of courts in achieving significant political or social change. As noted above, Scheingold cautions lawyers and scholars of legal and political change not to put too much faith in the transformative power of rights alone. He argued in his influential work, *The Politics of Rights*, that rights were limited and potentially backlash-inducing resources for progressive activists, especially when litigation strategies were the primary thrust of a movement. This stems from the fact that judges are highly constrained by majoritarian politics; therefore, judicial innovation will be "small and erratic."[17] Even though rights have tremendous rhetorical cache in U.S. politics, according to Scheingold, they, in reality, do little to shift the political status quo: "Rights are declared as absolutes [by courts], but they ripple out into the real world in exceedingly conditional fashion."[18]

Scheingold does not assert that rights have no utility. They can be a source of mobilization by planting seeds for political, not legal, action. The problem, as Scheingold sees it, is that lawyers are bad at mobilizing, since they never, as a result of their training, place much faith in routine politics. Ultimately, he argues, "Power cannot be purged from politics by a legalization of the political process."[19]

Gerald Rosenberg, in his book *The Hollow Hope*, builds on Scheingold's work and that of the political jurisprudence approach in arguing that courts merely react to politics; they do not transform it. Consequently, according to Rosenberg, activists who fail to understand this waste time on litigation strategies. Instead, their efforts should be focused on the political arena.[20] Rosenberg illustrates his case by comparing two views of the role of courts in the United States: the "dynamic" and "constrained" (which he favors) court models. The dynamic model sees courts as important catalysts, stemming from their neutral position (Chayes) and the political potency of their reasoning and language. This, Rosenberg argues, does not empirically reflect reality, since U.S. courts operate under enormous constraints. He argues, under the constrained court model, that courts do not have the proper tools to implement significant change and that courts are naturally conservative. This conservatism is grounded in the fact that, despite the Founders' best intentions to create an independent judiciary, U.S. courts are strongly hemmed in by public opinion. Only when opinion shifts can courts ever have a voice. As Rosenberg bluntly, and sweepingly, states: "U.S. courts can *almost never* be effective producers of significant social reform. At best, they can second the social reform acts of the other branches of government."[21] Rosenberg acknowledges that courts can achieve limited, localized change, but like Dahl and others, he asserts that courts cannot challenge dominant political majorities. He applies his framework to the famous cases of *Brown v. Board of Education* and *Roe v. Wade*, arguing, in both instances, that public opinion was already shifting in the direction of the court decisions and that the Court was only confirming this trend.[22]

Furthermore, Rosenberg asserts that counter-mobilization is the most likely mobilization triggered by litigation. Opponents of group-initiating litigation feel threatened and mobilize in response.[23] In the case of gay rights litigation, Jonathan Goldberg-Hiller reaffirmed this perspective in arguing that opponents of same-sex marriage in Hawaii were galvanized by litigation to sanction such marriages.[24] Although counter-mobilization is certainly a reality, especially with same-sex marriage litigation, I argue that important benefits stem from litigation strategies that can ultimately trump the counter-mobilization. Finally, Rosenberg argues that, given the lack of potential for litigation, civil rights groups waste time and resources on litigation strategies and may weaken their efforts in the long run.[25]

The perspective of Donald Horowitz is also in the tradition of critiques of court power. Contrary to Chayes, Horowitz argues that courts as institutions are ill-suited to making policy decisions.[26] Judges are generalists with little policy expertise, according to Horowitz. Litigation is often narrowly focused and disregards wider policy considerations. Judicial decision making is gradual and ad hoc, with courts as passive players relying on litigation brought to them. Thus, according to Horowitz, "Judicial decision becomes a chance occurrence, with no guarantee that the litigants are representative of the universe of problems their case purports to represent."[27] In addition, these litigants are not representative in the legislative sense, and courts are not equipped to ascertain policy or *legislative* facts, only *legal* facts, nor is there a mechanism for policy review in adjudication. In short, judges and litigants do not stack up well against legislators, bureaucrats, and interest groups. According to Horowitz, their ability to make sound policy is severely constrained. This critique is reflected in broader critiques of judicial activism, from a wide array of scholars and commentators, who assert that courts should not be involved in certain kinds of issues, nor should they overstep the "proper" boundaries of their authority.[28] I argue, however, that Rosenberg's sweeping assertions and Horowitz's normative disapproval of judicial decision making ignore important developments on the gay rights front, thereby causing them to disregard the "constitutive" side of the equation in this policy area and others.

## Constraints on Courts

Scholars such as Horowitz, Scheingold, and Rosenberg highlight a crucial element in judicial politics. Courts often operate under real constraints. I do not argue that courts and judges can always do what they want and radically change policy quickly and with lasting effect. Indeed, politics often matters for judges. Their path to the bench is influenced by politics, whether they are appointed or elected. Appointed judges can bring with them their own social and political biases and the political agendas of those who appoint them, while elected judges may obviously factor electoral concerns into their decisions. For instance, in Chapter 2, I describe the U.S. federal courts' relative lack of responsiveness to gay rights claims. This stems from wide societal homophobia through the middle to latter part of the twentieth century from which judges were not immune, as well as the dominance of conservative presidents in U.S. politics since 1968 and their ability to appoint generally conservative judges to the federal bench.

Beyond the selection process, judges also face direct and indirect limits to their power. Directly, they often possess limited tools of enforcement and often need to rely on other political actors to carry out their commands. Indirectly, they are subject to budget and jurisdiction changes from legislatures and executives, as well as the constitutional amendment process, which is the ultimate check on their power.[29] Judges may also constrain themselves out of concern for values more important than the policy choices in front of them, particularly a concern for allowing the fullest range of majoritarian decision making.[30] Public opinion also affects the decisions of judges. Given their lack of enforcement power and exposure to politics through the appointment or election process, judges often pay attention to public opinion, especially the U.S. Supreme Court.[31]

Trial and appellate court judges are often constrained by concerns for career advancement. Since they do not want to be seen as outside the judicial mainstream as a result of a high turnover rate on appeal, they tend to engage in "norm enforcement" adjudication, in which they apply previously established or settled doctrine, instead of innovative policy making.[32] However, as we shall see, this is not always the case. Many pro–gay rights decisions have come from lower court judges.

Indeed, many of these constraints are limited themselves by a sense of judicial independence in a polity. In states with well-developed judicial systems, polity norms protect the judiciary from excessive political influence—for example, the resistance to FDR's court-packing plan, appointment rather than election of judges, significant emphasis on nonpartisan elections, and a "higher law" understanding of constitutions. Judicial decision making is complex, and, I argue, many outcomes cannot simply be reduced to politics. In many cases, legal norms matter.

## THE CONSTITUTIVE PERSPECTIVE

As Michael McCann has noted, the perspective of Dahl, Horowitz, and Rosenberg is an heir to legal realism and its central notion that "judicially construed law is mostly epiphenomenal and derivative of, rather than an independent force shaping, social and economic life."[33] This study, along with the growing literature on courts and constitutive change, is an attempt to challenge the neorealist paradigm and enrich our view of the role that courts play in society. For instance, McCann argues that the law is not simply a set of neutral and distant rules for citizens to follow; it is an arena for change, "understood to consist of a complex repertoire of discursive strategies and symbolic frameworks that structure ongoing social intercourse and meaning-making activity among citizens."[34] Litigation and legal discourse can set new political and social agendas and change the terms of political debate by introducing new arguments and new methods of argumentation. Rather than being used instrumentally, legal norms and language become a forum for change. Legal norms can reinforce the status quo, but they can also undermine and transform it, especially as access to the law is democratized. As McCann again describes it: "judicial demarcation of 'what is possible' refers not to just those discrete options for actions that engaged political actors consciously access, but to the very frameworks of understanding, expectation, and aspiration through which both citizens and officials *interpret reality* or, to quote [Clifford] Geertz, 'imagine the real' around them."[35] Law and legal language has the power to transform politics by articulating new goals for a polity. And I argue that this dynamic is most powerful when this imagining is not completely foreign to a polity's political traditions but draws from and expands them.

Thus, the Rosenberg perspective is too "linear," as McCann puts it, in that it posits a direct, simple line between judicial decisions and social change, and thereby fails to capture the full picture of the role of courts.[36] Whereas Rosenberg asserts that courts have done little to effect positive change in the direction of same-sex marriage,[37] I argue that this is overly simplistic and fails to capture the complexity of the situation. Significant change has, in fact, occurred.

Litigation also provides more tangible tools beyond shaping discourse. Lynn Mather has noted the problems with Rosenberg's exclusive focus on the U.S. Supreme Court and argues that lower courts can be enormously powerful agenda setters, and the legal language used in litigation in these courts can shape and alter political discourse and lead to significant policy change.[38] McCann also notes that litigation can be used as leverage to increase the power of individuals and groups who may be powerless in the political arena. Also, this leverage may dissuade political and legal actors opposed to the agenda of a powerless group from further resistance to that agenda.[39] For example, some of the wind was taken out of the sails of opponents of gay rights in the United States after the *Lawrence* decision, which legally rejected the argument that same-sex intimacy is immoral and refused to continue to empower majorities with this argument in the legislative arena. After a string of same-sex marriage judicial victories in Canada, opponents have been marginalized.

Rosenberg also takes a narrow view of what constitutes social change. In addition to overlooking important developments, Rosenberg sets the bar for demonstrating social change too high by incompletely analyzing public opinion. Rosenberg's broad top-down approach fails to capture more subtle, yet critical, changes in a polity. A constitutive, "bottom-up" approach is more complex. As Troy Ridell puts it: "In this view, courts participate in a complex policy milieu that includes interest groups, executives and legislatures, state and local governments, bureaucrats, media, and the public."[40] Change, then, should not be measured by broad evidence, but by more detailed evidence of movement and change. For instance, Rosenberg argues that since national polling in the United States has not demonstrated a massive shift in the direction of same-sex marriage support, litigation has been ineffective at achieving change.[41] On the surface, this assertion appears correct; however, it ignores important conversations that have been taking place between courts and political actors. These conversations, I argue, have led to significant change. And, even by Rosenberg's broad measure, significant change has occurred in Canada.

Court skeptics also fail to appreciate the potential of courts to recapture lost political traditions or even create new ones grounded in marginalized traditions. Michael Kammen, who has a keen eye for American constitutional development, has predicted that "constitutional morality—that is the inclusion of social justice and fairness as legitimate criteria—will one day, not far distant, be broadly accepted as an appropriate underpinning for American jurisprudence."[42] Scholars like Rosenberg sees these values as more political than judicial. As I will demonstrate using the issue of gay rights, Kammen's prediction is being realized—more rapidly in Canada than the United States, but courts in the United States are moving in this direction. However, they are being challenged and constrained by a political culture that is dominated by a more restrictive liberalism.

Melnick points to another flaw in Rosenberg's framework. In analyzing rights expansion and significant policy change in welfare policy, Melnick asserts that "legal reformers are more politically astute than Rosenberg and most other court watchers have realized. Far from the naifs who relied exclusively on litigation," the reformers Melnick analyzed were politically astute and combined litigation with other, more "traditional," forms of political activity.[43] Similarly, many gay rights activists initially shunned litigation on the marriage issue, fearing a political backlash, and have chosen their legal battles carefully. Thus, Rosenberg's (and Schenigold's) "cause lawyer" caricature does not fit the case of gay rights.

This more sophisticated perspective on judicial policy making echoes recent assertions and findings by Malcolm Feeley and Edward Rubin. In the context of examining the judiciary's role in American prison reform, they assert that judges do indeed make policy, and this is not the dire situation that many commentators describe. They argue that viewing concepts like "the rule of law," separation of powers, and federalism as constraints on the actions of judges is outdated. Like Chayes, they are interested in the institutional capacity of courts to make public policy. They do not claim that judges are completely unrestrained; judges are also tied to legal doctrine and often justify their decisions with respect to this doctrine. But they also free themselves from doctrine when they wish to make policy. Feeley and Rubin distinguish this from mere interpretation:

> When a judge is interpreting a legal text, the opinion will be replete with textual references, and will attempt to link those preferences to the result by linguistic analyses, historical accounts of meaning, ... the drafter's intent, and citations of prior decisions.... When the judge is making public policy, such references will be absent, and in their place will be discussions of moral norms, social principles, nonlegal sources, nonauthoritative legal texts and citations of prior decisions that feature such discussions.[44]

This dynamic can clearly be seen in gay rights litigation. Court decisions that validate gay rights claims often turn on theoretical values that trump an interpretive approach and preserve the status quo. Whether it is a Millian concern for individual autonomy, which drives courts to strike down sodomy laws, or a concern for equality as a substantive value, which allows courts to require something like same-sex marriage, these decisions involve more than narrow, deferential interpretation.

However, this policy making is met with different reactions, both within and among nations. Sodomy law adjudication in the United States elicits little negative outcry, while same-sex marriage litigation stirs up a political hornet's nest. In Canada, court-driven same-sex marriage-like arguments are met with much more legitimacy than in the United States; political actors do not view court activity as illegitimately as do U.S. political actors. Indeed, there appears to be much more space for court policy making concerning gay rights in Canada. To understand the differences, however, we must first understand the new reality of judicial policy making.

## THE NEW INSTITUTIONALISM

This book echoes the statement made by Rogers Smith that "public law scholarship will not flourish if all scholars focus simply on spinning out their own normative legal theories."[45] A more promising approach to understanding courts is offered by the "new institutionalism," which attempts to go beyond the normative debates and views courts as institutions that impart an independent force on the legal and political process. According to Smith, "institutions are expected to shape the interests, resources, and ultimately the conduct of political actors, such as judges.... The actions of such persons are in turn expected to reshape those institutions more or less extensively."[46] There are certainly several strains of the new institutionalism, including rational choice and historical and social institutionalist approaches. However, the best approach is the least deterministic. It is influenced by neither structural-functionalist nor rational-choice reductionism, but takes history seriously and pays close attention to the development of legal and constitutional norms. It also recognizes that other institutions and political culture affect courts. According to Howard Gillman, the goal of this approach is to "reconstruct intentional states of mind and cultural or political contexts in the hope that we can induce with some confidence the reasons that led a particular person to adopt a particular course of conduct."[47] In this context, the "mission" of the institution becomes important, as institutional actors try to maintain the legitimacy of the institution. Judges thus see themselves as upholding the legitimacy of courts as institutions; they do not simply always impose their personal policy preferences. In doing so, the language of rights is often employed, since rights are increasingly the raw material of litigation. Courts, as institutions, are immersed in the language of rights, and this language can constrain and compel decision making. Although Glendon and Scheingold bemoan the use of rights, a new institutionalist approach sees rights discourse as a central component to understanding the nature of courts and their impact on social and political change. The way that legal arguments are developed and presented through the process of litigation is a central concern of this book. As the twenty-first century begins, rights discourse is firmly enshrined in the political and legal language of many nations and cannot be easily dismissed in the name of legal realism and its progeny or the preservation of "democratic" decision making.[48]

Another approach of new institutional institutionalism utilizes the concept of "path dependency" in explaining political change. Under this approach, according to Miriam Smith, "Political institutions and policy legacies open up certain opportunities for social movement politics while foreclosing others and these opportunities influence the policy agenda of each movement."[49] Ellen Andersen has explained the successes and failures of gay rights litigation in the United States in terms of "legal opportunity structure" which facilitates and constrains legal actors through the variation in access to institutional structures, power configurations among decision makers, the existence of allies and opponents, and historically and culturally rooted legal "frames" that allow or prevent change.[50]

These opportunity structure approaches tend to discount political culture as a variable and focus more on institutional arrangements. Indeed, Smith argues that the differences between Canada and the United States on gay rights are not sufficiently explained by differences in the political cultures of the two nations.[51] The approach of this book, however, sees these cultural differences as crucial. Ultimately, it may be necessary to view these developments through the dual prisms of ideas and institutions.

## LIBERALISM VERSUS MAJORITARIANISM

Because this book assumes a strong role for courts, it is perhaps necessary to comment on the legitimacy of their role, given critiques of judicial policy making. An argument against judicial activism (if this is a useful category) is that it allows judges to simply be moral philosophers, inserting their judgment for that of elected representatives. Legal discourse, then, becomes little more than abstract moral philosophy, unmoored from politics. One cure for the problem is original intent jurisprudence. This is not a real alternative, since it is far too minimal and gives short shrift to evolving constitutional principles. Instead, according to Harry Hirsch, "our philosophy of fundamental rights is not without content; it contains some propositions—historical propositions—that do bind us in certain ways. Thus 'history' and 'intent' are not the same thing. If we eschew a jurisprudence based on clause bound intent, we need not run headlong into a jurisprudence based on contemporary moral philosophy (as do Dworkin, and many others). . . . We must ask whether there is any space between these poles."[52]

One way to find that space is to ground interpretation in polity traditions. I argue that when judges utilize arguments and reasoning that are drawn from, and grounded in, a legitimate political tradition, they are not simply acting as Platonic guardians. Instead, they are trying to reconcile living under a principled constitutional order with democratic rule. Thus, finding Hirsch's space involves an exploration of competing and alternative political traditions to those held by current political majorities. This is particularly relevant for sexual minorities, since they come nowhere near to forming a numerical majority. And in the American and Canadian political traditions, groups need not be a majority to have their rights affirmed and be fully absorbed into the polity.

Indeed, this project is not obsessed with Bickel's "countermajoritarian difficulty."[53] Legal realism certainly had a point in rejecting a natural law-based jurisprudence, but a purely positivistic view of the law, a view to which advocates of a restrained judiciary subscribe, is incomplete. Majorities do not always have their way in American politics, nor even, increasingly, in Canadian politics. At any rate, the legislative arena is seldom a perfect reflection of majoritarian sentiment. As Epp puts it, "many legislative policies could not survive a popular referendum either."[54] In addition, legislatures and executives often care little about the rights of minorities. They respond to majoritarian or interest group power, not calls for justice.

The American constitutional structure is designed to protect minorities, or at least to soften the power of majorities. And with the adoption of the Charter of Rights and Freedoms in Canada, the protection of minorities is increasing as a political value in a political culture that has been largely noted for its belief in legislative supremacy. As Jennifer Hochschild has noted in her study of court-mandated school desegregation, "Liberal democracy has always relied on elites to save it from itself. If authoritative leaders see what is necessary to turn the semblance of democracy into real democracy, and the promise of liberal rights into their guarantee, the elitism (of a certain sort) is perfectly compatible with liberal democracy."[55] As she argues, school desegregation met with such popular resistance because it threatened the status quo of white privilege. The same is true with opposition to same-sex marriage: Heterosexuals are afraid of losing status by granting new rights to others. I argue that legal elites need to challenge the status quo by enforcing liberal rights for all. Epp also has noted that the "rights revolution" is not necessarily counter-majoritarian. The tendency for groups to assert rights in court resulted from a democratization of access to the judiciary. No longer are business groups the sole utilizers of the courts.[56]

As Feeley and Rubin argue, judicial policy making is a modern political reality, and fear of undermining "democracy" is misplaced. As they note in the U.S. context, "we are a massive modern state, not a Greek polis or a New England village."[57] Bickelian and Republican revival fretting is perhaps an important cautionary note; however, given the modern presence of judicial activism in the United States and Canada (and the fact that "activism" is usually in the eye of the beholder), excessive concern for the conflict between judicial review and democratic practice is normatively and methodologically misguided.

## RESCUING RIGHTS

This book also represents an attempt to revive the legitimacy of rights claims and rights-based litigation by emphasizing liberalism's capacity to accommodate rights claims by sexual minorities. Such claims have come under attack from the left and the right. Rights are either hollow, status quo reinforcing tools, destructive of majoritarian decision making, or tools of liberal judicial activism.[58]

In a sense, the issue of gay rights is a test for liberalism and its emphasis on rights. To what extent can a liberal political and legal order accommodate the acceptance of gay and lesbian relationships on a par with heterosexual relationships? In other words, can liberalism go beyond mere tolerance of private sexual acts and achieve recognition of lesbian and gay relationships for the purposes of extending public policy benefits like the extensive legal protections and benefits that come with civil marriage? Or, is liberalism essentially concerned with freedom at the expense of notions of equality and inclusion?

One of the most aggressive critiques of rights comes from the left. Legal realism not only spawned political jurisprudence; it also can count critical legal studies as its offspring. The claim that rights are hollow and, in reality, vehicles for the oppression of minority groups has gained prominence in the past several decades. The argument that liberalism is too limited to embrace fully the equality of sexual minorities represents a common critique of liberalism. It is far too focused on a narrow, procedural view of rights and fails to incorporate a true concern for equality. This critique is echoed by Joel Bakan who argues that despite the apparent potential for progressive social policy to result from the adoption of the Canadian Charter, the reality is that courts are fundamentally conservative institutions that use a "liberal form of rights" to limit social policy.[59] Conversely, I argue that liberalism is not simply a force of conservatism. In fact, through court enforcement of evolving legal norms, it can sustain a richer version of rights than commentators such as Bakan claim.

An example from the U.S. case is illustrative. As previously indicated, American state courts have been receptive to striking down state prohibitions of sodomy. But they have been more reluctant to move aggressively on the issue of same-sex marriage, although courts in Hawaii, Alaska, Vermont, Massachusetts, Oregon, New York and Washington have handed down decisions favorable to same-sex marriage. Not only have courts been more reluctant on the marriage issue, but the reaction from the political branches and the public has been quite different. In reaction to the striking down of sodomy laws, there has hardly been a stir from politicians and citizens. The vast majority of these decisions create no reaction; in fact, they often receive an implicit or explicit affirmation. Conversely, the public reaction to gay marriage decisions has been swift and vociferous at both the state and federal levels. A large majority of states have passed laws explicitly banning marriages between members of the same gender, with many constitutionalizing this policy, and the Defense of Marriage Act has made this national policy.

What accounts for this vast difference? A significant part of this gap can be explained by the distinction that J. David Greenstone makes between variants of liberalism. He distinguishes between "humanist" and "reform" liberalism, the former emphasizing negative freedom and the latter emphasizing a more positive form of freedom. Reform liberalism sees the individual in a richer context than does humanist liberalism; the individual is not to be simply left to his or her own devices. Rather, reform liberalism requires that an individual be allowed and encouraged to develop "abilities of body and mind, that come with the mastery of excellence in important human practices."[60] Most significantly, reform liberalism opens the door for a stronger notion of equality. Individuals are not simply autonomous individuals, unconnected with others, but are in fact a part of a greater whole. Society has a positive obligation to ensure that these individuals develop to their utmost capacity. Implicit in this view of liberalism is a strong emphasis on equality, not only freedom. As Greenstone noted, Abraham Lincoln's brand of this richer notion of liberalism led him to emphasize the issue of equality, while Stephen A. Douglas was only concerned with preserving the freedom of whites to decide for themselves the issue of slavery. This concern, which includes strong notions of equality in liberalism, is also reflected in the neo-Kantian arguments of political theorists and legal scholars like John Rawls and Ronald Dworkin, who advocate a richer, thicker notion of freedom and rights. This idea is not simply that individuals have a right to be left alone, but that they have a right to "equal concern and respect."[61] This strain of American liberalism has been dwarfed by the more prominent negative strain, but it nonetheless exists.

Rights, then, can serve as important tools, especially for marginalized groups. Martha Minow has argued forcefully for reclaiming rights as vehicles for political and legal change. Although noting that rights are not perfect tools, they nonetheless possess the power to transform the political status quo. As she states: "Rights pronounced by courts become possessions of the dispossessed."[62] Minow also noted that rights can be remade and reinterpreted; they don't always serve the powerful. This book demonstrates this in the context of rights claiming by sexual minorities.

## A Model of Judicial Decision Making

This book explores the process of decision making for a wide range of courts. What, then, goes into judicial decision making? A dominant explanation in political science is the attitudinal model. This model asserts that a judge's own views and attitudes drive and shape judicial decision making, so much so that one can predict judicial outcomes. "Simply put," according to the leading proponents of this perspective, Segal and Spaeth, "Rehnquist votes the way he does because he is extremely conservative; Marshall voted the way he did because he was extremely liberal."[63] Another view holds that legal doctrine determines outcome. Judges apply legal norms without regard to their own personal preferences or biases. Judicial doctrine and methods of interpretation play a central role in judicial decision making, according to this perspective.

This book relies upon an alternative framework that embraces some of both perspectives. It is clear that judges' ideology and background matter. Daniel Pinello has demonstrated that these factors play a significant role in the outcome of gay rights cases. Race, religion, gender, and party affiliation were some of the factors Pinello found salient.[64] Diversity is good for gay rights claims, with women, minorities, and Jews being the most favorable to gay rights claims, according to Pinello.[65] As he states, "when these judges from social groups with an extensive history of invidious discrimination . . . signed opinions in gay rights appeals, they spoke resoundingly in favor of the civil rights of another downtrodden minority."[66] However, Pinello also found that factors like *stare decisis* (doctrine), level of court (appellate versus court of last resort), and length of term (more than method of selection) played a role in outcomes.[67] Geography was also a powerful variable, with Southern judges least responsive to gay rights claims and judges in the Northeast and West most responsive.[68]

Pinello thus demonstrates that judicial decision making is complex and not always suited to the reductionism of the attitudinal model. Nor is legal doctrine always the driving force. But I share the criticism of Ronald Kahn that the traditions of realism, behavioralism, and attitudinalism miss a great deal in judicial decision making by neglecting the role of ideas as an independent force and by only seeing them as instruments used to further a judicial predisposition.[69] Kahn, following Greenstone, places constitutional interpretation, and thus a large amount of judicial decision making, in the context of American political thought and ideas. Constitutional interpretation is a conversation between alternative perspectives in the American political tradition. It is also a conversation between the courts and the scholars, journalists, public officials, informed citizens, and those involved with or affected by litigation, or what Kahn calls the "interpretative community."[70] This conversation is informed by Greenstone's variants of liberalism, noted above, as well as what Greenstone identifies as the republican strain in American political thought that places great emphasis on process and proper democratic procedures. Kahn refers to the republican concerns as "polity principles" and the more substantive liberal values as "rights principles."[71] For Kahn, constitutional adjudication involves the sorting out of these values and principles in each era. As he puts it:

> Justices seek coherence in polity and rights principles to increase their influence over the development of constitutional principles within the Court and wider society and thus make a place for themselves in history. They ask themselves what fundamental rights may be viewed as "in" the Constitution and how these principles are to be applied in a particular case, in view of their polity and rights principles, precedent, and the facts in the case. Justices create personal visions in which their views of polity and rights principles, their underlying moral values, and their attitudes toward the history of the Court and nation are central.... To achieve coherence, a justice cannot think only of the case outcomes, or the individual case, but must consider the implications of each choice for later applications of polity and rights principles.[72]

This dovetails with new institutionalist approaches by considering institutional mission and valuing ideas as separate influences on judicial outcomes.

The model of judicial decision making offered in this book takes attitudinal and institutional factors into account but also pays particular attention to legal norms and doctrine. And given that this study involves analysis of a mix of courts (state and federal, trial and appellate, U.S. and Canadian), I take a flexible approach to analysis, but ultimately argue that in many significant instances doctrine and ideas matter.

## JUDGES AS POLITY THEORISTS: BRINGING THE COURTS BACK IN

The framework outlined by Greenstone and Kahn invites a role for courts in national political and legal conversations. Courts are the institutions best able to recapture lost or subsidiary political traditions, since the more political branches tend to reinforce the ideological status quo. Through legal norms and arguments, courts can bring these traditions back into play and give them legitimacy.

Also, since judges are more removed from the political process, they are better able to reason abstractly based upon perceived notions of justice, not simply on the basis of who has the most political power. Michael Perry notes this capacity and has argued for the idea that courts should enforce human rights norms. Judges should play a key role in finding "right answers to political-moral problems. As a matter of comparative institutional competence," according to Perry, "the politically insulated federal judiciary is more likely . . . to move us in the direction of a right answer (assuming there is such a thing) than is the political process left to its own devices."[73] As we shall see, the U.S. federal judiciary is not the best example of a guardian of rights on the gay rights front. Other courts are playing this role. The larger point is that, institutionally, courts can bring this mode of decision making to the table.

In the legislative arena, it is hoped that outcomes will be rational, especially if true "deliberation" takes place. Courts, however, do more than hope; they often enforce the notion of rationality and apply it to political decisions. This is certainly true in the context of fundamental rights and equal protection jurisprudence in the United States. Even the minimal "rational basis" test is a rejection of the notion that majoritarian power is absolute in a constitutional democracy. This will be explained later in the book, as many judges begin to rule that prohibitions of same-sex intimate relationships and marriage do not make logical sense, but are only reflective of majoritarian morality and insufficient to pass constitutional muster.[74]

I do not argue that courts ought to be the final arbiter in all political controversies, only that they are important institutions in modern liberal democracies. They can especially be helpful in considering the full range of viewpoints and strains of discourse in a polity. At the same time, they are limited to those strains and the parameters of a polity's discourse. Judges should not be seen as philosopher kings, a caricature often used by opponents of judicial power, but as actors exploring and applying a nation's (sometimes forgotten) values, especially when political majorities, at a given moment in time, are not doing so.

My perspective echoes that of an earlier generation of scholars who were discontent with the lack of justice that is often present in legislative and bureaucratic decision making. Critical of mid-twentieth-century pluralism and its emphasis on procedure in legislative and bureaucratic policy making, rather than substantive considerations, these "critical pluralists,"[75] most notably Grant McConnell and Theodore Lowi, favor a larger role for courts in order to address a broader range of issues and arguments. McConnell argued that the U.S. polity was dominated by decentralized and local decision making that privileges private, economically powerful, interest groups. According to McConnell, "The tendency inherent in small [political] units to stratification of power relationships and to protection of established informal patterns of domination and subordination is most alien to equality."[76] The solution, then, is to emphasize nationalizing and universalizing institutions, like the federal courts, in order to develop "policies serving the values of liberty and equality," rather than the desires of powerful groups.[77] McConnell was trying to reassert a Madisonian vision of democratic politics, one that focused not on narrow considerations of power but on the notion of "justice and the general good."[78]

Theodore Lowi rejected the extreme positivism of pluralism and its elevation of nonlegal forms of decision making. He objected to the sterile, interest-group-driven politics of the United States in the latter part of the twentieth century. As he described it, this politics left no room for substantive consideration of justice or morality: "In a pluralistic government there is, therefore, no substance. Neither is there procedure. There is only process."[79] Lowi's solution was a turn toward "juridical democracy" that would lift politics above simple interest-group bargaining and empower more voices in politics, as well as allow for a "justice-oriented politics."[80] Lowi backed off his initial large role for courts in this process, later emphasizing that juridical democracy is not necessarily judicial democracy,[81] but Kahn effectively summarizes the pro-court thrust of McConnell's and Lowi's arguments. As he states, "they favor federal court intervention because they see that it may result in the expansion of the range of issues under discussion to include questions of rights, due process, and equal protection."[82] When applied to a fuller range of courts in both the United States and Canada, this accurately describes the role courts are playing in the area of gay rights.

## LEGAL MOBILIZATION

This book also addresses the way in which lawyers and litigation groups structure their efforts and the effect of those efforts on the legal and political systems. Marc Galanter noted in the 1970s that groups that consistently engaged in the practice of litigation (which he termed "repeat players") would find significantly more success than those that only occasionally accessed the legal system ("one-shotters"). This is due to greater expertise with, and knowledge of, the system, in addition to greater financial resources. These groups, therefore, can engage in long-term litigation strategies and develop bargaining power through this longevity, along with an understanding of informal modes of decision making that come from prolonged access to the system. "One-shotters," conversely, lack these resources and are more prone to settle early and do not have sufficient expertise and leverage to compete with the repeat players. This results in an imbalance in the system, with the established and wealthy having the upper hand in litigation; however, Galanter thought that certain reforms (increased funding for legal aid programs, class action lawsuits, active governmental support for one-shot litigants, outsider interest group litigation strategies, etc.) would level the playing field.[83]

An implication of Galanter's thesis is also that groups will have a natural advantage in litigation over individuals. Individuals and outsiders, to be successful, need to structure their litigation to take on the attributes of repeat players. And they have. As Epp puts it, "in recent decades, there has been a significant growth in the number and diversity of nonproducer advocacy groups claiming to represent the interests of one-shotters. As a result . . . *some* kinds of 'have nots' have gained *some* of the structural prerequisites for repeat playing."[84] Many have nots have become haves.[85] This includes a sophisticated network of gay rights litigators. Groups like this are able to bring a wide variety of resources and capabilities to assist "outsider groups," including expertise, money, publicity, legal and nonlegal research, and communication networks.[86] In addition to those qualities noted above, litigation groups can create a narrow focus on an issue or group of issues, thereby facilitating legal and political dialogue, use law review articles to put new legal arguments into play, and solicit amicus briefs from influential sources, including the government.[87] Also, litigation can have indirect, but important, "radiating" effects on policy. Litigation can, as McCann asserts, "help to redefine the terms of both immediate and long-term struggles among social groups."[88] Gay rights litigation, while not always fully successful in its aims, has profoundly changed the terms of the debate over gay rights.

Gay rights litigation has been a combination of gay interest groups, repeat player, and one-shotter litigation. And contrary to Galanter's thesis, it was one-shotter litigation, not one-shotters transformed into repeat players, that successfully launched the drive for same-sex marriage in the United States in the 1990s. By only focusing on financial and status resources, Galanter neglected to account for the potentially transformative power of litigation. Rather than disempowering individuals, litigation is a potent form of political participation that can transform law and politics,[89] especially when legal decision makers give greater support and standing to individuals and outsiders.[90] Litigation on behalf of outsiders, including sexual minorities, has been enormously successful in Canada and has had more limited, though arguably substantial, success in the United States.

## THE STUDY OF COURTS IN COMPARATIVE PERSPECTIVE

Scheingold has noted that inquiry into the politics of rights can benefit from national comparisons.[91] Although the main focus of this book is on the United States, a comparison to the Canadian case is useful for several reasons. First, in order to critique effectively the current approach of courts in the United States on the issue of gay rights, one must look outside the U.S. border. If, as I assert, arguments that go beyond libertarian conceptions of freedom have a difficult time finding a place in American political discourse, it is important to test whether or not this situation is unique. Through a comparative analysis, one can discover alternative approaches that demonstrate the plausibility of change. In this case, the type of liberalism that has developed in a country goes a long way toward explaining the capacity of that country's courts to adjudicate expansively on the subject of gay rights. If the dominant strain of liberalism conceives of rights narrowly, it may not be easy for courts to expand the notion of liberalism.

This is not a comparative study in the strictest sense of political science methodology. It is not a side-by-side, variable-by-variable, large-$N$ comparison but is, instead, a softer comparison. As noted above, I argue that a primary reason for the difference in policy outcomes between the United States and Canada is the difference in political cultures, particularly differing visions of liberalism. But other variables most certainly played a role in the different outcomes: the lesser influence of religious conservatives in Canadian politics, differences in party systems and legislative processes (which allowed for a more uniform policy response in Canada, since the Liberal Party was firmly in control of national politics), the greater role played by the Canadian federal government in marriage policy (in the United States, marriage is almost exclusively a state issue), and differences in legal norms and practices, despite a shared common law heritage. These are all examined later in this book. The latter variable, however, merges with the variance in liberalism, and, I argue, these two variables disproportionately drive the change. After the adoption of the Charter in 1982, Canadian courts have adopted American-style approaches to judicial review. The previous doctrine of parliamentary supremacy has given way to a judiciary empowered by a new constitution based on modern liberal values. This combination has been a potent force for change in the realm of gay rights.

Consequently, a comparison between these two nations, rather than only a U.S. state-by-state comparison, is necessary for understanding the future of same-sex marriage claims in the United States. Despite the perception that developments toward same-sex marriage in Hawaii and Vermont resulted from the uniquely progressive political climates of these states, change was actually driven by courts and the legal norms and values they articulated, and even imposed, on legislatures. Progressive political climates alone have not resulted in policy change. Climate can facilitate policy change after a court mandate, but the political process has not changed policy on its own. Therefore, the real story in the United States has been the influence of legal norms and values, not variance in state "political factors." For example, public opinion on same-sex marriage in Hawaii and Vermont differed little from national public opinion before the courts stepped in.

Carl Stychin has made the link between a nation's political culture as it relates to rights and issues of sexuality. He argues that rights are the link between national and sexual identity. The way a culture views rights can often heavily influence the way sexuality issues are addressed in public policy. Claims to rights are the link, since they are increasingly becoming universal. Given the rise of international human rights norms, the range of rights claimants is constantly expanding. Thus, according to Stychin, "rights claims are one means by which groups and individuals can play an active role in altering how the nation is imagined."[92] Stychin also argues, however, that a national culture's stance toward rights can also limit this alteration of the national imagination if those rights are conceived narrowly, a central premise of this project.

The notion of political culture is a disputed concept in political science. Many believe that it is a useless concept, even tautological.[93] However, the explicit assumption of this book is that political culture exists, it is definable (at least broadly), and it is a relevant explanatory variable. Certainly no national political culture is completely homogenous; multiple ideological traditions exist side by side in the same culture.[94] But this book assumes that broadly distinct political cultures exist and can affect policy outcomes by setting the broad terms of political debate. In particular, this inquiry is focused on the nature of liberalism in a particular nation and the manner in which a particular version of liberalism promotes a broad or narrow notion of rights.

Canada serves as an interesting comparison to the United States for several reasons. Prior to the adoption of the Canadian Charter of Rights and Freedoms in 1982, there was little history of judicial activism concerning individual rights in Canada. Parliamentary sovereignty, not judicial supremacy, was the hallmark of the Canadian political system. Seymour Martin Lipset has summed up the differences between the Canadian and American approaches to governing by highlighting the different political traditions that established the frameworks for each country: "The very organizing principles that framed these nations, the central cores around which institutions and events were to accommodate, were different. One was Whig and classically liberal or libertarian.... The other was Tory and conservative in the British and European sense—accepting of the need for a strong state, for respect for authority, for deference."[95] However, this distinction began to break down in the twentieth century. A Bill of Rights was enacted by Parliament in the 1960s, but it was only a statute, and courts could not use it to restrict the actions of Parliament.[96] With the adoption of the Canadian Charter of Rights and Freedoms, Canadian politics made a turn toward a politics of rights and judicial involvement in the determination of those rights. As F. L. Morton states, "The Charter has stimulated Canadian interest groups to adopt American-style litigation tactics to promote their objectives."[97] In particular, before the 1980s few cases existed that expanded the realm of gay and lesbian rights, but since the adoption of the Charter the situation has changed dramatically.[98] This rise in judicial activism has combined with a political tradition concerning rights that is not simply negative. As the Canadian Supreme Court stated in *M. v. H.*: "The exclusion of same-sex partners from the benefits of s. 29 [of the Family Law Act] promotes the view that... individuals in same-sex relationships... are less worthy of recognition and protection.... Such exclusion perpetuates the disadvantages suffered by individuals in same-sex relationships and contributes to the erasure of their existence."[99] This decision transcends mere privacy concerns and calls for the equal recognition of heterosexual and homosexual relationships.

This position contrasts starkly with the situation in the United States, a nation whose political culture is saturated with the notion of rights. These rights, however, have often been narrowly defined, negatively conceived, and have not been open to everyone.[100] Despite Greenstone's identification of a positive strain of American liberalism, it has mostly been conceived of in negative terms. The example of gay rights has been no exception to this reality. Federal courts in the United States have been quite uncomfortable with gay rights issues, having, until recently, refused to declare a right to privacy for sexual minorities and refused to view sexuality on par with race or gender for constitutional protection against discrimination.[101]

Indeed, the Canadian and U.S. polities appear to be diverging on social issues in significant ways, not just at the margins.[102] Canada is combining a richer liberalism with a more secular outlook on society, while in the United States negative liberalism dominates much of the political discourse, combined with a continued religiosity that cuts against secularism. This has made the Canadian polity much riper for legal and political support for same-sex marriage. And when courts in the United States enforce a richer liberalism, same-sex marriage claims gain traction.

## OUTLINE OF THIS BOOK

In the following chapters, I explore the issues outlined above. I begin in Chapter 2 with a brief history of U.S. federal gay rights jurisprudence to illustrate the lack of innovation in this jurisprudence and its tendency toward negative notions of freedom. I then turn to a discussion of liberalism's relationship to gay politics in Chapters 3 and 4, exploring the arguments of liberalism's critics and defining a liberalism that is accommodating of a full range of gay rights claims. In Chapters 5 and 6, I take up the question of U.S. jurisprudence concerning sodomy laws, arguing that decriminalizing sodomy is supported by the dominant liberal tradition in the United States, but that courts still need to achieve significant change in many parts of the country. Chapters 7, 8, and 9 examine same-sex marriage litigation in the United States and the political reactions to it. Chapter 10 examines same-sex marriage litigation and policy change in Canada as a source of comparison to the U.S. case. In Chapter 11, I argue that courts have contributed to significant social change and they should continue to invoke liberal arguments to do so. Chapter 12 then concludes this study.

Concerning the U.S. case, I have chosen to focus on sodomy and same-sex marriage litigation in order to highlight the potential of rights-based litigation and to show that variants of liberalism may shape the course and success of this litigation. Certainly, a larger array of litigation areas could be examined. For instance, litigation concerning same-sex parental rights would fit nicely into this discussion, but I chose to limit the inquiry to these two areas because I feel they offer a rich and useful contrast. In the Canadian case, sodomy laws were eliminated in the 1970s, thus eliminating a need for litigation but also demonstrating the difference between Canadian and U.S. political culture.

It is hoped that this book will not be seen as niche scholarship. Ultimately, the issue of gay and lesbian rights is not merely a side issue of significance to only a small segment of society. In many ways, the issue is a proxy for larger issues concerning tradition, morality, and rights and how these elements relate to one another in modern liberal democracies.

# 2    U.S. Federal Courts and Gay Rights

## *A History of Hesitancy*

THE ACTIVITY OF the U.S. Supreme Court and other federal courts demonstrates the influence of political culture on courts, in that even they are often unable to transcend the barriers of a dominant political discourse. The Supreme Court has been generally unwilling to view gay rights claims in a way that extends beyond a negative conception of freedom and rights (and has not even been willing to apply this negative conception in some cases) and has been, until quite recently, reluctant to offer a robust defense of gay rights claims. Indeed, extreme discomfort with gay rights claims, often tending toward animus, typifies the approach of the Court for most of the twentieth century.[1]

One of the earliest gay rights cases in the Supreme Court, *ONE v. Olesen*, turned out favorably for gay rights claims, but not because of increasing legal support for gay rights claims. Rather, the result was reflective of the Court's increasing freedom of expression-protective obscenity jurisprudence. In the 1950s, the Los Angeles postmaster seized and refused to deliver copies of a magazine about homosexuality, claiming it to be obscene under federal and state obscenity laws. The magazine was not pornographic in nature, it merely included letters, articles, and stories that dealt frankly with homosexuality. The editors of *ONE* challenged the postmaster's decision, but, agreeing with the postmaster, a federal district judge rebuffed their challenge, and the Ninth Circuit Court of Appeals upheld this ruling. Interestingly, the editors reached out to the American Civil Liberties Union (ACLU) for assistance but were denied support.[2] In finding the magazine obscene, the Ninth Circuit characterized the depiction of a lesbian relationship in one of the magazine's stories as "nothing more than cheap pornography calculated to promote lesbianism. It falls far short of dealing with homosexuality from the scientific, historical and critical point of view."[3] The magazine might be fine for homosexuals, the judges reasoned, but this was not constitutionally sufficient: "An article may be vulgar, offensive and indecent even though not regarded as such by a particular group of individuals constituting a small segment of the population because their own social or moral standards are far below those of the general community."[4]

This language is not surprising, given the political climate surrounding sexual minorities in the 1950s (indeed, the federal government was waging a campaign against sexual minorities),[5] but it was out of step with evolving First Amendment jurisprudence. A year before, the Supreme Court ruled in *Roth v. United States* that material bearing some relationship to social, political, or literary speech was immune from obscenity classifications and thus protected by the First Amendment.[6]

Consequently, when *ONE* was appealed to the Supreme Court, the Court over-turned the Ninth Circuit decision in a one-sentence per curiam opinion that used *Roth* as an authority.[7] The decision was clearly not, in the justices' minds, a gay rights case. In fact, the Court considered *cert* petitions from nudist maga-zines at the same time that it considered granting *cert* in *ONE*.[8] This reflected the Court's obscenity jurisprudence, a jurisprudence that was broadening the notion of freedom of expression, and its desire to police the boundaries of obscenity law. In this instance, then, gay rights claims were a beneficiary of the dominance of negative notions of freedom, not an affirmation of the legal status of sexual minorities.

This dynamic is also apparent in another gay-linked obscenity case, *Manual Enterprises Inc. v. Day*,[9] which ruled on another postmaster seizure of a gay mag-azine, in this case a "beefcake" magazine. Although some in the majority saw the case in terms of the proper extent of administrative discretion, the majority opinion by Justice John M. Harlan found that the nude male photographs in the magazine were not obscene under the *Roth* standard.[10] Again, negative freedom protected the distasteful material. Indeed, Harlan described the magazines as "dismally un-pleasant, uncouth, tawdry."[11] In fairness, the justices were prudish when it came to any kind of pornography, gay or straight, but there was a clear finding in the decision that gay men were not "normal." Harlan described the magazines as "read almost entirely by homosexuals, and possibly a few adolescent males; the normal male adult would not normally buy them."[12]

Although, as will be discussed in Chapter 5, legal elites were increasingly rejecting the notion that homosexuality was abnormal, this sentiment was not to be found on the Supreme Court in 1962. Astonishingly, Harlan quoted from the American Law Institute's Model Penal Code's (the ultimate reflection of legal elite thinking at the time) progressive definition of obscenity, but completely ignored the fact that the same document called for the elimination of legal penalties for gay sex based on the notion that homosexuality was "normal."[13] As a result of this bias of the Court, other types of gay rights claims did not fare as well, failing to ride the wave of nongay rights jurisprudence. After the "successes"[14] of *ONE* and *Manual* the Court entered into a phase of gay rights "dark ages."

A large segment of the antigay rights decisions dealt with immigration and federal employment issues, reflecting the way in which the U.S. government viewed sexual minorities. For instance, the Court upheld the federal government's policy of withholding employment to openly gay people and deporting sexual minorities who were not citizens. The Court refused to overturn a ruling validating the federal government's dismissal of a civil service astronomer, Franklin Kameny, for being gay.[15] The Court also denied *cert* in other similar cases, always siding with the government's arguments that sexual minorities were a security risk and prone to blackmail.[16]

In *Boutilier v. INS*, the Court affirmed the Immigration and Naturalization Ser-vice's policy of deporting gays and lesbians on the grounds that homosexuality was evidence of a "psychopathic personality." The Court held that Congress intended for this to be the policy.[17] Thus, the majority relied on statutory, not constitutional, interpretation for its decision, but Justice William O. Douglas, one of four dissenters, saw a due process violation. Arguing that the term "psychopathic personality" was akin to calling someone a communist, Douglas saw the policy as irrational and violative of the freedom of sexual minorities.[18] Since the case was decided a few years before the American Psychiatric Association declassified homosexuality as a disorder, Douglas relied on the then-common Freudian theory of sexuality, noting that gays and lesbians were the "product of an arrested development." In spite of this, however, Douglas was unwilling to eliminate sexual minorities from constitutional protection, unlike the majority who did not consider their personhood. *Boutilier* was a dramatic turning point for the Court but not a good one for gay rights claims. As Murdoch and Price describe it, after the decision, "the Supreme Court literally stopped listening to homosexual rights arguments. . . . With that ruling, the U.S. Supreme Court joined the government war against homosexuals."[19]

Indeed, until recently, the Court read protection for sexual minorities out of constitutional jurisprudence. *Bowers v. Hardwick* in 1986 declared that same-sex sex acts were not provided constitutional protection under the privacy jurisprudence that had developed in cases such as *Griswold v. Connecticut* and *Roe v. Wade.* Michael Hardwick was arrested for violating Georgia's sodomy law (which applied to same-sex and heterosexual sex acts) in his home. The Eleventh Circuit saw this case as a part of the privacy moving stream, declaring that a consensual sex act between persons of the same gender in a private home is "quintessentially private and lies at the heart of an intimate association beyond the proper reach of state regulation."[20] In particular, the court noted that while initial cases in this line of jurisprudence involved marital privacy, subsequent cases broadened the privacy principle to include intimacy concerns other than procreation.

The Supreme Court, however, refused to take such a broad view of privacy jurisprudence. The majority did not feel that this line of cases "established a fundamental right to engage in homosexual sodomy,"[21] since marriage and procreation still anchored the right to privacy. Heterosexual marriage was historically validated, the Court argued, but "[p]roscriptions against sodomy have ancient roots."[22] Chief Justice Warren Burger concurred with the opinion, but felt that the majority did not go far enough in condemning homosexuality, citing Roman law and Blackstone, who called sodomy "a malignity worse than rape."[23] Justice Lewis Powell also concurred with the decision, but he later expressed regrets at doing so, claiming that it was one of his greatest mistakes on the Court.[24] Critics of liberal legal thought who argue that it is inherently conservative would appear to find strong evidence here. However, this decision was completely illiberal; it was grounded purely in Burkean conservatism.

Justice Harry Blackmun dissented vigorously. He saw the Georgia statute as a violation of the right to privacy that, in his view, protected sexual intimacy, regardless of the gender of the persons involved. He rebuked the majority for deceptively focusing on homosexuality when the statute made no such distinction, arguing that Hardwick's claim "does not depend in any way on his sexual orientation."[25] Placing his position in line with the views of Louis Brandeis and Oliver Wendell

Holmes and the development of privacy jurisprudence, Blackmun argued that this jurisprudence was not tied to the preservation of an institution, like marriage, but was designed to protect a rich sense of personhood. Privacy, in this view, is not a mechanism for the public good, as the majority asserted; rather, privacy rights are protected "because they form so central a part of an individual's life." Blackmun continued: "we protect the family because it contributes so powerfully to the happiness of individuals, not because of a preference for stereotypical households."[26] Blackmun was thus defending a liberalism that incorporated a rich account of what individualism requires. He saw the right to privacy as neither the right to simply be left alone nor an instrument for social control. For Blackmun, it was the essence of modern, liberal personhood.

Indeed, in his dissent, Blackmun cited an article by Kenneth Karst in the *Yale Law Journal*, calling for a richer right to privacy, or what he called a "right to intimate association." This right placed at its core the idea that intimacy was central to modern personhood and cannot be separated from individual identity. Using heterosexual marriage as a starting point, Karst extrapolated to encompass other similar relationships, particularly same-sex relationships. Although he argued in favor of same-sex marriage, he also argued that, at a minimum, same-sex intimacy should be constitutionally protected.[27] This line of argument clearly falls in line with Greenstone's reform liberalism and modern liberalism's concern for equal concern and respect. However, Blackmun fell one vote short of enshrining this rich liberalism constitutionally. Neither would this idea be used even when state courts began to challenge sodomy laws in the 1990s, as will be explored in later chapters. Their view of the right to privacy would be explicitly more negative but would resonate politically.

The behind the scenes maneuvering of the Court in *Bowers* illuminates how the justices arrived at a decision. Since the Court had largely avoided gay rights cases since *Boutilier* nineteen years earlier, the decision to grant *cert* was noteworthy. Initially, only Justices Byron White and William Rehnquist (both gay rights foes) were interested in taking the case, and *cert* was denied. They wished to reject the lower court's application of privacy jurisprudence to sodomy, both of the justices being staunchly opposed to the trajectory of privacy jurisprudence. White circulated a dissent from the *cert* denial in an attempt to persuade his colleagues to reconsider. After a second vote, four voted to grant *cert*: Rehnquist, White, and the liberals William Brennan and Thurgood Marshall. Brennan then changed his vote while Chief Justice Burger voted to accept the case. Brennan initially may have thought he had the votes to affirm the lower court, but was apparently convinced by Blackmun that the opposite was true and the case could potentially overturn *Roe* itself. The liberals' miscalculation, then, resulted in another blow for gay rights, even though, contrary to Blackmun's fears, privacy jurisprudence for heterosexuals was not disturbed.[28]

Once *cert* was granted, attorneys for Hardwick, including Lawrence Tribe, targeted their arguments toward the justice they felt was the crucial vote, Lewis Powell. Powell was skeptical of the Georgia law, but did not wish to use due process to strike it down. Powell favored viewing the case as an example of cruel and unusual punishment, since prison is an excessive punishment for private, consensual sexual activity. And, in an initial conference vote, Powell voted to overturn the Georgia law, causing a 5 to 4 split in favor of Hardwick.[29] Powell, however, changed his vote. Murdoch and Price attribute the switch to several factors. Both Chief Justice Burger and a conservative Powell clerk lobbied Powell to rule against Hardwick. Even though Powell rejected Burger's extreme viewpoint, he had no particular sympathy for sexual minorities, despite having gay clerks (who never came out to him). He could not affirm their humanity the way that Blackmun's dissent did. Ultimately, Powell abandoned his Eighth Amendment objections, noting this in a memo to the other justices, since this was a novel legal argument and he was not comfortable affirming the due process and privacy arguments of the eventual dissenters.[30] The switch, of course, drastically changed the outcome and empowered the Burkean traditionalism of White and Burger, rather than the gay rights affirming philosophy of Blackmun.

*Hurley v. Irish-American Gay, Lesbian, and Bisexual Group of Boston* (GLIB) clearly illustrates the variant of liberalism dominant in Supreme Court decision making on gay rights. An Irish gay group applied to march in the South Boston St. Patrick's Day parade, but was ultimately turned away by march organizers in 1993. The group went to court, claiming discrimination under Massachusetts's public accommodation law that banned discrimination based on sexual orientation. The trial court found that the parade was a public accommodation, since it received money and city support, including police and parking control, and the parade took place on city streets.[31] The Massachusetts high court affirmed the decision.[32] Both courts saw this as a discrimination issue and emphasized equality concerns over the First Amendment rights of the parade organizers, who claimed a free speech right to control the content of the parade. As the lower court asserted, "On its face, the statute does not seek to suppress speech. Rather, its goal is to eliminate discrimination which is unrelated to the suppression of expression."[33] In the conflict between equality and freedom, the Massachusetts courts favored equality.

Their voice was not unanimous, however. In a vigorous dissent, Justice Joseph Nolan saw the decision as a clear violation of the First Amendment rights of the parade organizers and foreshadowed the decision by the U.S. Supreme Court. For Nolan, the court was going too far, regulating the content of speech in the name of equality. He asserted: "Our holding today, while, to some, seemingly pushes us forward, really pushes us back over 200 years, to an era that lacked the protection guaranteed by the First Amendment."[34]

Following this line of argument, the U.S. Supreme Court, in a 9 to 0 decision, overturned the Massachusetts high court. Justice David Souter argued that the parade was clearly expressive under the First Amendment and the attempt of the gay group to march was also expressive—the issue was one of conflicting First Amendment claims, not free speech versus equality. As a consequence, the free speech rights of the parade organizers prevailed. Souter argued that the presence of GLIB in the parade was clearly a form of expression that could be kept out by the parade organizers' views on homosexuality. The decision, then, "boils down to the choice of a speaker not to propound a particular point of view, and that choice is presumed to lie beyond the government's power to control."[35]

Indeed, for Souter and the Court, the use of the Massachusetts public accommodation law in this instance was nothing more than state-sanctioned political correctness, an attempt to force parade organizers to agree with speech with which they explicitly disagree. As applied by the Massachusetts courts, according to Souter, the law's "apparent object is simply to require speakers to modify the content of their expression to whatever extent beneficiaries of the law choose to alter it with messages of their own."[36] Gone from this opinion is any discussion of the mandates of equality. The discussion is placed in starkly negative terms, with the Commonwealth of Massachusetts inserting itself into the sacred realm of the near-complete freedom from the state in the First Amendment. Absent were any arguments that the parade might be a remotely public event; it was viewed by the Court as completely private, despite its use of public funds and resources. Also absent from the discussion was the fact that the parade organizers discriminated on little else than sexual orientation, with various religious, civic, and political groups participating without controversy. The Massachusetts courts, to carve out space for equality arguments, used all of these arguments, but this space was completely missing in the holding of the U.S. Supreme Court.

Similar dynamics prevailed in *Dale v. Boy Scouts of America*. James Dale was expelled from the Boy Scouts after Scout leaders learned of his homosexuality. He sued under New Jersey's public accommodation law that included sexual orientation protection, and, after initial defeat at trial, he found success in the New Jersey courts. The Superior Court found the Scouts to be a public accommodation and found their action to be an illegal form of sexual orientation discrimination.[37] The New Jersey Supreme Court agreed.[38] Both courts cited a New Jersey precedent that referred to the "cancer of discrimination" in previous public accommodation cases, and both courts, like the Massachusetts courts, placed great emphasis on equality concerns. The New Jersey Supreme Court emphasized the history of group exclusion in U.S. history, and noted that "The human price of this bigotry has been enormous. At a most fundamental level, adherence to the principle of equality demands that our legal system protect the victims of invidious discrimination."[39] This concern for equality led both courts to interpret the Scouts' First Amendment rights narrowly and Dale's equality rights broadly. As the supreme court again declared: "To recognize Boy Scouts' First Amendment claim would be tantamount to tolerating the expulsion of an individual solely because of his status as a homosexual—an act of discrimination unprotected by the First Amendment freedom of speech."[40] The invocation of "status" is interesting here: Privacy lost to equality in this instance—an equality grounded in the notion that individuals ought not simply be left alone but should be valued for certain identities, especially those subject to social disfavor.

As with *Hurley*, the U.S. Supreme Court disagreed with the state courts and favored free speech claims over equality claims, but the Court lacked *Hurley*'s unanimity, with four justices dissenting. Despite the fact that opposition to homosexuality is not a main stated goal of the Scouts, the Court agreed with the Scouts' assertion that they do have an antigay policy and this should be preserved in the name of free speech, particularly the right of association, or the right to choose group members.[41] The dissenters argued that this decision misread precedent. Justice John Paul Stevens noted that "we have squarely held that a State's antidiscrimination law does not violate a group's right to associate simply because the law conflicts with that group's exclusionary membership policy."[42] Indeed, cases in the 1980s had established the precedent that private groups could not violate state antidiscrimination laws unless the basis for discrimination was directly linked to group membership. Stevens argued that a group's assertion alone on this point was not sufficient; the Court had to decide if there was a genuine connection. He felt that there was no such connection with the Scouts. Further, he argued, antigay animus is harmful and is a legitimate concern of states: "That harm can only be aggravated by the creation of a constitutional shield for a policy that is itself the product of a habitual way of thinking about strangers."[43] Thus, Stevens was at least hinting, if not declaring outright, that the negative freedom of privacy is not the primary constitutional value and indeed can do great harm if exclusively privileged.

However, it should be noted that the dissenters were also part of the unanimous *Hurley* Court. Indeed, even Stevens distinguished the cases, arguing that the groups involved in the *Hurley* litigation were clearly expressive, while "Dale did not carry a banner or a sign . . . he expressed no intent to send any message."[44] This was the crucial difference: status versus expression—a seemingly thin account of the personhood of sexual minorities. When you speak out, your right to antidiscrimination protection ends.

In *Romer v. Evans* (decided before *Dale*), the Court appeared to make some headway on the gay rights front, ruling in 1996 that Colorado's Amendment 2, which outlawed sexual orientation antidiscrimination protection, was unconstitutional since it was based on nothing more than animus toward sexual minorities.[45] But this appearance is deceptive, since no hard doctrine was invoked, again pointing to the lack of willingness of the Supreme Court to embrace gay rights and equality claims.[46] State courts in the *Romer* litigation were also more protective of gay rights claims. The Colorado Supreme Court struck down Amendment 2 on political process grounds, instead of using traditional equal protection analysis, thereby not considering sexual orientation a suspect classification triggering strict scrutiny. A high level of review was invoked nonetheless, since Amendment 2 infringed a fundamental constitutional right, that of political participation. Citing John Hart Ely and his political process model of constitutional jurisprudence, the court declared: "We conclude that the Equal Protection Clause of the United States Constitution protects the fundamental right to participate equally in the political process, and that any legislation or state constitutional amendment which infringes on this right by 'fencing out' an independently identifiable class of persons must be subject to strict judicial scrutiny."[47] Amendment 2 thus amounted to unconstitutional disenfranchisement, according to the Colorado court.

Justice Anthony Kennedy wrote a majority opinion for the U.S. Supreme Court that, while striking down Amendment 2 and containing some powerful language in defense of sexual minorities, did little to break new constitutional ground in the name of gay rights. Echoing the Colorado court, Kennedy declared that "[i]t is not within our constitutional tradition to enact laws of this sort," laws that fence out a group from the political process.[48] Kennedy rejected the use of strict scrutiny review, however, choosing to apply a rational basis test—a test that Amendment 2 failed. It failed, Kennedy argued, since there was no rational basis for the law and because it was based simply on animus. It was, in his words, "a status-based enactment divorced from any factual context from which we could discern a relationship to legitimate state interests."[49]

This holding, while constitutionally minimal, provoked a vigorous dissent from Justice Antonin Scalia, with Thomas and Rehnquist joining. Although the majority can be viewed as at least inching toward equality concerns, the dissent appears to be little more than a restatement of the judicial antigay sentiments of *Bowers*. Assigning sexual minorities no constitutional protection or privilege (especially after *Bowers*), Scalia argued that Amendment 2 was simply an instance of the people of Colorado protecting themselves and society against harmful conduct, as they do for murder. Essentially, he argued, supporters of gay rights were asking for special protection for deviant behavior. And, reflecting what Richard Hofstadter described as the "paranoid style in American politics," Scalia launched into a tirade that deserves to be quoted at length:

> When the Court takes sides in the culture wars, it tends to be with the knights rather than the villains—and more specifically with the Templars, reflecting the views and values of the lawyer class from which the Court's Members are drawn. How that class feels about homosexuality will be evident to anyone who wishes to interview job applicants at virtually any of the Nation's law schools. The interviewer may refuse to offer a job because the applicant is a Republican; because he is an adulterer; because he went to the wrong prep school or belongs to the wrong country club; because he eats snails; because he is a womanizer; because she wears real-animal fur; or even because he hates the Chicago Cubs. But if the interviewer should wish not to be an associate or partner of an applicant because he disapproves of the applicant's homosexuality, *then* he will have violated the pledge which the Association of American Law Schools requires all its member schools to exact from job interviewers: "assurance of the employer's willingness" to hire homosexuals.[50]

The fact that three members of the Supreme Court hold such disdain for the idea of equality for sexual minorities makes clear the reason that state courts have overtaken the federal courts in civil rights.

Evan Gerstmann notes that *Romer* is consistent with the evolution of equal protection jurisprudence in the United States, given the Supreme Court's backing away from the expansion of protected classes since the early 1970s. The Court has done so because of the potential for equal protection doctrine to invalidate a sweeping amount of legislation. As he notes, "the Court's power to declare that some groups are suspect classes is something like the constitutional equivalent of the atomic bomb."[51] As a result, according to Gerstmann, gay rights claims are not protected by clear constitutional doctrine, but are instead subject to judicial whim and sympathy on the part of judges. This is the best that can be said for federal constitutional jurisprudence in the United States on gay rights matters.

Murdoch and Price note that, starting with *Hurley*, the Court began to lose its overt hostility toward gays and lesbians, using affirming language even when deciding against gay litigants.[52] Thus, the justices' attitudes were changing, but this did not result in uniform success for gay litigants. Doctrinal issues, particularly the importance of negative freedom over other values, trumped personal attitudes for many of the justices. This is exemplified by the 9 to 0 decision in *Hurley*.

In 2003, the Court appeared to change its mind more uniformly on sexual minorities. In *Lawrence v. Texas*, the Court overturned *Bowers* and held that the state's same-sex-only antisodomy law violated the right to privacy. In doing so, Justice Kennedy used the language of rich liberalism and rejected the moralism of the *Bowers* majority. Indeed, the case was a direct repudiation of *Bowers*, with Kennedy declaring that "*Bowers* was not correct when it was decided, and it is not correct today."[53] Seemingly, then, the Court is evolving on gay rights questions, but this is a recent development. *Lawrence* and its implications will be explored in greater detail in Chapters 6 and 12. I will argue that, with this decision, the U.S. Supreme Court is becoming more Canada-like and appears to be reviving a richer liberalism in the context of gay rights jurisprudence, but only time will ultimately tell.

The rest of the U.S. federal judiciary has a mixed record on gay rights claims. This is to be expected, given the larger number and greater variety of these courts. For the most part, however, these courts have been generally unwilling to get too far in front of the Supreme Court in this area. For instance, federal courts have, with one fleeting exception, been unwilling to apply high standards of review to sexual orientation classifications. In a series of cases concerning marriage,[54] security clearances,[55] and the ban on gays in the military,[56] federal courts have used the rational basis test to allow discriminatory policies to pass equal protection review. The Ninth Circuit did, for a time in the late 1980s, find the ban on gays in the military unconstitutional. In doing so, the court ruled that sexual minorities were a suspect class—an innovative decision for the time, but an en banc panel of the Ninth Circuit quickly overturned this innovation.[57] Additionally, the federal courts have uniformly repelled suits challenging the heterosexual definition of marriage.[58] As one federal judge put it: "There has been for centuries a combination of scriptural and canonical teachings under which a 'marriage' between persons of the same sex was unthinkable and, by definition, impossible."[59] As will be discussed in later chapters, until recently, U.S. judges were largely unwilling to change marriage policy from the bench.

When the federal courts were liberal, antigay animus drove much federal judicial decision making. As the animus subsided somewhat, the federal courts became more conservative and were unwilling to expand jurisprudence for the protection of sexual minorities. In addition, powerful legal norms reinforcing the emphasis of notions of negative freedom dominated many gay rights cases. Where negative freedom fit gay rights claims (*ONE* and *Manual*), the result was good for gay rights, but where the federal courts were asked to view liberalism differently, gay rights claims were not successful (*Boutilier*, *Hurley*, *Dale*). Even when negative freedom appeared to control a decision, antigay animus in the courts was often powerful

(*Bowers*). Any move in the direction of more support for a wide range of gay rights claims is only a recent phenomenon in the federal courts (*Lawrence*). And this trend is not yet on solid ground. In July 2004, the Eleventh Circuit upheld a Florida law banning adoption by gay couples.[60]

## STATE COURTS AS POLICY MAKERS IN THE UNITED STATES

Most of the favorable gay rights decisions, then, have come from U.S. state courts, particularly in the past decade. Indeed, state courts are institutions to be reckoned with in the development of state law. As Henry Glick states, "within the boundaries of their own political systems, state supreme courts perform a substantial judicial review function, and combined, the fifty state supreme courts have a considerable impact in state law."[61] Unfortunately, Tarr and Porter point out "state supreme courts tend to operate in relative obscurity."[62] Indeed, given the sheer number of state supreme courts, it is difficult to monitor their activities in the same manner that one may monitor the activities of the U.S. Supreme Court. State courts are also more difficult to monitor than federal courts, given the diversity of state law and state constitutions. Nonetheless, Tarr and Porter put forward several main premises about the nature of state supreme courts. First, federalism deeply defines their role and relationships with other legal and political branches. They point out that state supreme courts interact with federal courts (in what they refer to as vertical federalism), other state courts (horizontal federalism), and other branches of state government. These relationships are defined by both legal and extralegal factors, like political culture. These relationships are highly dynamic and are almost constantly in flux. Finally, Tarr and Porter argue that there is tremendous diversity among state supreme courts. This, of course, makes it difficult to develop uniform models for state court activity. They state, "Because there is no typical state supreme court, there can be no typical role for a state supreme court in either the state or national arenas."[63]

Despite this diversity, it is possible to view state courts as makers of policy within and among states. As Baum and Canon have demonstrated, state courts were instrumental in effecting fundamental changes in American tort law.[64] Most interesting in their study is the role played by a handful of highly activist courts, particularly California, Michigan, and New Jersey, in leading the way for reforms of tort law by other state courts.[65] Thus, despite the diversity among state courts and state laws, some element of policy coordination often takes place over state lines. The most likely reason for this is the importance of precedent in legal reasoning. Even though state courts are not bound by the decisions of other state courts, they often cite one another to justify the outcome of their decisions.[66] Porter and Tarr argue that policy change and reform in state courts are often initiated in those states that are more receptive to public interest litigation, such as states that have minimal standing requirements.[67] As they describe the sweeping changes in tort law, "a few courts created a momentum that carried less adventurous courts along the path to reform."[68] Glick has also noted policy innovation by state high courts concerning the "right to die."[69]

As we shall see, however, this model of a few activist courts, created by low standing requirements and other factors that lead to more receptivity to public interest litigation, leading the way in reform for less activist and more conservative courts does not fully describe gay rights litigation. Often, courts viewed as traditionally more conservative have been at the forefront of changes in laws concerning lesbians and gay men. Additionally, some reforms have not exactly spread like wildfire among state courts after their first articulation in one or a handful of state supreme courts.

However, precedent and the citation of other state court decisions have indeed played a key role, especially in the case of sodomy law reform, and, increasingly, with the issue of same-sex marriage. Thus, as Glick argues, focusing on cross-court citations can indeed help us to see that state courts are not completely distinct from one another, but to attribute too much significance to this phenomenon is a mistake. Even attempts to control for factors such as ideology, political culture, and judicial professionalism do not always predict which courts will become policy innovators. This is primarily because courts only react to the cases brought before them by litigants; they do not control the policy agenda. This results in, according to Glick, "a high degree of idiosyncrasy in opportunities to decide cases and, consequently, in the resulting diffusion of policies among the states."[70]

The need for studying state courts has developed particularly in the past several decades. As Porter and Tarr indicate, we are currently in a period of state court activity that began in the early 1970s and has led to "a reinvigoration of state constitutional law by state supreme courts (the new judicial federalism), as some courts sought to provide more extensive protection for individual liberties in the wake of retrenchment by the Burger Court."[71] State courts have often found raw material for this new activism in their own state constitutions, many of which provided more explicit protection for individual liberties and guarantees of equality than the U.S. Constitution. As Porter and Tarr state, "seventeen state constitutions contain 'little ERA's,' ten expressly protect privacy rights, and several others in some form guarantee a right to environmental quality."[72] Given the fact that the U.S. Supreme Court has no jurisdiction to review cases that involve questions of state constitutional interpretation, state supreme courts often make rulings that are well out in front of federal court policy. The "new judicial federalism" is no longer new but continues to describe the role played by state courts in the United States.[73]

This is a relatively recent phenomenon for state courts, since until the 1970s very few state supreme court cases revolved around individual civil liberties, especially as these liberties have been defined in the twentieth century. In the nineteenth century, when state supreme courts were fairly active, their dockets were largely filled with property and business cases. These courts were not great protectors of religious liberty, freedom of speech, and the rights of the accused.[74] When the Burger and Rehnquist Courts began to back away from the heightened concern for civil liberties of the Warren Court, state supreme courts often stepped in to fill the void. Particularly encouraging to state supreme court judges were the arguments of Supreme Court Justice William Brennan who encouraged civil rights activism in state supreme courts.[75] The resulting plethora of state supreme court decisions regarding individual civil liberties has spawned a wealth of legal scholarship.[76] Regardless of the merits of this development, U.S. state court activism in the realm of civil liberties is a modern political and legal reality.

Since federal courts in the United States have not been responsive to gay rights claims, much of the discussion of the U.S. case will involve the activity of state courts. Because of the unique system of federalism in the United States, significant opportunity exists for state courts to develop or contribute to the development of public policy, policy that may be more progressive than national public policy. This can result from more explicit protections for individual rights in state constitutions or institutional arrangements and a political culture that encourages judicial activism. This has certainly been true in the realm of gay and lesbian rights. Particularly since the early 1990s, state supreme courts have been at the forefront of shaping state policies concerning the legal status of lesbians and gay men, primarily in striking down laws against sodomy and, in several significant cases, finding that bans on same-sex marriages are unconstitutional. These decisions have often extended beyond the parameters of federal policy, especially in the case of sodomy laws that were upheld by the U.S. Supreme Court until 2003. Concerning gay rights, state courts are currently the most innovative policy makers in the United States and are bringing about changes in the legal status of lesbians and gay men. Indeed, despite retrenchment in activism by federal courts in recent decades, state court activism is alive and well. Concerns for privacy rights and equality are more pronounced at the state level. The issue of gay and lesbian rights is a further example of the new judicial federalism that has evolved in response to the more conservative jurisprudence of the Burger and Rehnquist Courts and the more conservative turn of the federal courts in general, which have been reshaped by Republican presidents.[77]

In a recent study, Daniel Pinello has confirmed that state courts are more receptive to gay rights claims.[78] He also found that gay rights claims found the most success when state courts relied on state constitutional provision rather than the federal constitution.[79] Location was also a significant factor, with the West and the Northeast as the most receptive regions for gay rights claims.[80] Consequently, Pinello calls for a state approach to gay rights litigation, despite the cost and coordination barriers, since his findings "unveil virtually no empirically based reason to anticipate success for lesbian and gay rights litigants in federal fora as they are constituted currently or in the foreseeable future."[81] The findings of this study echo Pinello's but from a more qualitative perspective.

As will be seen in Chapter 10, the Canadian judicial system does not reflect the federal/state dichotomy. Therefore, it makes more sense to view Canadian courts as a whole, and a direct comparison is perhaps problematic. This book, then, uses a three-part comparison: U.S. state courts versus U.S. federal courts versus Canadian courts. However, before this analysis continues, I will devote the next two chapters to a fuller exploration of the relationship between liberalism and gay and lesbian politics. This is a crucial discussion, since courts in the United States and Canada rely on liberal arguments in making decisions.

# 3   Liberalism and Gay Politics: Rights and Their Critics

MY ARGUMENT in this book is that liberalism is an ideology capable of accommodating claims of lesbian and gay equality, particularly the claims associated with same-sex marriage, and that courts can be effective vehicles for promoting this equality. But liberalism is, and continues to be, under attack. Queer and critical theorists view liberalism as a mask for power and oppression of minorities, while communitarians, both left and right, see liberalism as a thin ideology, overly concerned with the individual at the expense of the needs of society. Increasingly, few commentators are willing to embrace liberalism. This is ironic, since courts traffic in the language of liberalism and rights. Many of these critical commentaries, then, are divorced from political and legal reality; while commentators disdain rights, judges continue to use and apply them. This chapter will explore these critiques and defend liberalism as an ideology that can be receptive to lesbian and gay rights and equality. Although this chapter ultimately deals with political philosophy, it is not a chapter of pure philosophical reasoning. Instead, I outline recent developments in liberal thought and the thought of liberalism's critics and discuss the historical development and the prominent strains of liberalism in the United States.[1] Critics of liberalism score points when they offer a minimal caricature of liberalism; they paint liberalism in its thinnest and most unsubstantial form. Following David Greenstone, I argue that U.S. liberalism possesses multiple strains. These strains have waxed and waned over time, but they are fair game for political and legal discourse.

This and the following chapter will illustrate two points: (1) liberalism's utility, compared to other political ideologies, for the future success of lesbian and gay rights, and (2) the necessity to view liberalism as more than mere negative libertarianism. In this chapter, I outline some important aspects of liberalism for gay politics and assess critical and queer critiques of liberalism, followed by communitarian and traditionalist critiques.

## LIBERALISM'S IMPORTANCE FOR GAY RIGHTS

Liberalism is an ideology that emphasizes the importance of the individual. In classical and medieval thought, the individual was not a primary focus of concern, only the good of the state or society. Born of the Enlightenment's emphasis on empiricism and opposition to social and political hierarchy, liberalism holds that all human beings are free and equal and their main purpose is to pursue their individual tastes and interests and not exclusively be concerned with the good of society. Over time, liberalism has come to represent a wide variety of positions. Individual rights, legalism, equality, and a public/private distinction are all central tenets of liberalism. An emphasis on liberalism is important for this discussion, since the United States and Canada are nations where liberalism is the dominant political tradition. Indeed, as Louis Hartz has noted, the United States is almost completely liberal, lacking a feudal past that might nourish alternative ideologies such as conservatism and Marxism.[2] Although the U.S. political tradition is more complex than Hartz describes,[3] an overriding emphasis on individualism and rights is the historical and contemporary hallmark of U.S. politics. And in the past century, U.S. courts have become increasingly interested in questions of individual rights, having been almost silent on the issue in the nineteenth, save for the right to contract. Canadian courts are following their U.S. counterparts, particularly after the adoption of their Charter. Increasingly, then, litigants and judges are adopting the language and principles of liberalism.

However, liberalism is not always easily pinned down. Some versions are quite negative, in that they emphasize the need for the individual to be almost completely free from governmental restraint and coercion. This is, of course, classical liberalism or modern libertarianism. Even contemporary liberal theorists like John Rawls attempt to preserve an individualism that steers away from moral content; indeed, this perspective requires the state to be neutral on questions of individual morality and notions of the good life. Individualism has little independent substantive moral value in this approach. This might be useful for some areas of gay rights, like sodomy laws, but same-sex marriage requires the state's promotion of a value—the value that marriage contributes to a better, more fully developed individual.[4]

Another version of liberalism, perhaps more accommodating of this value, sees the individual as more socially situated and reliant on the state and society to develop fully as an individual. This version emphasizes positive, rather than negative, liberty. This latter view of liberalism is the intellectual centerpiece of this project. A rich liberalism, it will be argued, is the best foundation for furthering lesbian and gay politics. It is the version of politics that is most likely to sustain reform efforts while not alienating majorities by going too far outside the parameters of a political culture.

Isaiah Berlin was critical of the ideal of positive liberty. With twentieth-century totalitarianism in mind, he rejected variants of liberalism that tried to make humans free, instead of merely interfering with their lives. Berlin feared a liberal paternalism, grounded in Kantian thought, which stated that individuals have affirmative duties to make good choices, choices that generally lead to self-improvement. As he argued, "Paternalism is despotic, not because it is more oppressive than naked, brutal, unenlightened tyranny . . . but because it is an insult to my conception of myself as a human being, determined to make my own life in accordance with my own (not necessarily rational or benevolent) purposes, and, above all, entitled to be recognized as such by others."[5] Berlin cautioned against confusing liberty with equality and community. He adhered to Benjamin Constant's distinction between the liberty of the ancients versus the liberty of the moderns. The former was concerned not with the individual, but with the good of the community. Indeed, in classical thought individual liberty was a little-discussed concept. Ultimately, Berlin rejected any notion of positive freedom, since it would lead to totalitarianism as a result of its paternalism. Freedom should demand nothing more than state noninterference.

Berlin was correct to stress individual autonomy, but his distinction between negative and positive liberty is too stark. Even Constant, a great theorist of modern liberalism, wished to soften the edges of extreme negative individualism. He noted that modern liberal states were less ambitious in regard to their citizens, whereas the ancients required the complete obedience and subjugation of the individual to society.[6] This is no longer possible or desirable in modern times when a new ordering principle is prevalent. "Our freedom must consist of peaceful enjoyment and private independence," Constant noted.[7] So far, this line of thought comports with Berlin. However, Constant was not comfortable with complete private independence. His individualism is somewhat tempered by classical notions of freedom, since "far from renouncing either of the two sorts of freedom . . . it is necessary to learn to combine the two together."[8] The way to do so, Constant argued, was through representative government in which self-interest and individualism could be augmented and tempered. Representative government brings individuals and classes together and promotes a sense of the whole. It tends to mitigate against powerful groups ignoring the political claims of the powerless. In defending direct election of representatives, Constant argued that "[i]t is this election which requires, from the classes in power, a sustained level of consideration for the lower orders. It compels wealth to dissimulate its *arrogance*" (italics added).[9] Although Constant certainly does not wish to reestablish the ancient polis and all that it demands of citizens, his thought reflects a discontent with an exclusive emphasis on negative freedom and a recognition that liberalism, if not properly constrained by institutions, can be harmful to political minorities. Despite attempts by modern critics of liberalism to caricature it as a thin, useless ideology, prominent liberal theorists have maintained otherwise.

## LIBERALISM AND MAJORITARIAN POLITICS

Constant's use of the term arrogance is fitting, since a crucial reason that liberalism is the best ideology for lesbian and gay politics is that it is an ideology that disfavors arrogance, particularly the arrogance of political majorities. Arrogance is used in this context more descriptively than pejoratively by describing a dynamic where a majority takes its position for granted. This arrogance is marked by an absolute refusal to consider arguments and positions of political minorities, even when those arguments appear to fit rationally with already-established political discourse. For instance, opponents of same-sex marriage in the United States (a current political majority) refuse to consider that lesbians and gay relationships can create the same stable, monogamous, loving, child-rearing dynamic found in the heterosexual marriage ideal. Hypocritical arguments are recited as fact, even when they are clearly challenged by logic. A good example of this is the argument of same-sex marriage opponents that marriage's purpose is for procreation, and since gay couples cannot naturally procreate, marriage should not be open to them. This argument is undercut by the example of sterile and elderly heterosexual couples who are allowed to marry. The reality is that modern Western marriage has come to emphasize the emotional bond between two people, but same-sex marriage opponents still arrogantly cling to the outdated procreation argument, even as their own relationships reflect the modern reality.

William Galston has also identified the elimination of hypocrisy as an important element of liberalism. According to Galston, a virtue of liberalism "is the disposition to narrow the gap . . . between principles and practices in liberal society. For leaders, this means admitting and confronting social imperfections through a public appeal to collective convictions. For citizens it can mean either such a public appeal, or quiet acts that reduce the reach of hypocrisy in one's immediate community."[10] Arrogant majorities act with utter disregard for alternatives to their way of knowing and living. Liberalism can arm minorities with the tools to chip away at this arrogance and force an understanding of those outside the majority. The richer the liberalism, the more powerful the tools at the disposal of minorities.

Arrogance also blinds people from fully considering the claims of minorities and often leads them to caricature these claims. Such is the case with Jean Bethke Elshtain, who bemoans the state of contemporary politics as being too concerned with private matters, reflected in the feminist slogan, "The personal is political." She admires Berlin's emphasis on negative liberty and wishes to keep a strong distinction between public and private, with the public sphere limited and certainly not open to discussion of intimate matters. Her self-professed goal is to save democratic government, since discussions of lifestyle and sexuality open the door to moral concerns that are not easily resolved in the public sphere. Crucially, according to Elshtain, if the government chooses sides in this debate, it will inhibit those on the losing side of the argument from participating in the public sphere. As she states, "there *must* be within a world of democratic politics, ways for people who differ in important, not trivial ways, to come together to 'do' practical politics in a shared public arena. For this to be possible, we must recognize that public action and private intimacy have different requirements."[11] Elshtain views the political claims of lesbians and gay men as nothing more than a desire to legitimate sex—not as claims to civil equality in the treatment of relationships. "Militant gay liberationists [Elshtain identifies no other kind of gay rights advocates] . . . seek government protection and approval, not so much to prevent intrusion as to legitimate public assertion of private behavior."[12] Elshtain, of course, does not consider that the state confers public approval and benefits on private relationships in the form of marriage laws. Many of those laws are based on the explicit assumption that the persons in those relationships will be having sex. Should this lead, under Elshtain's framework, to a position that calls for the elimination of the legal approval of heterosexual marriage? Granted, she voiced her concerns in an essay in 1987, before arguments for same-sex marriage were a prominent part of the gay rights movement, but her willingness to see all claims of gay rights as illegitimate forays into the public arena illustrates the limitations of arrogance when applied to political philosophy.

## THE INSUFFICIENCY OF NEGATIVE LIBERTY

This book attempts to shed light on the paucity of dominant strands of American liberalism. The comparison of U.S. sodomy and same-sex marriage litigation to developments in Canada will illustrate that U.S. liberalism is generally too minimal, negative, and libertarian. Although richer strains of liberalism have existed in U.S. political traditions, this strain predominates. It is the U.S. "knee-jerk" political philosophy. Consequently, sodomy laws rather easily fall under the banner of sexual privacy, a negative liberal concept, while attempts to legalize same-sex marriage meet fierce political resistance, despite often being well received in the legal process. Marriage requires more than just being left alone within that relationship. It is an institution, at least as currently developed, that requires the official recognition and sanction by the state, since so many legal rights and benefits come with it. As Nancy Cott states:

> To *be* marriage, the institution requires public affirmation. It requires public knowledge—at least some publicity beyond the couple themselves; that is why witnesses are required for the ceremony and why wedding bells ring. More definitively, legal marriage requires state sanction, in the license and the ceremony.[13]

And yet, because of heterosexual arrogance, the point is seldom grasped. Since marriage is so common for heterosexuals and is such an ingrained institution, it does not seem like a positive affirmation by the state of certain relationships. It is just the way things are. As Cott asserts, "The majority . . . can parade the field, taking public affirmation for granted."[14] The question becomes how to eliminate this myopic view. I argue that liberalism can, and needs to, be the most appropriate ideological tool in this effort.

The liberalism at the center of this project is one influenced by neo-Kantian versions of liberalism developed in the past thirty years by Rawls, Dworkin, and David A. J. Richards. This brand of liberalism is attractive because of its attempt to revive rights claims as a legitimate part of modern politics. Particularly in the first half of the twentieth century in the United States, utilitarian/majoritarian views of law and politics tended to deemphasize the importance of rights. Legal realism was an understandable antidote to the Lochner era, but it gave far too much deference to political majorities in all areas of political life. Neo-Kantian thinkers attempt to revive rights claims. My goal here is not to engage in a philosophical defense of such thinkers. Instead, my view in this book recognizes that theoretical arguments can become the raw material of law and politics. Lawyers and judges, especially, use broad arguments, often articulated by political philosophers, to guide legal arguments. They are not concerned with nuance or minor particulars, but the general trend of an argument—in this instance, a concern for "equal concern and respect" and a refusal to defer to majoritarian sentiments.

Richards articulates the neo-Kantian perspective and asserts that it calls for the affirmation of same-sex marriage. Rejecting utilitarian liberalism and its minimal view of persons as animal-like pleasure/pain calculators, Richards argues that this richer liberalism views individuals "in terms of personhood, the capacity of each person self-critically to evaluate and give order and personal integrity to one's system of ends in the form of one's life."[15] This principle of "autonomy" is not simply a freedom to be left alone; it posits that individuals make decisions and arrange their lives for personal self-development. A large part of this ordering, for Richards, includes love and sexual intimacy. Whereas Rawls, from whom Richards draws, never directly addressed this issue in *A Theory of Justice*—his concerns were primarily economic[16]—Richards gives it central consideration.

> Because of the profound relation of sexual autonomy to basic self-respect, the following principle of obligation and duty, defining correlative human rights, would be accepted in the original position—*the principle of love as a civil liberty*. Basic institutions are to be arranged so that every person is guaranteed the greatest equal liberty, opportunity and capacity to love, compatible with a like liberty, opportunity and capacity for all.[17]

Articulated in the early 1980s, when the gay rights movement was mostly relying on arguments grounded in negative liberty (as with sodomy decriminalization efforts), this call for an ordering of an equitable society, which includes institutional arrangements and protections for the right to love by all, including sexual minorities, was certainly a bit ahead of its time. But less than two decades later, courts in the United States and Canada would use similar arguments to push in the direction of state recognition of same-sex unions.

## THE QUEER CRITIQUE

By the 1970s, the New Left was losing its allegiance to Marxism, which had been its intellectual foundation for decades. The reason for this change is stated by Steven Seidman: "Marxism may have initially facilitated social criticism and political mobilization in the . . . [New Left], but its epistemic and political privileging of working-class politics rendered racial, gender, sexual, and other nonclass struggles secondary and marginal."[18] Indeed, even gay liberationism came under fire. For many activists and intellectuals, its emphasis on a common cause neglected the diversity that existed in the realm of sexual minorities. Difference was to be the mantra, even within the gay and lesbian community.[19] As an example of this critique, based on diversity, lesbian-feminism insisted that the gay liberation movement was far too male-centered. Instead, lesbians were distinct from gay men, this critique argued. Lesbianism is a concept open to all women and has little to do with sexual orientation; it has more to do with women's liberation from the patriarchal society. In Seidman's words, "Lesbian-feminism encourages women to become aware of their ties to other women; it intends to promote the growth of female values and modes of being by building an autonomous 'womansculture.'"[20] Yet another group challenging the unity of gay liberation was gay people of color, who criticized the racism and white male domination and elitism of the movement.

Concurrently, social theory was providing a framework that would support the emphasis on difference and diversity. In particular, the theories of Michel Foucault opened the door for a new type of analysis about sexuality. Foucault maintained that the very notion of sexuality has changed throughout time. Sexuality is not fixed and immutable but changes with particular historical and social circumstances. Indeed, as Jonathan Ned Katz describes Foucault's position, "Sexuality ... is a uniquely modern phenomenon and idea, constituted by a historically specific, in-stitutionalized practice and ideology."[21] Rejecting the idea of sexual repression that epitomized much of the early New Left views of the politics of sexuality, Foucault argued that sexual repression was only a small part of modern sexual-ity. Contrary to the repression thesis, according to Foucault, "We have not only witnessed a visible explosion of unorthodox sexualities; but ... the proliferation of specific pleasures and the multiplication of disparate sexualities."[22] The prob-lem, then, is not repression but state power that promotes one version of sexuality. Foucault thus poses a direct challenge to the liberal distinction between the public and private realms. As David Halperin describes Foucault's view of power, "civil society, scientific research, intellectual activity, and personal life are not in fact free zones from which power has progressively retreated since the Enlightenment but colonized spaces into which it has steadily expanded, proliferated, and dif-fused itself."[23] Or, as Foucault himself put it: "Power is everywhere."[24] Politics since the Enlightenment, in this view, has been the story of the expansion of power into private matters like sexuality. The modern state required a population base, so procreation and the regulation of sexual norms increasingly became the busi-ness of government. According to Foucault, "Through the political economy of population there was formed a whole grid of observations regarding sex."[25] Thus, heterosexuality is not a given, but a construct used by the state that reinforces a capitalistic, bourgeois ethic.

The ramifications for politics based on this theory are profound. Sex and sexual orientation are not private matters, and the goal of this politics is not merely inclusion or acceptance. Like liberationism, the goal is a direct challenge to the norm of heterosexuality. Since power is everywhere, sex is not a private act but a political one. If heterosexuality is merely a social construct, it is easily destroyed and remade. Consequently, the door is wide open for a type of radical politics; the socially constructed nature of sexuality invites direct challenges once this fact is recognized. In fact, according to Halperin, "our task is to become queer."[26] Simply being different is a challenge to the sexual power structure, and this assertion of difference opens the path to remake the system based on the diversity of sexual norms and practices that are the mark of modern society. The diversity must be embraced and not stifled in the service of the needs of the modern state. Exactly how this is done is demonstrated though the examination of several political thinkers influenced by Foucault's analysis.

## MARK BLASIUS, MICHAEL WARNER, AND QUEER POLITICS

Furthering the trends of the 1970s, the gay liberation movement of the 1980s came under increasing attack. There appeared to be serious limits to the ethnic group paradigm, which held that gays and lesbians are common groups looking for political and social liberation. The right-wing backlash to the progress made in the 1970s and the rise of the AIDS epidemic quickened the impulse to rethink the nature of gay and lesbian politics. Based largely on the writing of Foucault, the queer political movement came into its own.

Mark Blasius attempts to formulate a vision of gay and lesbian politics in his book *Gay and Lesbian Politics: Sexuality and the Emergence of a New Ethic*. Blasius argues strongly for the abandonment of traditional, assimilationist politics for sexual minorities. Indeed, he argues that simply being gay or lesbian "is by definition political."[27] There can be no hiding from politics under the guise of privacy. Reflecting Foucault's argument that power is everywhere, Blasius argues that sexuality is not something that belongs in the corner of political discourse and activity; it permeates political space. Blasius also shares Foucault's view of the power dynamic of heterosexuality. "They [heterosexuals] create, within the structure of heterosexist domination, individuals who understand themselves as 'heterosexual' and, as such, can have access to the structure of domination to attain and maintain privilege and unequal social status."[28] As a result, the only avenue for political change is challenging this heterosexist domination directly. It does not involve asking to be included; one should not require the permission of heterosexual oppressors to assert one's independence or respectability. Those on the outside should not simply buy into the established social and political structure, in Blasius's view.

Consequently, Blasius calls for a politics that goes beyond the traditional civil rights paradigm—indeed one that even goes beyond the idea of liberation and its assumption of homogeneity among sexual minorities. Traditional legal rights, privacy, and equality are not enough. Liberal discourse must be abandoned in favor of a "cultural politics directed at the social conditions underlying regulative norms, as well as at the disciplinary mechanisms of power through which norms are inculcated upon individual bodies . . . ; new ethics, a new relational ethos, would result in new cultural forms."[29] The individual must be freed from a power structure that imposes sexual norms. Not surprisingly, for Blasius, sadomasochism is the type of sexual practice that best challenges these norms. Instead of being a deviant sexual behavior, it is a legitimate and useful practice, since it allows individuals to play with power relationships in a situation of fantasy with an element of reality.

> Although it is a fantasy situation, it could become real: the . . . physical sensations are real. Even though the power is consensual, it could become nonconsensual and real. It is at this threshold between reality and fantasy that participants understand how a power relation "works" and how one's subjective desires allow it to work or not work, and then carry this understanding over into the rest of their lives.[30]

Sexuality that teaches about the pervasiveness of power also provides a civics lesson. It is more difficult, however, to ascertain what direct political action Blasius wants to achieve through this new state of affairs. He calls for a new "relational right," which "should involve a right to self-determination of one's relationships with others."[31] Pockets of queer sexuality will challenge the dominance of heterosexuality and its conventionality, in his view. But this sounds less radical and more in the tradition of classical liberalism. Indeed, it sounds more like Mill's "experiments of living"[32] than Foucault's deconstruction. Remarkably reminiscent of Mill, Blasius states that, in acknowledging the openness of contemporary gay lives, "what we are doing is something historically new, an experiment in living that must be recorded."[33] Mill's position is not merely to leave individuals alone to pursue their own interests and pleasures, but that society benefits from this social experimentation. Societal norms, or "common modes of thinking,"[34] as Mill referred to them, would be challenged by this process and would hopefully evolve for the better. Despite the postmodern rhetoric, it appears that Blasius comes to a conclusion that, in the end, differs little from a liberal like Mill.

As Morris Kaplan points out, Blasius dangerously skirts the boundary of an overly narrow focus on the sexual practices of urban white middle-class males. "After all," according to Kaplan, "one needs to enjoy a certain measure of economic power and social privilege to be able to identify oneself primarily with one's erotic activities and community."[35] Indeed, the type of analysis in which Blasius engages faces the danger of being less about politics than about the justification of sexual practices. Is this type of analysis truly radical or merely selfish?

Michael Warner has provided a recent articulation of a politics that is somewhat more strident. He bristles at the idea of a politics based in "a rainbow coalition, or in trickle-down acceptance."[36] The contemporary gay movement, according to Warner, does not do nearly enough to address what he call the politics of shame, or the dominant heterosexual norms that treat sex as mostly bad and those who deviate from the norms as outcasts. The gay movement's focus on identity without addressing the issue of shame makes the movement too antiseptic and lets the enforcers of the norm off far too easily. Instead, shame must be turned into pride; the oppressive norms must be rendered irrelevant through the assertion of different sexualities. According to Warner,

> only when this indignity of sex is spread around the room, leaving no one out, and in fact binding people together, that it begins to resemble the dignity of the human.... That, I think, is the premise of queer culture.... But I'm speaking now of sluts and drag queens and trannies and trolls and women who have seen a lot in life—not the media spokesman and respectable leaders of the gay community.[37]

The politics of the dispossessed, those living outside legitimate social and political boundaries, is the true mark of a radical brand of politics. There is something more urgent, more visceral about Warner's words. He certainly cannot be accused of defending only white middle-class sexual practices.

This is a politics that refuses to buy into traditional forms of political activity. Direct confrontation, not lobbying, voting, or even litigation, is its tactic. This politics has no use for even an ounce of accommodation to heterosexual norms. "Queer politics is scandalous politics; queers materialize as the dreaded homosexual other imagined by straight society that had invisibly and silently shaped straight life but now do so openly, loudly, and unapologetically."[38] No fear, no hesitation encumbers this politics, and it is a far cry from even the most progressive liberal politics. And yet, as Martha Nussbaum has noted, Warner also calls for a Millian solution to liberate sexual minorities from the oppression of dominant sexual norms.[39] The liberal paradigm appears hard to escape.

## A NOTE ON LESBIAN POLITICS AND THE REJECTION OF LIBERALISM

So far, this discussion has centered on male political theorists and activists. As was previously noted, lesbian politics, derived from feminist theory, also developed as a reaction to the traditional civil rights paradigm of gay politics. Recognizing that issues of sexual oppression were intimately linked with issues of gender, feminist lesbians have developed a body of political thought that parallels, though not directly mirrors, that of Foucault and his progeny. Feminist-lesbian politics broadly falls under the queer umbrella, but with some differences.

In *Getting Specific: Postmodern Lesbian Politics*, Shane Phelan articulates a version of feminist lesbianism. Like those inspired by Foucault, Phelan views sexism and heterosexism as power structures. Thus, any attempt to ask for inclusion into this power structure is self-defeating, since it does not challenge the nature of the power itself. Indeed, the traditional language of liberation is limited, since it "has been inextricably bound to modernity and its forms of power and has been unable to address contemporary configurations that are not recognizable within that framework,"[40] suggesting that a liberal framework of rights and inclusion can still be oppressive toward women.

She continues this critique in a more recent work about citizenship. It is clear she has no use for liberalism, or at least the liberalism she caricatures. Typical of many queer theorists, Phelan paints liberalism as a thin ideology, one that is completely incapable of sustaining the cause of gay and lesbian rights and equality. She criticizes the "neutral procedural republic so fondly imagined by liberal theorists."[41] For Phelan, liberalism is the nineteenth-century variant that simply masks power and oppression and is seldom a force for positive change. This description of liberalism takes place in a discussion of citizenship, and Phelan feels that liberalism cannot accommodate citizenship's demands of sexual minorities, since it is "about participation in the social and political life of a political community, and as such it is not confined to a list of legal protections and inclusions."[42] Indeed, according to Phelan, liberalism's obsession with rights is distracting from the reality of power dynamics and allows liberals to be duped by sexual majorities unwilling to deconstruct their sexual mores and institutional arrangements.

Instead, Phelan calls for a "queer citizenship," one that is not content with assimilation or accommodation. "Rather than becoming 'virtually normal,' Americans must seek out the strange and the unexpected in themselves and others."[43] Nothing less than a direct, frontal assault on heterosexuality and heterosexual institutions is required. Gradual change will not lead to change at all; it will only result in further oppression. One must attack "pre-existing networks of cultural power and meaning."[44] For example, the idea that elimination of sodomy laws will open the door to more progressive change is naïve, in Phelan's view. She argues that courts will still privilege heterosexual relationships and continue to stigmatize only same-sex sodomy.[45] This assertion, of course, overlooks the actual change that has taken place over the past decade. Heterosexual privilege was eventually broken down by many courts under a liberal framework, as will be discussed in later chapters. Unfortunately, Phelan falls victim to the binary nature of queer thought. She cannot get beyond the insider/outsider intellectual construction to see the reality of the situation. In fact, the repeal of sodomy laws often leads to greater change, like same-sex marriage or domestic partnership arrangements.[46]

Despite this more radical critique, Phelan has called for a more inclusive model of political change. She calls for an egalitarian pluralism where lesbianism is recognized and valued. But a first step toward this goal is practical, not radical. "Thus as uninspiring as it may sound in a world of cultural warfare and subversion," Phelan argues, "lesbians need to fight for civil rights legislation. These rights are a part of our collective empowerment. . . . [W]e need to do this quite simply because without the safety afforded by these minimal guarantees we will never get to change anything else."[47] She may have become disillusioned with this tactic, however. Most recently, as noted above, she calls for much more radical change. A queer citizenship will look little like its heterosexual predecessor.

Ultimately, this tension between theory and action that many of these theorists exhibit can be explained by the fact that queer theory, and postmodern thought in general, is a poor foundation for political change in a democracy. Indeed, Phelan recognizes that democratic change can only occur when a majority decides when change will occur, but she believes that deconstructing the majority's norms is the best way to get it to change its mind. This would appear to be a difficult path in democratic politics. Change usually comes when a majority is persuaded that it is not living up to its ideals—not that its ideals are corrupt and oppressive. At any rate, courts using liberal arguments may be a better source for this change than academics armed with a theory, the goal of which is confrontation and destruction of political traditions.

Rhonda Copelon makes a similar argument to the one I present within a feminist framework. She critiques the male-influenced, largely negative-rights tenor of the Constitution and constitutional interpretation as not sufficiently attentive to the full range of issues involved in modern personhood. In particular, the public/private distinction has resulted in the oppression of women and other politically weak groups. The right to privacy, which is grounded in the public/private distinction, is a particularly dangerous right, since it distracts from the legitimate claims of women and sexual minorities. By expropriating the rights rhetoric of traditional male-centered liberalism while infusing it with a richer sense of rights, feminists, according to Copelon, "have both challenged the patriarchal structure and contributed to the progressive revelation of the thoroughgoing transformation that feminist principles require."[48] But, again, the critique and prescription for change differ little from an approach derived from liberalism itself. Interestingly, then, modern liberalism and some brands of "radical" politics ultimately differ little.

In this discussion, I do not intend to completely dismiss the perspectives of feminist and queer perspectives. These perspectives often effectively point out liberalism's blind spots. As Judith Baer states, "Liberalism's presumption of free will and consent denies women's vulnerability . . . . Individual rights exercised by women may be good for them, but individual rights exercised by people with power over women can oppress them."[49] I agree with Baer that liberalism properly attuned to power configurations and a richer notion of rights can be a framework for the elimination of oppression and inequality.

## THE CRITIQUE OF MODERN COMMUNITARIANS AND TRADITIONALISTS

Liberalism has also come under significant attack by those who argue that it does not take sufficient account of the extent to which individuals are defined by their communities or by tradition. To separate individuals from these elements, it is argued, is to misunderstand the socially constituted nature of human interaction in the name of abstract reasoning. One cannot be concerned, the argument goes, only with the individual self-realization of lesbians and gay men; their relationship to their communities and the ways in which they have been regarded by tradition are also important.

Michael Sandel is a leading voice of the communitarian critique. Like queer theorists, he is dissatisfied with liberalism's seeming thinness. Sandel bemoans liberalism's neutrality toward the good life, its emphasis on the public/private distinction, and the central placement of rights as trumps against the state. This tendency of liberalism, over time, has led to an "impoverished civic life."[50] The remedy, for Sandel, can be found in republican principles. Instead of moral neutrality, the state must be explicitly concerned with individual morality and must actively cultivate it, since "republican politics regards moral character as a public, not merely private, concern."[51] Indeed, Sandel explicitly calls for more of Constant's "ancient liberty."

Sandel directly relates his views to lesbian and gay politics. He criticizes arguments in favor of same-sex sexual autonomy as generally being too focused on privacy, as was Harry Blackmun's dissent in *Bowers v. Hardwick*. According to Sandel, this focus does not do enough to equate lesbian and gay relationships with heterosexual relationships and emphasize their commonality. In the end, it only further marginalizes gay relationships by keeping them outside the realm of the normal, albeit protected with rights. As he states, "A fuller respect [for gays] would require, if not admiration, at least some appreciation of the lives homosexuals live. But such an appreciation is unlikely to be cultivated by a legal and political discourse conducted in terms of autonomy alone."[52]

Sandel is certainly on to something here. As I have argued, libertarian liberalism is not sufficient to sustain fully gay rights claims. But his emphasis on republicanism as the way out is misguided, since communities are inherently exclusive, not inclusive. Communities clearly define their boundaries and are generally hesitant to alter or abolish them. Sandel, however, feels that through public discourse, any change can be made in a political community. Outsiders can easily become insiders. This view is, of course, far too hopeful and analytically thin. Community boundaries are complex and often layered with deeply held racist or sexist practices. Phelan has astutely pointed out the inherent masculinity of republican fraternal aspirations. Calls for brotherhood generally do not include same-gender intimacy, since this would undermine the nonsexual fraternal bond. As she states, "The homosexual man becomes the spoiler, the wet blanket at the fraternal slumber party."[53] Given this, I maintain that the outsider can only be fully protected through a liberal scheme of rights that is beyond the manipulation of the majority. Or, as Harry Hirsch asserts, "The *polis* can perhaps serve as a metaphor for the modern polity; it cannot serve as its model."[54]

William Eskridge argues that liberalism and communitarianism should merge on gay rights questions. The formulation he calls "equality practice" responds to the fact that liberalism does not fully accommodate all gay rights claims, but communitarian concerns often neglect gay rights claims. Yet, Eskridge wishes to let communitarianism inform remedies to liberal gay rights claims. Or, as he puts it, "Rawlsian rights and Sandelian remedies." Eskridge privileges these remedies because, he argues, liberalism doesn't have the best arguments for same-sex marriage claims. Rather, communitarian notions of the common good are preferable. As he states, "Same-sex marriage is good for many gay, lesbian, bisexual, and transgendered (GLBT) people and is on the whole a good idea for the larger community." Although he grants that communitarian arguments are often made in opposition to same-sex marriage, he claims that the "public goodness of same-sex marriage" argument convinces political actors in the middle of same-sex marriage debates to decide in favor of same-sex marriage rights. As I will argue in a later chapter, this is an incorrect assessment of the dynamics of same-sex marriage litigation and its political aftermath. I assert that same-sex marriage policies have only prevailed after clear judicial declaration of liberal legal rights along with a judicial mandate to change policy. Legislators do not act without judicial intervention. Communitarian arguments do not act as an independent political force for positive political change on same-sex marriage policy. Their overwhelming use is to maintain the status quo.

Carlos Ball also argues for augmenting liberalism in order to support fully the political demands of sexual minorities. He faults liberals like Kant, Rawls, and Dworkin for privileging reason at the expense of emotion. Relying on the arguments of Martha Nussbaum, he calls for a "moral liberalism" that transcends a sole reliance on rationality and focuses on emotions, and, therefore, relationships and their role in individual fulfillment and development. "As moral liberalism sees it," according to Ball, "political philosophy must grapple directly with the broader domain of human needs and capabilities associated with the body, emotions, and relationships."[55] Moral liberalism is a new liberalism for Ball, since it rejects the public/private distinction and neutrality about the good life. It builds on feminism and communitarianism to build a fuller liberalism. Ball has tried for some time to improve on liberalism on the basis of communitarian critiques.[56]

In many ways, Ball's moral liberalism looks a lot like the reform liberalism based on positive freedom that Greenstone notes has been a significant part of the U.S. political tradition. This liberalism sees individuals as socially situated and requiring affirmative support from society and by the state to fully develop as individuals. Or, as Ball describes moral liberalism, "human relationships and attachments, rather than being relegated to a private sphere . . . are instead an integral part of that morality because they are an integral part of the way in which individuals lead autonomous lives."[57] The problem is that this is not only a perspective driven by feminist and communitarian considerations. The development of liberalism in the twentieth century, as I explore in the next chapter, also takes account of a fuller person than libertarianism itself or the caricature that contemporary critics of liberalism invoke. At any rate, court decisions tend to be grounded in liberal discourse; judges in the Anglo-American tradition are much more focused on promoting liberal rights than tearing them apart and deconstructing them.

The perspective of Robert George illustrates the danger of relying on community and tradition for the furthering of gay rights claims. George comes from a tradition that views morality instrumentally as a source of social control. Like Leo Strauss and his followers, George emphasizes the social value of morality, rather than believing in the morality itself. He echoes Patrick Devlin's opposition to individualism (which will be explored more fully in Chapter 5) and any political ideology that allows individuals to spin off the societal center. Indeed, according to George, "In Devlin's view, the truth or falsity of a putative moral obligation is irrelevant to the question of whether it may legitimately be prohibited by law. Acts that are contrary to the core morality around which people have integrated themselves, thus constituting a society, threaten that morality and thus imperil social cohesion and the very existence of society."[58]

As with Strauss's (and Plato's) "noble lie," truth means little; morality merely serves as a source of social control. The individual, then, is required to be guided by state paternalism to ensure that societal norms are not violated, not only to protect society but to preserve the dignity of individuals by "prevent[ing] them from demeaning, degrading, or destroying themselves by their own wrongful choices," that is, homosexual acts.[59] Here George draws upon the natural law tradition represented by John Finnis. This presents an interesting connection between neo-Kantian theory and the natural law tradition. Both, to some extent, emphasize individual dignity and worth. However, the Christian elements of the natural law version of dignity and worth necessarily implicate Christian morality and, in this instance, its general disapproval of homosexuality. Therefore, committing a homosexual act (or any act outside of procreation) is self-defilement both unworthy of the individual and harmful to society for its potential to interfere with procreation.

However, nonprocreative sex is not always self-defilement. Instead, sexual pleasure and intimacy are innate parts of human activity and the pursuit of them is the pursuit of self-fulfillment. This has been well argued by Stephen Macedo. Macedo challenges Finnis's view that any sex outside of procreation is essentially masturbation—for no use other than personal pleasure—and thus is illegitimate. He rightly points out that Finnis and others generally do not have a problem with sterile heterosexuals couples having sex. And Macedo rightly claims that Finnis conceives of sex too narrowly. As Macedo asks, "Is it even remotely plausible that all homosexual acts—including the most loving sexual acts within long-term monogamous relationships—embody nothing more than a quick trip to a prostitute?"[60] Here, again, arrogance is at work. Natural law theorists and traditionalists/communitarians wish to elevate heterosexual sex, even if it does not directly link to procreation, while portraying all forms of same-sex intimacy as cheap and tawdry. The first kind of sex is thought to be integral to personhood, while the latter is destructive of it. The notion that sexual intimacy is a universal human good is not explored. This analysis also leads to logical contortions and almost absurd assertions by natural law theorists. For example, to justify sex among infertile or elderly heterosexual couples, natural law theorists argue that these couples at least have the biological "tools" that correspond with sex as procreation. This functionalist reasoning conveniently ignores advances in technology and fences out any consideration of the value of same-sex sexual intimacy.

In the above discussion, I do not mean to collapse totally communitarianism and traditionalism. Communitarians on the left, like Sandel, certainly support a more progressive social agenda than George and Finnis. My point is that communitarianism has, as a part of its nature and logic, a tendency toward privileging community judgments and definitions over the individual. These judgments can be progressive and supportive of individualism, but, as I have noted, they often are not. Michael Walzer, a left communitarian, illustrates this dynamic in the context of discussing citizenship, the line between insiders (community members) and outsiders: "communities must have boundaries; and however these are determined . . . they depend with regard to population on a sense of relatedness and mutuality. Refugees must appeal to that sense. One wishes them success; but in particular cases . . . they may well have no right to be successful."[61]

We can analogize to the same-sex marriage issue: Opponents of same-sex marriage say this is our (heterosexual) institution, and, to paraphrase Walzer, we wish you success in your relationship, but we are unwilling to include you in our community of marriage. Certainly, critics of liberalism have focused attention on its tendency toward excessive selfishness, but to ground an approach to gay politics in communitarianism takes away a powerful tool for change—the request by outsiders to become insiders by invoking liberal rights and transforming community boundaries.

## THE REJECTION OF RIGHTS IN CONTEMPORARY POLITICAL AND LEGAL COMMENTARY

Contemporary liberalism views rights as central to the preservation of individual freedom and autonomy. These rights are "trump cards held by individuals . . . to protect equal concern and respect,"[62] as Ronald Dworkin describes them, tools to be used by individuals to make claims on government to ensure that they are not erased from the polity and that they receive the same treatment in law and policy as other citizens. However, a significant thrust of the criticism against liberalism is the claim that its emphasis on rights is misplaced and destructive. Critics bemoan "rights talk," or the saturation of rights rhetoric in modern political discourse. Critical theorists view liberal rights as instruments of power that actually repress individuals, and communitarians see rights as barriers to the discovery of the communitarian ideal and good public policy. Unfortunately for these theorists, rights continue to be used by courts to define judicial outcomes, so an understanding of liberal rights, properly understood and not merely caricatured, is crucial to this inquiry.

Contemporary criticisms of liberal rights mirror the general objections to liberalism articulated by conservatives/communitarians and postmodern/critical theory discussed above. The critique of the latter maintains that rights, rather than being universal and powerful as liberalism generally posits, are socially relative, indeterminate, and toothless, hollow vehicles for political and social change. And, because "rights-talk is indeterminate," according to Mark Tushnet, a leader of the critical critique, "it can provide only momentary advantages in ongoing political struggles."[63] This seemingly mild criticism appears to differ little from critics of rights-based litigation like Gerald Rosenberg, who claims that it actually does little to independently further policy and may even produce a backlash.[64] Critical theorists go an important step further, however. The core critique of this perspective states that rights are not only poor vehicles for change but are, in fact, barriers to change and tools used by those opposed to change. Rights-based liberalism is a tool of oppression and is used by the privileged and powerful to mask their power.[65] This is reflected in Joel Bakan's assertions, discussed in Chapter 1, that the Canadian Supreme Court used the Charter of Rights and Freedoms to thwart the political claims of political and social minorities. But this myopic view of rights neglects the quite different role that rights-based litigation and politics are playing in the realm of gay rights in Canada today. In general, critical theorists ground their critique in historical examples and extrapolate these to all present and future cases. Certainly, rights have been used as masks for power, especially in service of a strictly negative account of freedom. But richer notions of rights are being used in the opposite manner, as this book will demonstrate.

Mary Ann Glendon states the communitarian critique of rights forcefully. Like Sandel and other communitarians and traditionalists, Glendon finds liberalism's individualism unsatisfying and incomplete. In particular, the use of "rights talk," an almost rabid use of rights-based discourse in all realms of politics and law, in U.S. political culture "heightens social conflict, and inhibits dialogue that might lead toward consensus, accommodation, or at least the discovery of common ground."[66] There is validity to this argument, especially since the liberalism Glendon discusses is of the negative variety. She aptly notes that "[i]n its relentless individualism," rights talk "fosters a climate that is inhospitable to society's losers." Certainly, sexual minorities have been on the losing end, as the negative freedom of the *Bowers* decision combined with the imposition of majoritarian values indicates. However, the solution to this dilemma is not to reject rights and liberalism in favor of communitarianism, as the earlier critique of Sandel argues, since this cure can be worse than the disease. Glendon, like others critiqued in this chapter, underestimates the ability of liberalism, especially when conceived of in richer terms, to sustain fully the claims of minorities. However, privileging communitarianism loses sight of the individual and can revert to exclusion. The limitations of community are not transcended merely by advocates of community possessing a more progressive political and social agenda.

# 4    Toward a Better Liberalism

IN CHAPTER 3, I critiqued opponents of liberalism and examined why their approaches may not be useful for gay rights claims. In this chapter, I outline the version of liberalism most able to sustain a full range of gay rights claims. I will present an alternative approach to liberal thought grounded in the strain of U.S. political thought articulated by Abraham Lincoln. I also discuss the liberalism of Andrew Sullivan, arguing why his approach to liberal politics is limited and is an example of the need for a richer view of liberalism in this context.

## TRADITIONS OF RICHER LIBERALISM IN AMERICAN POLITICAL DEVELOPMENT

The negative/positive freedom distinction has been a prominent part of U.S. political discourse. Although freedom in the United States has generally been conceived of in negative terms, a distinct strain of thought that includes more positive conceptions of freedom also has been present, as David Greenstone noted. According to Greenstone, two strands of liberalism have been present in the United States: humanist liberalism and reform liberalism. The former emphasizes negative freedom, since it holds that "the satisfaction of self-determined preferences is central to human well-being."[1] Hence, for the most part, humans should be free from external restraint to fulfill their own preferences. The latter type of liberalism, reform liberalism, emphasizes a concept of positive liberty. This is a strain of liberalism "rooted in the New England Puritan tradition and according to which individuals have an obligation—not just an option—to cultivate and develop their physical, intellectual, aesthetic, and moral faculties. Importantly, the obligation extends to helping others to do the same."[2] Reform liberalism places individuals in society and closely links them to it. The community sets the standards for excellence, while the humanist liberal's community merely provides for the equitable pursuit of individual preferences.

Although Greenstone acknowledges that humanist liberalism has been dominant in the United States, he argues that it has never achieved complete dominance. He illustrates this incomplete hegemony by discussing the views on slavery of dominant eighteenth- and nineteenth-century political figures. Whereas the humanist liberal Thomas Jefferson was generally tolerant of slavery near the end of his life, John Adams, with his Puritan background, became highly critical of the institution.[3] The humanist/reform distinction also was reflected in the differences between Stephen Douglas and Abraham Lincoln. Douglas's doctrine of popular sovereignty was grounded in humanist liberalism. Indeed, Douglas "believed in negative liberty.... He bitterly opposed the moralistic meddling of the political community in private affairs."[4] According to this view, local control of slavery was the best way to maximize individual preferences. Lincoln, on the other hand, according to Greenstone, is the ultimate embodiment of reform liberalism. For Lincoln, true liberty could only be achieved through a strong Union. He did not separate individual development from society. In fact, "he combined citizenship with morality.... He was convinced that an acceptable ethic must seek to redeem both the American republic and particular individuals within it."[5] The Union should not merely ensure the maintenance of a system of atomistic individualism. It must define the parameters of individualism, according to Lincoln. And these notions of positive freedom allowed Lincoln to view slaves as human beings, deserving of inclusion in the political order. Equality is richer with positive freedom; it requires that each member of a community be given due consideration by the state and public policy, not that he or she simply be divorced from the state. According to Greenstone, Lincoln "accepted but went beyond Webster's and Douglas's description of the Union. Lincoln's version ... included the Union's commitment to equality of rights, to the love of justice, and to the extension of positive liberty to all."[6]

In contrast, Robert George uses Lincoln as an example of the use of morality politics. He argues that Lincoln's moral superiority to Douglas stemmed from the fact that Lincoln argued the illogicalness of having a moral right to do something (vote on the legality of slavery) that is morally wrong (slavery). Thus, to update the discussion, the claim to have the right to engage in sexual practices that are deemed immoral is not a moral claim. Lincoln would therefore not say that the rights of sexual minorities are analogous to the slavery question, according to this view. This argument, however, misstates Lincoln. For Lincoln, slavery was immoral because it violated the Declaration of Independence and its principle of equality and because it violated a slave's right to full self-development. Likewise, the notion of sexual intimacy as an integral part of personhood dictates that prohibitions on same-sex marriage are immoral for the same reason. Lincoln's morality came from a secular faith in the Declaration and his Whig political thought, not biblical morality, as George implies. If anything, interpretations of biblical morality at the time justified slavery.[7]

Lincoln's brand of liberalism can also be seen in the politics of the Progressive and New Deal eras. Woodrow Wilson's strain of Progressive politics was largely grounded in a Jeffersonian, negative conception of liberty, but he, too, recognized the necessity for updating this view: "Freedom today is something more than being let alone. The program of a government of freedom must in these days be positive, not negative merely."[8] A positive notion of liberty is also reflected in Franklin Roosevelt's proposal for a second bill of rights that emphasized rights beyond the mostly negative rights listed in the original Bill of Rights.[9] Thus, a liberalism beyond libertarianism is not "un-American" or even "illiberal." Policies that have envisioned a fuller individual have been a real part of the U.S. political tradition, although they have not always been embraced by the courts.[10]

## LINCOLN AS A MODEL FOR CHANGE ON SAME-SEX MARRIAGE IN THE UNITED STATES

Lincoln's thoughts on the importance of more positive notions of liberty and rights are not the only ones important for this discussion; his approach to political change is also illuminating, especially in the context of the same-sex marriage debate. Lincoln's approach to the slavery issue, which was an affront to his positive liberty-inspired ideals, can provide insight into how to draw upon nondominant political traditions in the face of majorities who oppose a normative goal, like the eradication of slavery or the approval of same-sex marriage.

Lincoln has been criticized for being too much of a politician—too willing to compromise principles, especially the principle of full equality for racial minorities.[11] This in an incomplete assessment of Lincoln. He used political positions (such as his desire to prevent the immediate emancipation of slaves before the Civil War versus policies that would lead to slavery's eventual, gradual elimination) as a starting point to effect a transformation in the concepts of union and liberty in American political thought. With a strong Whig background, the idea of union was seldom absent from Lincoln's mind. Yet, he extended Whig notions. Daniel Webster declared "Liberty AND Union, now and forever, one and inseparable,"[12] but Lincoln defined why this was true. By linking the Declaration with the fate of the Union, he gave more concrete meaning to the nebulous Whig notions of organic social unity. The Union is a structure that ensures fulfillment of the ideals of the Declaration; it has an instrumental purpose. It is the framework in which to realize the central tenet of Lincoln's thought: the equality of the Declaration. This is what Lincoln referred to as the "standard maxim for free society . . . constantly looked to, constantly labored for, and even though never perfectly attained, constantly approximated, and thereby constantly spreading and deepening its influence."[13] The universalism and gradual, yet principled, change explicit in this statement reflects the best of Lincoln's liberalism.

An analogy can be drawn to the same-sex marriage debate: Calls for same-sex marriage often confront overwhelming popular opposition, but approaches like domestic partnership laws and civil unions are often more popular and have been enacted into law, as will be discussed in later chapters. Domestic partnership laws are the equivalent of opposing the expansion of slavery—an intermediary position, grounded in a judgment about the need for equality and based upon a richer notion of liberalism, but one that takes account of political reality. Many in the activist community have called this approach second-class citizenship. But, reflecting the Lincolnian approach, William Eskridge asserts, "If the civil unions law [in Vermont] is not equality, it is at least equality in practice. Full equality should be the goal for a liberal polity, but a polity that is a democracy and whose citizens have heterogeneous views about important matters is one where immediate full equality is not always possible, not practical, not even desirable."[14] As Lincoln emphasized, principled political change is a process, and I argue that courts are useful and legitimate vehicles toward full equality for sexual minorities.

ANDREW SULLIVAN'S DEFICIENT LIBERALISM:
A CASE STUDY IN THE PITFALLS OF NEGATIVE
LIBERTY AND GAY RIGHTS

Andrew Sullivan has become an influential commentator on contemporary lesbian
and gay rights issues, but his political thought presents some problems. In particular, his account of liberalism is often inconsistent and contradictory. Certainly,
political thinkers are allowed some inconsistency, since it is nearly impossible to
provide a perfectly clean political theory. But Sullivan's contradictions are particularly interesting for this discussion and problematic. For instance, he provides a
rich justification for the legalization of same-sex marriage, one that is grounded
in a lyrical defense of personhood and a rich individualism. At the same time,
however, he rejects seemingly less radical and controversial elements of the gay
rights movement, like antidiscrimination and hate crime laws. He claims that these
laws violate the public/private distinction central to liberalism—reflecting a strictly
thin, libertarian view that is at odds with his richer account of individualism. As
this chapter argues, a more consistent and fruitful approach involves emphasizing richer notions of liberalism in all areas of gay rights. I will also attempt to
explain Sullivan's contradictions by exploring important intellectual influences
on his thought: Straussianism and the political thought of Michael Oakeshott.
Indeed, Sullivan's thought reflects many of the hallmarks of modern conservatism: its mix of libertarianism and moralism that are often at odds with each
other.

In *Virtually Normal: An Argument about Homosexuality*, Sullivan critiques various approaches to gay rights: prohibitionists who wish to use the power of the
state to eliminate or control sexual minorities; conservatives who do not object
to sexual minorities in private but feel that the good of society is promoted by
their regulation in the public sphere; and liberationists,[15] a term he uses for queer
theorists. The bulk of his discussion, however, involves a fourth category: modern
liberals. According to Sullivan, contemporary liberals have strayed from classical
liberalism. In particular, they have fudged the public/private distinction that was
central to liberal thought. They have abandoned classical freedoms (speech, contract, religion) in favor of governmental policies designed to protect groups, not
individuals, from real or perceived harm, abandoning Mill and Constant in favor
of Dworkin. Contemporary liberals, Sullivan argues, have replaced a politics of
cool reason and acceptance of certain amounts of private injustice, with hysteria
designed to eliminate all forms of injustice, public and private. They want laws that
regulate private thoughts and behavior, antidiscrimination and hate crime laws, and
extend the state's reach to stifle private thoughts and actions that might negatively
affect sexual minorities. Contemporary liberals, therefore, have more in common
with classical conservatives who were not afraid to use the power of the state to
enforce morality. According to Sullivan:

> Liberalism is designed to deal with means, not ends; its concern is with liberty, not
> a better society. The impatience of liberals with antidiscrimination laws reveals how
> broad the scope of their project now is. It is to refashion society in the same way (for

different purposes) as conservatives want to refashion society; it is to use the law to prevent and deter actions in society that have nothing to do with the state; and to frame the law as a means to educate the citizenry into more virtuous behavior.[16]

In this view, a line has been crossed by contemporary liberals, which threatens the status of liberalism as the anti-ideology—the thin ideology that claims to do little but preserves much.

Sullivan also argues that liberalism is poorly equipped to deal with irrational antigay sentiment. "If the law is designed to solve this problem, it will be forced into being a mixture of moral education, psychotherapy, and absolution."[17] He also maintains that antidiscrimination laws simply do not work and are mere legal window dressing. This would be harmless if not for the negative reaction they generate. The loss of freedom is always greater than the good of protection against discrimination, especially for lesbians and gay men whose discrimination is less severe than that of racial minorities, according to Sullivan. "Homosexuals can pass," and they do not have to deal with centuries of economic exclusion.[18] Therefore, according to Sullivan, antidiscrimination laws based upon race may be justified in their restriction on freedom, but laws based on sexual orientation only unnecessarily restrict freedom and usually result in a backlash by those in the majority.

Hate crime laws are even more problematic for Sullivan, since they represent the most pernicious side of contemporary liberalism: thought control. Liberals are not simply content with protection from discrimination; they are determined to root out and eliminate every impulse of antigay sentiment. In addition to downplaying the incidence and severity of hate crimes, Sullivan argues that the motivation behind a crime and the crime itself can never be truly separated, nor should they be. "The truth is," according to Sullivan, "the distinction between a crime filled with personal hate and a crime filled with group hate is essentially an arbitrary one. It tells us nothing interesting about the psychological contours of the specific actor or his specific victim. It is a function primarily of politics, of special interest groups carving out particular protections for themselves."[19] And as with antidiscrimination laws, Sullivan is willing to endure something distasteful (hate) to preserve freedom: "A free country will always be a hateful country."[20] The public/private distinction is just too important to be tampered with, even if it means turning a blind eye to hatred and violence. Good liberals simply must tolerate bad things in the world in order to preserve their delicate, but all-important, line between public and private.

This perspective reflects a significant tradition in American political thought, echoed by Elshtain and extending back to James Madison in *Federalist* No. 10. This tradition attempts to remove from ordinary politics large questions of morality. Madison noted that, historically, democracies had failed because irresolvable conflicts and the political factions that resulted from and fed these conflicts wracked them. Madison wished to replace "[a] zeal for different opinions concerning religion, concerning government, and many other points,"[21] with the more mundane concerns of property and commerce. Consequently, Madison envisioned U.S. democracy avoiding this tendency by grounding politics in economic self-interest.

Recall, too, Elshtain's argument for the preservation of a realm for moral disagreement not resolved or arbitrated by the state.

Sullivan echoes Madison and Elshtain: "Liberalism works—and it is the most resilient modern politics—precisely because it . . . seeks to avoid these irresolvable and contentious conflicts. It is the only politics that can bridge all citizens, whatever their sexuality or religion or race or gender."[22] Sullivan believes that some laws should exist that violate the liberal ideal in order to protect groups, like racial minorities. As we have seen, this is based on a utilitarian calculation where the harm to liberalism is not greater than the good of this legal protection. However, sexual minorities do not meet the threshold. For Sullivan and Elshtain, this group can be sacrificed to the good of preserving modern liberal democratic practices. Their claims for equality, unlike racial minorities, are to be ignored so that religious freedom can be preserved. Sullivan and Elshtain seem to easily forget, however, that slavery and segregation had strong religious and moral justification and approval. For instance, political leaders like Stephen A. Douglas used exactly this argument in regard to slavery when he stated that new states should be allowed to vote for or against the legality of slavery. He wished to make the moral debate about slavery a simply political one, resolved by a democratic vote. The federal government and the Constitution were to remain silent on the issue in order to avoid a national conflict. And so Sullivan and Elshtain say that lesbians and gay men are outside constitutional and legal protection, since they are afraid of the consequences of inclusion.

This conclusion is misguided. It privileges private moral and religious judgment over civil equality, and it is based on the mistaken assumption that liberalism loves nothing more than a strong distinction between public and private realms, with a curtailed public authority. Not even John Locke took this position. In *A Letter Concerning Toleration* Locke defends religious freedom and the idea that it is futile for governments to control religious thoughts of its citizens. Indeed, religious and civil matters were entirely separate issues in his view. For Sullivan and Elshtain, this means that religion should nearly always be deferred to, in order to ensure that government does not infringe on religious thought and practice and to remove contentious moral debate from the public realm. Locke, however, took the opposite view. Where religious doctrine and civil authority collided, he felt it was religion that should give way. As he stated, "the private judgment of any person concerning a law enacted in political matters, for the public good, does not take away the obligation of that law, nor deserve a dispensation."[23] Only when the government is acting outside its realm of authority and is explicitly mandating a certain religious practice or particular faith are citizens not obligated to recognize the law. Thus, the test is the proper extent of the legislative power, not a special reserve of religious liberty. Any infringements on religious liberty are the price paid for the separation of the secular and spiritual realms (whereas for Sullivan and Elshtain, limitations on secular authority are the price to pay). Otherwise, the civil authority is useless if it is constantly subject to the objections of private citizens.

Indeed, Locke gives broad range to the properly constituted civil authority. He argues that only God ultimately can resolve the conflict between private religious practices and legislation that purports to act in accordance with the public good.

"For there is no judge upon earth between the supreme magistrate and the people."[24] His scheme does not include a temporal authority beyond the legislative power. Granted, Locke was likely not thinking of antidiscrimination or hate-crime laws, just as Madison was only thinking of economic minorities when concocting the elaborate scheme to preserve their rights in *Federalist* No. 10. But liberalism is able to use its general principles to accommodate new circumstances, and modern liberalism values the rights of minorities broadly defined.

Ultimately, then, Sullivan and Elshtain incorrectly conflate liberalism's public/private distinction with classical democracy's need for homogeneous consensus. But we have come a long way from ancient Greece. Using this as a model for modern democratic practice ignores a large part of the trajectory of Western political thought since Hobbes. Our contemporary political goal is not merely the smooth functioning of democratic deliberation; it is also the protection of minorities from the results of this deliberation through, at least in the United States and an increasing number of democracies, a written constitution and judicial review. A new safety valve on the democratic pressure cooker is the use of the law and constitutional principles as a way to resolve previously irresolvable moral conflicts.

## SULLIVAN AND SAME-SEX MARRIAGE: A DIFFERENT APPROACH TO GAY RIGHTS?

Sullivan's thin description of individualism and liberty detailed above stands in stark contrast to his discussion of individualism concerning same-sex marriage. Whereas the antigovernment stance of Sullivan conceives of individual liberty negatively, with a great deal of room to act in the private realm, he also creates a much stronger vision of personhood when he argues in favor of same-sex marriage. Indeed, the difference is striking. Sullivan would argue that this difference stems from the fact that marriage properly falls within the realm of what is "public," and therefore calls for a consideration of the state's treatment of the individual in more positive terms.[25] However, the reality is that Sullivan creates two very different conceptions of the political individual that are at odds with each other, and this leads to very different policy outcomes on the issue of gay rights. A more fruitful and consistent approach, I argue, would be to create a more unified account of individualism that does not vary based upon the policy issue in question.

For Sullivan, the legalization of same-sex marriage is the most important element of the gay rights movement, and his support for this policy brings forth an eloquent description of what it is to be an individual and why marriage is central to this description. Even though Sullivan appears most sympathetic to those he labels "conservatives" in his previously described typology, he clearly rejects a neoconservative-style argument for same-sex marriage: that it serves to rein in gay male promiscuity and leads to stability in the gay community. According to Sullivan, marriage is about much more than this:

> It is also the deepest means for the liberation of homosexuals, providing them with the only avenue for sexual and emotional development that can integrate them as

equal human beings and remove from them the hideous historic option of choosing between their joy and dignity. It is about deepening and widening and strengthening the possibility of true intimacy between human beings.[26]

Sullivan also emphasizes the central role that marriage plays in Western society. It is a reflection of the value placed on love and family and is often the seminal event in a person's life. In fact, according to Sullivan, "It is the mark of ultimate human respect; and its automatic, unthinking, casual denial to gay men and women is the deepest psychological and political wound imaginable."[27] These are words that only a neo-Kantian, modern liberal could love. The rich description of personhood and individual dignity are eloquent and striking, especially when compared to Sullivan's minimalist account of liberalism. Indeed, one wonders if Sullivan's classical liberalism would accommodate the pairing of psychology and politics with such ease.

In order to fit his advocacy of same-sex marriage into his classical liberal framework, Sullivan claims that since marriage is a public institution, state involvement is valid. But he fails to note that there is nothing necessarily "public" about marriages. Governments have chosen to recognize them and offer benefits to them because of their importance for individual development (which Sullivan eloquently describes) and the perceived benefit of familial stability. None of this, however, is required by classical liberalism's minimal state and sweeping private sphere. A classical liberal would argue that marriage should be the sole domain of private religion.

## EXPLAINING SULLIVAN'S POLITICAL THOUGHT: THE INFLUENCES OF STRAUSS AND OAKESHOTT

Sullivan's approach to lesbian and gay politics places him at odds with many in the contemporary lesbian and gay rights movement. Antidiscrimination and hate-crime laws are seen by most in the movement as crucial political and legal reforms. Sullivan has also been criticized for being highly critical of sexual liberation in general, while conducting a personal life that reflects liberationist values. Although the privacy of one's personal life should generally be respected, this controversy sheds light on Sullivan's intellectual influences and indicates how and why he can think in seemingly contradictory terms. In particular, this section examines the influences of two political philosophers on Sullivan's thought: Leo Strauss and Michael Oakeshott.

Sullivan's political thought is an often contradictory mix of intellectual influences that is not uncommon among modern conservatives.[28] These conservatives flow comfortably from libertarianism to a reliance on societal morality and tradition, largely as a result of the rather successful fusion of these two notions by the neoconservative movement of the past thirty years. The patron saint of neoconservatism, Leo Strauss, can help us understand Sullivan's contradictions. Strauss emphasized, among other things, the importance of public virtue and the need for politics primarily to seek and preserve this virtue. A citizenry needs a strong moral code to hold itself together. Strauss had no particular moral code in mind, as long as it served its purpose. Catholicism is a special attraction for Straussians in this regard, given its reliance on symbol and ritual, which make it easier for its adherents to follow.[29] Picking up on this, neoconservatives demonstrate an almost obsessive attachment to public morality, particularly the cultural mores of a citizenry. Gertrude Himmelfarb's relentless praise for Victorian shame is an example. And this is why neoconservatives decry the democratic personal liberation of the 1960s that lives on.[30]

Along with this concern for public morality, however, Straussianism also calls for the liberation from this morality for great thinkers. The masses need a strong moral code to make sense of their lives and to ensure that their decisions promote, not undermine in a selfish way, the needs of society. The great thinkers, however, know better. They are freed from the mundane and have the luxury of exploring the great personal virtues of love and pleasure. But to give this luxury to the masses would be to undermine the moral foundation of society. This is Strauss's notion of the "noble lie": The great thinker must come up with a moral code that he or she knows is not true but is for the good of society.[31]

In the novel *Ravelstein*, Saul Bellow provides insight into this mode of thought. The central character in the book, a disciple of the great professor Davarr (Strauss), is patterned after Bellow's good friend, the late Allan Bloom. Bellow shows us how the same man who was perhaps the harshest critic of the emptiness of contemporary morality and who was the mentor of a good number of influential conservative political players could also be obsessed with sexual pleasure, usually of the same-sex variety.[32] Straussian and Strauss-influenced thinkers often easily accommodate contradictory thinking.

Sullivan was undoubtedly affected by Straussian thought. Though his writings display a range of intellectual influences, it is significant to note that Sullivan studied at Harvard under a prominent Straussian, Harvey Mansfield. This is not mere guilt by association, however. In his 1998 book, *Love Undetectable*, Sullivan ruminates on the meaning of friendship, weaving classical and medieval notions of friendship into a discussion of a friend who died of AIDS. In the essay, Sullivan bemoans the modern emphasis on physical intimacy and pleasure and is nostalgic about the classical elevation of friendship as the ideal human relationship. Indeed, he notes that few modern philosophers have treated friendship as a legitimate realm of inquiry. Only in ancient and medieval times was friendship seen "as a critical social institution, as an ennobling moral experience, as an immensely delicate but essential interplay of the virtues required to sustain a fully realized human being."[33] Aristotle, Sullivan notes, spent a fifth of the *Nicomaehaen Ethics* on friendship and pays little attention to romantic love, "an experience we moderns have elevated to the height of our aspirations and concerns." And, in the classical worldview, friendship is even "bound up inextricably with the notion of virtue."[34] Thus, Sullivan does not like the modern emphasis on love over friendship.

I mean love in the banal, ubiquitous, compelling, and resilient modern meaning of love: the romantic love that obliterates all other goods, the love to which every life must apparently lead, the love that is consummated in sex and celebrated in every part of our popular culture, the love that is institutionalized in marriage and instilled as a primary and ultimate good in every Western child.[35]

Pondering the meaning of friendship, particularly in the context of classical and medieval thought, as well as the rejection of all things modern, is quintessentially Straussian.

In fact, Sullivan's seeming contradictions fit perfectly with the Straussian approach. In this context, these contradictions do not represent mindless hypocrisy. It is perfectly reasonable for him to reconcile the moral condemnation of the promiscuity and sex obsession of gay male culture and its emphasis on sexual intimacy, not friendship, while at the same time embarking on his own journey of sexual liberation and exploration of Eros. As with Bloom, a Straussian can explore hedonism while arguing that society should reject it, but Strauss perhaps did not anticipate that these great thinkers would become public media personalities.

Sullivan's doctoral dissertation at Harvard was an analysis of the political thought of Michael Oakeshott, a strong influence on contemporary British conservatism. From this analysis, broad themes emerge that indicate possible influences on Sullivan's own thought. The themes identified in the analysis of Oakeshott are also reflected in Sullivan's writings, especially his vision of lesbian and gay politics in *Virtually Normal*: a minimal state, a deemphasis on the primacy of politics, and a strong reliance on "private" institutions, especially religion, in organizing and propelling a society.

Sullivan begins his analysis of Oakeshott by noting profound contradictions in his thought. Most relevant for this discussion, he notes that Oakeshott "seems to embrace a conservatism which ends by affirming a radical liberalism,"[36] which can be seen as a shorthand description of Sullivan's own politics, at least as it relates to antidiscrimination and hate-crime laws. Oakeshott's ideal regime, according to Sullivan, "is a limited constitutional state, where the most fundamental guarantee of the liberty of Oakeshott's individual is the dispersion of power," and where the right to property is paramount.[37] The state should not be involved in inculcating moral virtue or even educating its citizens, only keeping a free market going and protecting the nation from attack or invasion.[38]

This template for Oakeshott's politics is minimalist for a reason. It is needed, according to Sullivan, to create a particular type of state that fits with the modern political world.

Oakeshott's political philosophy can be seen as a quintessential attempt to construct a theory of justice in a modern European state which manages to avoid any foundationalist underpinnings. He is, in short, tackling the essential problem of most modern political philosophy: how to construct a notion of a just politics in a radically disenchanted world. He does so . . . while eschewing anything but a persuasive story of the historical emergence of a particular conception of the modern state—civil association—and an attractive account of the kind of human personality which that conception encourages and allows.[39]

Indeed, in Sullivan's assessment, the concept of civil association is central to Oakeshott's politics and is grounded in the notion that politics is a peripheral human endeavor. "It is at best a distraction or an irrelevance to the life of a society and, at worst, a corruption of it."[40] The life of a society is driven by other factors, like tradition and religious practice. Sullivan asserts that for Oakeshott, "The 'communal' is prior to the 'political.'"[41] Politics is a defensive, not creative, endeavor. It "guards values; it does not make them."[42] In modern politics, civil associations acting through tradition are the institutions that generate and preserve these values, unlike the classical world where this was the explicit role of the state. And, according to Sullivan, "Although Oakeshott makes no claim for civil association as the triumphant form of modern politics (far from it), there is an intimation that it should be."[43] The wide range for private activity and influence certainly coincides with Elshtain's limiting of the scope of public authority and inquiry.

Sullivan's description of Oakeshott's views on religion is also telling. He notes another apparent contradiction in Oakeshott's thought: his skepticism of any eternal truths and his embrace of religion. In fact, this is not a contradiction at all, according to Sullivan, since religion is used by Oakeshott instrumentally—"a way of rendering more coherent the mode of practical experience, of sustaining a coherent way of living, without any recourse to transcendental truth."[44] Here Oakeshott merges with the Straussian/neoconservative position that religion is needed for the masses to make sense of their lives, despite the fact that elites may know that religion is false. Indeed, Sullivan claims that Oakeshott's account of the nature of religious practice is powerful. "The religious temperament, amounts . . . to something close to a trance, in which all moral uncertainty, practical deliberation, and prudential wisdom are banished in favor of 'intensity and strength of devotion and by singleness of purpose.'"[45] Sullivan is somewhat fearful of this account, since it removes the concept of choice from morality, in that religious beings are fairly unthinking. Nonetheless, according to Sullivan, religion is central to Oakeshott's description of civil association: "It provided the nerve necessary for a civil existence."[46]

The foregoing account appears to be a direct intellectual forerunner of Sullivan's own views, or at least a validation of them. An unwillingness to use state authority for other than narrowly prescribed ends (certainly not hate crime laws), a willingness to dismiss politics as an effective tool for societal change (for example, the assertion that antidiscrimination laws will not eliminate private prejudice), and a strong appreciation for the importance and utility of private institutions (most notably religion) make Sullivan's views almost a carbon copy of Oakeshott's. That is why Sullivan's discussion of same-sex marriage is so striking in contrast. One would think that an Oakeshottian view of marriage would certainly not include a role for the state, as Sullivan maintains, given the large sphere reserved for religion.

## A MORE USEFUL AND CONSISTENT APPROACH TO LIBERALISM AND GAY RIGHTS

Rather than Sullivan's conflicted account of liberalism, a more fruitful approach would be to recognize that liberalism accommodates multiple elements of the gay rights movement. There need not be a difference between calls for antidiscrimination and hate-crime laws on the one hand and same-sex marriage on the other. All rely on a rich view of individualism. If the individual is viewed as requiring a certain amount of societal support to develop fully, these policies appear more consistent. If a neo-Kantian individualism replaces a strictly negative account, antidiscrimination laws become not illegitimate attempts by the state to intrude into the private sphere, but attempts to guarantee that all individuals have equal access to society's benefits. Hate crime laws, then, are not attempts at thought control but attempts to ensure that individuals can express their identities without fear of violence based on these identities. Same-sex marriage, as Sullivan describes, allows individuals the emotional stability and support that comes from a committed relationship, as well as all of the legal benefits that sustain economic prosperity. These laws are all variations on the same theme; they all express the sentiment that individuals require more than just freedom from government authority to live good lives.

Sullivan attempts to escape this consistency by caricaturing the laws he disfavors, especially hate-crime laws. He provides as an example of a hate crime a dispute between neighbors about grass clippings that resulted in a gay man being beaten and called a faggot.[47] Sullivan claims that this was more of a neighbors' dispute than a hate crime, and it probably was. But Sullivan fails to recognize clear examples of violence and intimidation of lesbians and gay men that were intended to prevent political expression and activity simply based on hatred and fear. One of the assumptions made by Sullivan is that hate crimes would always happen without the hate. Violence is simply violence, and motivations are too complex to sort out fully. This position allows the preservation of a sharp public/private distinction, but it does not reflect reality. Violence is often used as a political tool that is intended to suppress and silence individuals making political claims based on their sexual orientation.

Sullivan's liberalism is especially problematic in the United States. Rhetorical libertarianism and a fear of the state have always been the United States's populism and the political discourse most easily referred to when facing policy questions.[48] And commentators like Sullivan use such rhetoric quite effectively. The use of this discourse usually begins by asking the question, "Do you really want the government to . . . ?" and strikes a collective political chord, ending further consideration of policy alternatives based on a richer liberalism. Greenstone argued "against simplicity" in understanding the U.S. political order, urging us not to forget the richness of that tradition, despite the dominance of a particular form.[49] Sullivan ultimately does nothing to remedy this situation, but the success of the gay rights movement may require it.

This framework can also be applied to other areas of identity-based politics. A fuller discussion of these areas is beyond the scope of this book, but it is useful to note the applicability of this framework to other problematical areas of civil rights policy.

Recall that Greenstone focuses heavily on the issues of race and slavery and differentiates between "humanist liberalism," which was hostile to racial equality, and "reform liberalism," which was much more attentive to the personhood of slaves. This also can be applied to contemporary political and legal discussions about race, particularly the issue of affirmative action. Recent critiques of affirmative action policy in the United States heavily emphasize the need for government neutrality when it comes to race and an emphasis on "color blindness." This, like Douglas's emphasis on the importance of popular sovereignty, a nice sounding principle of democracy, potentially ignores more substantive consideration of the legal and political status of racial minorities. Neutrality can, in fact, perpetuate racial inequality by ignoring deeper historical and socioeconomic factors that actually create inequality. A focus on protecting full personhood, then, may require government to act affirmatively, not simply be neutral when it comes to race. Not surprisingly, then, in Canada, where a richer liberalism is more prevalent, protection for affirmative action programs is enshrined in the constitution.

The political and legal status of women may also benefit from the application of this framework. Feminist scholars have argued that the libertarian approach to the regulation of pornography may be harmful to women, since women are often depicted in demeaning and degrading ways in pornographic material.[50] In the United States, where the libertarian approach is dominant, courts and policy makers have largely rejected these arguments. Although I am somewhat sympathetic to the libertarian approach, especially since it benefited the emerging gay rights movement in the United States, asking the substantive question of what pornography does to the dignity and personhood of women can assist in the creation of a fuller understanding of the status of women in contemporary society. Again, interestingly, the feminist argument has gained much more traction in Canadian policy.

This brief sketch demonstrates that moving beyond "simplicity" can be useful for other areas of social policy. Powerful majorities may find simplicity appealing, but, especially in the United States, we must be attentive to the ways in which dominant principles can inhibit the fullest development of each individual in a polity.

# 5    Sodomy Laws, Courts, and Liberalism

STARTING IN THE EARLY 1990s, many state courts began to question the constitutionality of sodomy laws, generally using a libertarian defense of privacy. This has been, in large part, in response to litigation strategies of gay rights groups to eliminate sodomy laws. These events have particular relevance for this discussion: First, when courts have struck down sodomy laws, there has been little political backlash. But when courts are less aggressive, political battles between those who favor and oppose sodomy laws become more pronounced. Generally, arguments favoring privacy rights win out, but they have a more difficult time gaining resonance without court intervention. Additionally, these arguments are successful not because of a concern for gay rights, specifically the need to allow sexual minorities the same right to intimacy as the majority in the name of developing the full person; rather, because opposition to sodomy laws has found success grounding itself in starkly negative terms. Fear of the state animates these claims, almost exclusively. This line of precedent illustrates the nature of liberal discourse in the United States, especially when placed beside the less than successful attempts at same-sex marriage advocacy. This discussion will also illustrate the power of legal norms and arguments as agents of political change, especially in the context of a liberal, rights-based framework.

## A HISTORY OF SODOMY LAWS

Before being invalidated by the U.S. Supreme Court in *Lawrence v. Texas*, sodomy laws were seldom enforced; however, they strongly affected the legal and political status of sexual minorities. They served as a barrier to gay rights legislation, since opponents of such measures argued that it is wrong to grant civil rights protection to a group whose conduct is illegal. Additionally, they were often used as shields to prevent genuine discussion of gay rights. As Richard Mohr described the situation, "sodomy laws afford an opportunity for the citizenry to express its raw hatred of gays *systematically* and *officially* without even having publicly to discuss and so justify the hatred."[1] Thus, when courts struck down sodomy laws, they were doing much more than destroying harmless or irrelevant laws; they, for good or ill, were paving the way for further gains in the realm of gay rights.

As recently as 2003, fourteen states criminalized adult consensual sodomy through legislation.[2] This is quite different from the 1950s when all fifty states had such statutes and all but two classified sodomy as a felony.[3] These statues often dated to colonial times[4] and were a legacy of the English crime of buggery, punishable by death, which was adopted by Parliament in 1533. Before this legal classification, sodomy was considered an ecclesiastical offense and was dealt with by the Church. But in his war with the Church, Henry VIII wished to use the legal classification to attack Catholic monasteries in England.[5] Buggery came to be interpreted by English courts as anal sex between men or between a man and a woman. It also included sex between humans and animals.[6] The English law was adopted by the colonies, and by 1830 all states had outlawed sodomy or buggery.[7] Despite this long history, for most of the nineteenth century, sodomy laws were not explicitly intended to regulate homosexual behavior. Instead, they reinforced attitudes toward all nonprocreative sex. Most laws did not speak about specific acts, but instead referred to "crimes against nature."[8] In general, then, these laws represented a statement on the "naturalness" of heterosexual vaginal intercourse. Anything outside this realm was deemed to be unlawful and immoral—not just sexual activities between men. Interestingly, these laws typically did not mention or include sex between women or oral sex of any kind. Oral sex was not considered a crime until the end of the nineteenth century, and sex between women was not illegal until the early twentieth century.[9] Courts, as well as legislatures, reinforced the notion that sodomy laws preserved the "naturalness" of procreative sex. In 1915, the Montana Supreme Court unanimously held that fellatio was covered by the state's "crime against nature" statute, arguing that every "intelligent adult person understands fully what the ordinary course of nature demands or permits for the purpose of procreation, and that any departure from this course is against nature."[10]

Not until the late nineteenth century, when gay subcultures began to develop in urban areas, were gay men singled out as objects of sodomy laws. Indeed, until the 1880s, few people were in prison as a result of sodomy laws. According to William Eskridge:

> Pre-1881 prosecutions overwhelmingly focused on male-female, adult-child or man-animal relations rather than same-sex intimacy. To the extent crime against nature laws were mechanisms of social control, their objects were either predatory men assaulting children, women, and animals, or were people of color and foreign-born individuals, all "alien" to middle-class WASP America.[11]

However, by the late nineteenth century, as gay subcultures began to form in large cities,[12] homosexuality became more visible and was increasingly seen as a distinct phenomenon. Individuals began to more openly challenge traditional gender roles, and laws for cross-dressing, public indecency, and obscenity sprang up in response to this openness.[13] Additionally, sodomy laws began to incorporate oral sex. Pennsylvania was the first to do so, followed by New York, Ohio, Louisiana, Wisconsin, Iowa, Washington, Missouri, Virginia, and Minnesota—largely states with significant urban centers.[14] Thus, by the early twentieth century the regulation of homosexual conduct was well established.

World War II further accelerated the growth of gay culture. According to John D'Emilio, the war "created something of a national coming out experience."[15] During the war, gay and lesbian service personnel connected with one another in ways that were not previously possible, especially those from rural locations. After the war, many of these lesbians and gay men settled in port cities like

San Francisco and New York, which led to the rise of a group identity for sexual minorities. The Kinsey Report, with its rather stunning assertions of the prevalence of homosexuality, "gave an added push at a crucial time to the emergence of an urban gay subculture. Kinsey also provided ideological ammunition that lesbians and homosexuals might use once they began to fight for equality," according to D'Emilio.[16] It is no surprise, then, as noted above, that all but two states in the 1950s treated sodomy as a felony.

Indeed, from the 1930s through the 1950s, there was something of a national political obsession with sexual deviants. Homosexuality was seen as a direct threat to the nation's well-being and was also linked directly to the sexual abuse of children. In particular, gay men were seen as subversives and child molesters. For these reasons, according to Eskridge, "Following World War II, conventional society sought to eliminate homosexuality in the United States."[17] The force of state power was used to flush out and identify homosexuals, largely using sodomy laws as a pretext. The depth of the hysteria is reflected in the fact that gay men were generally seen as the sole perpetrators of sex offenses against children, both male and female. A strong concern for combating sex crimes against children dovetailed with antigay hysteria and led to additional legislation, with Congress taking the lead. During this time, the District of Columbia did not have a sodomy law, so Congress passed the Miller Act, which made sodomy a felony punishable by up to ten years in prison. The penalty was twenty years if the sodomy was committed with a minor under the age of sixteen. Twelve states followed suit.[18] Certainly legislation to protect children from abuse is a legitimate exercise of state power, but the fact that the use of this power was so closely linked to the repression of sexual minorities is a relevant point for this discussion. During the middle part of the twentieth century in the United States, homosexuals, particularly gay men, were seen as severe threats to society—in fact, the main threat to children. The law was put to use in combating this threat without too much regard for the consequences.

However, in the 1950s a closer look at the situation by several states began to challenge this notion,[19] and there was increasing momentum among legal elites to reform sex laws. Beginning in 1961, with Illinois adopting general criminal law revisions from the Model Penal Code, many states began to repeal their laws against consensual sodomy.[20] Led by Herbert Wechsler, the American Law Institute (ALI) developed the Model Penal Code as a way to clarify and unify state criminal law.[21] The ALI was founded, despite criticism of its conservatism, mostly under the influence of progressive and realist principles among legal elites. The idea of bringing leading legal thinkers together to reformulate substantial areas of the law was certainly grounded in the assumption that the law was in serious need of reform.[22]

One of the main goals of the ALI's restatement of criminal law was explicitly liberal, even Millian, in that it declared that conduct should only be deemed criminal "that unjustifiably and inexcusably inflicts or threatens substantial harm to individual or public interests."[23] The ALI took up the issue of sex crimes early in 1955. Despite the ALI's reformist impulse, this was not a subject with which all members were comfortable. In a letter to Learned Hand, ALI Director Herbert

Goodrich ends with the provocative line, "On Saturday we shall talk sex. Any comments?"[24] To which Hand replied, "The 'sex talk' on Saturday! . . . I am a little antique to be deeply interested, but I may be there just the same."[25] Indeed, Hand was initially skeptical of decriminalizing sodomy, but he ultimately supported reform.[26]

The report dealing with sexual offenses submitted to the Criminal Law Advisory Group was much less equivocal, coming from reformist "experts." Reflecting the influence of legal realism, the report relied a great deal on sexual research of the previous decade, like the Kinsey Report, which sought to demystify sexual behavior that was outside the norm. Although still conceiving any sexual activity that transcended traditional heterosexual practices as "deviant," the report did speak in a matter-of-fact manner in describing sexual variation. And the report asserted that "[s]ubstantial members of males and females find themselves drawn to members of their own sex." The report also attacked the recent sexual hysteria and the legislation that resulted from it, stating that "evidence does not support the hypothesis that this generation suffers from a special 'wave' of serious sex offenses."[27]

The impulse to decriminalize sodomy found some receptivity among the ALI membership, but not as much as the parallel effort to decriminalize adultery. A substantial majority approved this latter effort, while the vote on sodomy decriminalization was closer, 35 to 24. The ALI membership was less enthusiastic about eliminating the criminalization of sodomy than were the ALI reporters and researchers who proposed decriminalization. Nothing in the debate reflected a desire to validate sexual minorities as individuals deserving of equal sexual determination. Many members made moral arguments against homosexuality and for the usefulness of having sodomy laws on the books as moral sanctions. Judge Parker was adamantly opposed to sodomy law repeal, since "it is important that they [immoral acts] be denounced by the Criminal Code in order that society may know that the state disapproves."[28] However, the debate focused primarily on the efficacy of enforcement. Hand supported decriminalization on the grounds that a bad, unenforceable law was worse than no law at all. This was a change from his previous support of keeping the sanction against sodomy, and his statement is reflective of the general ambivalence of even those members who supported decriminalization. He stated: "Criminal law which is not enforced practically . . . is much worse than if it was not on the books at all. It is merely an expression of moral disapprobation. . . . I think it is a matter of morals, a matter very largely of taste, and it is not a matter that people should be put in prison about."[29] This is not exactly a ringing endorsement for sexual freedom from this esteemed jurist. Many members were also concerned that decriminalizing sodomy would be so controversial that it would undermine their overall efforts at reform. As Parker stated, given that sodomy was seen as a crime in all states, "If we should . . . eliminate this as a crime . . . the attitude of the Institute would be largely misunderstood and that its work would largely be discredited in the minds of many people whose good opinion we should desire to retain."[30] Reform of sex laws in the 1950s was indeed a complicated game.

The Model Penal Code reforms were quite clearly directed at heterosexual consensual relations. In rejecting the concept of "deviant sexual behavior," the ALI appeared to be making the world safe for sexual experimentation within heterosexual relationships. As they declare: "Both the popular literature and available empirical data reveal that such practices are anything but uncommon. Moreover, current scientific thinking confirms that so-called deviate sexual intercourse may be part of a healthy and normal marital relationship."[31] Thus, according to this view, the state does not have a legitimate interest in regulating this activity, since it is not inherently damaging to society but can be beneficial to these relationships. However, the regulation of homosexual relations, according to the ALI, "is arguably more plausible."[32] This activity is more violative of social norms and thus is more suspect and more amenable to governmental regulation. The ALI nonetheless proposed to eliminate the classification of private homosexual relations as a crime, again, only on utilitarian grounds. "The criminal law cannot encompass all behavior that the average citizen may regard as immoral or deviate.... Economic resources are finite.... It seems sensible, therefore, that the criminal justice system should concentrate on repressing murder, robbery, rape and theft, and other crimes that threaten security of person or property."[33] Homosexual activity may be immoral, unlike heterosexual activity, which is healthy, but it should not be regulated because it may prove too difficult to do so, according to the ALI. Despite the varying standards accorded the two types of sexual activity, the ALI ultimately relied upon a libertarian sentiment to ground its justification for reform. "Any exercise of the coercive power of the state against individual citizens," according to the ALI, "diminishes freedom."[34] In the end, then, Millian arguments and the emerging approach of using more science and less morality when considering homosexuality won the day.

The discussion in the *Moral Penal Code and Commentaries* concerning reform of "deviate sexual conduct" law reflects a common and powerful thread of American political discourse relating to privacy and lesbian and gay rights. However distasteful or morally offensive homosexuality may be to a majority of citizens, regulation of homosexual conduct necessarily implicated heterosexual conduct. In the name of preserving the autonomy of heterosexual relations, the sexual activity of lesbians and gay men was included in the name of preserving the principle of privacy. State regulation of morality is such a loaded issue that preference must be given to preserving individual sexual autonomy. Homosexuality is not affirmed; it is included under the larger umbrella of sexual privacy and autonomy.

In the 1950s the British Wolfenden Committee mirrored the actions of the ALI. The Wolfenden Report also illustrates the approach of liberals of the time on the issue of homosexuality. Like the ALI recommendations, the Wolfenden Report was explicitly Millian in trying to carve out a broad realm for private, consensual sexual activity. Although the authors of the report did not deny the need to enforce morality in the law, they wished to defend that which was "private." According to the report, "Unless a deliberate attempt is to be made by society, acting through the agency of law, to equate the sphere of crime with that of sin, there must remain a realm of private morality and immorality which is, in brief and crude terms, not the law's business."[35] However, this did not mean that the Wolfenden Committee was willing to recognize sexual minorities in the positive sense. Understandably for the 1950s, they still carried a lot of antigay baggage. Indeed, the report addressed prostitution in addition to homosexuality, since both "rank high in the kingdom of evils."[36] But they were trying to be good liberals, looking at the "ugly facts of this evil . . . calmly, persistently, reflectively."[37] In fairness, they established some progressive stances, such as not categorizing homosexuality as a disease and dispelling the myth that homosexuality was a disproportionate phenomenon of the intellectual class. On the other hand, there was still a strong pull, especially by the medical professionals on the committee, to treat gays and lesbians as if they were ill. The nonmedical members rejected treatment of gay prisoners with estrogen, but the medical members did not want to give up on labeling some homosexuals as having "severely damaged personalities," such as "effeminate and flauntingly exhibitionistic individuals; grossly inadequate, passive, weak-willed persons; or deeply resentful antisocial types."[38]

The Wolfenden Report, then, reflects the limitations of a strictly negative conception of freedom. Although liberals were able to see a bit beyond the prejudices of the day in their quest to carve out a zone of privacy from which the hapless homosexuals would benefit, they were not completely able to embrace gay men (very little of the report addresses lesbianism) as individuals on par with heterosexuals. As they were declaring noble Millian principles, they were still uncomfortable with homosexuality.

Of course, the ALI and the Wolfenden Committee were not operating in a vacuum. Their reforms were part of a mid-century legal push toward the elevation of privacy, particularly sexual privacy, to constitutional doctrine.[39] Again, however, the right to privacy first elevated heterosexual, marital sexual privacy. As Justice John M. Harlan stated in his dissent in *Poe v. Ullman* in 1961, the right to privacy "is not absolute. Thus, I would not suggest that adultery, homosexuality, fornication and incest are immune from criminal inquiry, however privately practiced." However, "the intimacy of husband and wife" must be protected by the state through the right to privacy.[40] This position, of course, became law in *Griswold v. Connecticut* and would be used to affirm a woman's right to choose in *Roe v. Wade*. But it also would be used to uphold Georgia's sodomy law in *Bowers v. Hardwick*. In fact, on the Supreme Court, Harlan's assessment remained largely unchanged for forty years. Any attempt to include lesbians and gay men in the right to privacy was not going to come from the highest court in the land.

## SODOMY LAWS AND LIBERALISM

In a series of speeches given in the early 1960s, the legal scholar H. L. A. Hart sharply criticized a movement that he saw among English judges to enforce notions of sexual morality. So disturbed by this development, in fact, he compared it to legal approaches of Nazi Germany.[41] To critique this movement, Hart relied largely on John Stuart Mill. Although he did not fully accept Mill's arguments, he strongly felt that private sexual acts should be beyond the reach of government regulation.

He praised the Wolfenden Report and the actions of the ALI. Indeed, he stated, in reference to these two reform efforts, that it is "clear . . . that Mill's principles are still very much alive in the criticism of law."[42]

One of Hart's primary goals was to counter the argument, made by Lord Patrick Devlin and others, that a state has a right to preserve itself, and preserving proper morality is a necessary part of this right.[43] Hart did not disagree totally, but he argued that not all morality was alike. He made a crucial distinction between ordinary crime and sexual activity. The criminal impulse, he argued, is quite unlike the sexual impulse. As he stated, "Resistance to the temptation to commit these crimes is not often, as the suppression of sexual impulses generally is, something which affects the development or balance of the individual's emotional life, happiness, and personality."[44] By linking the expression of sexuality to emotional happiness and well-being, Hart puts forth a richer notion of individualism, one that respects the autonomy and self-fulfillment of the individual. In a sense, Hart is arguing for an equal right to sexuality, a right that is integral to the full development of the individual. Consequently, homosexuality is not something so distasteful as to be regulated out of existence or even tolerated merely in the name of the preservation of heterosexual sexual liberty. Instead, it is something to be valued and appreciated for its capacity to allow those for whom it is a part of their sexual and emotional makeup to lead lives as fully developed individuals. This is a rather remarkable statement for the times, but it illustrates liberalism's capacity to accommodate more than the notion of a mere "night-watchman" state. Here Hart is saying that the law must recognize (homo)sexuality as an integral part of individual dignity. Additionally, allowing for the diversity of sexual expression is good for society, not destructive of it. As Hart stated, "we must beware of following Lord Devlin in thinking social morality as a seamless web. . . . We should with Mill be alive to the truth that . . . society can not only survive individual divergences in other fields from its prevalent morality, but profits from them."[45] In retrospect, Hart's views are not really a surprise, since a recent biography chronicles Hart's struggles with his sexuality.[46]

It has already been demonstrated that most mid-century reformers did not share Hart's richer view. Most advocated a purely negative conception of liberalism and adopted a certain laissez-faire attitude toward homosexual sex, but were far from fully accepting sexual minorities as full and equal members of society. Many contemporary commentators argue that this approach was not merely benign; it resulted in the oppression of lesbians and gay men while masquerading as an attempt to help them. Larry Cata Backer provides a forceful critique along these lines. Backer argues that the philosophy behind the Model Penal Code and the Wolfenden Report is deceptively oppressive toward sexual minorities. It gives the impression that society is tolerant and just, but this impression "simultaneously permits this tolerant society the luxury of continuing to regulate the manifestation of the object of its tolerance in a manner that confirms to all but the dead that the conduct is disgusting, filthy, deviant, sick, and not worthy of emulation."[47] For Backer, there is little, if any, difference between Hart and Devlin. Both provide room for moral disgust and social exclusion, but one is just more upfront about it. The liberal position is nothing noble; it is nothing but a utilitarian calculation. "Thus," according to Backer, "the lofty ideal of decriminalizing private expression should not bar society from continuing to marginalize that which is offensive, but to merely tolerate that which appears not worth the economic effort to eradicate."[48] Consequently, the lesbian and gay rights movement since the middle part of the twentieth century has been stagnant, and lesbians and gay men have been prevented from achieving true liberation, since liberalism's efforts have not prevented their marginalization. "As long as offense, and particularly moral offense, remains a legitimate source of governmental power to regulate, no decision of any court will truly liberate sexual nonconformists from the darkness of the private spaces the government and society have assigned for them."[49]

Unfortunately, this position vastly undervalues the reformist power of liberalism and does not reflect the legal and political reality of the past decade.[50] This view is grounded in a postmodern critique of modern liberal society, especially as it relates to sexual regulation of the state. In this view, the liberal distinction between public and private is a construct that allows the state to exert formal and informal power over that which it considers deviant. The logic of this argument is well stated by Backer:

> Liberal toleration and sexual liberation of the contemporary variety steals the power of identity from the beneficiaries of its beneficence. It preserves, in the dominant society, the power to create identity. Dominant culture dictates the existence of groups; having constructed them ("us" and "them"), it then creates the descriptive differences between the "us" and "them" created. . . . Dominant culture takes for itself the power to describe the characteristics of these groups, where they live and what they do.[51]

This, of course, ignores the fact that liberalism is rooted in the principle that there are some things the dominant culture may not do. Liberalism is not simply a facade and an instrument of oppression; it also provides the seeds for remarkable political and social reform. Although the liberalism of the Model Penal Code and Wolfenden Report was certainly limited, it at least set forth a process that led to a richer rights claiming by lesbians and gay men—a claim to which courts are increasingly sympathetic. This is not to argue for a Pollyannaish view of progress. It simply reflects the course of affairs. As was noted in Chapter 3, postmodern analysis may be a powerful tool for critiquing, but it struggles to provide a blueprint for political action. If nothing else, liberalism provides for its own growth and evolution by expanding the notion of individualism. Backer, unfortunately, presents only a caricature of liberalism. A goal of this project is to rescue liberalism from such characterizations.

## CONCRETE, BUT LIMITED, RESULTS OF REFORM

The Model Penal Code did prompt state action, but not at first. In fact, states that were reforming their penal laws while the ALI was acting on this front often retained sodomy sanctions while liberalizing other parts of the criminal law. Wisconsin, New Mexico, New York, Minnesota, Georgia, and Kansas refused to follow the

ALI's recommendations.[52] Illinois was the first state to adopt the Model Penal Code in 1961 with the sodomy law repeal included. Not all states were as thorough or progressive as Illinois.[53] Between 1961 and 1980, thirty-five states used the Model Penal Code as a guide for revising their criminal laws, but only sixteen of these repealed their sodomy laws. The 1970s was a particularly active decade for the legislative repeal of sodomy law, with twenty states doing so. However, after 1980, legislative sodomy law repeal slowed considerably, with only four states repealing their sodomy laws through the legislative process in the 1980s and 1990s.[54]

More tolerant public attitudes on same-sex intimacy and relationships do not explain this wave of legislative repeal. Instead, continued public disapproval of such relationships likely explains the reluctance of legislatures in the 1950s and 1960s to go along with the ALI recommendations, since in a poll taken in 1970, 86 percent of respondents showed some type of disapproval of same-sex relations.[55] This attitude remained fairly constant throughout the 1970s and even saw an increase in the late 1980s. Respondents who viewed same-sex relations as "always wrong" remained near 70 percent in the 1970s and peaked at 75 percent in 1987, falling off sharply in the 1990s to the mid-50 percent range.[56] Thus, prior to the 1990s, approval of same-sex relations did not dramatically increase, pointing to the influence of legal norms articulated by the ALI and enacted by legislatures, until, in the 1990s, when the courts became the impetus for policy change.

Donald Haider-Markel and Kenneth Meier have noted that gay rights claims often fare best when shielded from broad-based, majoritarian politics. Legislative victories tend to occur when policy elites are able to shield laws meant to protect sexual minorities. When the scope of the conflict is expanded and the power of these elites is diminished through greater exposure to hostile public opinion and morality politics, the claims of sexual minorities are defeated.[57] In this case, much of the legislative repeal of sodomy laws came as a result of more comprehensive criminal law reforms inspired by the Model Penal Code. Legislative repeals of sodomy laws, then, were not just about sexual morality, a topic in which sexual minorities would have been at a severe disadvantage in an expanded conflict. Broader criminal law reforms allowed repeal to occur, despite continuing public disapproval of same-sex relations. In this instance, legislators were the agents of change, but the legal norms defined by the ALI likely triggered and guided reform. After the legislative process played itself out, courts would step in to further contract the scope of the conflict in the 1990s.

Sodomy law reform in the state legislative arena paralleled attempts by many states to define a state constitutional right to privacy both out of old constitutional clauses and out of clauses adopted in more recent times. According to Dorothy Toth Beasley, "Between 1968 and 1990, seven states—Hawaii (twice), Illinois, South Carolina, Louisiana, California, Montana, and Alaska (for a second time)—amended their constitutions to include a right to privacy. In doing so, they joined Florida, Washington, and Arizona, which had already included privacy protections in their constitutions."[58] As will be chronicled, state courts responded to this trend by taking over the cause of sodomy law repeals.

This is, of course, quite different from the policy of the U.S. Supreme Court, which upheld the validity of Georgia's sodomy law in 1986.[59] In *Bowers*, the Court held that the line of precedents that had established a right to sexual privacy for heterosexuals did not apply to gays and lesbians.[60] As will be shown, however, state courts would ignore *Bowers*, claiming that sodomy laws violate state constitutions and may be struck down without regard for the federal precedent.

## The Courts Step In: Early Sodomy Law Litigation

Despite the presence of an organized, national lesbian and gay political movement in the United States beginning in the 1970s, litigation was not a tool used by national activists on the sodomy front until the 1980s. Virginia's sodomy law was challenged in the early 1970s, but local gay men initiated this litigation. Their challenge failed when a federal court refused to apply *Griswold v. Connecticut* to same-sex sexual activity, and the U.S. Supreme Court affirmed this decision.[61] This imposed a chilling effect until increasingly mature gay rights advocacy and litigation groups began to reassess the efficacy of sodomy law challenges. Before this time, groups like the American Civil Liberties Union (ACLU) were hesitant to fully embrace the cause of gay rights. In fact, in the 1950s the ACLU affirmed the constitutionality of sodomy laws and generally stayed away from sodomy challenges, since they implicated "conduct" and not traditional First Amendment protections like speech or belief.[62] By the late 1960s, however, the ACLU adopted a policy that all forms of sexual intimacy should be protected under cases like *Griswold*. The group created the Sexual Privacy Project in 1973, the goal of which was to challenge laws restricting sexuality.[63] In 1977, the ACLU, along with the Lambda Legal Defense and Education Fund, which was founded in 1972, began a sodomy law challenge in New York that was ultimately successful. And by 1983, both groups held a national meeting designed to develop a strategy for challenging sodomy statutes nationwide.[64]

## Early Litigation Attempts Repelled by the Supreme Court in *Doe* and *Bowers*

Litigation designed to invalidate Virginia's sodomy law reached the U.S. Supreme Court in *Doe v. Commonwealth's Attorney* in 1976. An anonymous individual who had been arrested and prosecuted under the law originally filed the case in U.S. District Court. The initiative behind the suit came from Bruce Voeller, a gay rights advocate, after a conversation with William O. Douglas. Douglas indicated that the Supreme Court might be receptive to extending privacy protection to sodomy in the wake of *Roe*.[65]

Due to scheduling problems, two retired judges were brought in to hear the case, in addition to a third active judge. The retired judges voted in the 2 to 1 majority upholding the Virginia statute.[66] In doing so, the judges made it clear that, in their view, the right to privacy recently developed by the Supreme Court was limited only to sexual acts and practices within the parameters of marriage.[67] The judges also made a point of the law's long-standing tradition on the books in Virginia and quoted scripture. "It [banning sodomy] is not an upstart notion," the majority declared, "it has ancestry going back to Judaic and Christian law."[68] The dissent took a different view of the privacy precedents, arguing that "private consensual sex acts between adults are matters, absent evidence that they are harmful, in which the state has no legitimate interest."[69] The majority, according to the dissent, took a far too literal view of *Griswold* in limiting it to the creation of a right to marital privacy, instead of a general sexual privacy right.

However, a majority of the Supreme Court thought otherwise, since only three justices were in favor of hearing oral arguments. Douglas was gone from the Court at this time, and Thurgood Marshall, William Brennan, and John Paul Stevens were the only justices who were potentially in favor of overturning the Virginia law. The Court had to make a decision on the case, since all appeals from three-judge panels required a decision.[70] The Court merely issued a one-sentence decision on the appeal: "The judgment is affirmed."[71] The decision outraged Marshall, and, according to an account described by Randy Shilts:

> Brennan posted a newspaper cartoon in his office depicting a couple in bed in a brick house called "The Rights of Individuals"—while a smiling Associate Justice William Rehnquist served on a wrecking crew that was demolishing the structure. "We are told they were 'strict construction-ists,'" said the man in bed. ... Brennan kept the cartoon on his office wall until Chief Justice [Warren] Burger saw it.[72]

Many in the scholarly world were also upset with the decision, with Gerald Gunther calling the decision "irresponsible" and "lawless."[73] Nonetheless, it was a sign that the federal judiciary was hesitant to address the issue, despite the efforts of others in the legal community. And with *Bowers*, this negative trajectory continued in the Supreme Court.

## KENTUCKY: A WATERSHED IN SODOMY LITIGATION

In 1992, the Kentucky Supreme Court was the first state high court to strike down a sodomy statute since the U.S. Supreme Court upheld the Georgia statute in *Bowers*. Interestingly, the law was fairly new compared to the history of sodomy laws, having been passed in 1974.[74] In 1985 Jeffrey Wasson was one of twenty-five individuals arrested for approaching undercover police officers for sex. In the process of reviewing the case, a state district court declared the sodomy law unconstitutional on privacy grounds. The decision was affirmed by a state circuit court and appealed to the state supreme court.[75] The court, by a 4 to 3 vote, declared that the state's prohibition against homosexual sodomy violated both the privacy and equal protection provisions of the Kentucky Constitution.[76] In doing so, the court first disposed of the precedent of *Bowers*: "We are not bound by the decisions of the United States Supreme Court when deciding whether a state statute impermissibly infringes upon individual rights guaranteed in the State Constitution so long as state constitutional protection does not fall below the federal floor."[77] The majority then took up the privacy issue, arguing that although the Kentucky Constitution did not contain an explicit privacy provision, Kentucky judicial precedent created one. The majority cited the case of *Commonwealth v. Campbell*, decided in 1909, which adopted a libertarian interpretation of the Kentucky Constitution in regard to a right to privacy. The majority drew special attention to quotations by Mill in the *Campbell* decision. Indeed, as Justice Charles Leibson stated for the majority, "there is little doubt but that the views of John Stuart Mill, which were then held in high esteem, provided the philosophical underpinnings for the reworking and broadening of protection of individual rights that occurs throughout the 1891 Constitution," which was the basis of the *Campbell* decision.[78]

In striking down the sodomy law, the court saw itself as part of a larger movement providing greater protection for individual liberties, especially in terms of sodomy law reform. The majority opinion cited several instances of both state supreme and lower courts finding sodomy laws unconstitutional. Thus, rather than being policy innovators, the majority saw itself as "but a part of a moving stream."[79] As a dissenting opinion pointed out, however, most of the movement in this stream came from legislative repeal, not judicial enactment.[80] Despite their assertions to the contrary, the majority in *Commonwealth v. Wasson* was clearly making new policy for the State of Kentucky and acted in a novel manner in the realm of sodomy law reform.

Since the Kentucky statute singled out same-sex sodomy for criminal sanction, the majority also found the law unconstitutional on equal protection grounds. The opinion went to great lengths to establish the immutable nature of homosexuality, quoting Lawrence Tribe (who helped to argue the case against the state) and relying on the evidence presented in amicus briefs.[81] Having established this fact, the majority emphasized that the right to be treated equally before the law was an even more fundamental right under the Kentucky Constitution than the right to privacy. Consequently, the statute failed rationality review, since it was based simply upon the approbation of homosexuals. "Simply because the majority, speaking through the General Assembly, finds one type of extramarital intercourse more offensive than another, does not provide a rational basis for criminalizing the sexual preference of homosexuals."[82]

The dissenters clearly saw the majority as making policy in a manner inappropriate for the judiciary. Generally taking a restraintist and strict constructionist approach, those in the minority saw the decision as a slippery slope leading to increased activism. In words that could have been uttered by Robert Bork, Justice Robert Stephens declared that "the decision is a vast extension of judicial power by which four Justices of this Court have overridden the will of the Legislative and Executive branches . . . and denied the people any say in this important social issue."[83] This rhetoric, typically found in U.S. Supreme Court decisions, is also visible at the state level, confirming that states have become the new battlegrounds in the contest over the scope of individual rights.

The author of the majority opinion, Justice Leibson, was seen, before his death in 1995, as a leader of the Kentucky Supreme Court. Indeed, according to one account, he was "arguably the most important jurist in recent Kentucky history."[84] It is no surprise that Leibson quoted Mill in the decision, since he favored a libertarian approach to issues of individual rights. Indeed, a newspaper account noted his "impassioned advocacy of individual rights."[85] He was a registered Republican who was reelected with 72 percent of the vote in 1990,[86] and, interestingly, taught a course at the University of Louisville law school that emphasized using the state's constitution as a source of law protecting individual liberties[87]—a combination of advocacy and jurisprudence that centered around Millian notions of individual rights.

For a decade leading up to the sodomy decision, the Kentucky Supreme Court had become more activist and interpreted the Kentucky Constitution as affording more protections than the U.S. Constitution. In 1983, the court struck down a law allowing the state to supply textbooks to students in nonpublic schools; in 1989, the court found a right to equal educational funding in the state constitution; and in 1990, the court found that the state constitution provided more extensive protection against double jeopardy than the federal constitution.[88] After *Wasson*, in 1993, the court found a "right to die," allowing the family of a comatose woman to take her off life support.[89]

Thus, the decision in *Commonwealth v. Wasson* can be seen as part of a larger trend on the part of the courts to expand individual rights under the Kentucky Constitution.[90] This libertarianism also came from some interesting sources. An amicus brief filed by the Presbyterian Church (U.S.A.) in support of striking down the sodomy law stated that the law "constitutes an impermissible infringement upon the rights of privacy."[91] This reflects how profoundly imbedded libertarianism had become in the U.S. political psyche. Even some prominent religious groups valued privacy over morality.

## KENTUCKY: THE POLITICAL RESPONSE

Shortly after the decision in *Wasson*, Kentucky Attorney General Chris Gorman asked the Kentucky Supreme Court to reconsider its decision. Although the court was not likely to do so, the attorney general used the opportunity to voice concern over the antimajoritarian nature of the court's decision. As the brief for the attorney general asked, "On what basis will the courts of the commonwealth . . . override the collective judgment of the elective representatives of the people . . . the traditions of western civilization, the history of the U.S. and the history of the commonwealth of Kentucky?"[92] Similarly, on one level, public reaction to the decision was quite strong, including an anonymous death threat against the four justices who voted to strike down the sodomy law. And in a clever melding of the debate over judicial activism and cultural conservatism, Kent Ostrander of the Family Foundation called the ruling the "*Roe v. Wade* of sodomy." There was also some discussion in the legislature about starting a ballot initiative to classify homosexuality as "abnormal, wrong, unnatural and perverse." This talk went nowhere, however.[93]

This issue did not completely die, as attempts were made in 1994 to propose a constitutional amendment overturning the decision; however, these attempts failed to get out of the legislature. An amendment was passed by a House committee but was killed by Democrats. The amendment would have required a three-fifths vote of the legislature before being placed on the ballot for popular ratification. Despite the efforts of activists opposed to *Wasson*, there appeared to be little political will to pass a constitutional amendment to overturn the decision.[94] Another constitutional amendment was considered in 1996 by conservative legislators, but was not even voted out of a committee. The senate majority leader, a Democrat, understood the contemporary politics of privacy. A constitutional amendment could, said David Karen, overrule the courts, but "The only way to make an amendment work . . . is to make it apply to everyone. That means it would have to apply to husbands and wives. My feeling is that there is a growing number of people who believe government does not need to be in the family's bedroom."[95] This was not an affirmation of same-sex sexual privacy but a reflection that this type of sex generally is subsumed by concerns for heterosexual privacy. One wonders what the senate majority leader's position would have been had this linkage not been developed by legal elites like the ALI and had Mill not become the patron saint of sexual privacy.

## TENNESSEE: THE TREND CONTINUES

According to one commentator, the Supreme Court of Tennessee "has become one of the most activist courts in the nation."[96] A part of this activism is the case of *Campbell v. Sundquist*, where the court let stand the invalidation of Tennessee's Homosexual Practices Act, which states: "It is a Class C misdemeanor for any person to engage in consensual sexual penetration . . . with a person of the same gender."[97] This form of the statute was passed by the legislature in 1989 as a part of a comprehensive criminal law reform effort, when sodomy was downgraded from a felony to a misdemeanor. The legislature affirmed the decision by the Tennessee Sentencing Commission to remove vague "crime against nature" statutes and specifically singled out same-sex sexual conduct,[98] because the legislature was convinced that "there were deleterious effects from a homosexual lifestyle," according to the Tennessee attorney general.[99] Thus, in this case reform meant reducing the penalty but keeping the moral sanction against sexual minorities. The statute was challenged by local attorney Abby Rubenfeld, with support from the ACLU.[100] A Nashville circuit court judge found the law unconstitutional, stating: "The right to privacy . . . includes the right of sexual expression with another consenting adult regardless of the gender of the sex partner."[101] Recognizing the politics of sodomy laws, Rubenfeld stated after the decision, "This case isn't about endorsing homosexuality. It's an endorsement of the fundamental right to privacy, which . . . is valuable to all Tennesseans, whether or not they're gay."[102] This argument apparently resonated with the public, because there was no overwhelming negative response to the decision, save for a few letters to the editor.[103]

The Court of Appeals and the Tennessee Supreme Court affirmed the decision. In declaring the act unconstitutional, the court of appeals first dismissed, like the Kentucky court, citing the precedent of *Bowers*, since (quoting another case) "state supreme courts, interpreting state constitutional provisions, may impose higher standards and stronger protections than those set by the federal constitution."[104]

Unlike the Kentucky court, however, the Tennessee court relied exclusively on the right to privacy to declare the Homosexual Practices Act unconstitutional. Although the court recognized that no explicit right to privacy existed in the Tennessee Constitution, it declared that this right is to be inferred from several provisions of the Tennessee Constitution, such as freedom of worship and speech provisions and provisions prohibiting unreasonable searches and seizures and the quartering of soldiers.[105] The court first defined this right to privacy in 1992 in the case of *Davis v. Davis*, where the court declared a right to privacy in defending a father's right not to procreate from frozen embryos.[106] In justifying this line of precedent, the *Campbell* court declared, citing *Davis*, that while the framers of the Tennessee Constitution could not have foreseen in vitro fertilization, "there can be little doubt that they foresaw the need to protect individuals from unwarranted governmental intrusion such as the one now before us, involving intimate questions of personal and family concern."[107]

In allowing this decision to stand, the supreme court perhaps was affirming a sentiment it expressed in 1975 when, after upholding a sodomy law conviction, it opined that it "would not be amiss for the legislature to take a new and fresh look at Tennessee's . . . "crime against nature" statute. Such a re-evaluation, in the light of modern mores . . . would be in the public interest."[108] The legislature did reevaluate, but not to the court's liking. The legislature had not gone far enough in the direction of reform, thereby causing the courts to step in. Once again, Millian libertarianism trumped majority will as expressed by the Tennessee legislature. And in this case, like Kentucky, the direct beneficiaries were sexual minorities, no longer dependent on heterosexual goodwill.

Thus, by the early 1990s, legal norms first articulated in the 1950s began to take root in U.S. state courts. The next chapter will explore the continuation of this phenomenon as other state courts took up the issue, often with mixed results. Many state high courts continued the work of sodomy law reform, but this was not guaranteed. The reasons for this inconsistency shed light on the role of courts as agents of political and social change.

# 6    Lessons from Continued Sodomy Adjudication

As LITIGATION EFFORTS spread to other states, a mixed record developed. Some state high courts went the way of Kentucky and Tennessee, while others were more hesitant, not wishing to challenge political and legal moralism. However, sodomy law repeal efforts without litigation achieved even fewer results for reformers. This demonstrates the significant power of courts to achieve change, especially when that change is framed in a way that reinforces powerful strains of a political culture.

## TEXAS

Although the U.S. Supreme Court invalidated the Texas sodomy law in *Lawrence v. Texas* in 2003, developments in Texas before this decision provide an excellent example of the role that liberal legal arguments can play in contemporary U.S. politics, as well as the continued salience of morality politics, especially in socially conservative states where courts are more reluctant to act aggressively. Until recently, Texas was one of four states to criminalize sodomy for persons of the same sex only. A sodomy law dating from 1860 relied on common law interpretations from the courts to give it effect, since the wording of the statute was quite general.[1] The law was given specificity by the legislature in 1943, when a discussion of specific body parts and specific sexual acts, including oral sex, were included in the definition of sodomy.[2] This expansion of the law was upheld by the Texas courts as a legitimate exercise of legislative authority and not violative of any fundamental rights.[3]

In 1969, the revised law was challenged in federal court. The case first involved a gay man (or as the case opinion stated "a confessed homosexual") who had been arrested for having sex with another man in a public restroom in Dallas. The case was soon overshadowed with the concerns of heterosexuals, however, since a married couple and a heterosexual male who claimed they lived under the threat of future prosecution joined the case.[4] The case was heard in a U.S. District Court, which declared the law unconstitutionally overbroad in that it implicated the sexual acts of married couples. Relying on the recent precedent of *Griswold v. Connecticut*, the court held that marital privacy was protected from such intrusion. Additionally, the court adopted a Millian approach to the regulation of private morality.

> Sodomy is not an act which has the approval of the majority of the people. In fact such
> conduct is probably offensive to the vast majority, but such opinion is not sufficient

reason for the State to encroach upon the liberty of married persons in their private conduct. Absent some demonstrable necessity, matters of (good or bad) taste are to be protected from regulation.[5]

Among the examples from case law that the court cited in defense of this position were cases involving nudism, hair regulation, distribution of political literature, and receiving communist literature by mail.[6] Thus, it was not the rights of lesbians and gay men the court was defending, but the marital privacy and a general right to be free from the moral judgments of society. In fact, the case is remarkable for its lack of discussion of homosexuality, despite initially involving the actions of gay men. But privacy was clearly on the mind of this court, and it was offended by the reach of the Texas sodomy law.

The Texas Court of Criminal Appeals was not happy with this decision. In a separate sodomy case in the same year, the state court explicitly refuted and refused to apply the holding of the federal court. Fundamentally, the Texas court disagreed with the characterization of *Griswold* by the federal court: It was not privacy in general that was implicated, but the distinction between birth control and the practice of sodomy. Laws prohibiting the former were much more shocking and offensive than those prohibiting the latter, since even the dissenters in *Griswold* were offended by the birth control statute, the Texas court argued.[7] Consequently, the 1943 revisions to the sodomy law were given the stamp of approval by the highest criminal court in Texas.

But politically the tide was turning in favor of decriminalizing heterosexual sodomy, and the Texas sodomy law was, in fact, revised in 1974 to eliminate penalties for heterosexuals.[8] The 1974 law made it a Class C misdemeanor to engage in "deviate sexual intercourse" with members of the same sex. The penalty for the infraction was a $200 fine. The revision of the law stemmed from a general Penal Code revision begun in 1965. In 1968, the Texas State Bar Committee on the Revision of the Penal Code specifically addressed the issue of same-sex sodomy. At this time, a draft revision was put forth that did not make same-sex sodomy a crime. Drawing on the precedent of the Model Penal Code and the efforts of other states' repeals of sodomy laws, the staff of the committee made this recommendation.[9] After some discussion, the committee eventually decided to keep the criminal provision, but reduce the offense to a misdemeanor. This provision passed by a 5 to 4 vote. The committee readdressed the issue in 1970, but the position did not change, despite the hopes of the staff who had pushed for the provision's reconsideration. The changes were first presented to the legislature in 1971 but died in committee. It finally passed two years later as a Class C misdemeanor that removed the threat of jail time and provided for a maximum $200 fine. The original proposal had been for a Class A misdemeanor, a more severe infraction.[10]

Questionnaires given to the members of the committee reflect a fairly predictable set of motivating factors. The four who voted to decriminalize generally justified their vote on libertarian grounds and a belief in the right to privacy. They also thought that decriminalizing sodomy would be good for the mental health of gays and save taxpayers money in law enforcement efforts. Those opposed to decriminalization feared the impact on families and were convinced that it would lead to increased homosexual activity and persons. They also did not want to remove the general moral stigma. All members of the committee realized the political dynamic of the situation and feared that decriminalization would jeopardize the entire reform effort.[11]

Thus, even if the committee's recommendation had gone the other way, there is little chance that complete decriminalization would have survived the legislative process, even though it did so for heterosexual sodomy. And despite the more progressive elements of the committee, no one put forth a strong defense of the dignity and equality of lesbians and gay men. Indeed, according to Randy Von Beitel, "one of the most striking conclusions to be drawn from reading the minutes of the Committee's deliberations is the total absence of the view that homosexual acts and relationships are just as morally valid and correct as their heterosexual counterparts."[12]

Nearly two decades later, several plaintiffs brought suit against the law, and it was declared unconstitutional by a state district court judge in Austin. The plaintiffs argued that the sodomy law violated due process, privacy, and equal protection provisions of the Texas Constitution.[13] On appeal, the Third Court of Appeals affirmed the ruling, largely relying on privacy arguments. According to Chief Judge Jimmy Carroll, "We can think of nothing more fundamentally private and deserving of protection than sexual behavior between consenting adults in private."[14] The court alluded to an equal protection problem as well. After they established the privacy right, the judges declared that "it cannot be constitutional, absent a compelling state objective, to prohibit lesbians and gay men from engaging in the same conduct in which heterosexuals may legally engage." And the court rejected the state's interest in preserving public morality as a compelling interest, asking, "If lesbians and gay men pose such a threat to the state, why then does the state not enforce the statute on a regular basis?"[15]

The court, then, presented a rather sweeping renunciation of the Texas sodomy law and the state's efforts to preserve it. This is perhaps no surprise, since the Austin court is generally considered to be one of the most liberal in the state.[16] But the fact that the court relied on the right to privacy was politically controversial in Texas beyond the issue of gay rights. Many pro-life groups were concerned that a strengthened right to privacy could endanger some abortion laws still on the books in Texas. The right to privacy was still not fully defined in Texas law, having been first articulated by the Texas Supreme Court in 1987 in a case involving a mandatory polygraph test for state employees in certain agencies.[17]

In that case, *Texas State Employees Union v. Texas Department of Mental Health and Retardation*, the supreme court admitted that the Texas Constitution contained no explicit provision defining a right to privacy. But like Justice William O. Douglas's reasoning in *Griswold v. Connecticut*, the court maintained that various provisions of the Texas Constitution create a "zone of privacy."[18] It was the privacy argument upon which the Third Court of Appeals ultimately relied in *State v. Morales*, declaring: "The State has not met its burden of showing that a compelling government objective justifies the intrusion §21.06 [the specific statutory provision] makes into appellees' private lives.... We expressly decline to determine whether §21.06 violates the state guarantees of due process or equal protection."[19] Even this aggressive pro-gay decision could not bring itself to embrace equal protection claims, instead relying on the bulwark of Millian jurisprudence.

The issue of standing was also implicated in *Morales*. Since there was no arrest of any of the plaintiffs, the state argued that they lacked standing to sue. Especially since, in Texas law, civil courts generally do not have jurisdiction to overturn criminal statues on constitutional grounds. The Court of Criminal Appeals maintains this jurisdiction. An exception to this rule was created in *Passel v. Fort Worth Independent School District*. This 1969 case held that when property rights are implicated, a civil court could overturn a penal statute. The plaintiffs in *Morales* argued that this also applied to personal rights, and the Third Court of Appeals agreed. The court also agreed with the plaintiffs, against the state's arguments, that they faced actual harm, even though prosecution was unlikely, since, according to the court "they have shown that the statute causes actual harm which goes far beyond the mere threat of prosecution."[20] Thus, the court clearly wanted to make a statement about the validity of the Texas sodomy law. Otherwise, they could have ruled narrowly and dismissed the case due to a lack of standing. Also, a year later in the case of *City of Dallas v. England*, the Third Court of Appeals (made up of three judges different from those who ruled in *Morales*) upheld a lower court's finding that §21.06 was unconstitutional. In this case, the statute was used as the basis for the denial of employment in the Dallas Police Department of an admitted lesbian.[21] This aggressive adjudication, however, would not continue up the ladder of the Texas court system.

As previously indicated, in Texas law, there are two courts of last resort: the supreme court, which hears civil and constitutional matters, and the criminal court of appeals, which has jurisdiction in all criminal appellate matters. Texas Attorney General Dan Morales decided to appeal to each court to cover the state's bases. It was not clear which was the appropriate court, since the parties that originally challenged the sodomy law were never prosecuted. Ultimately, the criminal court of appeals rejected the case, since no crime was committed, but the supreme court agreed to hear the appeal. On January 3, 1993, the Texas Supreme Court heard ninety minutes of oral arguments on the appeal. As an indication of the attention given to this litigation, Court TV taped the arguments for later broadcast. The oral argument took a predictable course, with the attorney for those challenging the statute presenting Millian arguments. As Patrick Wiseman told the court, "You ought to have a damn good reason to poke around in someone's bedroom," obviously appealing to the majoritarian concern with the right to privacy. Assistant Attorney General Harry Potter III put forth two main arguments: the law is never enforced and posed no threat, and the law is reasonable since it represented the moral judgment of the citizens of Texas. The topics of questioning ranged from abortion, drugs, and witch-burning to gay and lesbian psychology. Under questioning Potter admitted that he could not argue that lesbians and gay men were psychologically suspect, largely because he could find no credible experts to testify.[22]

However, this position was put forth by a group of thirty Texas legislators in an amicus brief. The legislators argued that homosexuality "endangers the public health," since it is a psychiatric condition that is "closely associated with other anti-social, deleterious behavior."[23] Indeed, the brief rejected the judgment of the psychiatric community on homosexuality and argued that "The only reason the American Psychiatric Association had delisted homosexuality as a mental disorder is the relentless intimidation and political pressure applied to the APA by militant homosexual activists."[24] Interestingly, then, opponents of sodomy law repeal were more confident refuting rather unanimous professional medical and scientific judgment than refuting the right to privacy.

During oral arguments, the judges appeared to be divided, asking questions that were both skeptical and supportive of the government's position. Justice Craig Enoch was concerned that overturning the sodomy law would lead to the invalidation of other criminal laws. He was also skeptical of the distinction that attorney Patrick Weisman made between sodomy and growing marijuana. Wiesman argued that the state had an interest in regulating the growth of marijuana, but not sodomy, since drug trafficking is a real social problem, whereas private, consensual sex is not. Enoch argued that someone growing marijuana for his or her own use would not pose a threat to society—essentially trying to poke a hole in the "harm principle" argument. Justice John Cornyn was also skeptical of the merits of the case and inquired why homosexuals were harmed, since the sodomy law was never enforced. Conversely, Justice Robert Gammage brought up the equal protection issues, asking Potter why the state was able to justify enforcing sodomy laws only against lesbians and gay men. Obviously, the court was not of one mind on the appeal.[25]

While the Texas Supreme Court was mulling over the decision, the Texas legislature was thrust into the sodomy debate. According to a law passed by the legislature in 1991, all state criminal laws were slated to expire in 1994. The legislature had begun the process of rewriting these laws two years prior, and the issue of the sodomy law resurfaced as a part of this process.[26] One legislator wished to extend the sodomy prohibition to heterosexuals, thus reversing the earlier decision of the legislature decriminalizing sodomy for heterosexuals. Representative Warren Chisum's proposal was adopted by the House by a vote of 74 to 48—not exactly a ringing endorsement for Millian principles. The Senate had already voted to remove the same-sex sodomy provision, so the House was making a particularly distinctive statement. In defending his proposal, Chisum argued that the law would fight the spread of sexually transmitted diseases like AIDS.[27]

In a conference committee convened to come up with a final version of the criminal law revision, the House conferees rejected the will of the House and eliminated Chisum's proposal, but they voted 3 to 2 to keep the same-sex sodomy prohibition. The Senate conferees conversely voted 4 to 1 to eliminate the law. This issue, along with hate crime legislation, threatened to torpedo the entire criminal law revision. The House was being recalcitrant on both issues, since the hate crime law would have provided for stiffer penalties for crimes motivated by race, religion, or sexual orientation. One legislator stated: "I think the Senate will approve the penal code if that provision [the prohibition of same-sex sodomy] is in there or not in there. I don't think the House will. That's the difference."[28]

This turned out to be a prescient statement, since the next day the House and Senate conferees unanimously agreed to keep the same-sex sodomy prohibition while eliminating the heterosexual prohibition, thereby affirming the statutory status quo. On a previous vote, only two House conferees wished to eliminate both provisions, leading the chief Senate conferee, Senator John Whitmire, to see the writing on the wall. Ultimately, Whitmire did not think defending the rights of lesbians and gay men was important enough to thwart the entire penal code revision. He stated: "I thought it was too important to solve those problems and get on about making Texas a safe place, versus getting pulled down in the gutter with . . . proponents of a political and social agenda." He also indicated that although he thought the reconciled version of the law perpetuated bigotry, he deferred to the process that was taking place in the judiciary. In optimistic support of judicial action in the area he stated, "the (Texas) Supreme Court is dealing with it, and it's been struck down by two (other) courts."[29]

Despite Whitmire's optimism, the Texas Supreme Court dismissed the appeal from the Third Court of Appeals. By a 5 to 4 vote, the justices decided that they did not have jurisdiction in the matter, since none of the plaintiffs had been charged with a crime, and "there is no allegation . . . that the statute will be enforced." The oral arguments were a good harbinger of what was to come, since those justices most critical of the plaintiffs' claims, Cornyn and Enoch, voted with the majority, while Justice Gammage, who posed the equal protection concerns, voted with the minority. But the skeptics obviously won the day. The decision technically invalidated the lower court decision, and in the confused aftermath, both sides declared limited victories: Those opposed to the sodomy law could point to another lower court decision that struck down the sodomy law in *City of Dallas* (the lesbian discrimination case). Most significantly, however, the court ducked the issue, leaving the decision ultimately up to the political branches. According to the only openly gay member of the legislature at the time, "I find it reprehensible that the gutless majority of the Texas Supreme Court has found a way to sidestep the issue."[30]

Due to the court's ducking, the issue was thrust into the ongoing gubernatorial race between Governor Ann Richards and George W. Bush. Richards declared that she would not oppose its repeal. According to a spokesman, "What it [the sodomy law] really is, is an unenforceable law that has no place in Texas. Our law enforcement officials have plenty of real crimes to worry about."[31] Thus, Richards was unwilling to defend the rights of lesbians and gay men positively, especially in a close election campaign. The sodomy issue was simply a way to emphasize her "law and order" message. Her opponent was more forthright, however. George W. Bush said he would definitely veto a sodomy law repeal, stating, "I think it's a symbolic gesture of traditional values." Jeff Fisher of the American Family Association echoed this position: "I think pigs will fly before you'll see the sodomy statute overturned in a normal legislative process. I think it's pretty clear that the people of Texas want that law on the books."[32] He was right. The Texas legislature did not repeal the law. The United States Supreme Court would be required to invalidate the law.

## MONTANA

A year after Tennessee's sodomy law was invalidated, the Montana Supreme Court struck down the section of the state's deviate sexual conduct statute that criminalized sexual conduct between persons of the same gender.[33] Gay rights advocates in Montana attempted a legislative repeal in 1991 but were rebuffed. According to Nancy Gryczan, who became lead plaintiff in the litigation, "We heard horrible abuse in the Legislature . . . . We saw we were getting nowhere, so we took it to the courts."[34] Based on a suit filed in 1993, Montana District Judge Jeffrey Sherlock invalidated the law on privacy grounds, the main argument put forth by the plaintiffs. In Millian terms he declared, "Since Plaintiffs' activities do not harm anyone, it is hard to understand why anyone needs to be concerned with what these people do in private."[35]

The Montana case is interesting, since there is an explicit privacy provision in the Montana Constitution that was at the time relatively new, in constitutional terms, having been drafted in 1972. Article 2, Section 10 states: "The right of individual privacy is essential to the well-being of a free society and shall not be infringed without the showing of a compelling state interest."[36] Indeed, the provision is a reflection of Montana's unique concern for individual rights. Its framers wished to update the Montana Constitution by adding an explicit privacy provision.[37] But the relationship between the adoption of this provision and the protection of the privacy of sexual minorities is not clear. There is evidence that concern over the legitimization of homosexuality led to a change in the privacy provision. During debate over the privacy clause in the Montana Constitutional Convention of 1971–1972, concerns about homosexuality may have led to the narrowing of the proposed privacy provision. The initial privacy clause was unanimously adopted, and it merely asserted the importance of the right to privacy. However, after a proposal was made to decriminalize all consensual sexual conduct (which was soundly defeated), the delegates reconsidered their initial vote on the privacy clause, now deciding to narrow it by adding that the right to privacy could be infringed given a "compelling government interest." It is likely that fear of decriminalizing sodomy led to a narrowing of the provision. Indeed, as further evidence of the fact that sexual minorities were outside of privacy protection in Montana, the legislature adopted a revision of the criminal code in 1973 that retained sodomy law violations as a felony and made the crime applicable only to same-sex acts.[38]

Reversing a trend that saw Montana courts defer to the legislature and local prosecutors on the sodomy issue, the Montana high court affirmed the lower court's decision. Like other state courts, the justices dismissed the federal precedent of *Bowers v. Hardwick* and found its justification in the Montana Constitution alone.[39] The court's decision was a strong affirmation of the right to privacy that began with a discussion of the privacy jurisprudence of Louis Brandeis and ended with a rather unequivocal statement:

> Quite simply, while legislative enactments may reflect the will of the majority, and, arguably, may even respond to perceived societal notions of what is acceptable conduct in a moral sense, there are certain rights so fundamental that they will not be denied to a minority no matter how despised by society.[40]

The court was also aware of developments in other states, as it explicitly cited the litigation in Tennessee.[41] And the court was unanimous on the outcome, with one judge preferring to rely on equal protection arguments, not privacy.[42]

Thus, unlike the Tennessee court, the Montana court was on surer footing in defending the right to privacy, though perhaps no less controversial in applying it to same-sex sexual conduct. Nothing in the political events in the decades leading up to *Gryczan* would indicate that the court was responding to increasing political liberalization on gay rights. Indeed, political activity since *Gryczan* demonstrates that court decisions invalidating sodomy laws are not always unquestioned by political actors. During the 1990s, the Montana legislature voiced strong opposition to homosexuality. In 1995, the Senate passed a bill, by a margin of 32 to 18, that would have required persons convicted of violating the gay-only sodomy law to register with local law enforcement for life.[43] Only after statewide and national negative reaction to this provision and a veto threat from the Republican governor, Marc Racicot, did the Senate back down.[44] As of the 2001 session, the legislature refused to take the invalidated sodomy law off the books. Votes have been close but not successful. Legislators, determined to keep the perceived moral sanction in place, as well as the hope of future prosecution, have refused to accept fully the supreme court's decision. According to one legislator, "There still is potentiality, and probably should be potentiality, for prosecution."[45] But the larger story is of an aggressive judicial decision that staked out a claim for gay rights in Montana politics in a state not particularly receptive to gay rights claims.

The litigation over Montana's sodomy law provides an interesting and telling glimpse into the dynamic at the heart of this inquiry: liberalism and gay rights claims. Whereas in *Gryczan* the Montana Supreme Court relied on a strictly negative conception of freedom, arguments were presented to the court advocating a richer notion of individualism and freedom. In particular, Montana's "dignity clause" led lawyers opposed to the sodomy law to put forth neo-Kantian arguments. However, reflecting negative liberalism's dominance in the United States, the court did not listen.

The plaintiffs' brief first outlined the standard privacy arguments and tied them to the Montana Constitution and the litigation preceding *Gryczan*, but it also provided "an alternate basis for affirming the lower court." The basis lay in the "dignity clause" of the state's constitution that reads: "The dignity of the human being is inviolable." The brief argued that this clause should be an independent, freestanding clause for courts to use to judge legislation beyond the privacy or equal protection clauses of the Montana Constitution. To define "dignity," the brief used a definition that requires each individual to "be permitted to participate equally in the honor and opportunities available in the society," thereby grounding the opposition to sodomy laws in a richer notion of personhood.[46]

An amicus brief from the Women's Law Caucus of the University of Montana School of Law argued the neo-Kantian perspective more aggressively. The brief pointed to the fact that delegates to the convention who wrote the current constitution explicitly relied on Kantian arguments, citing the philosopher in a report on the dignity clause. The brief noted that the report "quotes a passage from Kant in *Foundations of the Metaphysics of Morals*. In this passage, Kant makes clear his belief that the 'inner worth' of each human being, his or her dignity, is found in his or her capacity to act as an 'autonomous member of the realm of ends.'"[47] The direct citation of Kant by lawyers reflects the capacity of the law to push the boundaries of political discourse: It makes sense that members of a constitutional convention used these arguments in the neo-Kantian 1970s and that lawyers trained in this tradition would use these arguments in litigation.

It also illustrates the limits of this dynamic, however, since the court refrained from using this argument, instead grounding its decision in a strictly negative freedom framework. The court asserted the strong, but clearly negative, principle that

> all adults regardless of gender, fully and properly expect that their consensual sexual activities will not be subject to the prying eyes of others or to governmental snooping or regulation.... Moreover, while society may not approve of the sexual practices of homosexuals... that is not to say that society is unwilling to recognize that all adults, regardless of gender or marital state, at least have a reasonable expectation that their sexual activities will remain personal and private.[48]

In other words, society may strongly disapprove of homosexuality, but it must, out of fear of government intrusion, let consenting sex be private and protected as such. Nothing here reflects Hart's arguments about the central role that sexuality plays in personhood. Rather, the court's statement is one that Learned Hand would have embraced wholeheartedly.

## GEORGIA

In *Powell v. Georgia*, the Georgia Supreme Court invalidated the very law that the U.S. Supreme Court upheld in *Bowers*. According to the Georgia Supreme Court in *Powell*, Georgia has a long history of privacy jurisprudence "which is far more extensive than the right of privacy protected by the U.S. Constitution."[49] The court also asserted that "consensual, private, adult sexual activity... is at the heart of the Georgia Constitution's protection of the right of privacy."[50] This case marked an abrupt change in the thinking of the Georgia Supreme Court in regard to the constitutionality of sodomy laws. Only two years earlier, the court upheld Georgia's statute that prohibited the solicitation of sodomy in *Christenson v. State*.[51] The court was divided, with a three justice plurality declaring: "The right to determine what is harmful to health and morals or what is criminal to the public welfare belongs to the people through their elected representatives."[52] Obviously, the position was not a strong one in the court, since it would soon be replaced by a more important concern for the right of privacy. As Andrew Jacobs presciently wrote in 1996, "The extreme fragmentation of the Georgia court leaves the door ajar to future challenges to the statute, and likely portends future challenges in other jurisdictions."[53] Change can happen quickly in state courts, making them receptive arenas for policymaking based on rights claims. Additionally, *Powell* provides no better example of the role currently being played by judicial federalism. A law upheld by the U.S. Supreme Court was found to be unconstitutional using a higher standard of review at the state level; the same law led to two very different outcomes.

The Georgia court has become less conservative in recent years. Indeed, five of the seven justices were appointed by Democratic Governor Zell Miller, although the justice most perceived as being conservative was also appointed by Miller. In addition to the sodomy ruling, the court has reversed several death penalty cases and has begun to scrutinize the actions of police and prosecutors. It also invalidated a state law that banned outdoor advertising by businesses engaged in adult entertainment.[54]

As with decisions in other states, a bit of political activity followed, but nothing was done to challenge directly the court's decision. The lieutenant governor elect, Mark Taylor, stated: "I think there needs to be a law of some sort on the books." But he also hinted at the political reality, stating, "[i]t's an issue the Legislature would rather not deal with."[55] Although overruling the decision was a high priority for conservatives, the political reality was perhaps best articulated by Georgia House Judiciary Chairman Jim Martin: "I'd hate to think we'd be silly as to try to amend the Georgia Constitution to take away a person's individual liberty rights in this area. There is a point of personal liberty beyond which government shouldn't intrude."[56]

## LOUISIANA

Like Texas, Louisiana presents more of a mixed bag concerning sodomy law adjudication and points to the effects of court ambiguity. Lower courts have struck down the state's sodomy law, which makes no gender distinction, in recent years, but the state high court has upheld the law, as recently as 2002. Before the U.S. Supreme Court settled the matter in 2003, a struggle took place in the state, with lower courts repeatedly taking up the issue while the clearly conservative supreme court repelled attempts at sodomy law liberalization. The legal arguments made some headway in the legislature, where advocates saw some movement while emphasizing privacy arguments, especially since the law is so broad. But the fact remains that morality politics was still quite salient, given that the high court was unwilling to interpret the Louisiana Constitution in a matter that would challenge the legislature.

After early challenges to the sodomy law were rebuffed by the state high court in the 1970s,[57] little happened on the litigation front until the 1990s. In the early part of the decade local attorney John Rawls brought two challenges to court.[58] In one, a trial court struck down the law under the Louisiana Constitution's privacy provision, generally defending the "privacy of the bedroom." On appeal the supreme court used a standing argument to avoid direct consideration of the sodomy law as it related to consensual sex acts. The trial court had argued that the entire law was implicated. Two justices were uncomfortable with the law, however. Justice Revius Ortique agreed with the majority on the standing issue, but urged the legislature to update the law, stating that "[m]orality statutes should reflect the moral standards of the era and not those of the turn of the *previous* century."[59] Chief Justice Calogero dissented, arguing that standing should have been granted, since "[f]ew areas of personal autonomy are more private than sexual intimacy between consenting adults."[60] Calogero was accustomed to being in this position, having dissented in the cases upholding the sodomy law in the 1970s. His opposition to the law was longstanding.

The case was remanded to the trial court for reconsideration given the court's holding, but it was clear that the trial judge did not like the law and was out to strike it down under any rationale. Consequently, he reacted favorably to the plaintiffs' claim that the law was unconstitutional on nine grounds other than privacy, finding validity in three of these claims: equal protection, cruel and unusual punishment, and the sodomy law as a bill of attainder. The supreme court again overruled (*Baxley* II), asserting that these grounds were a bit of a stretch constitutionally (for instance, the law applies equally to persons regardless of sexual orientation) and asserting the right of the legislature to preserve a sodomy law, especially given its historical precedent. Any changes in the trajectory of history were up to the legislature to make, according to the high court. Calogero again dissented, stating his privacy objection to the law and specifically finding the punishment for violating the law excessive.[61]

This tug-of-war between lower courts and the high court continued. In the same year as *Baxley* I, a judge granted an injunction against enforcement of the sodomy law on privacy grounds, but the state supreme court refused to hear the case.[62] The injunction was eventually dropped after law enforcement officials in the parish where the case originated agreed not to enforce the law.[63] Despite the vocal objections of some of its members, the Louisiana Supreme Court was not willing to back down from its tradition of defending the state's sodomy law.

This, however, did not deter more challenges. In the late 1990s, two prominent challenges began making their way through the Louisiana courts. One case was the continuation of litigation begun in 1994 by Rawls in *LEGAL v. State*; the other was the result of a criminal conviction for heterosexual date rape. In this case, Michael Smith was charged with rape and aggravated crime against nature. He was acquitted of the rape charge but found guilty on the crime against nature count (in this case, oral sex). The encounter involved heterosexual sex. The Louisiana Fourth Circuit Court of Appeal overturned Smith's conviction as a violation of privacy under the Louisiana Constitution.[64] The unanimous three-judge panel, citing the Georgia decision, stated: "There can be no doubt that the right of consenting adults to engage in private, non-commercial sexual activity, free from governmental interference, is protected by the privacy clause of the Louisiana Constitution."[65]

Not surprisingly, the Louisiana Supreme Court reversed. Resistance to judicial activism grounded the decision. As the majority opinion summarized, "The court is not inclined, and does not intend, to discover new constitutional rights in the Louisiana Constitution."[66] Consulting the historical record, the court found no evidence of a constitutional right to privacy, especially as it related to sexual matters. The court pointed out that the crimes against nature law in Louisiana dates to 1805, and a constitutional right to privacy certainly cannot include long-proscribed criminal activity. In typical fashion of failing to separate a wide range of sexual activity from other private activities typically under the purview of the criminal law, the court declared that if such a right to privacy existed, "the state could no longer enforce laws against consensual incest, fornication, prostitution, drugs, etc."[67] In fact, the decision is explicitly anti-Millian.

> By equating the general constitutional guarantees of "liberty" or "privacy" to all Louisiana citizens with the right of each individual citizen to engage in self-indulgent but self-contained acts of permissiveness, this court would be calling into constitutional question any criminal statute which proscribes an act that, at least to the satisfaction of a majority of this court, does not cause sufficient harm to anyone other than the actual participants.[68]

The court, then, sided with Patrick Devlin and against John Stuart Mill and H. L. A. Hart on the question of the public harm of private actions and clearly saw the value in regulating such actions. It is striking to see a court so forcefully adopt this position in the face of the opposite trends of the past half century.

Interestingly, the Louisiana Supreme Court cited *Powell v. Georgia*, but it did so negatively and disapprovingly. The majority cited a dissent rejecting a right to privacy and dismissed the majority in *Powell*, citing the Georgia court's flip-flop. In a moment of candid parochialism, the Louisiana court declared: "We are not bound by foreign courts."[69] The court indicated, in a footnote, that the Fourth Circuit Court relied on *Powell*, *Commonwealth v. Wasson*, and *Campbell v. Sundquist*, but it refused to take part in such a policy innovation.[70]

Rawls's challenge further exemplifies the back-and-forth nature of the litigation in Louisiana. After a trial in which thirty-one witnesses were called by the plaintiffs to demonstrate the legitimacy of homosexuality and the negative effects of the law on lesbians and gay men, a judge found the law to be unconstitutional. New Orleans district court judge Carolyn Gill-Jefferson found after the trial that "[t]he state has presented no evidence, much less the required compelling state interest, to justify its intrusion on plaintiff's constitutionally protected right of privacy." Indeed, the state only presented three witnesses at trial, one who claimed to be able to cure homosexuality.[71] Given the holding in *Smith*, however, the supreme court, on appeal, remanded the case to Gill-Jefferson for clarification. But Gill-Jefferson did not change her position and issued a permanent injunction against enforcement of the law.[72]

Since Gill-Jefferson's decision was based on privacy alone, and Louisiana's sodomy law is broad, Rawls appealed her decision to the Fourth Circuit Court of Appeal on more specific gay rights claims. Generally using discrimination and cruel and unusual punishment arguments, Rawls claimed that the law unfairly targets same-sex relations. Gill-Jefferson had ruled that the sodomy law only implicates conduct, not status. Taking a more substantive view, Rawls argued before the court of appeal that "[t]his law has no more to do with conduct than Jim Crow did with seats on the bus; they had to do with status, who was on top and who was on the bottom."[73] Relying on reasoning like that of Hart's, Rawls argued that same-sex couples cannot engage in anything but sodomy and are thereby denied access to intimacy, even though the law applies to heterosexual sex as well.[74] But given the supreme court's reluctance to embrace minimal privacy arguments, this would have been an unlikely path. Indeed, the supreme court overruled Gill-Jefferson on the privacy issue but remanded the case to an appellate court to consider other constitutional challenges.[75] This court rejected equal protection arguments, holding that there is no evidence that the law is used to discriminate against sexual minorities.[76]

There also was little political support for Rawls's position in Louisiana. Even critics of the law generally did not frame the opposition in terms of substantive gay rights but privacy. The leading newspaper, in criticizing the supreme court in *Smith*, called the law "big government at its worst," and called for the legislature to repeal the law "and keep the government's eyes out of Louisiana's bedrooms."[77] Even Rawls knew where the political argument was anchored, stating after *Smith*: "This is an equal opportunity court. They think it is all right to have the government invade everybody's bedrooms, not just gay people's."[78] But he hoped to add to this with his legal arguments, indicating that there is a separation between political and legal language and rhetoric—at least in the eyes of legal elites.

The legislature did, in fact, respond to the discussion created by the litigation. In May 2001, a House committee voted 5 to 3 to eliminate the sodomy law. Echoing the *Times-Picayune*, the bill's sponsor stated: "This bill is a privacy bill. It says 'Big Brother, we don't want you in our bedroom.'"[79] The full House voted 47 to 45 to follow the recommendation of the committee, but this was six votes short of a required fifty-three for a majority of the chamber (twelve members did not vote). The privacy issue was clouded by concerns over the need to combat public sex and prostitution, as well as religious and moral concerns. As one Republican supporter of the repeal stated: "A lot of you have told me in private, 'Man, I can't vote for this bill—those religious people back home will kill me.'"[80] Perhaps demonstrating that privacy arguments do not always spell success, especially when courts do not take the lead, opponents framed the issue around the acceptance of homosexuality. According to one legislator, "The heart of this legislation has nothing to do with what married couples choose to do. This has everything to do with legitimizing homosexuality."[81] Interestingly, opponents and attorney Rawls were in agreement on this point. The Senate voted by a margin of 23 to 12 to decriminalize sodomy, thereby forcing the House to reconsider this issue.[82] But House members were not willing to do so, rejecting the Senate's position by a vote of 104 to 0. One round of controversy was enough.[83]

Indeed, advocating for lesbian and gay rights in Louisiana can be difficult. Despite the presence of a large gay community in New Orleans and some progressive laws in the city, the rest of the state reflects a conservative morality. In 1999, Governor Mike Foster reflected this sentiment by stating that pending antidiscrimination bills based on sexual orientation "don't sound like Louisiana-type bills."[84] Any ground gained by lesbian and gay rights advocates has been gained with some courts in Louisiana articulating a right to privacy that broadly encompasses almost all consensual sexual activity. Advocacy groups are attempting to build coalitions with other progressive forces in the state, like labor and abortion rights groups,[85] but before the *Lawrence* decision, attempts at liberalization in Louisiana were destined to flounder on the shoals of morality politics.

## TEXAS: ROUND TWO

Despite assurances from the Texas Supreme Court in *Morales* that the sodomy law would never be enforced, two men, John Geddes Lawrence and Tryon Gardner, were arrested in September 1998 after police entered Lawrence's home and found the two engaged in consensual sodomy. The police were responding to a report of an armed intruder—a false report given to the police by Gardner's roommate.[86] The case was taken up by Lambda as part of a coordinated effort to eliminate discriminatory sodomy laws. The group was simultaneously working on the sodomy law challenges in Louisiana and Arkansas, both of which, like Texas, had "gay only" sodomy laws. The previous litigation in Texas was not coordinated from a national litigation organization, but was fueled by the effort of local lawyers. Energized by the decision of the Georgia Supreme Court, Lambda decided to get aggressive with sodomy laws still on the books. Referring to the Georgia case, Susanne Goldberg of Lambda stated: "That should help lay the groundwork to overturn the Texas law."[87]

At the original trial, Lawrence and Garner pled no contest and were fined. They appealed the decision to the Fourteenth Court of Appeals in Houston. That court reversed the trial court's decision and held that the Texas sodomy law was unconstitutional.[88] Lawrence and Gardner had challenged the law on four grounds: federal equal protection, state equal protection, state privacy provisions, and federal privacy provisions.[89] The majority were reluctant to rely on privacy arguments, since, as they noted, the Texas Supreme Court ruled in 1996 that the right to privacy was not very broad.[90] Therefore, the court focused on the Texas Equal Rights Amendment and equal protection concerns. The Texas Constitution states that "equality under the law shall not be denied or abridged because of sex, race, color, creed, or national origin."[91] In a similar manner to that of the Hawaii Supreme Court in *Baehr v. Lewin*, the 1993 same-sex marriage case (which the Texas court did not cite), the majority claimed that the Texas sodomy statute was unconstitutional because it outlawed activity based on gender: If a man and a woman can legally practice sodomy, the majority argued, and it is illegal for two men or two women to do so, the prohibition is based on the gender of one of the latter pairings. The state argued, like the state of Virginia in *Loving v. Virginia*, that gender discrimination was not implicated, since the statute applied equally to men and women. But the court rejected this claim.

We . . . reject the equal application argument. . . . Merely punishing men who engage in sodomy with other men and women who engage in sodomy with other women equally does not salvage the discriminatory classification contained in this statute. The simple fact is, the same behavior is criminal for some but not for others, based solely on the sex of the individuals who engage in the behavior. In other words, the sex of the individual is the sole determinant of the criminality of the conduct.[92]

One of the three judges dissented, arguing that the Texas Equal Rights Amendment was not intended to protect same-sex sex acts. In what he referred to as the majority's "farcical interpretation," Justice Harvey Hudson argued that this position was used by opponents of the amendment who "theorized it would mandate the construction of unisex restrooms . . . decriminalize homosexual conduct, and legalize same-sex marriages."[93] The majority replied that its duty was to apply the plain language of the amendment and not be concerned with moral judgments about the nature of homosexuality. They were merely compelled by the language of the constitution and the circumstances of the case at hand. "Our Constitution does *not* protect morality; it does, however, guarantee equality to all persons under law."[94]

In his dissent, Hudson also took an explicitly Devlinian position on morals legislation, citing cases from the early twentieth century on the proper scope of the police power. He cited Montesquieu's and Blackstone's condemnations of sodomy, and, clearly reflecting his normative position, stated rather strikingly that "[if] good and evil are to be anything other than relative, highly mutable concepts, they must rest upon divinely instituted principles." Curiously, Hudson noted the trend of decriminalization of consensual sexual conduct nationwide, but didn't appear to apply this trend to homosexuality. Indeed, he declared, "Whether this trend will ultimately encompass homosexual conduct remains to be seen."[95] Remarkably, the political legal activity on the sodomy decriminalization issue of the past fifty years was completely lost on Justice Hudson. It seems odd that he neglected to discover that, at the time, Texas was only one of five states that criminalized same-sex sodomy.

The decision sparked an outcry from some Texas politicians. The executive director of the Texas Christian Coalition stated: "It shows a further coarsening of our culture, and a lack of respect for the traditional family, as it has been defined for thousands of years."[96] Additionally, in an unusual affront to the independence of judges, some Houston Republican Party leaders wrote a letter asking one of the judges who voted to strike down the sodomy law to change his ruling or resign. This letter targeted Justice John S. Anderson, a Republican, but some party leaders refused to sign on. Harris County party chairman Gary Polland initiated the campaign against Anderson, but other county leaders were more willing to defer to the judges. As Brazoria County chairman Mike Golden stated, "these judges are intelligent guys, they are highly educated, they are experienced in the law, or else they wouldn't be judges."[97] The party did, however, include a rebuke to Justices Anderson and Paul Murphy, the other judge who voted to overturn the law, in their platform at the state convention in June.[98] It is unlikely that the efforts would have resulted in tangible results, since Anderson was running unopposed in the upcoming election.[99] In response to the party's actions, a state district judge called for a criminal investigation, but the case was never pursued.[100] Legislative hearings were held on the matter, but ultimately First Amendment concerns outweighed any proof of coercion.[101]

This episode is an interesting case study on the role that judges play in the political process. An activist decision was met with some resistance, but attempts to alter the legal process and interfere with legal decision making was seen as illegitimate by many political leaders who disagreed with the court's decision. In this instance, deference to legal authority and reasoning played a real role in the reaction to the decision. In the eyes of many, the law is a separate sphere from politics. As the prosecutor of Lawrence and Garner stated, "I think we are going to win this case on the merits and I want it to be . . . won on the merits and not because of any political pressure. I think anybody who attempts to affect the outcome by other means might be doing a disservice."[102]

However, the political activity affected the case dynamics. The State of Texas, instead of appealing to the Court of Criminal Appeals, reserved its right to appeal to the full complement of the Fourteenth Court of Appeals. On full panel review, the court reversed its earlier decision and upheld the sodomy law. Justice Hudson, in the minority before, authored the court's opinion, and Anderson and Murphy were now on the other side of the majority and dissented—a complete reversal of outcomes, since the rest of the court sided with Hudson. The political controversy was directly discussed in the case. An amicus brief included the letter from the Houston Republican Party and argued that political pressure would likely influence the outcome. Justice Yates took strong issue with this assertion in a concurrence: "There is simply no place for suggesting that members of this Court are pandering to certain political groups or deciding a case as a means to achieve a politically desired end. . . . We have done so [upheld the sodomy law]—not because of political pressures, as amicus curiae has suggested, but despite them."[103] Perhaps the justice protested too much. The court is completely Republican, and media accounts emphasized that the full court heard the case because of the political pressure.[104] Conversely, legal norms appear to have motivated the dissenters Anderson and Murphy less than politics, since they, too, are Republicans.

At any rate, the court found no validity in any of Lawrence's or Gardner's claims, rejecting equal protection and privacy arguments and stressing deference to the legislature, taking an explicitly Devlinian stand on the role of morality in legislation. The decision, like the original dissent, emphasized the long-standing disapproval of sodomy (citing *Bowers* in this context) and argued, consequently, that the legislature was justified in singling out same-sex sodomy. Whereas we have seen judges who strike down sodomy laws cite information from pro–gay rights sources, this court relied on antigay scholarly literature.[105] An editorial in the *Houston Chronicle* called Hudson's opinion weak and largely based on his personal bias.[106]

The case was appealed to the Texas Court of Criminal Appeals, which refused to hear the previous challenge to the sodomy law due to a lack of standing. Many commentators familiar with the court indicated that a recent election would make the court receptive to overturning the sodomy law. Two conservatives, Michael McCormick and Steve Mansfield, left the court and the two judges elected to replace them, Charles Holcomb and Barbara Parker Hervey, were both considered to be moderates, although both are Republicans. According to a Houston lawyer, "The complexion of the court could be entirely different by the time this case gets up there. For the first time, in a long time, there could be people listening. There's no telling what they are going to do and how they are going to do it."[107] The optimists were mistaken; the court, without comment, refused to hear the appeal, letting the previous decision stand.[108]

## ARKANSAS

A Lambda-initiated suit to overturn Arkansas's same-sex-only sodomy law achieved success. The suit was filed in the Chancery Court of Pulaski County in Little Rock, where the plaintiffs argued that the law contradicts state and federal privacy and equal protection concerns.[109] Sodomy was a misdemeanor, punishable by up to a year in prison and a $1,000 fine.[110] The law was adopted by the Arkansas legislature in 1977 after a sodomy law, covering both heterosexual and same-sex acts, was repealed in 1975.[111] The repeal was part of an American Law Institute (ALI)-inspired criminal law repeal, and the sodomy law repeal slipped under the radar until one legislator, at the height of the Anita Bryant controversy in 1977, decided that the law needed to be reinstated, since it was "aimed at weirdos and queers who live in a fairyland world and are trying to wreak [sic] family life."[112] Attempts at legislative repeal have been markedly unsuccessful. A repeal bill in 1991 died in the Senate judiciary committee after failing to get even one vote, and the same thing happened in 1993 after only one vote was gained.[113]

The chancery court ruled in favor of the plaintiffs on their standing to bring the case, but the Arkansas Supreme Court reversed that decision, claiming that the chancery court lacked jurisdiction to hear a criminal case. In Arkansas law, this is the jurisdiction of the circuit courts. The supreme court did not deny the validity of the plaintiff's claim, however. The court unanimously held that they did have standing to challenge the statute, but the claim must be made in a circuit court.[114]

A circuit court judge ruled that the case could go forward, and oral arguments were heard on the merits of the case on January 28, 2001. Predictably, the attorney for the state argued that the state has the right "to express the moral indignation of its citizens," while the Lambda lawyer stated, "The police simply do not belong in consenting adults' bedrooms." But Lambda also relied heavily on equal protection arguments—arguments reinforced by the diversity of the plaintiffs: "young, old, white, black, male and female, a minister, a teacher, a nurse."[115]

The judge appeared skeptical of the state's claims, responding to the state's lawyer, "You say, 'Well, we think it's immoral, so we're not going to let you do it.' The problem is that with most other laws based on morality, you can find some discernable harm. I really have trouble finding some reasonable harm here."[116] Indeed, his decision was a total victory for the plaintiffs and Lambda. Judge David Bogard cited the plaintiff's experts' affidavits on the legitimacy of homosexuality and that heterosexuals engage in the same acts that are proscribed by the law. He also relied on *Wasson*, *Campbell*, and *Bonadio* in striking down the law on privacy grounds. He found the law suspect on equal protection grounds under the Arkansas Equal Rights Amendment, since "the Sodomy Statute criminalizes the conduct solely on the basis of the sex of the participants, thereby violating the ... prohibition against denying equality under the laws on the basis of sex." As a result, he applied strict scrutiny and found that the state could not prove a compelling interest.[117]

The Arkansas Supreme Court affirmed the lower court and handed down a rather sweeping decision. The court found that the law violated privacy and equal protection provisions and relied heavily on the precedents in other states, citing and generously quoting from the Georgia, Montana, Kentucky, and Tennessee decisions. The court also noted the position of the ALI. The court's privacy arguments followed that of other courts, but its equal protection analysis was somewhat more forceful. Particularly with a same-sex-only sodomy statute, this was a more prominent issue. On the substantive analysis, the court was unanimous; differing rationales came from a justice who wished to keep sanctions for public sex acts and another who felt that no justicable issue was involved.[118]

## VIRGINIA

As was discussed in the previous chapter, the U.S. Supreme Court upheld the Virginia sodomy law, and efforts to eliminate the law since then have not been successful. The law is over two hundred years old and classifies as a felony oral or anal sex between any two people, regardless of gender. The law is mostly ignored, but some police departments, like those in Richmond, Charlotte, and Roanoke, began in recent years to use the law to clamp down on gay sexual activity in public parks and restrooms. Some legislators have tried to change the "crime against nature" statute to only include sex with minors, relatives, or animals, but none of these attempts were successful. The legislature was generally unwilling to bring up the issue of sex, particularly to be seen as being in favor of perceived sexual deviants. According to one legislator, "People wanted to stay out of the way of the whole thing."[119]

Given this political situation, opponents of the law took a less aggressive approach. In 2000, the House of Delegates approved a bill that would reduce the law from a felony to a misdemeanor. According to the bill's sponsor, it is unjust for a felony to be the charge for "[a] private act of love that occurs every day in homes across the commonwealth."[120] The bill passed the House by a vote of 50 to 49, but it was killed in a Senate committee.[121] Later, an attempt to reduce the classification of the crime was rejected by the House courts of justice committee by a vote of 13 to 9. The bill's sponsor refused to include a provision maintaining a fine for private, consensual sodomy, in order to keep the moral sanction in place. The bill would have likely gotten through the committee with this, but was instead voted down. Opponents were again afraid of appearing to be pro-sodomy. According to a Republican delegate, "Changes to the law such as this begin to nibble away at the edges of laws that have been in place for centuries.... Whether this is changed or not in the law, I will never be an advocate of anal intercourse."[122] Thus, there existed no political will in Virginia to change the felony sodomy law. Millian arguments do not make much headway in this state. Whereas public opinion in the United States as a whole has liberalized on same-sex relations, particular states have not responded to the changes.

As a result of the police crackdowns on gay sex in public restrooms and parks in several Virginia cities, numerous men were charged with sodomy in Roanoke. They challenged their convictions on several grounds: The sodomy law violates their right to privacy under the Virginia Constitution; it violates state and federal constitutional protections from cruel and unusual punishment; and it violates state and federal prohibitions against the establishment of religion, since most of the objections to sodomy are biblically inspired.[123] The Virginia Court of Appeals rejected all of these arguments. The three judges claimed that the actions of the defendants were not private, since they took place in public places.[124] They also quickly dismissed the cruel and unusual punishment and establishment claims.[125] Overall, the court was simply not inclined to challenge the validity of the statute in any way. All points of law were construed narrowly, and complete deference was given to the judgment of the legislature.

A request for a review by the entire Court of Appeals was rejected, and the attorney for some of the defendants filed for a hearing by the Virginia Supreme Court. This filing also included a case of heterosexual sodomy in a hotel room, in an attempt to broaden the issue from just that of public gay male sodomy. According to attorney Sam Garrison, "There seems to be a widespread misperception that sodomy is something that is committed by gay people. The overwhelming majority of violations of this statute ... are committed by straight people. In effect, this law makes every adult Virginian an unindicted felon."[126] The supreme court took its cues from the court of appeals and refused to hear the case.[127] Liberal arguments against sodomy laws need a foothold somewhere to have legal and political salience, but the State of Virginia lacked such a foothold. The *Lawrence* decision, of course, made this a moot point, but that decision demonstrates the importance of litigation in this area. The political process was not going to respond to calls for reform.

## OTHER LEGAL CHALLENGES TO SODOMY LAWS

The American Civil Liberties Union successfully challenged sodomy laws in Maryland and Minnesota. The Maryland law was found not to apply to the private sex acts of heterosexuals in 1990,[128] and the ACLU sought to eliminate its application to same-sex relations in a lawsuit filed in 1997.[129] A lower court was receptive to this attempt and interpreted the statute to not include private, same-sex sex acts.[130] After this decision, the state agreed not to use the law, essentially making it a dead letter without an appeal.[131] Similarly, in Minnesota a lower court invalidated the state's sodomy law on privacy grounds, and then-Governor Jessie Ventura decided not to appeal the case.[132] A similar course of events took place in Michigan in the early 1990s, where a lower court invalidated the state's sodomy law and state officials agreed not to appeal or enforce the law,[133] but this decision was later overturned, leaving the status of the law in question until *Lawrence*.[134] Prompted by a GLAD (a New England litigation group) lawsuit, the Supreme Judicial Court of Massachusetts sharply limited that application of the state's sodomy statutes in 2002, though, for technical reasons, did not strike them down.[135] State courts in Oklahoma and Missouri, however, rejected challenges to sodomy laws.[136]

## NONJUDICIAL SODOMY LAW REPEAL: THE CASES OF ARIZONA, RHODE ISLAND, AND NEVADA

Three states have repealed sodomy laws through the legislative process since the early 1990s, when judicial repeal commenced. These cases provide more insight into the role played by courts in this process and specifically demonstrate that clear judicial repeal generally has resulted in much less political controversy. Purely legislative repeals have expanded the scope of the conflict and have resulted in more political opposition, since liberal legal norms do not go unchallenged. Not even the most negative conceptions of liberalism are completely privileged in the Unites States because of the power of moralistic arguments.

Nevada was the first state to repeal its sodomy law after 1990. The repeal effort met diminished political resistance, passing the state senate by a 2 to 1 vote margin in 1993. This was likely a reflection of changing demographics in the state, especially with the population growth in southern Nevada. A state with a relatively moralistic political tradition is beginning to see a more progressive political environment, thereby diminishing the necessity for litigation.[137]

Legislative repeal of Rhode Island's sodomy law followed a court decision that upheld the law. In *State v. Lopes*, the Rhode Island Supreme Court relied on *Bowers* and one of its own precedents, which asserted that "a decision of unmarried adults to engage in private consensual sexual activities is not of such a fundamental nature and is not so implicit in the concept of ordered liberty as to warrant its inclusion in the guarantee of personal privacy."[138] Thus, the court held that privacy most fervently protects procreation. The Rhode Island law dated from 1896 and came to include fellatio, cunnilingus, or anal sex, thereby implicating a broad range of sexual activity.[139] Ultimately, its broad nature led to its downfall: Whereas the supreme court did not view the law as sufficiently violative of privacy and downplayed a right to sexual intimacy outside of marriage and procreation, the legislature ultimately felt otherwise. The first attempt to repeal the sodomy law was made by local activists in 1984, when a repeal passed the House but died in the Senate.[140] Legislators had attempted repeals throughout the 1990s, but only after many attempts was the effort successful.[141] In particular, several legislators from Providence's liberal East Side kept the initiative for legislative repeal alive.[142] The breakthrough came in 1998 when Democratic legislator Edith Ajello finally received a sufficient number of commitments from House Judiciary Committee members for repeal.[143] After testimony and some wrangling in the committee, the repeal bill was passed on to the full House, where it was approved by the less than overwhelming margin of 49 to 40 to 11.[144] The bill eventually passed the Senate by a margin of 26 to 17.[145]

For advocates of repeal, the issue was strictly one of privacy broadly defined; it was not presented as a gay rights issue. Certainly, the broad nature of the law facilitated this approach, and advocates knew that this was their best political argument. As one stated: "What is personal is personal, and what is private is private. It has always been the same issue: government doesn't belong in anyone's bedroom."[146] Or, as the *Providence Journal-Bulletin* editorialized, "end this unwarranted intrusion into a sphere that should remain private."[147] No arguments were made about intimacy being a part of personhood. Opponents, on the other hand, viewed the issue as one of diminished morality and public approval of homosexuality and cast the repeal law as the equivalent of changing Providence's name to Sodom and trying to "legitimize homosexual behavior."[148] They maintained significant political ground (especially in the most Catholic state in the nation) but were ultimately outdone by libertarian arguments.

The legislative repeal in Arizona reflected similar dynamics. Legislation, sponsored by the openly gay member of the Arizona legislature Steve May, to repeal sex laws was passed without court intervention. These laws included prohibition of "infamous crimes against nature," "open and notorious cohabitation," or any nonprocreative sex and dated from the early 1900s.[149] Several aspects of this repeal are notable. First, the repeal was presented largely as a tax issue, since nonfamily dependents cannot be claimed for federal tax purposes if local laws are being violated by the relationship, as in the cohabitation law.[150] This was obviously an attempt to "de-sex" this issue. Also notable was the existence of significant opposition to repeal, as was the case in Rhode Island. The vote for repeal in the House was 31 to 24, while the Senate vote was 17 to 11.[151] Whereas political reactions to judicial repeal have been rather muted, the opposition in the purely political arena was more forceful. Indeed, intense pressure was exerted on Governor Hull to veto the repeal. E-mail against the repeal dominated that in favor by nearly a three to one margin, and conservative leaders mounted a grassroots campaign to urge a veto.[152]

Ultimately, the governor signed the repeal, with her spokesperson stating, "Fundamentally, it came down to government doesn't belong in people's lives."[153] Despite efforts to focus on the tax issue, the debate ultimately revolved around a familiar debate of privacy versus family values, with supporters of the repeal siding with the sentiments of the governor. Opponents of the repeal, however, saw it as a dangerous precedent. According to one Senator, "We have a cultural war here. This is a direct attack on the family."[154] This is not significant for the novelty of the argument, but the fact that it was made so vociferously and received support from policymakers is noteworthy.

The cases of Arizona and Rhode Island indicate that the absence of court involvement in opposition to sodomy laws appears to embolden those opposed to sodomy law reform as the scope of the conflict is expanded. When repeal is not given judicial imprimatur, privacy concerns are not as dominant. Nonetheless, they still carried the day, particularly when framed in starkly negative terms and when the sexual practices of heterosexuals were implicated. However, in states more conservative than these two, when courts do not take the lead, morality politics dominates and locks the prohibitive status quo into place, as was seen in Virginia. Additionally, activists in North Carolina were frustrated in their attempts at reform since the early 1990s without the assistance of litigation.[155]

## *LAWRENCE V. TEXAS*: THE U.S. SUPREME COURT FOLLOWS THE LEAD OF STATE COURTS

Following the lead of state courts, in 2003 the U.S. Supreme Court overturned *Bowers*. The *Lawrence* decision was the result of the political and legal wrangling over the sodomy law in Texas. Recall that neither political actors nor the highest courts in Texas were willing to eliminate the state's sodomy law. The U.S. Supreme Court did not hesitate, as has been noted, and struck down the Texas law, as well as all remaining sodomy laws in the United States. In the few short years since *Bowers*, legal elites clearly shifted away from the moralism at the center of that decision.

The majority opinion by Justice Anthony Kennedy strikingly relied on a rich notion of personhood and affirmed the relationships of same-sex couples, when a reliance on negative notions of freedom might have sufficed to strike down the Texas antisodomy law. This latter approach is certainly more in line with the dominant version of liberalism in the United States. In fact, U.S. same-sex marriage activists and opponents alike argued that the decision appeared to open the door to judicial acceptance of same-sex marriage (it was cited heavily by the Massachusetts Supreme Judicial Court), and the decision received an enormous amount of media attention, sending shockwaves through the polity.

The shockwaves were indeed the direct result of the sweeping nature of and gay supportive language in the decision. The direct repudiation of *Bowers* ("*Bowers* was not correct when it was decided, and it is not correct today")[156] rested upon the evolving jurisprudence in state courts and the legal norms first articulated by the ALI and the Wolfenden Report. The Devlinian moralism of *Bowers* was completely swept aside by the majority. Furthermore, Kennedy placed the rights of sexual minorities squarely within the tradition of privacy jurisprudence the Court had carved out for heterosexuals in cases like *Griswold* and *Roe v. Wade*. But, like the right to privacy in those decisions, this was not simply a libertarian right to be left alone. Sodomy laws, according to Kennedy, violated the modern, richer right to personhood. "When sexuality finds overt expression in intimate conduct with another person, the conduct can be but one element in a personal bond that is more enduring,"[157] Kennedy mused. Finally, H. L. A. Hart's arguments were accepted by the highest U.S. Court.

He went on to apply the right to privacy to sexual minorities, equal to that of majority heterosexuals, relying on the Court's description of this right in *Planned Parenthood v. Casey*: "'These matters, involving the most intimate and personal choices a person may make in a lifetime, choices central to personal dignity and autonomy, are central to the liberty protected by the Fourteenth Amendment.'"[158]

Even though, on the surface, some might see this as an articulation of negative free-dom, Kennedy's language about the central role that sexuality plays in personhood clearly points in the direction of a liberalism that envisions a fuller person than stark libertarianism. That approach might have achieved the same result by stating, "The government has no business in the bedroom. Case closed." But Kennedy's language goes far beyond this and led to the accusation by Justice Antonin Scalia in dissent that the decision opened the door for Court recognition of same-sex marriage. After all, if gays have the same rights of intimacy and personhood as do heterosexuals, Scalia asked, and the heterosexual right is protected and extended by the institution of marriage, what, legally, can prevent gays and lesbians from claiming a right to the institution?[159] Gay rights activists asked the same question.

Kennedy's desire to affirm same-sex relationships is also reflected in his rejec-tion of Justice Sandra Day O'Connor's approach in the case. Rather than overturn *Bowers*, she preferred an equal protection path, similar to Kennedy's approach in *Romer v. Evans*. Under rational basis review, O'Connor found the Texas law based on nothing more than moral disapproval and therefore unconstitutional.[160] Kennedy thus rejected his own previous formulation, because it was too weak in this instance. He noted that O'Connor's approach would not invalidate sodomy laws, which also applied to heterosexuals and did not technically discriminate. Thus, he abandoned the weaker equal protection approach for the rich privacy route, perhaps mindful of O'Connor's noting that not all laws that treat sexual minorities differently were constitutionally suspect, that is, marriage laws. Under O'Connor's framework, marriage discrimination might easily meet rational ba-sis review, but Kennedy's elevation of gay relationships seems to make marriage discrimination less tenable—if true, a genuinely transformational decision.

## WHAT IS TO BE MADE OF SODOMY ADJUDICATION?

As has been noted, part of the critique of rights-based politics involves the critique of "cause lawyering"—pursuing political ends through litigation strategies by na-tionally funded and based lawyers descending on the court system, and pushing through their nonmajoritarian agendas in clever legal arguments relying on "rights talk."[161] The case of sodomy adjudication paints a very different, and much more subtle, picture, however. After the Supreme Court upheld the Georgia sodomy law in *Bowers*, legal efforts to overturn sodomy laws turned to state courts. This strategy did not always prove successful, with several state supreme courts rejecting argu-ments in favor of the unconstitutionality of these laws. But, overall, the trend was toward declaring these statues unconstitutional according to state constitutional provisions or judicial traditions, as the Georgia reversal demonstrates. National gay rights litigation groups eventually came to the forefront of this process, but early challenges were not coordinated. Lambda Legal Defense and Education co-ordinated litigation in the early 1980s but was stung by the defeat in *Bowers v. Hardwick* and only reengaged in a coordinated litigation strategy after the success in Kentucky.[162] This was also a clear example of the have-nots benefiting from litigation. Sexual minorities are clearly outsiders in U.S. politics (even more so in certain states), and this litigation provided them with enormous legal and political leverage.

Nevertheless, the arguments of these groups are usually well received by political actors and judges. Indeed, these decisions were relatively uncontroversial, especially in comparison to the response generated by judicial decisions concerning same-sex marriage. Some elected officials have expressed disapproval with the decisions, as when Georgia's lieutenant governor stated in response to *Powell* that "there needs to be a law of some sort on the books."[163] Overall, however, state elected officials have been perfectly willing to allow antisodomy laws to fall at the hands of state supreme courts. Even below the Mason-Dixon Line, this arena of judicial activity is greeted with diminished resistance, and, I argue, this demonstrates the extent to which the right to privacy has become a fundamental point of consensus in U.S. politics. But it has required action first by legal elites then by judges to remind the U.S. polity of this basic value. And where courts did not act, repeal efforts stalled or were not even initiated, overshadowed by morality politics.

There were, however, limits to the political potency of privacy arguments. When the emphasis shifted from abstract arguments about privacy, public sentiment and political actors favored maintaining sanctions against same-sex intimacy. Many court decisions, then, did not follow public opinion but lead it. Despite the love of privacy, the U.S. public was still often ambivalent about the legality of same-sex intimacy. During the 1990s, when the state courts were most aggressive, opinion on the legality of same-sex intimacy was split, with support for criminalization ranging between 43 percent and 47 percent in the Gallup poll, and opposition to criminalization ranging between 44 percent and 50 percent. This was similar to the responses in the late 1970s to the early 1980s. By the mid-1980s, after *Bowers*, significant majorities favored criminalization. When state courts pushed back against *Bowers*, opinion went back to being more divided. And by the 2000s, majority support for decriminalization began to emerge.[164] Support continued to climb for decriminalization to a high of 60 percent just before the *Lawrence* decision. In the immediate aftermath of that ruling, support dropped significantly, likely due to the same-sex marriage implications of the decision, but began to climb back to early 2000–2001 levels.[165] Also, opinion in some conservative states is not reflecting the libertarian trend of the nation on this issue. A 2004 poll in Alabama found that 47 percent of respondents favored the criminalization of same-sex intimacy, and only 40 percent supported decriminalization.[166] Thus, state courts were not simply "seconding" shifts in public opinion. A legal elite-driven privacy consensus had emerged, but privacy rights for persons of the same-sex were far from attaining majority support in the public when these courts were acting.

In these decisions, one also sees elements that are reflective of characteristics of the trend toward state court activism. Most significantly, courts have been keenly aware of what has been happening in other state courts. Almost all of the sodomy decisions quote similar decisions in other states, relying upon the precedents of their own states and the precedents of other states as well. In *Powell*, the Georgia court cited the Montana, Tennessee, and Kentucky decisions, even going back to one of the first decisions of its kind in New Jersey in 1977. The Tennessee court made particular reference to the decision of "our neighboring state" of Kentucky. Clearly, judicial policy coordination occurred among states' supreme courts in regard to sodomy law adjudication, and it occurred in a rights-based, libertarian framework.

In these decisions, one also sees the dynamic described by Feeley and Rubin at work. Decisions striking down sodomy laws were often quite philosophical and utilized highly principled language about rights and equality. Courts unwilling to strike down these laws ruled more formally and narrowly, emphasizing the importance of majoritarian decision making.

Additionally, courts appear to be increasingly relying on the arguments put forth in pro–gay rights amicus briefs. In *Campbell*, the Tennessee court used strict scrutiny to assess the validity of the Homosexual Practices Act. The State of Tennessee offered five "compelling state interests" in favor of upholding the law, among which were arguments concerning the encouragement of nonprocreative activities, encouraging a stigmatized and unhealthy lifestyle, encouraging short-lived and shallow relationships, preventing the spread of infectious disease, and preserving the moral values of citizens. All of these arguments failed strict scrutiny analysis, many as a result of information provided in amicus briefs from the ACLU, the American Psychological Association, and the Lambda Legal Defense and Education Fund. The court relied on the pro-gay briefs rather than those of the State of Tennessee in most of its findings of fact, from which its arguments flowed. Negative arguments about homosexuality have much more staying power in purely political settings.[167]

The outcomes of these cases were not influenced by the mode of selection of the judges, election, or appointment. Election was the method of selection for state high courts on both sides of the sodomy question. In fact, many of the antisodomy decisions came from elected judiciaries. This may be because these decisions were not all that out of step with public opinion. Conversely, the Virginia high court, which refused to take the sodomy challenge, is appointed by the legislature. Interestingly, the dividing line was not election versus merit selection but merit selection/nonpartisan election versus partisan election/legislative appointment.[168] In this case, exposure to partisan or more direct politics appears to have made judges less willing to overturn sodomy laws.

This finding slightly challenges other recent scholarship on the relationship between gay rights decisions and method of selection. Recall that Pinello has found that the length of term in office rather than the method of appointment affects judicial outcomes on gay rights claims.[169] Additionally, most state high court decisions endorsing relationship equality, as will be discussed in the next several chapters, were the products of merit selection. The link between method of selection and outcomes on gay rights needs to be further studied to discover any causal link. However, the parameters of U.S. political culture seem to affect judicial independence in challenging the legal and political status quo concerning gay rights. Where litigation invokes legal and political norms more integrated into the dominant culture, elected, rather than only appointed, judges may feel more comfortable confronting political majorities. When judges are asked to be more aggressive in confronting the political status quo, the highest level of independence may be necessary to affirm fuller gay rights claims.

Indeed, almost all of the sodomy decisions relied on the right to privacy, with judges generally shying away from the more potentially consequential and majoritarian-challenging equal protection arguments. Issues of privacy, then, have a tremendous amount of legal cache in many state courts. Most courts saw privacy as a fundamental right, one that held up to the rigorous challenge of strict scrutiny review. The political theories of John Stuart Mill are alive and well in state court jurisprudence. Indeed, the Kentucky high court even quoted Mill in arguing for the need for a large realm of personal autonomy. Although not quoting Mill directly, most courts used the same line of reasoning, and given the lack of a strong back-lash, U.S. political culture appears to support this, despite pockets of opposition and more hesitation about extending privacy rights to sexual minorities. One might argue, then, that courts did nothing notable, given the support of the political culture, in this case a belief in the negative right to privacy. However, since sodomy law reform was never fully driven by majoritarian politics, courts were required to continue to push the reform efforts. The link between policy and political culture is perhaps not always direct. Court review may be necessary to ensure that policy coincides more fully with the ideals of political culture, and, in some cases to push the boundaries of political culture itself.

Ellen Andersen argues that the post-*Bowers* successes were the result of a change in legal opportunity structure. "Turnover in the membership of the Supreme Court, the widespread disparagement of the reasoning in *Bowers* in the legal community, the new legal frame provided by *Romer* v. *Evans*, the 'normalization' of AIDS, and shifts in the cultural framing of homosexuality" explain the shift from *Bowers* to *Lawrence*.[170] While some or all of these factors were at play, I assert that the power of legal and political arguments were most influential. After all, libertarian legal norms almost prevailed in *Bowers*; it just took their continued use and development in the state courts to convince the Supreme Court to quickly reverse itself.

Finally, the trend of state courts invalidating sodomy laws indicates the extent to which courts, previously at the federal level but now in the states, are used in our political system to protect and promote individual rights. Many scholars, like John Dinan, argue that we should not view courts as the primary guardians of individual rights, and indeed doing so is a relatively recent historical phenomenon.[171] Interestingly, Dinan uses sodomy law reform to support his thesis that rights protection has not always, nor is it now, the exclusive domain of the judiciary. He correctly asserts that much of the effort behind sodomy law reform has been aimed at legislatures, but he minimizes the role played by state courts, especially after *Bowers*.[172] He also fails to account for the fact that sodomy law reform began as a result of the liberal arguments of legal elites, not elected officials. This demonstrates the continuing and unique role played by courts in our constitutional system. Sodomy law reform may previously have appeared to fit Dinan's model of rights protection as primarily the province of legislatures, but now courts have taken the initiative. However, the parameters of U.S. political culture may sharply limit this phenomenon from bleeding into other areas of the gay rights movement, most notably the call for same-sex marriage.

Ultimately, this chapter has demonstrated the appeal of rights-based litigation in the realm of gay rights, but it has also noted the limits of defining these rights too negatively. From the reluctance of the ALI to view the sexuality of all citizens as a part of personhood, as Hart did, to the tendency of both legal and political advocates to frame repeal efforts in terms of the starkly negative right to be left alone, we can see the unwillingness in U.S. political culture to embrace difference affirmatively in public and social policy. The tide may be turning with *Lawrence*, but this is far from certain, especially given the political resistance to the push for same-sex marriage.

# 7    Courts and Same-Sex Marriage in the United States: Hawaii and Alaska

THE DYNAMICS SURROUNDING same-sex marriage litigation are quite different from the litigation concerning sodomy laws. Unlike sodomy law cases, the political reaction to gay marriage cases has been significantly more pronounced. In the 1990s, courts began to find in favor of same-sex marriage claims. Yet, the political reaction to legal rulings favorable to same-sex marriage has provoked a tremendous national political response. Why has this been so different from sodomy law reform? As this book argues, the nature of marriage and its shift from a purely negative notion of liberty to a requirement of government sanction that implicates notions of positive liberty and equality strains the boundaries of U.S. political culture. Same-sex marriage threatens the libertarian truce between heterosexuals and homosexuals that sexual privacy reinforces. Instead of being confined to the bedroom, gay marriage demands a public recognition of gay and lesbian relationships—a recognition that the dominant form of U.S. liberalism has not been willing to accommodate. At the same time, however, same-sex marriage litigation has resulted in substantial change. In the United States, the terms of the debate have shifted on the issue, public support for relationship equality has increased, and significant policy change has occurred. The next several chapters explore these developments.

## EARLY SAME-SEX MARRIAGE LITIGATION

In the early 1970s, the first attempts were made to litigate the issue of same-sex marriage. These suits were likely the result of two developments of the late 1960s: the Stonewall Riots and the Supreme Court case of *Loving v. Virginia*. The Stonewall Riots of 1969 marked a clear shift in the gay and lesbian rights movement, from a small movement mostly centered in a few large cities to a more legitimate, national movement. As Arthur Leonard states: "After the 1969 Stonewall Riots, and the increased willingness of lesbians and gay men to be open about their sexual identity, it was natural that some same-sex couples would be emboldened to seek official recognition...from the state."[1] In 1967, *Loving* struck down Virginia's statute against interracial marriage and applied the equal protection clause of the Fourteenth Amendment to the institution of marriage.[2] Following these events, suits were brought in Minnesota, Kentucky, and Washington challenging the prohibitions on same-sex marriage, but they were of little consequence. Since the lesbian and gay rights movement was in its infancy and the legal arguments in favor of same-sex marriage had yet to be fully developed, these cases were largely overlooked and easily dismissed by the courts.

Interestingly, these suits were not the result of a concerted litigation strategy—in fact, there was nothing concerted about this process. Despite the increased visibility of the lesbian and gay rights movement, the movement's leaders did not see same-sex marriage as an important issue. The focus of activists was to stop police harassment and begin the passage of antidiscrimination laws. They knew that advocating same-sex marriage was not politically wise. In fact, marriage was seen by leading activists as an institution tainted by its connection with heterosexuality. One can hardly be liberated in marriage, the argument went. But the increasing numbers of openly lesbian and gay couples wishing to have their relationships sanctioned by the state did not necessarily take their cues from the leadership of the movement.

The Minnesota Supreme Court decided the first case, *Baker v. Nelson*, after two men applied for a marriage license and were refused. Jack Baker and Michael McConnell were together for three years by the time they applied for a marriage license. Both were local gay rights activists and wished to use the application for a marriage license to provoke a reaction in the media. It worked; they were profiled in *Look* magazine in 1971. After the refusal, they retained a local attorney, not concerned that most activists did not want to push the issue of same-sex marriage.[3] Theirs was a more traditional perspective than that of the liberation-minded activists of the time.

They sued for a writ of mandamus, compelling the clerk of the district court to grant them a license, but a trial court quashed this writ and the case was appealed.[4] Before the Supreme Court of Minnesota, the male couple first put forth a textual argument: They argued that without an explicit textual prohibition of same-sex marriages, such marriages were valid under Minnesota law. Second, they attacked the constitutionality of the refusal to grant a marriage license to same-sex couples, relying on the legal precedents establishing a right to privacy, especially as it related to marriage, in cases like *Griswold v. Connecticut*. They also relied on equal protection arguments similar to those in *Loving v. Virginia*.[5]

The court rejected both lines of reasoning and anchored its decision on an opposite textual interpretation. They argued that common usage of the term "marriage" connotes an arrangement between a man and a woman. In fact, in a footnote, the court included definitions of marriage from *Webster's* and *Black's* dictionaries that proved its point. The court was unwilling to take a novel, expansive look at the definition of marriage. As the opinion declared, "It is unrealistic to think that the original draftsmen of our marriage statutes . . . would have used the term in any different sense."[6] Dismissing the constitutional arguments, the court refused to apply the *Griswold* reasoning, since, the court declared, marriage is about procreation and child rearing.[7] Finally, the court dismissed the precedent of *Loving* as only dealing with "patent racial discrimination."[8] On all counts, the Minnesota court refused to break any new legal ground. These judges were unwilling to see any other purpose for marriage and were unwilling to tamper with this entrenched institution.

In *Jones v. Hallahan*,[9] the Kentucky Court of Appeals similarly rejected an attempt by two women to obtain a marriage license. The court rejected all constitutional arguments in a rather brief opinion and, like the Minnesota court, relied on a textual, common usage interpretation of the Kentucky marriage statute. "In substance, the relationship proposed by the appellants does not authorize the issuance of a marriage license because what they propose is not marriage," the court declared.[10] In this case, tautology passed for legal argument.

A case in the State of Washington foreshadowed later litigation. In this case, the appellants, in addition to textual and federal constitutional arguments, argued that the denial of a marriage license to same-sex couples violated the recently passed Equal Rights Amendment in the state, by asserting that the denial of same-sex marriage licenses is a form of sex discrimination.[11] The Washington court rejected this argument, but it was the same line of reasoning that would later be used successfully in the Hawaii litigation. In 1974, however, this argument was far too radical for any court to accept. Novel legal arguments are not guaranteed success.

Another interesting aspect of the Washington case is the strategy used by the appellants in an effort to persuade the court of the validity of their position. They did so not just through legal arguments, but also through the submission of a forty-page brief that argued for the acceptability of homosexuality, and same-sex marriage in particular, from the perspective of sociology, theology, science, and medicine—in essence, a Brandeis brief for same-sex marriage.[12] Also, realizing that they had little case law upon which to rely, the appellants cited a law review article that specifically addressed the issue of same-sex marriage to buttress their claims.[13] Although the court gave the appellants high marks for submitting such material, they found it to be irrelevant. Like previous courts, they rejected all constitutional arguments and held that marriage was self-defined as an institution between a man and a woman, and any effort to challenge the institution on constitutional grounds, no matter how original, was fruitless. Although recognizing that the procreation rationale was somewhat problematic, the Washington court nonetheless grounded its decision in such an argument.

> In the instant case, it is apparent that the state's refusal to grant a license allowing the appellants to marry one another is not based upon appellants' status as males, but rather it is based upon the state's recognition that our society as a whole views marriage as the appropriate and desirable forum for procreation and the rearing of children. This is true even though married couples are not required to become parents . . . . The fact remains that marriage exists as a protected legal institution primarily because of societal values associated with the propagation of the human race.[14]

In this decision, one gets the sense that the court was trying to jump out of an interpretation based solely on tradition and trying to point in the direction of the recognition of the validity of lesbian and gay relationships. However, in 1974, the jump was more like an extended leap, and lesbian and gay rights activists saw the reality of the situation. According to Leonard, "These simultaneous losses convinced public-interest lawyers working on lesbian and gay issues (who had not represented the petitioners in these cases) that further attempts to seek same-sex marriage were futile."[15] The movement shifted its focus to other issues, like the elimination of sodomy laws. The AIDS crisis also took much of the movement's energy in the 1980s. At any rate, a largely unorganized litigation strategy that had met fierce resistance from the courts in the early 1970s remained dormant until the early 1990s.

Indeed, by the mid-1980s, same-sex marriage was a dead issue for legal activists. In 1986, the American Civil Liberties Union (ACLU) created its Lesbian and Gay Rights Project with no mention of same-sex marriage. Lambda Legal Defense and Education Fund established the Legal Roundtable, a group of gay rights lawyers who began to strategize on lesbian and gay rights issues. Same-sex marriage became a topic of discussion and produced rather contentious debates. Members of the group, like Evan Wolfson and Tom Stoddard, felt that a same-sex marriage strategy should be pursued. Many lesbian feminist lawyers in the group, like Paula Ettelbrick and Nancy Polikoff, disagreed, arguing that marriage was a sexist institution. Others, like Nan Hunter and Matt Coles, did not agree with the feminist argument, but they argued that pursuing same-sex marriage was not politically pragmatic. Consequently, the decision was made not to adopt a litigation strategy to legalize same-sex marriage. Litigants seeking that goal who came to these lawyers were turned away. Contrary to the "cause lawyer" caricature, these lawyers were quite politically prudent and restrained, not crusading for lesbian and gay rights at any cost.[16]

## HAWAII: THE LITIGATION AND POLITICAL REACTION

The second wave of litigation in the 1990s began as lesbians and gay men were increasingly becoming "mainstream." The liberationist impulses of the movement in the 1970s had given way to a more inclusive, assimilationist approach. Like the earlier cases, the new round of same-sex marriage litigation was not a coordinated effort, largely due to the decision of the Legal Roundtable. Lambda became involved in a few suits only after the initial litigation and opposed suits in other states.[17] In the early 1990s, several suits were brought to obtain marriage licenses for same-sex couples, most notably in Washington, D.C., and Hawaii. In both cases, the litigation was brought by solo lawyers based on the claims of local litigants, not large national organizations.[18] As Barbara Cox described the situation, "Without waiting for the long struggle involved with the petitioning of state legislatures to expand the marriage statutes, a few courageous same-sex couples decided that they wanted to marry and wanted the option of having that marriage recognized."[19] Ironically, the D.C. case attracted more media attention, since Hawaii was more isolated geographically and politically.[20] The D.C. case ended unsuccessfully for the plaintiffs in the D.C. Court of Appeals in 1995,[21] but the Hawaii litigation found great success.

In December 1990, Nina Baehr and Genora Dancel and two other same-sex couples applied for marriage licenses in Hawaii. The road to this point began earlier in the year when a local gay rights activist, Bill Woods, decided to promote the same-sex marriage issue by identifying about twenty-five couples interested in obtaining marriage licenses. By November, Woods and several couples were ready to make their claim, but the ACLU was not. Woods requested support from the organization, but local representatives, reflecting the decision of national leaders not to pursue a same-sex marriage litigation strategy, were not as enthusiastic as Woods. Indeed, the couples were ready to make their claims in the summer of 1990 as part of gay pride celebrations but held off to wait for the ACLU to deliberate. However, the ACLU was not willing to take a lead role in this process. An ACLU staff attorney, Carl Varady, sent a letter to leaders in the gay community to gauge support, rather than support the efforts outright. And a member of the ACLU Hawaii Board, Tom Humphries, was publicly ambivalent, stating: "People are very reluctant to come forward with a case because cases have all been lost in the past and it's a long and tedious battle . . . . I think if any individual case were brought forward there would be no hesitation on the part of the ACLU" to support such litigation. In other words, "we are not going to stick our necks out, but you can do it." Instead, Humphries was more willing to emphasize legislative efforts to pass a domestic partnership law. Thus, the pragmatism of the national gay litigation organizations was reflected on the ground in Hawaii. A local activist like Woods saw the ACLU as "dragging its feet" and ceding too much to public opinion.[22]

The granting of the licenses was put on hold, while officials at the health department awaited an opinion on the matter from Attorney General Warren Price III. They had seen earlier newspaper accounts of the couples' potential action and consulted Price.[23] In a letter to the director of the Department of Health, John Lewin, Price clearly did not think that the laws of Hawaii supported same-sex marriage:

> In view of the complex social issues surrounding marriage and the interest of the state in the marriage relationship, we doubt that the Hawaii courts, given the paucity of precedent, would be any more inclined to be the means by which the right to marry is extended to same-sex couples than it was to find a common law right to marry.[24]

Price had precedent on his side. In 1981, a male couple applied for a marriage license, with one of the men dressed as a woman. Once it was discovered that he was indeed a man, the license was revoked.[25] But Price was not unsupportive of gay rights in general. He hoped that the legislature would address the same-sex marriage issue, since, as he stated, "There's a need for us as a society to understand better and offer compassion to the gay community."[26] But he was working for a governor who did not support same-sex marriage and did not feel politically able to reason as abstractly as a legal advocate. The majoritarian politics of the situation were clearly constrictive, not expansive, of gay rights. As a result, the applications were denied, and the couples sued the State of Hawaii.[27]

The lawsuit was not litigated directly by the ACLU but by a local attorney, Daniel Foley. In bringing the suit, Foley primarily relied on privacy arguments. A privacy provision was written into the Hawaii Constitution in 1978 and Foley saw this as the best vehicle for success. In particular, Foley relied upon the case of *State v. Kam* in which the court protected the sale of pornography using this provision, even though the court had also ruled that prostitution and police immunity from drug testing were not covered by the privacy clause.[28]

Despite Foley's efforts, the privacy argument never proved successful. During proceedings in the circuit court, Judge Robert Klein stated that the privacy argument was weak and the better argument was grounded in equal protection jurisprudence. Ultimately, however, this was not even dispositive for Klein, since he dismissed the case. In doing so, he first dismissed the privacy argument, asserting that the delegates to the 1978 Constitutional Convention did not intend to cover same-sex marriage as a fundamental right protected by the right to privacy. Nor did the limiting of marriage to heterosexuals violate due process, since "[t]he law does not infringe upon a person's individuality or lifestyle decisions." Thus, lesbians and gay men have the freedom to be left alone, but this does not require governmental affirmation. But Klein spent most of the decision eviscerating the claim that he had previously said held the most promise: equal protection. He refused to grant that gays were a suspect class or anything that resembled one. Gays were nothing like African Americans, according to Klein, and they certainly did not face historical discrimination in a state like Hawaii, "with its history of tolerance for all peoples and their cultures." Furthermore, Klein asserted, the recent passage of an employment antidiscrimination law on the basis of sexual orientation proved that gays were not politically powerless. And, citing federal court decisions, he denied that homosexuality was immutable. As a consequence, the Hawaii marriage law passed constitutional muster, "because the law is obviously designed to promote the general welfare interests of the community by sanctioning traditional man-woman family units and procreation."[29]

On appeal, however, Baehr and the other plaintiffs won a stunning victory in the Hawaii Supreme Court. The supreme court rejected the circuit court's view of equal protection jurisprudence, stating, "We conclude that the circuit court's order runs aground on the shoals of the Hawaii Constitution's equal protections clause."[30] The court began its analysis with a rejection of the idea, proposed by the appellants, of same-sex marriage as a fundamental right, on par with the heterosexual right to marriage articulated in cases like *Griswold*. It is not "so rooted in the traditions and collective conscience of our people that failure to recognize it would violate . . . fundamental principles of liberty."[31] But this did not prevent the court from confronting the legal precedents of the 1970s. In laying the groundwork for a constitutional affirmation of same-sex marriage, the court sharply criticized the earlier courts for stopping after plain language analyses reflecting the traditional man/woman view of marriage. In fact, the court characterized the reasoning in cases like *Singer v. Hara* as "tortured and conclusory sophistry."[32] Instead, the supreme court of Hawaii felt it was necessary to go beyond mere tautology and examine the constitutional implications of same-sex marriage denial.

Accordingly, the court refused to be limited by traditional equal protection analysis, as was the circuit court. Its goal was not to inquire as to whether gay men and lesbians belonged to a suspect class; rather, the question concerned discrimination on the basis of gender. Unlike the U.S. Supreme Court, the Hawaii Supreme Court had established that gender-based classification was always suspect and required

strict scrutiny review, since the Hawaiian Constitution contained a provision explicitly prohibiting gender discrimination. Consequently, the court asserted that the
law was unconstitutional unless the state could demonstrate a narrowly tailored,
compelling interest as to why the same-sex prohibition should stand.[33]

Although not directly stated, the court's reasoning was as follows: since a woman
cannot marry another woman under Hawaii's marriage policy but can marry a man,
the reason for the ban on same-sex marriages is discrimination on the basis of gender. Whereas previous decisions had been highly formal, simply looking at the text
to define marriage, the Hawaii Supreme Court, as stated before, was not content
with this approach. Its invocation of gender-based equal protection analysis had
been previously articulated in one of the court's earlier decisions, *Holdman v. Olim*.
That case involved a legal action by a female prison visitor who was barred from
the prison visiting area for not wearing a brassiere. The prison instituted the policy to discourage provocative dress. Although the suit was dismissed, the Hawaii
Supreme Court undertook a rather substantive discussion of gender discrimination
in its opinion. The court asserted that "[d]ress standards are intimately related to
sexual attitudes," and the policy was a direct result of these attitudes.[34] Theorizing
a connection between dress standards and sexual attitudes does not reflect conservative, formal reasoning. It was clearly an attempt to bring into adjudication more
substantive elements, even if some might argue that these arguments are more
fitting for the field of women's studies than constitutional jurisprudence. The same
thing can be said for the court's implicit reasoning in *Baehr v. Lewin*: Even though
it was presented in formal terms (i.e., the suspect nature of the same-sex marriage
ban derived from the woman-woman/man-woman distinction), the reasoning was
quite substantive. Focusing on gender discrimination was a unique path, given
that prior equal protection discussions in this area centered upon the nature of
homosexuality as a suspect classification.

A vigorous dissent came from Judge Walter Heen. He refused to grant the
plaintiffs any new legal ground. Relying on the precedents of the 1970s, Heen
declared that there is no constitutional imperative to grant same-sex marriage,
certainly not regarding gender discrimination, since men and women are treated
equally: neither gender can marry a person of the same gender (this, of course,
harkens back to the Virginia Supreme Court in *Loving*, which held, formally, that
antimiscegenation laws applied to whites and blacks equally). Thus, Heen used
a rational basis test, which the marriage statute met: "the statute's classification
is clearly designed to promote the legislative purpose of fostering and protecting
the propagation of the human race through heterosexual marriages and bears a
reasonable relationship to that purpose."[35] Heen also noted that the legislature
could address this issue "without rooting out the very essence of legal marriage,"
thus hinting at a domestic partnership law. He was also concerned about the fiscal
effects of the decision on the state and the nation.[36] Ironically, he was more willing
to consider public policy concerns than other justices; they generally stuck to
constitutional concerns. This was officially a lone dissent, since substitute Justice
Yoshimi Hayashi's term expired before the opinion was handed down. Hayashi
would have signed on to the dissent.[37]

The seeds of the court's argument were present at oral argument. Two judges who would eventually side with the plaintiffs, Steven Levinson and Walter Burns, were skeptical of the state's claims. Burns in particular asked the deputy state attorney general why the prohibition was not sex discrimination.[38] When she replied that the plaintiffs wished to change the Hawaii Constitution, Burns replied, "They want you not to discriminate against them." Burns and Levinson were also concerned that the circuit court made conclusions of fact without an evidentiary hearing.[39]

The path taken by the prevailing justices was not entirely novel. These arguments had been offered in the legal academy. In an article in the *Yale Law Journal* in 1988, Andrew Koppelman offered the argument that sodomy laws are unconstitutional not on privacy grounds, but because they are a form of gender discrimination. Koppelman argued that sodomy laws reinforced gender status and hierarchy, and he likened sodomy laws to antimiscegenation laws. White supremacy depended on racial segregation and differentiation, and sexism likewise relies on the differentiation of the sexes, with clear roles for each gender. Similarly, according to Koppelman, "Just as miscegenation was threatening because it called into question the distinctive and superior status of being white, homosexuality is threatening because it calls into question the distinctive superior status of being male."[40] Koppelman clearly saw the potential of his claims. As he indicated, "The thesis that laws directed against lesbians and gays discriminate unconstitutionally on the basis of gender has radical implications.... If... taken seriously, it follows that the equal protection clause forbids the denial of marriage licenses to gay couples."[41] Or, as he stated in an article soon after *Baehr*, "The courts... ought to ignore political pressure and do their job" and grant same-sex marriage.[42] Interestingly, however, this argument was never made in plaintiff's or amicus briefs. As was noted, Foley relied primarily on privacy arguments and generic equal protection and due process arguments—not the novel sex discrimination argument. The judges appear to have created that on their own.

The Hawaiian Supreme Court would indeed "do their job," but not quite yet, instead remanding the case to a trial court for the state to show a compelling interest.[43] Despite the lack of a final decision, however, the case put the issue of same-sex marriage on the political map. Since marriages in one state are, for the most part, honored in other states through the Constitution's "full faith and credit" clause, for the first time, it appeared that states other than Hawaii might be forced to recognize same-sex marriages performed in Hawaii.[44]

In some ways, the decision was not an isolated event in the jurisprudence of the Hawaii Supreme Court. Since the Hawaiian Constitution explicitly defines sex as a category protected from discrimination, unlike the U.S. Constitution, there was some legitimate ground for using equal protection analysis based on gender. *Baehr* was part of a larger trend on the part of the court to extend greater constitutional protections under the state's constitution than under the U.S. Constitution. For example, in October of 1993 the court barred some types of airport searches as violations of the protection against illegal search and seizure—searches that are permitted by the U.S. Supreme Court.[45]

Unique circumstances concerning the members of the court may have also affected the outcome. The court that heard the case was not the regular makeup. Judge Klein of the circuit court had been appointed to the supreme court and therefore recused himself. Chief Justice Herman Lum recused himself for an undisclosed reason, and Justice Wakatsuki had recently died. They were replaced by Burns, chief appeals court judge, Walter Heen, an appeals court judge, and a retired justice, Yoshimi Hayashi.[46] Given these rather chaotic circumstances, the outcome could have been quite different, especially since the holding of the court was initially only a plurality. With this somewhat unsettled nature of this state of affairs, the attorney general immediately appealed for reconsideration, arguing that there was no clear mandate from the court.[47] This motion was denied, and the court's plurality became a working majority when a new justice, Paula Nakayama, sided with Levinson and Ronald Moon.[48] These three represented a clear wing of an activist court, reflecting an attempt by Governor John David Waihee to appoint more activist judges.[49] Age was also a factor: At the time of the decision, Levinson was forty-six, Moon was fifty-two, and Burns was fifty-six. Heen and Hayashi were sixty-five and seventy-one, respectively. Nakayama, the new justice, was thirty-nine. Levinson called himself a "child of the '60s" and was seen by many as the court's most liberal justice.[50] Clearly, baby boomers carried the day, motivated by a substantive view of equality and an unwillingness to rely on the formal reasoning of the 1970s precedents.

## THE POLITICAL REACTION

After the decision, everyone was caught a bit off guard, since no one really expected the outcome. Advocates for lesbian and gay rights were certainly pleased, if not a little shocked, at the potential scope of the decision, given the dearth of past success. As William Rubenstein, who was then director of the ACLU's gay rights project, stated, "This is a major breakthrough. This is the first court decision to give serious consideration to gay marriage."[51] From the other side, a great deal of political pressure was exerted on the legislature to counteract the decision and preserve the institution of heterosexual marriage. Initially, legislators appeared to respond to both sides. In the legislative session after the court decision, legislators proposed a constitutional amendment to limit marriage to heterosexuals, while at the same time proposing a domestic partnership act.[52]

At the start of the 1994 session, after many hours of debate and public testimony, the House Judiciary Committee submitted a report to the full House that castigated the supreme court for its decision. The members of the committee claimed that the court's decision was based upon "a mistaken view of legislative intent" of the state's marriage laws. Therefore, the committee intended to state clearly that "the primary purpose of issuing marriage licenses is to regulate and encourage the civil marriage of those couples who appear, by virtue of their sex, to present the biological possibility of producing offspring from their union."[53] The Senate Judiciary Committee was more openly hostile to the court's decision, emphasizing its undemocratic nature. The committee's report declared: "The Hawaii supreme court's plurality opinion . . . has effectively supplanted the role of the Hawaii State Legislature on this issue by substituting its own policy judgment for that of the people of Hawaii."[54] Later in the process, however, the Senate would become more sympathetic to the principles and reasoning of the *Baehr* decision.

Much debate ensued on the floor of the legislature because of legislation proposed to define marriage as being only between a man and a woman and to assert that procreation was the justification for the state's marriage policy. Supporters of the measure echoed the sentiments of the committees' reports. Terrance Tom, the House Judiciary Committee chairman and a Democrat, stated that the bill "does not denigrate anyone's lifestyle," but, he continued, "I believe that if same-sex marriage licenses are to be issued, that policy decision properly belongs to us in the Legislature . . . . I cannot stand idly by and allow our Judiciary . . . to decide on issues of such importance."[55] Opponents of the measure based their opposition on several factors. Some were skeptical of the procreation justification. As one member asked, "What of seniors who would marry but are beyond childbearing age? What of the disabled? What of the sterile?"[56] Others simply appealed to antidiscrimination arguments and supported the court's actions as appropriate and noble. James Shon, a Democrat from Honolulu, stated his opposition this way: "A majority do not feel comfortable with people they fear or misunderstand. Is this the way to make public policy? Are we really willing to step back into our darker history? I choose to live in Hawaii . . . because it is generally a more tolerant place."[57] Some members, who supported a ban on same-sex marriage, were uncomfortable with the open rebuke to the supreme court. As Representative Thielen, a Republican, stated, "We cannot control nor should we try to control the judicial review of our legislative actions."[58] Notably absent from the debate was extreme antigay rhetoric. The legislators did not yet feel fully pressed against a wall; they simply were trying to clarify legislative policy in light of the court ruling. They were trying to reassert themselves in what Tom referred to as "this nuptial turf war" with the courts.[59] More heated rhetoric would come after the court pushed back a few years later.

To send a clear message to the supreme court, Tom urged a unanimous vote on the marriage definition bill, but, in the end, the House was somewhat divided. The final vote was 36 ayes to 12 nays, with a majority of the "no" votes coming from members from urban Honolulu, and only one "no" vote came from an island other than Oahu, the most urban of the islands. The vote did not fall along party lines, since the House in 1994 was made up of forty-seven Democrats and four Republicans.[60]

The Senate was more hesitant about the legislation. Initially, Senators voted against bringing the bill out of the Judiciary Committee, and some in the media accused them of trying to duck the issue.[61] Debate on the floor, after the bill made it out of committee, focused primarily on the role of the supreme court. Senator Randy Iwase referred to *Marbury v. Madison* and Thomas Jefferson in denouncing the court's judicial activism, while Senator Ann Kobayashi cited the same in defense of the court's decision. He did not like the idea of same-sex marriages, or other instances of judicial activism, but, he asserted, "We just don't write a law that shuts down the most important elements of our constitutional government to try to get the means to the end which we seek."[62] This deference to the court was echoed by Senator Richard Matsunga, who agreed with the court's reasoning and asserted, "Throughout out nation's history, courts have engaged in policy-making."[63] Whereas the mostly Democratic Senate stuck to a discussion of judicial activism, some of the Republican members feared the potential ramifications of the decision. As Senator Koki declared, "Now is not the time to embark in a bold new experiment that will take us further along that road of deterioration of family values."[64] Senator Reed was fearful of cultural ramifications as well, fearing that Hawaii would become "the homosexual marriage capital of the world," and "our schools would have to be changed to teach our children that homosexuality is a completely acceptable, alternative lifestyle."[65]

The Senate vote was a bit more one-sided than the House vote (it passed 21 to 4),[66] perhaps because the Senate insisted on the creation of a commission to study the issue of same-sex marriage in Hawaii, thereby giving some cover for a "yes" vote for those who were sympathetic with the *Baehr* decision. Also, the ultimate version of the legislation eliminated any reference to procreation as the primary justification for marriage laws. It only rebuked the supreme court, defined marriage as being only between one man and one woman, and called for the creation of the commission. The law stated that the state's marriage statute was intended "to foster and protect the propagation of the human race through male-female marriages."[67] This was an oblique reference to the procreation justification, not a direct endorsement of it. Even at this early stage, in the immediate shadow of the supreme court decision, some members of the Senate proposed a domestic partnership bill, indicating some support for *Baehr*, but this never got out of the Judiciary Committee, having been killed by the chair.[68]

This state of affairs was remarkable for its rather muted legislative reaction. No constitutional amendment directly challenging the courts was passed by the legislature, and, as noted above, antigay rhetoric was not extreme. Although some legislators were clearly upset, others took the *Baehr* decision seriously. As a result, Andrew Koppelman could write in 1995 that, "Hawaii hasn't panicked or risen up in hostility. In fact, the response there has turned out to be remarkably mild."[69] Additionally, the creation of the commission was a sign that the court's decision in *Baehr* did have an effect on policy toward same-sex marriage. There appeared to be a consensus in 1994, a year after *Baehr*, that same-sex marriage in some form would be the result of the litigation. The *New York Times* summed up the situation in the following manner:

> A result of this judicial and legislative jockeying, virtually everyone agrees, will be either legalization of gay marriage by the court or a broad domestic partnership act after the commission completes its work, and perhaps both. "That was something people thought was unattainable before May 5," said Daniel R. Foley, the lawyer for the three gay couples, citing the date of the supreme court's 3 to 2 decision. "And now the only question is how much, how soon."[70]

Perhaps Hawaii's progressive political tradition of dealing with multicultural-ism and inclusion helped to sustain this outlook a year after the court's decision.

Election year dynamics were also likely at play: Legislators did not want to take any extreme positions without further testing the political waters. The creation of a commission to study the issue was a particularly good way to take the heat off of themselves.[71] At any rate, it appeared that the court had effected a great deal of political change within a year of its decision. Before the litigation, there was no push for anything resembling same-sex marriage or domestic partnership in the legislature.

## THE POLITICAL REACTION OUTSIDE OF HAWAII: DOMA AND THE MINI-DOMAS

Outside Hawaii, the reaction was much less ambiguous. The prospect of same-sex marriages being recognized nationwide through the full faith and credit clause caused a majority of states to pass laws explicitly prohibiting same-sex marriages. Generally, if a state can demonstrate a public policy exception to the recognition of other states' laws, they are not legally bound to honor that law.[72] Consequently, starting with Utah in 1995, many states began enacting laws designed to prevent the recognition of same-sex marriages.[73] Additionally, the federal government passed the Defense of Marriage Act (DOMA), which asserts that "[n]o State . . . shall be required to give effect to any public act . . . of any other State . . . respecting a relationship between persons of the same sex that is treated as a marriage under the laws of such other State."[74] This is the first instance in which the federal government passed legislation concerning marriage, which has traditionally been the province of the states. Obviously, the litigation in Hawaii struck a national political nerve. Indeed, the report from the House Judiciary Committee cited the Hawaii litigation as the reason for Congress's action, noting the "nature of the orchestrated legal assault being waged against traditional heterosexual marriage by gay rights groups and their lawyers." The report mischaracterized the role played by advocacy groups, alluding to a nationwide litigation strategy in place since the early 1970s. Despite the falsity of this claim, it demonstrates the extent to which federal lawmakers felt they were under judicial assault from state courts and liberal legal norms.[75]

The debate on the floors of the U.S. House and Senate were marked by vigorous moral arguments by supporters of DOMA and a relatively weak, procedural and tactical response by opponents who always appeared to be on the defensive and only used principled equality arguments obliquely. Defenders of DOMA primarily grounded their arguments in the preservation of the family and the threat posed by changing the institution of marriage, while opponents fell back on technical arguments or arguments claiming that the law was nothing more than an attempt to score political points in an election year by demonizing an unpopular minority. For instance, Charles Canady opened the House debate with the following: "What is at stake in this controversy? Nothing less than our collective moral understanding—as expressed in the law—of the essential nature of the family—the fundamental building block of society."[76] Patrick Kennedy responded: "This is not about defending marriage. It is about finding an enemy."[77]

The position and arguments of Barney Frank, an openly gay Democratic member of the House who was the point person for the opposition, tells a lot about the political position of DOMA's opponents. Frank argued first that the bill was not yet needed, since the situation in Hawaii had not been resolved, thereby making the bill nothing more than an exercise in divisiveness. He also ridiculed the argument about the potential destruction of marriage. "They allow same-sex marriage in Hawaii and 5,000 miles away, marital bonds will crumble. That seems pretty silly, but that is what the bill says," Frank argued.[78] Indeed, Frank offered an amendment not to legalize same-sex marriage at the federal level but to mandate federal recognition of same-sex marriages where states have approved them. He was essentially arguing process over substance by allowing for a Brandeisian form of state policy experimentation on same-sex marriage without taking a firm stand on the demands of equality.

Interestingly, but perhaps not surprisingly, it was African American members of the House who made explicit equality arguments. Representative John Lewis, a leader of the civil rights movement, argued that DOMA was foreign to U.S. political tradition:

> This bill is a slap in the face of the Declaration of Independence. It denies gay men and women the right to liberty and the pursuit of happiness. Marriage is a basic human right .... We are talking about human beings, people like you, people who want to get married ... and spend their lives with the one they love .... I will not oppress my fellow human being. I have fought too hard and too long against discrimination based on race and color not to stand up against discrimination based on sexual orientation.[79]

Representative Sheila Jackson-Lee directly invoked the Fourteenth Amendment as supporting same-sex marriage.[80] But this was not the main thrust of the opposition to DOMA. Equality largely lost out in favor of procedure, tactic, and ridicule.

Debate in the Senate followed the dynamics of the House. Supporters of DOMA emphasized moral decline resulting from same-sex marriage, while opponents, even the chamber's most liberal members, like Barbara Boxer and Ted Kennedy, emphasized the law's divisive consequences and its potential unconstitutionality. Indeed, many of these members pushed for the passage of the Employment Nondiscrimination Act, which would have outlawed discrimination in employment nationwide, as a way to still support antidiscrimination while supporting DOMA. Like African Americans in the House, Senator Carol Moseley-Braun argued that the U.S. political tradition of equality and inclusion disfavored the exclusion of same-sex couples from the benefits of marriage, often quoting Martin Luther King, Jr.[81] Also making substantive arguments in opposition was Senator Chuck Robb of Virginia. Robb's speech was perhaps the most remarkable of the entire debate, coming from a senator of a Southern state. His speech went beyond tactical arguments, advocating full equality for sexual minorities and arguing that to oppose same-sex marriage is to "stand on the wrong side of history." He rejected the validity of "political" arguments, noting that many of his colleagues were personally opposed to the law but felt compelled to support it out of fear of constituent reactions. Instead, Robb argued, "A basic respect for the human dignity—which gives us the strength to reject racial, gender and religious intolerance—dictates that in America we also eliminate discrimination against homosexuals. I believe that ending this discrimination is the last frontier in the ultimate fight for civil and human rights."[82] Ultimately, politics won; DOMA was passed in the Senate by a margin of 85 to 14.

Thus, in the U.S. Congress in 1996, there was little genuine consideration of the view that liberalism supports same-sex marriage. Majoritarian morality politics dictated the outcome, pushing aside arguments intended to link same-sex marriage with the United States' inclusive political past that viewed antidiscrimination not just formally but substantively, with human dignity and its requirements at its core. Indeed, even opponents of DOMA invoked the language of negative freedom. Senator Ron Wyden, who voted against the law, stated: "Not once has a gay or lesbian Oregonian come to me and asked that the Federal Government endorse their lifestyle. They simply ask to be left alone. In this regard, they are very similar to what I hear from ranchers and small business owners and fishermen and scores of other of our citizens."[83] In other words, gays and lesbians are libertarians, too. As will be demonstrated in Chapter 10, this negative language, majoritarian morality, and small space for richer arguments about the requirements of liberalism will be quite different from national legislative debates in Canada. Strikingly, U.S. liberalism could not even sustain a much less demanding piece of legislation, the Employment Non-Discrimination Act, which would have outlawed workplace discrimination on the basis of sexual orientation. As was discussed, Democrats linked consideration of this legislation to DOMA, hoping to catch some crumbs of goodwill. The bill fell one vote short of passage in the Senate and was doomed to failure in the more conservative House.

## CONTINUING DEVELOPMENTS IN HAWAII: THE COMMISSION, LITIGATION ROUND TWO, AND THE POLITICAL RESPONSE

Events in 1995 through 1997 illustrate the complicated nature of the litigation in Hawaii. On the one hand, the supreme court had been rhetorically rebuked by the legislature. But a commission was formed to study the same-sex marriage issue, and many observers felt that change was imminent. Courts kept pushing the issue, but legislators were never willing to completely follow their lead; however, some took the decision's reasoning very seriously.

The charge of the Commission on Sexual Orientation and the Law was to "[e]xamine the precise legal and economic benefits" of marriage, "[e]xamine whether substantial public policy reasons exist" to extend these benefits to same-sex couples, and "[r]ecommend appropriate action" for the legislature.[84] Initially, the committee was composed of eleven members, including two each from the Catholic and Mormon churches. Most of the members appointed by the governor, however, were from groups supportive of same-sex marriage.[85] Indeed, legislators who favored the creation of domestic partnerships saw to it that this was the case.[86] Before it could fully get off the ground, however, the commission's membership was challenged in U.S. District Court as an improper mixing of church and state, and the judge permanently enjoined the church members from the body.[87] As a result, it fell apart and ceased to operate, since the members refused to submit a report without all eleven members.[88]

The legislature quickly responded to these developments in the next session, amending Act 217 to create a commission of only seven members, none explicitly coming from religious organizations. Neither were other appointees to be picked from specific groups, but two were to come from recommendations of the Speaker of the House and two from recommendations of the president of the Senate.[89] In making these changes, the legislature, especially the House, was looking to have more control over the commission, particularly attempting to replace the perspective of the religious groups. From comments during floor debates it is clear that the legislature was frustrated with the court challenge and the pro–same-sex marriage makeup of the original commission. Representative Tom stated: "It is my fervent hope that the selection process we are establishing will result in a commission comprised of truly diverse viewpoints. . . . If the report is one-sided, biased or incomplete, it will be of little use for us."[90] In other words, the commission had better not side completely with the supreme court.

Nevertheless, the makeup of the commission was still heavily tilted in favor of same-sex marriage. Several of its members had been active in local gay rights organizations, and the chair, Thomas Gill, was a former lieutenant governor and congressman who became quite supportive of same-sex marriage. Two members nominated by Speaker Souki became a vocal yet powerless minority: James Hochberg was an attorney with the conservative Rutherford Foundation and had represented the Rutherford Institute in an amicus brief in the original *Baehr* litigation.[91] Marie Sheldon was a noted antiabortion activist with ties to the foundation.[92]

In reestablishing the commission, the legislature still was more than willing to take the heat off of itself, and this was apparent during the 1995 session. In the Senate, no members proposed a constitutional amendment banning same-sex marriages, and only two members of the House did so.[93] Some legislators, especially in the Senate, were not yet willing to exercise the ultimate trump card; many, despite public opinion to the contrary,[94] still wished to explore alternatives following the reasoning of *Baehr*. In fact, the Senate would become the focus of efforts to explore the domestic partnership issue.

Governor Benjamin Cayetano also campaigned in the fall of 1994 with the position that the state should get out of the "marriage" business altogether and just administer domestic partnerships for same-sex and opposite-sex couples, thereby leaving the "marriage" question to private religious groups. Privately, however, he maintained that he would not act until the courts gave the final word on the constitutionality of the same-sex marriage prohibition.[95] He thus won the election with a position that generally was supportive of the supreme court's reasoning. Granted, he was a Democrat in a uniformly Democratic state, but not all Democratic legislators held such a progressive position.

The new commission got to work in September 1995 and hoped to submit a report to the legislature by the end of the year. The members were certainly aware of the political thicket in which they were enmeshed, but they also saw that they had a clear job to do, regardless of political concerns. As Thomas Gill stated at the first meeting:

> I think we are all aware that the questions being addressed are viewed by many members of the legislature as highly controversial and not a favored topic for an election year. Some would like the whole matter to be killed or, at least, just go away. Some would prefer to punt the issue into the constitutional arena. What the legislature does is its business. Our job is to give the members a sensible report outlining steps they can take if they want to do so.[96]

Through written and oral testimony from a wide variety of experts, advocates, and citizens,[97] the commission primarily focused on economic issues, particularly addressing two questions: (1) What is the economic nature of the benefits given to married couples and (2) What would be the economic impact of extending these benefits to same-sex couples?[98] For the most part, then, the commission assumed the validity of same-sex marriage claims and tried to investigate the legal and economic ramifications of including same-sex couples in the marriage laws. The minority strongly opposed this approach, instead choosing to focus on moral issues concerning homosexuality. A great deal of discussion arose when Hochberg and Sheldon wished to add to the appendix of the report testimony and articles critical of homosexuality. In an e-mail, one of the commissioners, Morgan Britt, described the situation this way:

> It turns out this was a ploy for him [Jim Hochberg] to go to Joe Souki, the man who appointed him . . . and Speaker of the House . . . and cry over the fact that the Chair . . . would not let him add ANOTHER 25 page appendix to the report . . . well after the deadline for the introduction of new materials . . . The proposed appendix was mostly material by long-time anti-gay propagandist Charles Socarides.[99]

The majority resisted, prompting Speaker Souki to send a letter to Gill, stating that he was "very concerned that the Commission render a complete report to the Legislature, fully addressing both sides of this important issue," and he did not like the fact that the minority was being blocked in its efforts—he was obviously sympathetic to their cause.[100]

Despite this political pressure and the efforts of the minority, the commission moved ahead with a final report that strongly supported extending marriage benefits to same-sex couples. Some members of the majority preferred a domestic partnership alternative[101] but, ultimately, the commission recommended for the legislature "to extend all the benefits to same-gender couples by allowing them to marry." The domestic partnership alternative was not fully supported, since, "Under the *Baehr* decision case, adopting domestic partnership would not grant equal protection under the law."[102] Of course, this position was too radical for Hochberg and Sheldon. In fact, the majority and minority began to meet separately to draft their respective reports, since the differences were so pronounced.[103]

The motivation of the majority is reflected in Britt's e-mail, in which she thanked the members of the same-sex marriage discussion group for their support "to ensure that [the] promise of America, freedom and justice for all, can come a little closer to reality."[104] Clearly, as indicated earlier, the majority was predisposed to recommend same-sex marriage. Indeed, the majority report reads like the supreme court's decision in *Baehr*, defining legal benefits that come with marriage, relying on equal protection arguments, making parallels to *Loving*, knocking down the state's "procreation as a compelling interest" argument, defining the separation between church and state, and generally not being at all concerned with political or moral issues.[105] Robert Stauffer effectively summed up the majority's feeling in a statement in the *New York Times*: "I hope, I pray we'll see the end of this apartheid against our gay and lesbian citizens."[106]

In the end, despite the legislature's attempt to pass the buck to and control the commission, they were given recommendations that they were unwilling to support, but the issue was back in their laps. When consideration of the same-sex marriage issue was sheltered from the political process, the outcome was support for allowing same-sex couples to marry. Now, however, the issue was going back to the political arena in an election year—a year that would see the courts push the process further.

Perhaps predictably, the legislative session of 1996 ended in a stalemate. The House ultimately wished to pass a constitutional amendment banning same-sex marriage, while the Senate favored a domestic partnership law. Both chambers held hearings on the commission's recommendations but responded differently. The House Judiciary Committee failed to report out a domestic partnership bill or a bill to legalize same-sex marriage, but the chair, Representative Tom, also did not wish to report out a constitutional amendment early in the session and deferred votes on this issue.[107] The Senate Judiciary Committee chair, Rey Graulty, decided to consider a domestic partnership bill, despite the House's actions.[108] The committee rejected same-sex marriage by a vote of 1 to 6 but approved a domestic partnership bill that was similar to the commission's recommendations by a vote of 5 to 2. The committee also rejected a constitutional amendment by a 3 to 4 vote.[109] Thus, the Senate was still on the side of recognizing the equality of its gay and lesbian citizens, and, ultimately, passed a domestic partnership law by a 14 to 11 vote. Meanwhile, the House leadership was committed to passing a constitutional amendment, and Speaker Souki suspended the rules and pulled the stalled amendment out of the Judiciary Committee. The chamber ultimately voted 38 to 14 to pass the amendment, meeting the two-thirds requirement for passing an amendment.[110]

By this time, the legislature was completely deadlocked, with Senate leaders refusing to hold hearings on the constitutional amendment, even though it had passed overwhelmingly in the House. Ultimately, the amendment was pulled from the Judiciary Committee by a floor vote driven by its supporters to overcome the committee's intransigence, but the tactic backfired and the amendment was defeated by a 15 to 10 vote.[111] Senator Graulty summed up his opposition to the amendment by stressing that the amendment itself did not address the issue of discrimination against lesbians and gay men—an issue that the Senate had emphasized consistently since *Baehr*. As he stated, "This issue is one of fairness.

Gay and Lesbian people are important members of our community, and we reaffirm, as they ask, that they be treated fairly."[112] This argument first derived from a judicial declaration but was now echoed in the political arena.

This stalemate was a part of a larger inability of the legislature to address substantial issues, like a budget crisis, auto insurance reform, and pension reform.[113] Indeed, the fact that this was just one of many issues addressed further illustrates the somewhat reasoned and reasonable reaction of Hawaii legislators to the same-sex marriage litigation. There was certainly a strong push to overturn the courts with a constitutional amendment, but there was an equally strong effort to ensure that same-sex relationships were treated in a manner similar to traditional marriage.

## BACK TO THE COURTS

The trial for the state to present arguments defining its "compelling interest" began on September 10, 1996, about the same time that the Defense of Marriage Act was passed.[114] The trial had been delayed while the legislature was sorting through the issue and to allow it to review the recommendations of the commission.[115] Kevin Chang, appointed to hear the case, was considered to be a moderate judge, with no clear disposition to one side or the other. He had been a prosecutor and corporate lawyer—not a labor or defense lawyer with a history of civil rights advocacy (like Thomas Gill, for instance).[116] The state tried to reargue the law on the equal protection issue, for instance holding that *Loving* was not applicable, since race and gender are different categories.[117] But this was not a realistic effort, since the supreme court limited the trial to only a consideration of the compelling interest question and was not open to a reconsideration of the law. The state also contended that its compelling interest in restricting marriage to opposite-sex couples was that of promoting the proper upbringing of children, since, it alleged, children develop best and most fully when raised by biological parents in a traditional marriage arrangement. "It is a mistake to consider the object of marriage to be love, commitment, devotion and nothing else," the state's brief argued. The state also asserted that the legislature had reaffirmed this position in Act 217, despite its backing away from this position in 1994.[118] Plaintiffs argued, conversely, that the quality of upbringing had little to do with the biology of the parents and relied a great deal on the findings of the commission. They also noted that the legislature did not explicitly declare that procreation was the purpose of the state's marriage laws in Act 217.[119]

Given this, the trial mainly addressed the question of same-sex parents. Both sides presented psychologists, family therapists, and sociologists who argued each side of the "fitness" question. Chang, in his decision, indicated that he found the plaintiff's witnesses "to be especially credible." In fact, he went to great lengths to note that despite defendant's witnesses' general holding that the best environment for child rearing was that of two opposite-sex parents, they all reaffirmed that same-sex parents can do just as well. As a result, Chang ruled that the state had not met the compelling interest test, reaffirmed the supreme court's ruling, and enjoined the state from denying marriage licenses to same-sex couples.[120] However, he suspended his order while the state appealed.[121]

Needless to say, advocates for same-sex marriage were delighted with the decision. The lead attorney for the plaintiffs from the start, Dan Foley, stated, "We got everything we asked for. We got 100%."[122] Indeed, many in Hawaii and around the nation thought that same-sex marriage was on the verge of becoming a reality, since no one thought the state had any chance of winning the appeal.[123] Things were looking good for same-sex marriage advocates: An independent legislative commission had recommended same-sex marriage and the courts had reaffirmed their previous position. Chang was compelled by the dictates of the supreme court on remand only to consider the compelling interest question, and, like a good judge, he followed these orders, looked at the evidence presented, and made his decision. Given legal norms and processes, this was almost a foregone conclusion after the original decision in *Baehr*.

## BACK TO THE LEGISLATURE—AGAIN

The legal momentum was on the side of the proponents of same-sex marriage, but the focus then turned back to the legislature. Those who opposed same-sex marriage urged the legislature to pass a constitutional amendment to head off a final decision by the Hawaii Supreme Court that would likely legalize such marriages. There was clear support for a constitutional amendment, since a poll showed that as many as 74 percent of Hawaiians opposed same-sex marriage, although many polls showed the opposition in the 60 percent range.[124] Yet, following the previous division, the House and the Senate were split, with the Senate also desiring a bill that would offer 200 state marital benefits to "reciprocal beneficiaries," or couples of any type that cannot be legally married.[125] Governor Cayetano indicated that he would sign such a bill, giving it added support. Despite his opposition to same-sex marriage, the governor stated that the bill would be "an historic step forward. You can't put a dollar figure on basic rights that should be extended to all."[126]

Most legislators viewed the constitutional amendment as a way to rebuke the supreme court once and for all. They were disappointed, to say the least, that the courts did not find their definition of marriage in Act 217 sufficient to withstand equal protection strict scrutiny. As Representative Tom argued from the House floor, "the judicial branch of government has . . . refused to recognize this legislative policy and continues on a path, which, if left unchecked, will represent a very dangerous departure from our democratic traditions." The situation was dire, according to Tom, and only a constitutional amendment "will completely and with finality address the constitutional crisis which our Supreme Court has inflicted upon this state."[127] This aggressive language reflected the level of exasperation felt by the majority of legislators in the House. The measure passed the House by a vote of 44 to 7, more than the necessary two-thirds vote and by a larger margin than in the previous session.[128]

Interestingly, the legislators were given a certain degree of motivation for their actions from the chief justice of the Hawaii Supreme Court. In an address to a joint session of the legislature at the start of the 1997 session, Chief Justice Ronald Moon, who had been in the majority in *Baehr*, addressed the proper role of the judiciary, especially in the wake of the previous controversial years. This was the first time that such an address had taken place, and Moon made note of the "historic event," one that marked the "beginning of a new dialogue and cooperative spirit among our three branches of government." Obviously, he saw room for improvement on this front, given the rhetoric of the previous four years. He did not feel that the courts were above criticism, but "[w]hat causes great concern is the type of uninformed, emotionally based criticisms that we've recently read in letters to the editor or heard about on talk radio shows." Moon's remarks squarely addressed the concerns over same-sex marriage litigation. First, he defended judicial independence, given that "our decisions must be solely based on the legal merits of a case," not popular input, thus clearly carving out an independent, nonpolitical role for the judiciary. However, perhaps seeing the political writing on the wall, he also gave deference to popular and legislative judgment. As he told the legislature:

> When deciding cases, judges often apply common law, statutory law, or constitutional law to new facts and circumstances. In so doing, we do not intend to usurp the legislative function. However, under our system of checks and balances, if we stray into legislative prerogative, the legislature has the ability to cure the trespass. As you know, in our legal system, statutes trump common law, and constitutions trump statutes. We are ever mindful that the legislature—the peoples' representatives—hold the highest trumps.[129]

In the four-year standoff between the courts and the legislature, the courts blinked. In fact, many legislators made explicit reference to Moon's remarks in speaking in support of the constitutional amendment later in the session.[130] The courts in Hawaii were beginning to see the real effects of a challenge to their legitimacy and did not want to push the issue further. Their legal norms could only take them so far when their version of liberalism was not close to being dominant, and morality politics was highly salient.

Despite the court's increased sensitivity to "legitimacy" issues, senators were still more careful in their consideration of the matter and did not simply wish to trump the courts; they also continued to take the equal protection considerations articulated in *Baehr* seriously. In fact, the constitutional amendment proposed by the Senate included language that was protective of the gender discrimination concerns voiced in *Baehr*. The proposed amendment read, "The State shall have the power to regulate and define the institution of marriage, including the reservation of marriage to couples of the opposite sex ... provided that ... the application of this reservation does not deprive any person of civil rights on the basis of sex."[131] The House's amendment did not include this qualification, and Senate Judiciary Co-Chairman Avery Chumbly called the House version "too blunt an instrument" and defended the Senate version for its principle of inclusion. "As citizens of the most successful multicultural society in the world, it is a reflection of who we are and what we promise our children."[132] House members strongly opposed this wording, with Souki and Tom stating that the amendment would "virtually guarantee" same-sex marriage.[133] Additionally, the House version of the reciprocal beneficiaries law included only four areas of legal benefits, as opposed to the 200 in the Senate version. Fearing the economic costs of such an extensive bill, the House limited the benefits to just a few, such as hospital visitation and joint ownership of property.[134]

A stalemate again ensued; however, unlike the previous year when the Senate held firm, members now felt more political pressure to compromise. In the preceding election, many members had been defeated, including Judiciary Chair Graulty, for perceived inaction on several fronts, including same-sex marriage. And Chumbley was up for reelection in the fall.[135] Standing on principle may have been noble for a while, but their position was clearly in opposition to public sentiment. The public wanted a clear ban on same-sex marriages. House conferees also gave a few, dropping objections to insurance benefits for reciprocal beneficiaries. The final bill that was approved extended about fifty benefits to such relationships. Some of the primary benefits included survivorship benefits, like inheritance rights; health insurance benefits; joint property rights; and legal standing concerning wrongful death actions and domestic violence issues.[136] Many observers, especially given the previous session's inaction, praised this compromise. A description of the role played by Senators Matsunaga and Chumbley by the *Star-Bulletin* reflects the political dynamics that were at play in the compromise.

> In the same-sex marriage debate, their teamwork was evident. They were like-minded in their approach to the issue, aware of its legal complexities and committed to giving gay and lesbian couples state marital benefits substantially similar to those given heterosexuals. Their personalities also complemented one another. Matsunaga, who still believes same-gender couples are entitled to equal protection, appeared the more idealistic of the two. Chumbley seemed more the political strategist, faster to lock horns with House Judiciary Chairman Terrance Tom.[137]

Not everyone was quite so pleased, however. Many gay rights advocates saw the law as creating second-class citizenship for lesbians and gays. As Dan Foley stated, "The irony is that all this was done to deny full equal rights to gays."[138]

Later that fall, the constitutional amendment passed overwhelmingly, 69 percent to 29 percent.[139] The political struggle over the amendment was intense, with both sides of the issue putting forth considerable effort and expense. As of October 18, 1998, groups in favor of the amendment had raised $1.26 million and opponents $1.15 million.[140] Much of the funding came from the Mormon Church, which favored the amendment and contributed $600,000. The Human Rights Campaign contributed nearly $1 million to the "no" campaign. The majority of money came from outside Hawaii. Spearheading the effort to ratify the amendment was the group Save Traditional Marriage-'98. It raised money, lobbied, and ran political ads in favor of the amendment. They were careful to limit their appeal to preserving the institution of marriage and not to try to respond to their opponents on civil rights grounds, where they might have been vulnerable. Conversely, those who opposed the amendment had a more difficult task, which was summarized by David Smith of the Human Rights Campaign, the leading group opposing the amendment. "They had an easy, emotional message. We had a complex, technical message about government and civil rights: If this [denying marriage to gays] can be done to us, discrimination can also happen to you." Supporters of the amendment were also careful to distance themselves from more extremist voices. The strident president of the Hawaii Christian Coalition stepped down and kept a low profile. As Linda Rosehill of Save Traditional Marriage stated, "We wanted our entire campaign to be moderate and the voice for the silent majority."[141] Potentially, a civil rights appeal could have tremendous appeal in largely progressive Hawaii. In fact, one group targeted by the "no" effort, in addition to young people and women, was Japanese Americans who remember the World War II internment.[142] Clearly, the notion of second-class citizenship was not a popular one in Hawaii, and proponents of the amendment made sure to steer clear of any arguments that could push the debate in this direction. Nonetheless, the litigation resulted in an effective counter-mobilization by opponents of same-sex marriage by painting calls for same-sex marriage as outside the religious and native traditions of Hawaii and not a part of the state's tradition of inclusion.[143]

The constitutional amendment ended the movement for same-sex marriage, with the Hawaii Supreme Court ruling in 1999 that the amendment had overridden their efforts to include same-sex couples in the state's marriage laws.[144] Ultimately, the courts in Hawaii were unable to sustain their attempt to legalize same-sex marriage in the face of popular and legislative opposition. Nevertheless, the litigation in Hawaii profoundly changed the nature of the debate concerning same-sex marriage. It put the issue on the map and started a political and legal discussion about the nature of discrimination against lesbians and gay men, infusing this discussion with serious concerns for their equal treatment. It also resulted in concrete public policy, policy that would be broadened in other states.

## SAME-SEX MARRIAGE LITIGATION IN ALASKA

Soon after the initial *Baehr* decision, a political and legal fight over same-sex marriage began in Alaska. Like Hawaii, a court found the state's exclusion of same-sex couples from marriage law constitutionally suspect. And, like Hawaii, voters approved a constitutional amendment that trumped court activity. Nonetheless, Alaska presents an interesting case for this discussion: Its courts have historically ruled in favor of gay rights claims, the reasoning used by the court that invalidated the state's same-sex marriage prohibition was novel, and the rhetoric used in the political arena illustrates the power of notions of negative freedom and morality in the United States and their ability to trump claims of positive freedom.

In August 1994, a male couple applied for a marriage license with the Alaska Office of Vital Statistics but was denied.[145] Jay Brause and Gene Dugan had lived together for fifteen years and were "married" in a religious ceremony in 1979.[146] Soon after the suit was filed, the Alaska legislature passed a mini-DOMA in direct response to the suit. The bill passed the Senate by a 17 to 3 vote and the House by a margin of 31 to 9.[147] The legislature felt especially vulnerable, since a revision to the marriage laws in 1974 changed the explicit reference to marriage as between a man and a woman to an arrangement between "persons." According to one legislator, "Marriage is a definition of what a family is, based on traditional culture."[148] Clearly, the Alaska legislature was trying to head off developments in Hawaii and at home and trying to preserve its view that marriage should not be opened to same-sex couples.

The legislation posed a dilemma for the Democratic governor, Tony Knowles. Like Democratic governors in Hawaii, Knowles did not favor the legalization of same-sex marriage, but he viewed the legislature's efforts as mean-spirited and was generally supportive of gay rights claims. His chief of staff summarized Knowles's position: "It seems like this is a bill to bash a group of Alaskans who are part of Alaska's family . . . . If that's the priority of this session, there's something sick about this place."[149] Ultimately, the governor allowed the bill to become law without his signature, stating:

> There is no confusion about the current marriage code or my administration's resolve to support it. [The bill] is nothing more than a thinly disguised ploy to pit Alaskans against one another for political advantage. [Alaskans should] reject the manipulation and opportunism of those who would divide us through intolerance.[150]

This is a fairly strong statement that reflects a strong pro–gay rights stance on the part of the governor. His status quo position on the marriage law likely reflected the reality of the political landscape, given the unpopularity of same-sex marriage, rather than a true lack of support for the issue. Democratic executives, despite personal support for same-sex marriage, are still limited by politics. Waihee, Cayetano, and Knowles all acted in a similar manner: They stayed away from an explicit endorsement of same-sex marriage while still trying to carve out a space for gay equality.

Four years after Brause and Dugan filed for a marriage license, an Alaska Superior Court judge ruled in their favor. Judge Peter Michalski found same-sex marriage to be a "fundamental right," subject to strict scrutiny review. Like the Hawaii Supreme Court, Michalski was unwilling to accept old, deferential, formal definitions of marriage. "It is not enough to say that 'marriage is marriage' and accept without any scrutiny the law before the court . . . . [T]his court cannot defer to the legislature or familiar notions when addressing this issue," he asserted. The counter-majoritarian difficulty did not appear to trouble him. The judicial deference prevalent on the issue in the 1970s was waning. Michalski grounded his analysis in the explicit privacy clause of the Alaska Constitution adopted in 1972. Relying on Alaska high court rulings made in the wake of the new provision, he held that the right to privacy included the right to same-sex marriage. Under his interpretation, however, the right to privacy means more than "seclusion, secrecy, or being left to one's personal affairs." Given that marriage is a public act, the notion of privacy needed to be expanded to fit this. Therefore, Michalski turned privacy from a strictly negative to a much more positive notion. To prove his point, he made the analogy to one of the privacy precedents, *Breese v. Smith*,[151] in which the Alaska Supreme Court struck down a high school hair length restriction. As he stated, "Though how one looks is a very public fact, the decision about one's personal appearance is personal, and therefore protected by the right to privacy." So too is the case with same-sex marriage: even though getting married has become a public act, its primary justification is the "choice of a life partner." Indeed, Michalski found the right to choose a life partner to be a fundamental right, no different from the fundamental right to marry articulated by the U.S. Supreme Court, irrespective of the gender of those involved in the relationship. "It is the decision itself that is fundamental, whether the decision results in a traditional choice or the nontraditional choice Brause and Dugan seek to have recognized." Michalski did not discuss equal protection ramifications in detail, since he saw the issue as moot, having already found a fundamental right that automatically triggers strict scrutiny review. He also felt, however, that the denial of same-sex marriage constituted gender discrimination, but this would only have triggered intermediate scrutiny under Alaska law.[152]

Rejecting tradition and deference to legislatures, another court used liberal legal reasoning and norms alone to invalidate a prohibition on same-sex marriage. This was perhaps not a surprise for an Alaska court, given a tradition of rather favorable judicial outcomes for gay rights claims as early as the late 1970s. The state's high court found a free speech and equal protection violation with a gay rights group's exclusion from a listing in an Anchorage municipal directory,[153] overturned a lower court ruling that prevented custody of a child for a mother because she was a lesbian,[154] and invalidated a referendum petition to overturn a gay rights ordinance that the court characterized as biased and misleading.[155] On several fronts, then, the Alaska Supreme Court was quite protective of gay rights claims, often before other courts throughout the nation. One can reasonably assume that the Alaska Supreme Court would have at least taken Michalski's arguments seriously had the legislature not quickly stepped in.

Reflecting developments in Hawaii, legislators called for a constitutional amendment overturning the decision, held a committee hearing on an amendment, and voted 5 to 1 in that committee in favor of the amendment within ten days of the holding in *Brause*.[156] Thus, quick work was made of the decision; there was no attempt, as in Hawaii, to accommodate the court's reasoning though a domestic partnership arrangement. By the fall election, voters approved the amendment by a 2 to 1 margin.[157]

Unlike Hawaii, where progressive forces were able to stake some political ground, Alaska had a tradition of effective and organized antigay political activity that was clearly at odds with the state's judiciary. For instance, during the Anchorage ordinance controversy in 1992 and 1993 intense debate and hostile opposition to the ordinance wracked the city. At one point, church leaders publicly appealed for calm. Much of the opposition can be traced to the influence of religious conservatives. As a conservative former Anchorage assemblyman who introduced the ordinance stated, "Dealing with homosexuals is such a volatile issue with the religious right. It is life or death, fall on your sword."[158] In a lightly populated state like Alaska, strong sentiment such as this can indeed go far. In the campaign over the constitutional amendment in 1998, the Mormon Church gave $500,000 to support the amendment on behalf of its 24,000 Alaskan Mormons.[159]

The political discourse used, especially by those opposed to same-sex marriage, was quite different from the discourse used by the courts. Rather than try to expand the view of privacy to include the choice of life partners, many opposed to same-sex marriage fell back on the negative/positive distinction. As one voter declared: "They are not family-oriented. What do they have to produce? They're non-contributors to society.... It's about sexual gratification."[160] This is a view of homosexuality that focuses just on the sex and neglects the role that intimate relationships play in individual development (or through heterosexual arrogance fails to see this dynamic at play in lesbian and gay relationships). An Anchorage Baptist minister perfectly articulated this dynamic: "People can do what they want in their private chamber, but when you force people as a whole to accept it, that's not right. [When the state sanctions same-sex marriage] the state is making all of us say it's OK, and it's not OK."[161] Even advocates of same-sex marriage in Alaska used this strain of political discourse to advance their cause. At a legislative hearing, the president of the Alaska ACLU told legislators that the government should stay out of the picture on marriage. "This is a simple matter of leaving people alone."[162] Whereas Judge Michalski could build on this argument to actually create a legitimate realm of state sanction of same-sex marriage, in the political arena, advocates fell back on strictly negative arguments about privacy. Nothing could be added to enlarge and enrich the argument.

The courts were not silent during the political campaign over the amendment, however. Opponents of the amendment brought suit to have it invalidated, arguing that it infringed on privacy and equal protection rights and limited the power of the judiciary to frame these rights. A lower court rejected this claim outright, but the supreme court took the appeal.[163] In considering the claim, the court tried to sort out the differences between constitutional amendments that are "add-ons" and constitutional revisions that require a constitutional convention. For example, in the same case, the court struck down a proposed amendment taking away rights of prisoners, since it would affect several provisions of the Alaskan Constitution. But the court ruled that the same-sex marriage amendment was sufficiently narrow, at least the part that defined marriage. The proposed amendment read: "To be valid or recognized in this State, a marriage may exist only between one man and one woman. No provision of this constitution may be interpreted to require the State to recognize or permit marriage between individuals of the same sex." The court struck the second sentence because of the "possibility that the sentence in question might be construed at some future time in an unintended fashion which could seriously interfere with important rights," particularly equal protection concerns.[164]

Clearly, the court could do little to directly confront the political process that played itself out in the previous months, but the justices were still willing to assert some control and authority on the process, preserving some space for the possibility of recognition of legal relationships short of marriage. As evidence, both sides of the political debate claimed victory, with opponents of the amendment vowing to litigate even if the amendment passed, especially since the court appeared to leave the door open to an equal protection challenge.[165] Courts may be aware of public opinion and unwilling to directly challenge it, but they also may try to challenge the political status quo if their norms and values dictate.

By 1998, then, uncoordinated same-sex marriage litigation was surprisingly well received in court in two states, with the courts embracing positive freedom and equality arguments. The litigation, of course, ran headlong into the political status quo of libertarianism and moralism, while gaining some momentum among political actors. Despite the opposition, this litigation could not be contained, and the expansion of litigation would continue to face resistance. But it would also begin to reshape the political landscape.

# 8    Courts and Same-Sex Marriage in the United States: Vermont

SHORTLY AFTER the Hawaii Supreme Court declared that the people of Hawaii had overruled its decision, the Supreme Court of Vermont handed down another landmark same-sex marriage case. In *Baker v. State of Vermont*, the court maintained that limiting marriage only to opposite-sex couples violated the Vermont Constitution, and the court compelled the legislature to remedy the situation.[1] This chapter examines this litigation, the political response that resulted in significant policy change in the state, and policy change that would have been unlikely in the absence of litigation.

In the decade preceding the litigation, the issue of gay rights had been a prominent topic in Vermont politics. In 1986, a proposed equal rights amendment was narrowly defeated, largely due to concerns that the amendment would legalize same-sex marriage.[2] Hate crime and antidiscrimination legislation was passed, with vocal antigay opposition (a dynamic that would also play in the debate over civil unions legislation), in the early 1990s.[3] A combination of a state high court decision and legislation extended adoption rights to same-sex couples.[4] Emboldened by these successes, activists broadened their fight. As David Moats describes it: "During the 1980s, the gay and lesbian community had been fighting for mainly negative freedom—freedom from violence and discrimination. During the 1990s, the community would begin to fight for positive freedom—freedom to live a life of their choosing, to form families, to raise children, to marry."[5] This required a turn to litigation.

Unlike the original litigation in Hawaii, the Vermont litigation was a coordinated effort influenced by the events in Hawaii. Beth Robinson and Susan Murray, two lawyers who were friends and worked at the same law firm, founded a political group in 1995, the Freedom to Marry Taskforce. They had been discussing a lawsuit for several years, but were emboldened to act by the events of the mid-1990s. In 1995 Murray and Robinson declined to assist a gay couple file a same-sex marriage lawsuit. In Robinson's words, "We felt the karma wasn't right."[6] Instead, they organized chapters around the state to begin laying the political groundwork to support the eventual litigation, including producing a video with same-sex couples describing their relationships and why they wished to marry.[7] Although the political groundwork was being laid, however, it was clearly the litigation that was central to the activists' efforts. No effort was made to address the issue legislatively; the litigation would be the battering ram, rather than pure deliberation and debate. Indeed, when the legislature inadvertently addressed the same-sex marriage issue early in 1997, Robinson and Murray urged legislators not to pursue the issue.

The House had passed a bill making it easier for residents of Vermont to get married in towns other than their own. In the process, they deleted the words "bride" and "groom" from the marriage statute. This, of course, had implications for same-sex marriage, since it would take the male-female definition out of the equation. During a Senate hearing on the matter, Murray claimed that final approval of the law would create legislative intent that could be used by the courts. As she stated,

> the gay and lesbian community has not asked the legislature to deal with this issue. . . . [I]t's a very complex issue. . . . It's a big social issue. We know that there is litigation in the state of Hawaii and there's all kinds of stuff going on in the country about it, and I don't think that this Senate should vote on this issue on such short notice at the very end of the session with virtually no input on it.[8]

This appears odd, given that Murray founded a group two years before to give input into this process—unless that input was designed to be mostly legal. Murray appeared to be saying, "Don't worry about it, the lawyers are working on it." Indeed, three months later, the lawsuit was filed. And the Vermont group pulled in Gay and Lesbian Advocates and Defenders (GLAD), a Boston-based lesbian and gay rights litigation group, bringing greater legal resources and expertise to bear on the litigation.[9] This point is detailed, since it might be tempting to emphasize that activists pursued a dual strategy of politics and litigation and this led to the positive results in the courts and in the legislature. However, from this evidence, it appears that the political strategy was quite secondary to the litigation and its desired effects. In fact, the Vermont lawyers were extremely disappointed when the Vermont courts did not fully give them what they wanted. As David Moats describes Robinson: "She had believed in the law and the law's power to shine a clear light on the constitutional requirements of equality and justice. But the law had let her down."[10] This description may play into the cause lawyer caricature, but these cause lawyers also achieved a great deal.

The decision to initiate litigation was made by Robinson, Murray, and Mary Bonauto of GLAD in 1996 in part because of the recent legislative success and because Vermont's constitution was difficult to amend, thereby making tangible, direct reaction to a court decision improbable.[11] When the litigants filed their suit, they put out a press release outlining their claims, which included their legal arguments, as well as biographical information on the three couples bringing suit. One couple, the press release emphasized, had been together for twenty-five years and another was described as "want[ing] to marry for the same mix of reasons that other couples choose to marry: they love each other, they want to make a public commitment to one another, and they seek the legal protections and obligations of civil marriage."[12] Clearly, then, the litigants were making more than just legal arguments. They were also focused on public opinion and were trying to lay the political foundation for their litigation by establishing the human element of same-sex marriage in showing how same-sex marriage is the same as traditional marriage. Indeed, legislators would eventually point to the personal stories of same-sex couples as the reason for supporting civil unions. However, these stories were only influential after the supreme court handed down a decisive decision and created a framework for political action. As we shall see in other progressive states, these types of stories do not carry the day in the absence of litigation. And these stories do nothing to persuade those who argue that homosexuality is immoral. In states where potential for change exists, the only response to this dynamic is aggressive liberal rights-based litigation.

## THE VERMONT COURTS HAVE THEIR SAY

Initially, the case was dismissed from the superior court in Chittenden, where the case was filed. Using a minimal standard of review more similar to the same-sex marriage cases of the 1970s than the Hawaii case, superior court Judge Linda Levitt tossed out the plaintiff's claim. In fact, her decision explicitly cited the 1970s precedents. Asserting a low standard of review, she declared that the legislature needed only to provide a "rational basis" to prohibit same-sex marriages. For Levitt, this rational basis was the state's interest in preserving procreation and child rearing.[13]

Obviously, the plaintiffs appealed, and the case was argued before the Vermont Supreme Court on November 18, 1998. Seventeen amicus briefs were submitted, seven supporting same-sex marriage claims and ten opposing.[14] At oral arguments, the justices were quite active in questioning counsel and, for the most part, seemed to accept the plaintiffs' position while pushing them in various directions, like exploring whether the case involved sex or sexual orientation discrimination. For instance, at one point Justice Marilyn Skoglund asked whether the state had already defined sexual orientation as a suspect class through legislation protecting gays from discrimination. Chief Justice Jeffrey Amestoy and Justice John Dooley explored policy options, such as giving rights to same-sex couples without calling it marriage (Dooley) or abolishing marriage and creating domestic partnerships for everyone (Amestoy). Conversely, the justices always appeared skeptical of the state's claims, especially the procreation justification. Justice James Morse asked whether the state could legitimately prohibit infertile couples from marrying, thus poking a hole in the state's main justification for opposite-sex marriage. In hindsight it is always easy to see a decision coming, but, clearly, the justices appeared sympathetic to same-sex marriage claims.[15]

Indeed, they were. The court held that the exclusion of same-sex couples from the benefits of marriage laws was impermissible under the Vermont Constitution. All five felt so, though they differed in their reasoning and remedies. The outcome was set almost immediately after oral arguments when all members of the court agreed that they would side with the couples.[16] They never gave the state's arguments serious consideration.

The decision is a remarkable example of a rich, liberal jurisprudence. Claims that lesbians and gay men were worthy of recognition by the state and deserved dignity under the state's constitution were easily accepted and supported. The words of Chief Justice Amestoy reflect Abraham Lincoln's aspirational liberalism and H. L. A. Hart's affirmation of intimacy as a part of liberalism:

> The past provides many instances where the law refused to see a human being when it should have.... The challenge for future generations will be to define what is most essentially human. The extension of the Common Benefits Clause to acknowledge plaintiffs as Vermonters who seek nothing more, nor less, than legal protection and security for their avowed commitment to an intimate and lasting human relationship is simply, when all is said and done, a recognition of our common humanity.[17]

And, reflecting liberalism's requirement of reasoned arguments, the court dismissed the state's justifications for a male/female only marriage policy as illogical and grounded in no rational basis.

Like the Vermont superior court, the supreme court rejected the statutory claim of the plaintiffs and held that the legislature assumed marriage to be between only a man and a woman.[18] But on the constitutional front, the Vermont high court found an abundance of reason to question the state's policy. The court found that the marriage policy ran afoul of the Vermont Constitution's Common Benefits Clause.[19] This clause held enormous significance for members of the court, and much of Chief Justice Amestoy's majority opinion is spent discussing the origins and application of the clause. Clearly taking a "living constitution" approach, Amestoy stated that the proper interpretative framework is to "remain faithful to ... [a] historical ideal, while addressing contemporary issues that the framers undoubtedly could never have imagined."[20] For him, the central ideal behind the clause is "the principle of inclusion."[21] Additionally, the Vermont Constitution was progressive in other ways: abolishing slavery and property qualifications and calling for direct elections.[22] Thus, for Amestoy the Vermont Constitution was a forward-looking document.

Amestoy was curiously unwilling to apply federal equal protection analysis to the Common Benefits Clause, which had been the practice of Vermont courts. Likely out of fear of creating a new suspect class, Amestoy rejected the "rigid" categories of federal jurisprudence in favor of a "balancing approach."[23] Amestoy used a rigorous rational basis test in evaluating the state's marriage policy. In doing so, he challenged the state's assertion that the marriage policy was linked to procreation. Noting that many married couples never intend to or cannot have children, Amestoy found that "[t]he law extends the benefits and protections of marriage to many persons with no logical connection to the stated government goal."[24]

Interestingly, Amestoy's decision closely follows the plaintiffs' brief in the case. From the discussion of the origins and development of the Common Benefits Clause, the analysis of relevant precedents, the claim that the court did not need to identify a suspect classification to invalidate the Vermont marriage statute, and the picking apart of the state's marriage policy rationales, reasoning, and language are remarkably similar. Indeed, in their brief and during oral arguments, the plaintiffs' lawyers played down gender and sexual orientation discrimination arguments, instead relying on a rational basis analysis. Perhaps out of fear of the barriers to breaking new legal ground, advocates shied away from grand claims.

In fact, an amicus brief by prominent law professors supportive of same-sex marriage claims argued that statutory interpretation alone justified same-sex marriage and avoided constitutional arguments altogether.[25]

But in discussing the remedy, Amestoy parted company with the plaintiffs who hoped for full same-sex marriage. He did not directly choose a remedy, but, instead, gave that role to the Vermont legislature. The legislature could either, according to the chief justice, grant full same-sex marriage or develop a strong domestic partnership law. As the court stated, "We do not purport to infringe upon the prerogatives of the Legislature to craft an appropriate means of addressing this constitutional mandate," but they noted that domestic partnerships would be a viable constitutional alternative.[26] In fact, Amestoy included in his decision a quotation from a prominent scholar of constitutional law, Cass Sunstein, who has argued for courts to tread cautiously in politically sensitive areas.[27] Thus, the Vermont Supreme Court wished to give the legislature some space and hoped to be a catalyst for, rather than a dictator of, social policy. Indeed, many commentators have praised this example of "judicial minimalism."[28] But it appears quite inconsistent with the holding. As Justice Denise Johnson stated in dissent, the majority made a clear constitutional statement, "yet it declines to give . . . any relief other than an exhortation to the Legislature to deal with the problem."[29] However, the court preserved its upper hand in the matter by retaining jurisdiction in the case if the legislature failed to act. This would prove to be decisive in framing the legislature's response, and, in a sense, was no abdication at all, merely a clever political maneuver to lessen negative political reaction. After all, at bottom, the court had delivered a clear mandate in favor of the rights of sexual minorities. The court did not simply advise the legislature; by maintaining jurisdiction it forced it to act along its outline. Perhaps a lesson had been learned from Hawaii where the legislature was shut out of the process, a backlash ensued, and there was little space for the preservation of legal language and ideals. By bringing the legislature in while defining its actions, the court got what it wanted, and its language and ideal were the driving force behind the eventual legislation. In addition to being clever politically, Amestoy's approach was likely a reflection of his more general approach as a judge. A moderate Republican who served for seven terms as Vermont's attorney general, he was known for consensus building and for a desire to avoid unnecessary conflict.[30]

In a concurring opinion, Justice John Dooley took the majority to task for abandoning traditional equal protection analysis and starting down a path of unnecessary judicial activism with its heightened rational basis review. He would have preferred finding that sexual orientation was a suspect classification. To not do so, Dooley argued, was to rely "too much on the identities and personal philosophies of the men and women who fill the chairs of the Supreme Court, too little on ascertainable standards."[31] A valid jurisprudential point, to be sure, but his outcome would have been the same. This project is less concerned with the quality of judicial arguments (which is certainly not easy to ascertain), than with the extent to which they reflect liberal principles and the specific strain of liberalism. For neither Dooley nor Amestoy is liberalism simply libertarian.

As noted above, Justice Johnson's dissent criticized the majority for its seeming lack of a remedy. She chose to apply the *Baehr v. Lewin* reasoning of sex discrimination to the case and called for an immediate remedy.[32] Moats notes that Johnson approached the decision from a purely legal perspective, while Amestoy, formerly an elected official, merged law and politics.[33] The other justices went along with Amestoy's approach that probably helped to keep a majority together. This political awareness, however, should not be mistaken for judicial timidity. The justices knew that the ruling was potentially explosive. Justice Skoglund called her daughter's school the day of the decision to be sure there were procedures to ensure her safety the day the decision would be handed down.[34]

Indeed, it is important to emphasize that no justices disagreed on the holding, only the reasoning and the remedy. This was not a great surprise, since the court was certainly considered to be liberal with a history of activism and sympathetic to gay rights claims. In 1993, the court ruled that a lesbian could adopt the children of her partner without terminating the partner's parental rights.[35] And the court had a history of lobbing legal and political bombs to the legislature. For example, in 1996, the court found the state's system of school funding unconstitutional using the Common Benefits Clause. The legislature was forced to pass legislation making funding more equitable.[36] This was undoubtedly a liberal court and one fairly removed from politics. Judges in Vermont are appointed by the governor, confirmed by the Senate, and retained through legislative votes.[37]

## THE POLITICAL REACTION

Immediate reaction to *Baker* seemed to indicate that the court had achieved a fait accompli. Politicians representing a broad range of ideologies coalesced around the idea of equality for same-sex couples. Governor Howard Dean declared: "This is simply the logical extension, the incremental extension, of civil rights to all. And I don't know that we should have a big problem with that, other than those who are caught up in homophobic teachings." One of the most conservative members of the legislature, Republican Julius Canns, initially supported a domestic partnership approach. "This is not terribly important, in my view. If two people want to live together, that's their business. Certainly, I don't want to get into their bedrooms."[38] Libertarianism was this conservative's first reaction (Canns, however, would eventually not support civil unions and proposed a constitutional amendment to overrule the Vermont Supreme Court). At this early point in the process, the opposition had not established their footing and seemed a little confused about the ramifications of the decision. Rev. Craig Benson, a member of Take It to the People, a group opposed to equality for same-sex couples, called the decision "a victory nationally because the sanctity of marriage is intact." Soon, however, the opposition would take the opposite view, arguing that the decision destroyed the meaning of marriage and usurped the legislature's and the people's authority. People like Canns would come to embrace this view. But, at this early stage, the force of liberal legal arguments was carrying the day.[39]

Public opinion concerning the decision was mixed. In a poll taken just weeks after the decision, 52 percent of respondents said they disagreed with the court and 38 percent agreed. A poll from the preceding October indicated that 47 percent of Vermonters opposed same-sex marriage, while 40 percent were in favor.[40] In the short term, the decision did not radically alter public opinion, but it was not in step with public opinion either.

Clearly, the Vermont Supreme Court challenged the political process and forced the hand of the legislature by mandating that it pass legislation legalizing same-sex marriage or creating domestic partnerships. If the legislature did nothing, the court would certainly declare a right to same-sex marriage on its own. In other words, the court left the legislature very little "wiggle room." This point was not lost on the person most responsible for the legislature's response, House Judiciary Committee Chair Thomas Little. Little, a Republican, took the charge from the court seriously, as indicated by a memorandum he sent to his committee on January 4, 2000, less than a month after the court's decision. Mindful of the court's authority looming overhead, he reminded his committee members that "The Court has retained jurisdiction of the case, in order to be able to issue a further ruling on the marriage statutes if the General Assembly fails to act in a timely fashion." Little was determined to tread a fine line between the decision of the court and the obvious public sentiment against its ruling. As he stated, "my goal is not only to keep the Committee's 'eye' on the Constitutional principles, but also to build consensus and avoid divisiveness within the General Assembly and throughout the state."[41]

Indeed, throughout the process, Little, a lawyer, showed tremendous respect for the Vermont Supreme Court's decision as legitimate and proper, and he denied that the court had usurped the legislature's power. Although not willing to sponsor full same-sex marriage, he found the legal arguments for the inclusion of same-sex relationships into existing legal protections found in marriage statutes persuasive and translated them into political action. As he stated later during the floor debate, "What we have here in front of us are Vermonters who are different from some other Vermonters (but) nonetheless equal members of our state under the law. . . . We're not asking anyone to grant special (protections) to anyone, we're only asking for equal protection under the law."[42] Ultimately, Little was guided by a statement made to his committee early in their deliberations: "Leadership requires a keen sense of what ought to be done in the context of what can be done."[43]

The Judiciary Committee began its work quickly, as was Little's plan. The committee took testimony from a range of witnesses, pro and con, including the counsel for the plaintiffs and the attorney general.[44] A public hearing was also held on January 25 with 1,500 people in attendance.[45]

Meanwhile, the committee undertook its own discussions and had been leaning toward drafting a domestic partnership bill that stopped short of same-sex marriage, but provided all of the benefits of legal marriage. A straw vote indicated that all committee members favored proceeding with some type of legislation, with eight supporting domestic partnership and three actually favoring same-sex marriages. No members wished to preserve the status quo. Little desired a "civil rights act" that mirrored heterosexual marriage but was separate from the marriage statute. Opinions from Judiciary Committee members varied: William Lippert, an openly gay Democrat, supported full marriage rights, stating that gay and lesbian relationships ought to be celebrated and "welcomed into the community." John Edwards, a Republican from a conservative and remote part of the state,[46] called for a "legal benefits bill." Democrat Michael Vinton vaguely called for "equal protection" for same-sex couples. Citing the need to accept same-sex couples as "full members" of society, Progressive Steve Hingtgen rejected the idea of domestic partnerships, since this "validates the hate" against sexual minorities by reinforcing their second-class status. Michael Kainen, a Republican, simply deferred to the will of the committee and would support either marriage or domestic partnership. He stated that unanimity from the committee was crucial. Democrat Alice Nitka emotionally called for legislation that would grant rights for same-sex couples as well as blood relatives. Republican Judith Livingston called for the separation of the civil and religious aspects of marriage and for the state to grant civil union status to all couples, leaving religions free to determine what is "marriage." Cathy Voyer, a Republican, favored the civil union approach as the best way to prevent the state from being torn apart. Democrat Bill Mackinnon fully supported marriage rights for same-sex couples. Noting that "it was an honor to have this [issue] handed to us," he regretted not having been a part of the civil rights struggles of the 1960s. He didn't want to be the one to water down the solution. Finally, Democrat Diane Carmolli advocated a civil unions path, noting Vermont's history of tolerance. She also stated that she had re-read the *Baker* decision the night before. Clearly she took the court's arguments seriously, as did the rest of the committee, since none rejected equality arguments. Indeed, Little asserted that the preamble of a draft of the committee's bill "echoes the language of *Baker*."[47]

Remarkably, then, the *Baker* court's mandate received full support from a legislative committee (contrast this with the legislative response in Hawaii). It was not an easy vote; the members related having many sleepless nights and stomach pains as they made their decision. Nitka described it in the following dramatic manner: "This was D-Day for us. We hadn't had to really put out all our cards...on the table. Today, we did."[48] But the Vermont Supreme Court dealt the hand. A comment by Edwards after the committee vote is telling: "Somehow, when you listen to the compelling stories of gay and lesbian people, it demystifies who they are, what they stand for and how valuable they are for our communities."[49] Thus, when richer liberalism is presented, either through legal arguments, rational discourse intended to break the grip of majority privilege and arrogance, or a combination of both, gay rights claims can have great salience. But when these arguments are not privileged and have to compete with morality, religion, and tradition (communitarian values), the end result is much more mixed for gay rights claims. So far, these claims were sheltered. After the sense of the committee was noted, they began drafting a civil unions bill that was patterned after the Vermont marriage statutes.[50] Indeed, Little's goal was to have no legal difference between the statute for same-sex partners and the marriage statute, save for the name.[51]

The committee reflected an interesting mix of backgrounds and personalities. Some were familiar with the law: two were retired state troopers and three were lawyers. Undoubtedly, for them the court's mandate carried great weight. Consider Thomas Little: He certainly could have scored political points by railing against same-sex marriage. Instead, he pushed a process forward that respected the Vermont Supreme Court's decision and the necessity of providing some form of legal equality for same-sex couples. His fellow committee members thought likewise. The members of the committee also reflected diverse family arrangements, which made them hostile to traditional defenses of marriage. Six were in long-term marriages; one was going through a divorce; one was a gay man in a seven-year relationship; two had been in long-term, unmarried heterosexual relationships; and one was a single mother who bristled at the notion that the traditional nuclear family was best for child rearing. Through their backgrounds and experiences, these committee members perhaps had an easer time "imagining the real" of same-sex marriage. As committee member Alice Nitka stated in considering the value of her own thirty-one-year marriage: "You think about your own experience. You think, 'Yes, you might want to be married.' "[52] In this statement one can see legal liberalism chipping away at heterosexual arrogance.

Part of the committee's deliberation, however, highlights the limits of liberal discourse in U.S. politics, especially when not directly related to litigation. An early version of the Judiciary Committee's bill used the word "intimate" in the bill's findings to describe same-sex relationships. Some members feared using this term would alienate moderates, and Alice Nitka, who favored granting benefits to relatives, felt this language would fence them out. Reflecting Hart's view of liberalism that acknowledged intimacy as a part of personhood, Lippert argued that the term "acknowledges the significance of the relationship." But he ultimately agreed to substitute "caring" for "intimate."[53] Recall Chief Justice Amestoy's use of the term in question: He said same-sex couples seek "legal protection and security for the avowed commitment to an *intimate* and lasting human relationship" (italics added). When the arena is no longer purely judicial, however, richer notions of liberalism are harder to sustain.

The committee also encountered the desire by many who testified (and one of its members) to de-gay the issue by providing benefits more broadly, as was done in Hawaii. Despite Little's reservations that this would detract from the Vermont Supreme Court's charge, the findings of the committee did contain a limited set of benefits for blood relatives. Representative Peg Flory strongly advocated for this expansion, testifying in favor of the creation of "family units." In her testimony, she was clearly uncomfortable with endorsing homosexuality and tried to demote same-sex relationships. She stated that the only difference between two loving aunts and a same-sex couple is sex.[54] This was a common tact of those who felt some responsibility to respond to the court's mandates but who did not wish to recognize the personhood of sexual minorities. Of course, this route never would have satisfied the court, but it was seen by some as more feasible politically, or all that the political culture could bear.

As was noted, the Judiciary Committee was not alone in favoring the domestic partnership route. Governor Howard Dean, a popular Democrat, also favored this approach. In fact, just after the decision in *Baker*, Dean indicted that he wanted the legislature to pass such a bill. As he stated, "It is in the best interest of all Vermonters, gay and straight, to go forward with the domestic partnership act, and not the gay marriage act."[55] Sentiment in the Senate was similar. The Senate President Pro Tem, Peter Shumlin, stated: "Realistically, I think a partnership bill is something we can pass."[56] This kind of talk coming only a day after the court decision indicates the strength of this position. Caught between the court and public opinion, the political leaders looked for a compromise. Luckily, the court gave them that option.

However, by the time that committee deliberations began in earnest in February 2000, opponents began a more aggressive campaign against any benefits for same-sex couples. In response to Little's desire to create a parallel institution to marriage, Michele Cummings of Take It to the People declared, "If it looks like marriage, acts like marriage, and talks like marriage, it's marriage." This approach of opposing a domestic partnership route ran counter to the advice of a lobbyist for a group who advised to accept this to prevent the Vermont Supreme Court from mandating same-sex marriage. But they were increasingly unwilling to compromise.[57] Indeed, opponents began giving out yellow rubber duck key chains as a symbol of their opposition to any favorable outcome for same-sex couples.[58] Also, an attempt was made to impeach the Vermont Supreme Court, although only twelve legislators signed on to the resolution. Additionally, a proposal was presented to call for a constitutional convention to respond to the supreme court. Unfortunately for opponents, no provision exists for such a convention in the state constitution, and the House, 103 to 45, eventually rejected this proposal. A proposal for a popular referendum was also defeated 91 to 56. Clearly, the legislature was not willing to entertain any frontal assaults on the supreme court's authority, or at least did not feel that they had any real options for this.[59]

Once the bill got to the House floor, an intense lobbying campaign commenced from both sides of the issue. Proponents of same-sex marriage or domestic partnership, organized under the Vermont Freedom to Marry Action Committee, hired two lobbying firms to assist in their efforts. Originally trying to put the pressure on legislators to legalize same-sex marriage, they would ultimately support the civil unions law.[60] As the scope of the conflict expanded, action became less and less certain and morality politics played a larger role. Neither the court nor the Judiciary Committee was concerned with these issues (theirs was mostly a legal mandate), but many legislators on the House floor were. And many were backing off earlier support for domestic partnerships, especially after they began to see fierce, concentrated opposition from their constituents. Indeed, in a state like Vermont, with a clear urban/rural political split, members from rural areas were seeing strong opposition to any benefits for same-sex couples. Whereas polls showed the state overall somewhat split on the issue, in parts of the state support or opposition was lopsided. As this became clearer, legislators became more fearful of electoral backlash. An example of this lopsidedness came a few weeks before consideration by the full House. On Town Meeting Day, 50 of the state's 246 towns considered the issue. None supported same-sex marriage and only 10 were supportive of any rights for same-sex couples.[61] In some towns the vote against same-sex marriage was 4 or 5 to 1.[62] Partisan divisions were also evident. Exit polls from a recent primary showed that a majority of the state's Democrats supported same-sex marriage and 70 percent supported domestic partnerships. Eighty percent of Republicans opposed same-sex marriage and 60 percent opposed domestic partnerships.[63] Rural, small-town Republicans and, to some extent Democrats, had a lot to lose in supporting same-sex marriage rights. Opposition was less amorphous at that point, and morality politics began to compete with liberal legal norms.

Consequently, House consideration was delayed because of a lack of votes for the Judiciary Committee's bill.[64] By the time the bill was taken up, there were no guarantees of passage. In fact, when debate began in the House, opponents were only a few votes shy of defeating the bill. But, at the last minute, a provision was added to reaffirm that marriage was to be only between a man and a woman, allowing those who voted for domestic partnerships to affirm traditional marriage. Also, some members were swayed by an impassioned speech given by William Lippert, the only openly gay member of the House. Indeed, many of Lippert's colleagues cried during his speech.[65] Defending same-sex relationships, Lippert told his colleagues:

> Who are we? We are committed, caring, loving individuals in a time when desire for greater commitment, greater love, greater fidelity is needed in our society, and I find it so ironic that rather than being embraced and welcomed we are seen as a threat. We are people, some of us, that in recent times endured the scourge of a terrible epidemic, and even in the midst of that epidemic have reached out and formed relationships, cared for each other, holding each other, sometimes as death arrived. Don't tell me about what a committed relationship is and isn't. I've watched my gay brothers care for each other deeply and my lesbian sisters nurse and care. There is no love and no commitment any greater than that I've seen, what I know.[66]

An opponent of civil unions was sure that this speech swayed some crucial votes,[67] thereby carving out enough space for passage. Thus, this rich liberalism was determinative, but only after the Vermont Supreme Court created the framework. A speech like this would have done little to affect public policy in the absence of the court's decision.

During the floor debate, opponents made two primary arguments: First, the supreme court has usurped its authority at the expense of the legislature and the people. In the words of one member, "We are not back in jolly old England.... We don't have to get down and kiss the shoes of the five royalty on the fifth floor [the Supreme Court]." Second, opponents made religious and moral arguments that homosexuality was sinful and destructive of the public good. Republican Nancy Sheltra, in a rambling, vicious speech, declared that by approving of same-sex relationships "we will be legalizing sodomy [Vermont repealed its sodomy law in 1977, a point obviously lost on Sheltra]," and this would lead to more disease, especially HIV. She also asserted that same-sex relationships always have problems, and the state was risking the wrath of God. A member questioned the relevance of Sheltra's comments, and she was instructed by the speaker to keep her comments to the civil unions issue. Supporters generally used arguments of inclusion and fairness and often made analogies to the other civil rights struggles and personal experiences of gay and lesbian friends and relatives.[68]

Ultimately, the House passed the bill by a vote of 79 to 68. The vote was largely along party lines, with fifty-seven Democrats and fourteen Republicans supporting the bill and fifty Republicans and eighteen Democrats opposing. Women were the decisive factor in the vote: They favored the bill by a 35 to 9 margin, while men voted against the bill by a margin of 60 to 41. Effective, united lobbying by same-sex marriage advocates also explains the bill's success. Recall that the Vermont Freedom to Marry Task Force had laid the groundwork for this outcome five years earlier by, in addition to the litigation, cultivating political support, speaking to local civic and religious groups, and putting together a modern grassroots lobbying campaign, with brochures, press packets, and videos (although, as I have indicated, the litigation was the centerpiece of their efforts). Take It to the People, on the other hand, was always playing catch-up and never spoke with a unified voice. Their message of saving the traditions of marriage often was drowned out by political and religious extremism, elements that do not sit well with most Vermonters.[69]

The Senate also approved the civil unions bill by nearly a 2 to 1 vote.[70] By this time, the large fights were over, and the momentum had clearly shifted in favor of civil unions. Some statements made by senators are useful to highlight for this discussion. Senator McCormack embraced the court's decision, emphasizing that the purpose of a constitution is to protect minorities from the majority. Indeed, in Dworkinian terms he declared that "[c]onstitutional rights trump the will of the majority." This is in contrast to opponents of civil unions who argued in purely majoritarian terms. Another senator urged the body to treat same-sex couples "with decency and respect."[71] Senator Julius Canns, who had been an early supporter of a domestic partnership approach, came to reject the idea that this issue was one of civil rights: "This is not a civil rights problem. This is a sex problem."[72] Governor Dean signed the law without much fanfare, in private with only fifteen staff members looking on[73]—an indication of the peculiar politics of this issue. A private signing is perhaps a direct consequence of judicially mandated, publicly controversial public policy. Despite this initial timidity, however, Dean bragged about his support of civil unions to lesbian and gay civil rights groups in his effort to gain the Democratic Party nomination for president. In Lincolnian terms he told one group: "It taught me a lot about public service, and it taught me a lot about this country—about how far we have to go, but most of all about hope, hope that we can get there."[74]

Political fallout from the civil unions bill was mixed. In a poll conducted soon after the law was passed and signed, only 24 percent of respondents said the law would be important in their choice for governor. Overall, a slight majority disapproved of the law, with 52 percent disapproving and 43 percent approving. Opponents of civil unions specifically targeted Republican members of the legislature who supported civil unions. Of the eight targeted, four were defeated in September primaries and four survived challenges.[75] In the general election, Republicans did take a majority of the seats in the House for the first time in nearly two decades. Five pro–civil unions Republicans lost, but a larger number retained their seats, including Little. In the Senate, only one pro–civil unions Democrat lost, while a handful of others survived significant challenges. Governor Dean was re-elected over an explicitly anti–civil unions challenger by a margin of 51 percent to 38 percent. A Progressive Party candidate who fully supported same-sex marriage received 10 percent of the vote, thereby giving marriage or civil unions advocates 61 percent.[76] The antiunions forces were disappointed with this result. Cummings bluntly stated, "I feel rotten." Exit polls showed the voters nearly evenly divided, with 49 percent supporting the law and 48 percent opposing.[77]

After the election Republicans quickly acted to amend the civil unions law to include other unmarried blood relatives.[78] The House passed a law explicitly banning same-sex marriage, but the Senate would not consider the legislation and Governor Dean felt the law was unnecessary.[79] The House also narrowly voted, 72 to 69, to repeal the civil unions law and replace it with a reciprocal beneficiaries bill. A bill outlawing civil unions without a replacement was more soundly defeated, since everyone knew that the court would likely step back in. But Republican leaders thought that a reciprocal beneficiaries bill would still pass constitutional muster. As one opponent of civil unions, Rev. Craig Benson, put it, "We see this [reciprocal benefits] as a step in the right direction. It's a bill that makes sense only in a world defined by Baker." Peg Flory, who replaced Little as chair of the Judiciary Committee, spearheaded this effort, as she had done in the original civil unions debate.[80] However, again, the Democratic Senate and governor were unwilling to go along. Although the law appears safe from repeal, there is still a lot of anger and frustration in the state from the usual suspects. Despite concentrated opposition to civil unions from the state's most conservative political voices, policy makers appear increasingly unwilling to alter the status quo. In the 2002 legislative session, Republican leaders declined to introduce repeal legislation, prompting the charge of "traitor" from conservatives.[81] In the 2002 elections, many anti–civil union legislators elected in 2000 were defeated.[82] Indeed, the reality of civil unions is becoming commonplace: Announcements appear in local newspapers and many merchants catering to weddings are advertising to same-sex couples.[83] Additionally, other states have been looking or will look to Vermont as a model for crafting their own civil union laws.[84] This is examined in greater detail in the next chapter.

Since the greatest difference between civil unions and marriage is the seeming lack of portability, couples taking civil unions outside of Vermont have begun to challenge this distinction in court. The Georgia Court of Appeals ruled that Vermont civil unions do not have marital status in the eyes of Georgia law, since nothing like this exists in Georgia, and Georgia passed a mini-Defense of Marriage Act. This decision appears unlikely to be overruled by the Georgia Supreme Court.[85] The Indiana Civil Liberties Union filed a suit on behalf of Indiana residents who obtained Vermont civil unions. The lead attorney for the case saw the challenge as a way to bring same-sex marriage rights to Indiana. "Our clients want to be treated just like any other citizens. They just want the same opportunity to build a life with someone they love that other Hoosiers have."[86] Legal liberalism, then, appears to see little qualitative difference between civil unions and marriage.

With more coordination and lessons learned from Hawaii and Alaska, legal activists achieved concrete policy change through the courts in Vermont. The legal process framed and controlled the political process, despite fervent opposition and a lack of willingness of the political process to act in support of relationship equality on its own. Although the immediate change was limited to one small state, the success in Vermont spurred further litigation, as well as continued backlash.

Developments after Vermont: An Evolving
      Jurisprudence and Its Backlash

INDEED, AFTER VERMONT, the process continued. Legal and political developments especially accelerated in 2003 with a decision by the Massachusetts Supreme Judicial Court mandating the recognition of same-sex marriages. This was followed by litigation in other states that resulted in decisions favorable to same-sex marriage advocates, legislative policy change in some states granting rights and recognition to same-sex couples, as well as a continued backlash in other states. Additionally, legal arguments led nonlegal actors to support same-sex marriage, as several local jurisdictions throughout the United States began to grant marriage licenses to same-sex couples early in 2004.

Following on the successful litigation in Vermont, a GLAD-sponsored suit in Massachusetts was filed in April 2001 by seven couples who lived throughout the state.[1] A year later, a superior court judge denied their claims. Like other courts that dismissed same-sex marriage claims, this court found that a plain reading of the Massachusetts marriage statute left room for only opposite sex marriage and that the history of the law confirmed this reading.[2] As for the constitutional claims, the judge refused to find a fundamental right to marry under the Massachusetts Constitution and rejected equality arguments, noting that the Massachusetts Constitution does not contain a clause similar to the "common benefits" clause of the Vermont Constitution. Judge Thomas Connolly also held that procreation was central to marriage; consequently, the legislature could rationally limit it to opposite sex couples.[3] Ultimately, the court preferred to keep the issue in the political arena, stating: "While this court understands the reasons for the plaintiff's request to reverse the Commonwealth's centuries-old legal tradition of restricting marriage to opposite-sex couples, their request should be directed to the Legislature, not the courts."[4] No legal argument could have prevailed with a court that saw the issue as a purely legislative one. Like the lower court in Vermont, this judge was unwilling to adjudicate aggressively, or bring in novel arguments, like noting changes in the nature of procreation. The case received an expedited appeal to the Massachusetts Supreme Judicial Court[5]—a court that has developed a liberal reputation, particularly when it comes to defining the family. In 1999 the court ruled that a lesbian partner was a de facto parent and granted her visitation rights.[6]

Despite the initial loss for same-sex marriage advocates, same-sex marriage opponents were committed to a process placing a constitutional amendment outlawing same-sex marriage, or any benefits for same-sex couples, on the ballot for voter approval. Conservative activists, through the group Massachusetts Citizens for Marriage, spearheaded the efforts for this "Super DOMA."[7] After a controversial signature drive in which there was evidence of misleading tactics on the part of signature gatherers (many signers thought they were signing a petition to ban the slaughtering of horses), enough signatures were attained to send the proposal to the legislature, where two consecutive sessions were needed to give it 25 percent approval—a seemingly low threshold even in a progressive state like Massachusetts.[8] Activists opposed to the amendment were anticipating approval by the legislature and braced for a fight in the electorate by 2004.[9] They also put pressure on legislative leaders, particularly Thomas Birmingham, the Senate president who was running for governor, to kill the amendment. Even though Birmingham opposed the amendment, he felt some pressure to allow the democratic process to take its course and not be viewed as a closed-door insider.[10] But he did everything he could to block a vote on what he called a "hateful" and "mean-spirited" action.[11] A joint committee also unanimously recommended that the legislature reject the amendment, the chair of the committee, Harriette Chandler, stating, "It just doesn't fit with the guarantees that [the state constitution] offers."[12] Ultimately, the amendment was killed on a procedural vote in July 2002, with the legislature voting 137 to 53 to adjourn a constitutional convention before a direct vote on the amendment was taken.[13] This was important for gay rights advocates, since the amendment likely would have been approved. Public sentiment was moving in the direction of support for same-sex marriage, but majority support had not yet emerged. The delay allowed more time to build political support, now framed by litigation.

The political tide was indeed shifting. All candidates for governor in the 2002 election supported some form of recognition for same-sex couples, even the Republican Mitt Romney, the eventual winner. One candidate, former Clinton Labor Secretary Robert Reich, supported full same-sex marriage rights. Certainly, Reich was trying to out-liberal his opponents in a five-way Democratic primary, but his position was unique. According to Reich, "It's the next frontier of civil rights, and I feel very comfortable with being supportive of gay civil marriage."[14]

An interesting dynamic developed in the opponent's strategy of the amendment. This strategy had less to do with affirming same-sex couples out of liberal equality than protecting the children of same-sex couples. GLAD lawyer Jennifer Levi, responding to Judge Connolly's decision, stated: "I think what's unfortunate here is this decision really highlights that children of same-sex couples are provided fewer benefits than other children in the state. What we are arguing is that all children deserve and need the same level of protection."[15] Levi's legal arguments in court had been about fundamental rights, equality, and privacy, but her political arguments were quite different with her focus on children. Certainly, other arguments more directly addressing the rights of sexual minorities were introduced into the political arena, but the upfront discussion of children reflects the relative inability of same-sex marriage advocates in the United States to address the legal issues head-on in the political arena. The resulting political dynamic, at least in Massachusetts, saw advocates of the same-sex marriage ban emphasizing that the amendment would not affect domestic partnerships and the like, when it almost certainly would, in order to play down the discriminatory nature of the amendment. At the same time, opponents downplayed the discrimination against same-sex couples and focused instead on potential harm to children. The politics of same-sex marriage in the United States can cause interesting role reversals on the part of policy advocates.

Another role reversal was evident in Massachusetts. The movement for the amendment was not triggered by the litigation; the reverse was true. GLAD decided to file the suit, after a decade of hesitation, in response to the anticipated amendment as a way to grab the political and legal momentum. In this instance, then, litigation was a response to political developments. As Mary Bonauto of GLAD put it: "We knew our opponents wanted to change the constitution. We know we'd be talking about marriage anyway. Hawaii ensured that, and Vermont double-ensured that. We didn't want to lose this opportunity."[16] Indeed, activist attorneys in New England had been meeting since 1993 to consider litigation options. The group decided to initiate the Vermont litigation in 1996 but held off in other states. It was the threat of the amendment in Massachusetts that triggered the lawsuit in that state.[17] These lawyers, then, were politically shrewd and cautious, trying to choose the right time legally and politically to initiate litigation.

The lawyers also learned from the Vermont litigation. They felt they had made a strategic mistake in the Vermont litigation by excessively focusing on the tangible benefits that come with marriage. This, in their judgment, allowed the Vermont court to see something like civil unions as an acceptable alternative. In the Massachusetts litigation, then, they shifted the thrust of their arguments. According to Mary Bonauto, "We spent more time . . . talking about how marriage is a basic civil and human right. . . . We talked about what marriage is in our culture."[18] Indeed, Bonauto made this clear to the court during oral argument.[19] Like Vermont, the litigants were carefully chosen to put the best "face" on the litigation and assist in the public education campaign.[20]

The opportunity was not wasted. In November 2003, after several months' delay, a divided Massachusetts Supreme Judicial Court ruled in favor of same-sex marriage and reversed the lower court. The 4 to 3 decision, like its predecessors in Hawaii, Vermont, and Canada, saw marriage rights as positive rights required by the Massachusetts Constitution:

> The individual liberty and equality safeguards of the Massachusetts Constitution protect both "freedom from" unwarranted government intrusion into protected spheres of life and "freedom to" partake in benefits created by the state for the common good. . . . Both freedoms are involved here. Whether and whom to marry, how to express sexual intimacy, and whether and how to establish a family—these are among the most basic of every individual's liberty and due process rights.[21]

In fact, the court argued that "the decision whether and whom to marry is among life's momentous acts of self-definition."[22]

Consequently, the court found, under a nondeferential rational basis review, that Massachusetts lacked any legitimate justification for restricting marriage to opposite-sex couples, and took the aggressive step of redefining marriage itself to include same-sex couples. Like its predecessors, the court rejected the procreation justification as logically suspect and not sufficient to prove a "rational basis."[23]

Like other courts affirming the equality of same-sex couples, the Massachusetts court noted that state constitutions are more protective of individual rights, and that the Massachusetts Constitution "affirms the dignity and equality of all individuals. It forbids the creation of second-class citizens."[24]

The decision was stayed for 180 days to allow the legislature to respond, but it was clear from the opinion that this was not to be a Vermont-style legislative solution. The legislature was directed to alter marriage statutes to fit the court's opinion, not to find an alternative "civil unions" solution.[25] Despite the sweeping nature of the opinion, the majority insisted it was merely building on previous adjudication: Citations of *Baker v. State*, the recently decided *Lawrence v. Texas* (*Lawrence* was handed down while the Massachusetts court was considering the case and likely gave impetus to forming the majority), and recent Canadian decisions were prominent in the opinion.[26] The majority also made a point to note the similarities to *Loving v. Virginia* and noted the California Supreme Court's role in laying the foundation for that opinion in 1940.[27] The majority thus saw itself in the same tradition of innovation in civil rights jurisprudence.

Justice John Greaney concurred with the outcome, but would have applied *Baehr*-style equal protection gender analysis, like Johnson's concurrence in *Baker*.[28] (One of the reasons, perhaps, the other judges in the majority did not take this route is that when Massachusetts's equal rights amendment was ratified it was understood that it did not invalidate the state's ban on same-sex marriage.)[29] This concurrence was a clear example of substantive reasoning. According to Greaney, "This case calls for a higher level of legal analysis. Precisely, the case requires that we confront ingrained assumptions with respect to historically accepted roles of men and women within the institution of marriage."[30] The judges in the majority, then, clearly did not see their role as one of deferentially applying formal legal reasoning. In fact, Greaney was clear about his normative motivation. As he stated, "Simple principles of decency dictate that we extend to the plaintiffs, and to their new status, full acceptance, tolerance, and respect."[31]

The dissenters mostly objected to the court's aggressiveness—they saw the question of same-sex marriage more appropriately addressed by the legislature.[32] They emphasized that the rational basis test was a minimal, deferential one. And, unlike the majority's substantive reasoning, they chose a more formal approach. For example, Justice Francis Spina distinguished the case from *Loving*, since, "the Massachusetts Legislature has erected no barrier to marriage that intentionally discriminates against anyone." In other words, if gay people wish to get married, they can marry someone of the opposite gender. The irony of the statement was apparently lost on Spina, since this is the same kind of formal argument presented by political and judicial defenders of antimiscegenation statutes: all races were equally discriminated against, since none could marry the other. The U.S. Supreme Court clearly rejected this view in *Loving*. Also, although the majority saw an evolving jurisprudence in support of same-sex marriage claims, stemming from *Loving* and the more recent same-sex marriage cases, the dissenters saw cases like *Baehr v. Lewin* as outliers in a jurisprudence that clearly views marriage as heterosexually defined.

Even though the dissenters noted that they would have little objection to legislative sanction of same-sex marriage, there was a conservative core to their arguments, most significantly evidenced by citation of a marriage precedent from 1810. That case, *Milford v. Worcester*, referred to marriage as an institution "intended to regulate, chasten, and refine, the intercourse between the sexes; and to multiply, preserve, and improve the species."[33] Justice Cordy's dissent (joined by the other dissenters) fully agreed with this view of marriage, while relegating changes in the institution to the status of quaint window dressing, which does not detract from the traditional essence of the institution. Thus, the two sides of the court not only disagreed about process; theirs was also a fundamental disagreement about the nature of marriage itself. In the majority opinion, Chief Justice Margaret Marshall described marriage as an "exclusive commitment of two individuals to each other [that] nurtures love and mutual support."[34] This was a fight between modern liberals who emphasize autonomy, liberation, and freedom and neoconservatives who value social institutions that impose limits on individuals and structure social intercourse.

Events surrounding the decision demonstrate that the result was far from a sure thing, since it occurred in the context of some bad blood between the court and the legislature, pointing to the likelihood that it was more of a legal than political decision. In 2002 the court endured a showdown with the legislature over a public financing law. The court had ruled that the legislature was in violation of the law, which upset many in the legislature, but the court lacked the authority to enforce its decision and, essentially, was forced to back down. As a result of the decision, legislators threatened to reduce the judiciary's budget and staff.[35] Given this, one might predict that another confrontation with the legislature was not in the cards, but the *Goodridge* decision demonstrates otherwise. The court was willing to take more political heat. The fact that the court took on the legislature demonstrates that the majority were motivated by law more than politics. Indeed, the author of the opinion, Chief Justice Margaret Marshall, is a civil rights progressive who pays attention to global civil rights developments and decisions of courts in other nations, especially in her native country of South Africa. Marshall was appointed by the socially liberal William Weld, on the basis of her civil rights activism, who praised her for her "passion for justice."[36]

Not all the judges were appointed to be socially liberal activists, and, in fact, the court is conservative on many issues, like crime and personal injury cases.[37] The two liberals, Roderick Ireland and Greaney, sided with Marshall, and the fourth vote came from Justice Judith Cowin, who is generally considered to be a conservative. In fact, Cowin appeared to be skeptical of the plaintiff's claims at oral argument, asking, "Why should we do something that virtually no other state has done?"[38] It is likely that the eight months the court took to render its decision was needed to secure this fourth vote through lobbying by Marshall.[39]

The political response to the sweeping decision left many policy makers confused. Leading law makers, the governor, and the attorney general thought that civil unions would suffice, despite the court's clear language to the contrary.[40] In fact, the court had to clarify its decision in a second ruling requested by the state, affirming that its intention was to have same-sex marriage legalized in the state.[41] Governor Mitt Romney put his political clout into starting the amendment process again in order to ban same-sex marriages. After considerable maneuvering and political tumult, the legislature narrowly passed an amendment that would ban same-sex marriage but allow for civil unions.[42] Equality was affirmed by the legislature, but many politicians in this heavily Catholic state took a traditional view of marriage. However, 2006 is the earliest the amendment would take effect (it needs to get through two legislative sessions), and after the court's 180-day stay expired, the state began granting marriage licenses to same-sex couples on May 17, 2004. Two years of legal same-sex marriages will likely make passage of the amendment more difficult because of the public education effects of the marriages and the potential unwillingness of voters to divorce these couples en masse.[43]

Romney was able, however, to limit marriages through the use of a 1913 law originally intended to allow the state to not recognize interracial marriages. The law, not enforced for decades until same-sex marriages were at issue, limits marriage in Massachusetts to residents of the state. Some county clerks defied the governor's order to enforce the law for same-sex couples, but a judge sided with the governor in August 2004.[44]

Public opinion in Massachusetts, unlike the nation as a whole, is clearly supportive of relationship equality. In the wake of the decision, a poll found 50 percent support for the court's decision with 38 percent opposed—a fairly strong public affirmation of the decision. In the same poll, opposition to a constitutional amendment stood at 53 percent with only 36 percent of respondents supporting such an amendment.[45] Another poll immediately after the decision found 49 percent support for same-sex marriage and 76 percent support for full marriage benefits just not called marriage, with 54 percent opposed to an amendment.[46] This level of support for the decision is consistent with polling conducted before the decision. A poll in April 2003, a month after oral arguments, found 50 percent of respondents supporting same-sex marriage rights.[47] And the decision itself appeared to soften opposition to same-sex marriage, from 44 percent before the decision to 38 percent after.[48]

It was only after legislators and the governor denounced the decision that support began to fall slightly. A poll in February 2004 found support for same-sex marriage at 42 percent (64 percent favored civil unions), and, by a split of 49 percent to 41 percent, respondents said that the court went too far in its decision.[49] Thus, the public backed off the "marriage" aspect of the decision, but still strongly favored equality for same-sex couples. In April a poll showed that 40 percent supported same-sex marriage, 28 percent supported civil unions, and only 17 percent favored no recognition.[50]

Undoubtedly, the media coverage of the litigation and the public relations efforts of GLAD and other groups shifted public opinion to a favorable position on same-sex marriage rights. Opinion in Massachusetts was divided over same-sex marriage (while strongly in favor of relationship equality), but much more supportive than most states. Consequently, it would be a mischaracterization to call the decision counter-majoritarian. Far from coming from left field, the decision was grounded in an evolving jurisprudence, taken from other state courts, the U.S. Supreme Court, and courts of other nations. And it was not radically out of line with public opinion in the state, but, arguably, slightly ahead of it with its clear support for full civil marriage equality. The litigation itself, and the public campaign surrounding it, helped to shift public opinion in favor of equality for same-sex couples.

## NEW JERSEY

The Lambda-sponsored suit in New Jersey is a clear example of forum shopping. As evidenced by *Dale v. Boy Scouts of America*, discussed in Chapter 2, the New Jersey Supreme Court is quite progressive on gay rights issues and has been at the forefront of family law changes favorable to sexual minorities. In 2000 the court unanimously ruled that same-sex partners who raise children together possess rights identical to married parents in the event of their separation.[51] The suit had been in the works for about a year prior to the filing in June 2002, and Lambda was hoping to capitalize on the visibility of the challenges facing same-sex partners in the aftermath of the September 11, 2001, terrorist attacks.[52]

The suit emphasized equal protection arguments but also saw the denial of same-sex marriage rights as violative of the right to privacy (this is the first count of the complaint), since "the right to marry involves one of life's most intimate choices, of a deep personal nature."[53] Again, advocates of same-sex marriage recognize the salience of this argument, but the constraints of U.S. political culture also serve as an impediment on this issue. Matt Daniels, executive director of the Alliance for Marriage (a national anti–same-sex marriage group), stated the apparent status of majoritarian political thinking: "Gays and lesbians have a right to live as they choose. But they don't have a right to redefine marriage for our entire society."[54]

Some political traction also exists in New Jersey for a favorable outcome from the perspective of gay rights claims, though probably not full marriage. Given the lawsuit and the state's burgeoning progressive political climate, a Vermont-style outcome is perhaps a possibility. Indeed, in this progressive state even Republicans competing for a Senate nomination in 2002 softened their opposition to same-sex marriage claims. Two candidates, Diane Allen and John Matheussen, opposed a national constitutional amendment (with one emphasizing the need to protect against sexual orientation discrimination), and the third, Douglas Forrester, hedged, saying that he needed time to study the issue further.[55] In addition, Democratic governor James McGreevey had planned before the litigation to submit domestic partnership legislation, but his advisors felt the suit would hurt this effort by creating a backlash.[56] McGreevey opposed the litigation. But reflecting the litigators' faith in their legal strategy, the lead Lambda attorney countered the governor by asserting, "This is a matter for the courts."[57]

However, the first round of court involvement did not go well for advocates. A lower court judge dismissed the suit but urged the legislature to address the unequal treatment of same-sex couples.[58] The decision is, of course, being appealed.[59]

Recall that lower courts in Vermont and Massachusetts ruled in a similar fashion. These courts are typically unwilling to aggressively make policy and are more deferential to legislatures. Such has been the case with recent court refusals to change policy on marriage in Arizona and Indiana.[60]

The domestic partnership legislation supported by McGreevey was approved by the legislature in January 2004 and offers a limited menu of rights to same-sex couples and persons over the age of sixty-two, thus falling short of Vermont's civil unions but still a significant policy change that recognizes same-sex couples. The legislation was narrowly approved in the House but sailed through the Senate on a 23 to 9 vote.[61] Given this legislative support for relationship equality and, as will be detailed in Chapter 11, the fact that public opinion in the state is also supportive of equality, if the high court rules in favor of same-sex marriage, one could expect an outcome similar to that in Massachusetts.

## RHODE ISLAND, CONNECTICUT, AND NEW YORK

Attempts to change policy are being made in states without the cover of litigation, but generally less successfully (with the exception of California, which is detailed below). Same-sex marriage/domestic partnership laws have been formally submitted in the New York and Rhode Island legislatures where they have stalled. In Rhode Island, a gay state legislator, Michael Pisaturo, has been symbolically submitting same-sex marriage bills since 1996 without calling for a hearing or a vote.[62] A hearing finally was held in March 2000 as a result of the developments in Vermont, but the bill was pulled for lack of support (recall the difficulty of the sodomy law repeal in Rhode Island only a few years earlier). "I have no doubt . . . that in five years' time, the bill will pass," the bill's sponsor Pisaturo stated, taking a longer-term perspective.[63]

Connecticut provides an example of the problematic nature of the legislative process for same-sex marriage claims in the United States. High legislative hopes have resulted in concrete legislation, but initial legislation was quite watered-down. The problem was not necessarily a lack of popular support, since polls showed majority support for significant legal rights for same-sex couples. Instead, rather than the noble forum for high-minded deliberation envisioned by contemporary republican revivalists, the process that played out in Connecticut reflected a minimalist approach to law making born out of often irrational short-term fear on the part of elected officials responding to a few loud voices opposed to marriage rights for same-sex couples. Ultimately, though, events next door in Massachusetts and progressive public opinion led to the enactment of a civil unions law in the state in 2005.

Motivated by developments in Vermont and the preceding year's activity in the legislature on gay rights (a law was passed and signed by the governor that allowed same-sex couples to adopt children), activists and legislators began a process toward a civil union-style approach in 2001.[64] A public hearing was held, but the bill never got out of committee. According to one legislator, Republican Peter Nystrom, opposed to the legislation, "It is something that I and other legislators would oppose by all means."[65] He did not say that he would support legislation that carried public support. His was a "fight at any cost and filibuster" approach. Also, opponents claimed to have public opinion on their side. A lobbyist with the Connecticut Catholic Conference, Marie Hilliard, asserted: "I think what we witnessed this year, and what polls indicate, is that the people of Connecticut are not in support of the legalization of same-sex unions. My hope is that legislators will represent the people who sent them to the General Assembly and not special interest groups."[66] However, it appears that this special interest group statement had things reversed. A poll taken a year later found that 47 percent of respondents in the state strongly supported a registry and rights for same-sex couples and 27 percent moderately supported that idea.[67] Recall the political reaction in Vermont: There was a backlash for certain legislators, but, overall, public opinion favored civil unions. Given that Connecticut is more urban and suburban than Vermont, one might surmise that the opposition would be even less powerful, though no less vocal.

Despite this, for several years the legislative result in Connecticut was far less satisfying from the perspective of gay rights claims than in Vermont, where legal language and principles framed the deliberation. Separate civil unions and marriage bills were submitted in 2002 that went nowhere, but a law was enacted that gives certain limited rights. The law received bipartisan support, for example, passing 30 to 6 in the Senate, but fell far short of Vermont's civil unions: It was de-gayed in that any two people could benefit from the arrangement and only allows medical decisions to be made by a legally designated person, allows private visits in nursing homes, and allows emergency phone calls in the workplace from the designee.[68] There likely was room for more in Connecticut, but the legislature was able to produce only this limited statute. In the absence of a framework created by legal arguments, real change in this area can be difficult. Likely sensing this, as well as a sympathetic judiciary, GLAD filed a same-sex marriage suit in August 2004.[69] And, in a rather quick turnaround, the legislature enacted civil unions legislation in 2005.[70]

Perhaps surprisingly, New York has lagged other progressive states on relationship equality. In 2002 the legislature finally passed an antidiscrimination law that had been pending for thirty years.[71] In August 2004 the legislature took a first step in approving hospital visitation rights for same-sex and opposite-sex domestic partners, lagging far behind other progressive states like New Jersey and California that have enacted more sweeping legislation without direct judicial mandate. There was only one vote against the hospital visitation legislation.[72] Neither, however, has New York passed a "mini-DOMA." Attorney General Eliot Spitzer said that New York would recognize same-sex marriages performed in Massachusetts.[73] Mostly, though, the state has been in a bit of a policy stalemate, caught between a liberal political tradition and Republican control of the state Senate and the governorship.[74] As a result, Lambda Legal and Empire State Pride, the state gay rights organization, initiated same-sex marriage litigation in 2004.[75] Lower courts in New York have ruled in favor of and against same-sex marriage claims.[76]

## CALIFORNIA: A DOMESTIC PARTNERSHIP LAW AND THE CIVIL DISOBEDIENCE OF MAYOR NEWSOM— IS MARRIAGE NEXT?

Numerous localities have instituted domestic partnership benefits or relationship recognition for government employees, but coverage for all citizens is rare. California, however, has joined the ranks of Hawaii and Vermont, starting in 2001 and expanding the policy in 2003 to rival the benefits offered by Vermont's civil unions. The process took several years and many convoluted turns, but it was initiated in the wake of the *Baehr* decision and illustrates the salience of the issue defined by courts in liberal language over the objections of traditional arguments. But it also points to the limitations due to a lack of direct legal intervention and rhetorical cover. California also became a forum for same-sex marriage debates when, in an act of civil disobedience, San Francisco Mayor Gavin Newsom granted marriage licenses to same-sex couples in February 2004. This triggered two avenues of litigation in the state: one challenging the mayor's authority to grant licenses and broader challenges to California's policy forbidding same-sex marriage. At the same time, a serious same-sex marriage legalization bill was being considered by the legislature.[77]

Bills to create domestic partnership policies were introduced in the early 1990s, but the opposition of the religious right in California prevented serious consideration.[78] Due to the developments in Hawaii and a change in tactics, a bill passed the legislature in 1994. The change in tactic involved a broadening of those included in the legislation to senior citizens who live together but do not choose to marry.[79] The legislation was introduced on Valentine's Day 1994. In language both reflective of America's love of privacy and free choice and the less dominant liberal strain of state affirmation, the bill's sponsor stated: "There are thousands of couples who live together and for one reason or another choose not to be married. It's about time the state of California recognized these relationships."[80] Opponents, of course, saw things quite differently. They were not willing to let stand the attempt to broaden the appeal of the law. As one legislator stated: "The real purpose of this bill is to establish a state-sanctioned relationship for all people, but particularly for the homosexual community, that is equal to marriage. It is an obvious attempt to (make) legitimate the homosexual lifestyle."[81]

The attempt to create a coalition outside the gay rights community by broadening the legislation was ultimately successful, to a point. A *Los Angeles Times* poll indicated that 52 percent of registered voters approved of the measure, while 37 percent opposed it. The legislature narrowly approved the legislation with each chamber registering the exact number of votes needed for a majority, largely along party lines with Democrats supporting the measure.[82] However, stating, "We need to strengthen, not weaken, the institution of marriage," Republican Governor Pete Wilson vetoed the bill.[83]

In sessions that followed, opponents and advocates of same-sex marriage/domestic partnerships reached a stalemate, with Republican attempts to define marriage as only between a man and a woman being linked to domestic partnership legislation. This combination was better for Democrats, since they could have the best of both political worlds. As then Lieutenant Governor Gray Davis stated: "I've always opposed gay marriages, but I support domestic partnerships."[84] In California, this was a politically viable position. By 1997, three years after Wilson's veto, public support for domestic partnerships had increased. A Field poll showed that 67 percent of Californians approved of granting basic rights, like hospital visitation, medical power of attorney, and conservatorship. Fifty-nine percent favored more extensive rights, including family leave, insurance coverage, and death benefits for domestic partners. According to a spokesperson for the Field poll, "The public feels the idea of two gays living together and committing themselves to each other and devoting years to that is something that should be recognized and favored."[85] Also notable was the comment of the leading advocate of domestic partnerships, Assemblywoman Carole Midgen. During debate on the issue in 1996 she stated: "Government ought not to interfere with the fundamental rights of consenting adults to form unions with each other."[86] Again, advocates of relationship equality felt the need to ground the defense of their position in privacy and the language of negative freedom. In 1994 the emphasis was on choice; two years later Midgen was emphasizing privacy.

Ultimately, Midgen's efforts were successful, albeit incrementally. In 1999 she was able to gain passage of a domestic partner registration bill that allowed same-sex couples and all couples over the age of sixty-two to register with the state and receive minimal benefits like hospital visitation rights. The original bill was stronger, but Governor Davis said he would sign only this watered-down version.[87] Opponents claimed that even this minimal victory opened the door to same-sex marriage, and Midgen put the most positive spin on the situation, stating "It's a truly precedent-setting, historic step."[88] She knew of what she spoke, since two years later a fuller domestic partners bill was passed and signed into law. The 2001 law was passed in the wake of Proposition 22, which outlawed same-sex marriage (by a margin of 61 percent to 39 percent, about 10 percent less than bans in Hawaii and Alaska), but it was only eclipsed by Vermont's civil unions law in its scope. Davis was now ready to support a substantive law. Approximately a dozen benefits were conferred, including the right to sue for wrongful death, the right to make medical decisions, adoptions of partner's children, the use of sick leave for partner care, the right to act as a conservator, and the right to keep unemployment benefits when relocating with a partner.

Advocates hoped to go even further and introduced civil union legislation.[89] However, the bill was withdrawn from consideration in January 2002 after its sponsor saw a lack of support in the legislature, especially in an election year.[90] Governor Davis appointed a task force to examine Vermont's civil unions law and see what could be taken from it for California.[91] In the 2002 session, the legislature also enacted, and Davis signed, a bill extending laws on intestacy to same-sex partners.[92] Following this pattern of incrementalism, the legislature passed, and Davis signed (in the midst of the recall effort), a further extension of benefits under the domestic partnership legislation. The list of benefits for California same-sex domestic partnerships approaches the scope of rights and benefits under Vermont's civil unions.[93]

In less than a year, events in California further accelerated. In February 2004, only a month after taking office, Mayor Gavin Newsom directed the county clerk of San Francisco to begin granting same-sex marriage licenses. Roughly 4,000 same-sex couples were granted licenses before the California Supreme Court imposed an injunction against San Francisco granting the licenses.[94] Other cities and counties throughout the United States followed Newsom's lead, including the mayor of New Paltz, New York.[95]

Although Newsom's act was not technically judicial, he claimed that his decision was based on constitutional principles of equal protection of the law, no doubt inspired by the Massachusetts decision. His act of civil disobedience expressed dissatisfaction with the majoritarian status quo and its arrogant (as defined in Chapter 3) refusal to consider the equality of same-sex couples. This political actor took a legal approach, and a local official thus engaged in constitutional interpretation.

Newsom's actions and Massachusetts's developments also stimulated legislative activity in California. For the first time in the United States, a legislative committee approved same-sex marriage legislation when the Assembly Judiciary Committee voted 8 to 3 to approve the bill.[96] The legislation stalled after that, but leaders plan to reintroduce the bill in 2005, and some are confident that it will pass, sending it to Governor Arnold Schwarzenegger who has made ambiguous statements about his support for marriage, while clearly supporting civil unions.[97] Public opinion also trended toward support for same-sex marriage in California. The Field poll found support in 1977 at 28 percent, in 1985 at 30 percent, in 1997 at 39 percent, in 2003 at 42 percent, and in 2004 at 44 percent.[98] Given that the largest jump occurred in 1997 when Hawaii was in the headlines and California policy makers began to address the issue in response, it appears likely that litigation has contributed to this shift in opinion.

The California Supreme Court ultimately invalidated Newsom's actions and the marriages that were performed. Although sharply critical of Newsom from a separation of powers standpoint, the court went out of its way to note that the substantive question of the constitutionality of the same-sex marriage ban was still unresolved. It simply asserted that the courts will ultimately make this determination. Although the court was unanimous on the question of Newsom's authority, two justices dissented from voiding of the marriage licenses. Using remarkably affirming language, Justice Joyce Kennard asserted: "Individuals in loving same-sex relationships have waited years, sometimes several decades, for a chance to wed, yearning to obtain the public validation that only marriage can give." Therefore, according to Kennard, it was premature to void the marriages until the constitutional question was definitively resolved.[99]

Certainly, developments in California, while not directly resulting from litigation, were an outgrowth of same-sex marriage litigation. The initial wave of legislative activity came in the wake of the *Baehr* decision, and the domestic partnership laws were enacted after the decisions in Vermont and Massachusetts. But the case also reflects the limits of political efforts without the direct cover of litigation. Initially, without the issue being directly framed by legal language, advocates in California had to "play politics," watering down and broadening the legislation, especially to include seniors. Despite public support, conservative political forces were able to frustrate efforts toward the creation of a domestic partnership framework for several years. And advocates chose their language carefully, reflecting this broad appeal, and they often relied on appeals to negative freedom and tried to emphasize that their goal was to get the government "off the backs" of committed relationships while actually seeking governmental recognition of these relationships. They knew well the parameters of U.S. political culture, especially that which is purely political and not augmented by legal language. Given the actions of Mayor Newsom and the ongoing litigation, this dynamic may change, providing more support for legislative and legal same-sex marriage claims.

## A TREND ON THE WEST COAST?

Events on the West Coast accelerated in 2004 where, bucking the trend of lower court wariness, trial courts in Oregon and Washington ruled in favor of same-sex relationship equality. They did not, of course, resolve the issue definitively, but their decisions and the events that led to them shed more light on the role of courts in this area.

Following Mayor Newsom's actions, Multnomah County (Portland) in Oregon granted marriage licenses to same-sex couples.[100] The county attorney submitted a confidential memo to the county commission stating that it was the county's obligation to grant marriage licenses to same-sex couples. Attorney Agnes Sowle maintained that the refusal of licenses to these couples contravened the Oregon Constitution, in particular Article I, Section 20—a privileges and immunity clause that acts as an equal protection clause in Oregon jurisprudence. At the center of the legal analysis was the case *Tanner v. OHSU*, in which the Oregon Court of Appeals found sexual orientation to be a suspect classification.[101] On this advice, the commissioners made their decision to grant licenses in a conference call, relying on the chair's executive authority. No vote was taken. The decision came from consultations with commissioners and Basic Rights Oregon, who requested such a decision in late January, interestingly, before Newsom's action but after the Massachusetts decision.[102] Critics argued that the move violated open meetings laws.[103] The commission acted quickly, they claimed, to avoid the possibility of a court enjoining them from granting the licenses.[104] Ultimately, the commission took a public vote affirming the action, but the political controversy lingered.[105] An effort to recall the commissioners was initiated, then abandoned, but the chair of the commission, Diane Linn, ultimately apologized for errors in handing the situation.[106]

Like San Francisco, the decision was perhaps not a surprise in a liberal city such as Portland. Indeed, most leading political figures in the city supported the substance of the decision.[107] In 2000 the county commission approved a domestic partnership registry for same-sex couples.[108] Another liberal jurisdiction in the state, Benton County (Corvalis), also decided to grant same-sex marriage licenses. But, after being threatened by the attorney general, the county made the interesting move of halting the issuance of all marriage licenses until the courts ultimately resolved the constitutional questions.[109]

A growing legal consensus began to emerge that Oregon courts, based on the recent evolution of state jurisprudence, would be skeptical of the denial of marriage rights to same-sex couples. Shortly after the county began issuing licenses, the Oregon attorney general issued an opinion that, while highly critical of the tactics of the Multnomah officials, predicted that the state high court would invalidate the policy, using basically the same analysis of Agnes Sowle.[110] The legislature's chief counsel came to the same conclusion.[111] Even a leading litigant against the county expected such an outcome, arguing that civil unions, not marriage, would satisfy the requirements of the Oregon Constitution.[112] The state's attorneys also argued this position in court.[113]

And the first court to adjudicate the question agreed with them. Suits initiated from both sides of the question were consolidated into a suit in the Multnomah County Circuit Court.[114] Two judges in that circuit affirmed the emerging legal consensus: Judge Dale Koch refused to grant an injunction to stop the issuance of licenses requested by an anti–same-sex marriage groups on the grounds that they stood little chance of proving that the licenses were unconstitutional, and, soon thereafter, another circuit court judge, Frank Bearden, found the denial of marriage to same-sex couples violated the Oregon Constitution.[115]

Bearden's decision followed the logic of Sowle and the attorney general, particularly the focus on *Tanner*.[116] The decision also relied heavily on *Goodridge* and *Baker* but most closely followed the tactics of the Vermont decision. Bearden found that limiting benefits that stemmed from marriage was a form of sexual orientation discrimination that triggered strict scrutiny, following *Tanner*, but he ordered the legislature to create a remedy that could include a civil unions–style approach.[117] Bearden also ordered the state registrar to register the marriages performed by Multnomah County (they had been in limbo) but ordered the county to refrain from issuing new licenses until the issue of constitutionality was finally resolved.[118] The Oregon Court of Appeals later fast-tracked the appeal to the supreme court, while also requiring the marriages to be officially recorded.[119] Ultimately, the legislature did not act, since a measure banning same-sex marriage qualified for the ballot in the November 2004 election, and legislative leaders were unwilling to call a special session to consider the issue, preferring to leave it to the voters.[120] The measure passed with 57 percent of the vote.[121]

Despite its history of civil rights innovation and its position at the forefront of the new judicial federalism,[122] the Oregon Supreme Court invalidated the marriage licenses of the same-sex couples and declined to rule on the civil unions issue, leaving it to the legislature. Given the civil union/domestic partnership emphasis of the Bearden decision, the high court could have a constitutional violation in the denial of benefits for same-sex couples. Indeed, the *Tanner* decision stipulated that the finding of sexual orientation as a suspect classification did not necessarily doom heterosexual-only marriage. However, the court narrowly ruled that county officials lacked the authority to grant marriage licenses and that the civil unions question was not the direct focus of the lawsuit, only the marriage question.[123]

There is also political support in Oregon for a California-style solution of same-sex domestic partnerships and heterosexual-only marriage. Polls show public support for domestic partnerships, and leading politicians have advocated this, including Governor Ted Kulongoski, who stated, "We are one state and one people, and we must treat all citizens fairly. . . . Those gay and lesbian couples should have all of the state-sanctioned rights and responsibilities that extend to heterosexual couples."[124] Significant policy change in favor of relationship equality is possible in Oregon despite the reluctance of the state's highest court. But the legal consensus has undoubtedly affected the political process.

Interestingly, whereas the California litigation was separated into two legal questions, the legitimacy of Newsom's authority and the constitutionality of the same-sex marriage ban, the litigation in Oregon did not focus on the authority question; rather, the emphasis was on the constitutional questions. All parties in the litigation agreed to this emphasis, and a challenge to the "authority" of the county officials was dropped (although it was picked up by the supreme court).[125] Thus, the concept of local officials making legal decisions based on their own interpretations was not as legally disputed, though it was politically controversial. Perhaps this is because the Oregon Court of Appeals provided a clear precedent about sexual orientation as a suspect class or because, as was noted, California strictly forbids the kind of interpretation in which a local official like Newsom engaged. At any rate, constitutional interpretation by local officials was given a bit of a temporary boost in Oregon.

This is, of course, a controversial development. Critics of such actions by local officials note that they are lawless and used by public officials on the political right, especially over church-state issues.[126] But a distinction can be made between actions of local officials in clear violation of well-settled judicial doctrine, like prohibitions against direct government sanction of religious doctrine or symbols, and new, contested, unsettled areas of the law like gay rights. Indeed, it may be that Newsom's and Linn's interpretations of the law will be validated by the courts (Linn's initially was). It is harder to envision that the courts will embrace Roy Moore's view on the display of the Ten Commandments in government buildings. Legal/civil disobedience by local officials may be another way to goad courts into a consideration of a fuller understanding of political traditions like positive freedom and its companion, antidiscrimination.

Oregon also demonstrates the fine line that is evolving on gay rights questions between law and politics, despite many scholars' and commentators' desire to keep them analytically distinct. Basic Rights Oregon (BRO) selected the Multnomah County Commission for lobbying in favor of granting licenses because of its liberal reputation, working closely with the commission behind the scenes to produce the maximum positive effect in the media. The group decided to engage in this tactic and the ensuing litigation because they saw an anti–same-sex marriage amendment coming. They, like activists and lawyers in Massachusetts, were trying to head off or blunt the effect of an amendment. According to Rochella Thorpe, BRO's executive director, "We could see the backlash coming no matter what we did." BRO spent the previous decade fighting at the grassroots level for gay rights. Lawyers did not just parachute in and start to sue. Sophisticated political-legal strategies are the hallmark of contemporary gay rights groups, not the cause lawyer caricature.[127]

Activity in the summer of 2004 was not confined to Oregon. In response to a suit filed by Lambda Legal, in conjunction with the Northwest Women's Law Center (the American Civil Liberties Union filed a separate suit around the same time), a Washington superior court judge found the state's ban on same-sex marriage to be unconstitutional but stayed the ruling pending review by the state supreme court.[128] The decision was striking in the way that it opened. From the start, Judge William Downing asserted the role of courts in protecting minorities from arbitrary state action and assumed the equality of same-sex relationships. Demonstrating how effective litigation strategies to "humanize" plaintiffs have been, Downing stated that "plaintiffs are eight pairs of individuals, each pair sharing a mutual commitment. . . . In a basic sense of the word, they are already married."[129]

The opinion was much more lyrical than Bearden's in Oregon and was strongly rooted in notions of positive freedom by its reliance on the fundamental right to marry. As Downing asserted: "That, then, is the right being asserted by the plaintiffs here—the autonomous right to have such a 'most important relation' in their lives and, in that relationship, to be able to make their own unique contribution to the foundation of society."[130] Applying traditional "fundamental right" analysis, Downing concluded that the state had no compelling state interest in preventing same-sex marriage, rejecting morality, tradition-based, and procreation arguments. He, like other courts that ruled similarly, found that the procreation defense was full of logical inconsistencies.[131] And, fully seeing courts as players in the discussion over evolving polity ideals, Downing asserted that "[a]s time marches inexorably on, human society—its collectively felt needs and its ability and inclination to provide for those needs—evolves."[132] Downing took note of what his fellow (international and U.S.) jurists had been doing on the question of same-sex marriage and saw his decision as part of that evolving judicial trend.[133] Unlike his Oregon counterpart, Downing was unwilling to entertain a domestic partnership compromise, arguing that this would degrade the institution of marriage for same-sex and opposite-sex couples.[134] All of this is fairly aggressive for a trial court judge.

And he was not alone. A month later, another superior court judge declared the state's Defense of Marriage Act unconstitutional. Judge Richard Hicks interestingly looked more to Oregon jurisprudence than that of his own state. He refused to overrule the Washington case of *Singer v. Hara*, instead choosing to argue around it, noting that it was dated and irrelevant. "The community has changed" since the 1970s when that decision was handed down, he argued.[135] Rather than focus on the fundamental rights approach, as did Downing, Hicks found gays to be a suspect class under the Washington Constitution. He did so by relating Washington's privileges and immunities to that of Oregon, which he noted was the inspiration for the Washington clause. Then, relying on *Tanner* (the Oregon case discussed above) and placing his analysis in line with *Baker* and *Goodridge*, Hicks found that the state's procreation justification was not a compelling state interest, noting the evolution of the family in recent decades.[136] In fact, he called the state's position a

"Lilliputian view" that "does not reflect our common reality." [137] This was yet another aggressive lower court decision, rooted in clear and evolving jurisprudence, in the U.S. Northwest. Indeed, the decision took cross-citation so far as to ignore state boundaries.

The Washington Supreme Court has recently ruled in favor of gay rights claims, including a decision that affirmed the granting of part of the estate of a gay man's deceased partner. But, unlike Hawaii, Vermont, and Massachusetts, Washington high court judges are elected, not appointed. Thus, the political response to the decision could directly affect the legal process, though this is not guaranteed. Political reaction in Washington appeared more muted than in Oregon, but one legislator did promise to propose a one man/one woman constitutional amendment in the next legislative session. This would require a two-thirds vote in the legislature before a popular majority vote, a larger legislative hurdle than Massachusetts or Oregon where political reaction has been swifter and more vociferous. [138]

## LITIGATION PROLIFERATES POST-*LAWRENCE* AND *GOODRIDGE*, CREATING MORE BACKLASH

In the months following *Lawrence* and *Goodridge*, litigation challenging bans on same-sex marriage proliferated in state and federal courts throughout the United States. At the same time, legislative and popular efforts to prevent same-sex marriage continued and even accelerated. By August 2004, twenty same-sex marriage lawsuits in eleven states were alive in the United States. [139] Lawsuits by Lambda, ACLU, or GLAD were pending in New York, New Jersey, Connecticut, Maryland, Washington, Oregon, and California, in addition to the successes in Vermont and Massachusetts. All except those in New Jersey were initiated post-*Goodridge*. These states were carefully chosen, as was the case in Vermont and Massachusetts. However, litigation is also taking place outside the national strategy. Local lawyers and litigants have filed suits in Indiana, Arizona, and Florida. These, of course, stand less of a chance of success. In fact, a famous, media-loving Florida lawyer initiated the Florida litigation, challenging the state's ban on same-sex marriage as well as the federal DOMA, and national groups strongly oppose the litigation out of fear of the creation of bad precedent, especially in the federal courts. [140]

Litigation in Arizona demonstrates the need for a careful, coordinated litigation strategy. A couple in Maricopa County applied for a marriage license and were denied. They were eventually supported by the Arizona Civil Liberties Union but no national groups gave any type of support. [141] The Arizona Court of Appeals upheld the state's opposite-sex only policy in a decision highly deferential to the legislature, using neither equal protection nor fundamental rights claims and applying traditional (minimal) rational basis review. Indicative of a court unwilling to adjudicate aggressively, the court sided with more settled, not evolving, jurisprudence. The decision limited the relevance of *Lawrence*, *Baker*, and *Goodridge*, and focused exclusively on Arizona jurisprudence in finding that the procreation justification was sufficient to pass rational basis review. The three judges did not at all try to take apart the logic of the state's position, as other courts have. The

Arizona Supreme Court refused to hear the case, letting the lower court decision stand.[142] Arizona seems an unlikely place for either political or legal traction on same-sex marriage. Domestic partnership legislation was proposed there in 2002, but failed to get out of the legislature. The House Judiciary Committee approved limited domestic partnership legislation 7 to 3, but supporters lacked votes on the floor.[143]

By the summer of 2004, thirty-nine states had statutory or constitutional bans on same-sex marriage and several states, post-*Goodridge*, moved to enact constitutional bans. In Missouri, an amendment passed with 71 percent popular support the same day of the Washington decision.[144] In the November 2004 elections, constitutional bans on same-sex marriage were enacted by referendum in eleven states.[145] The opposition to same-sex marriage also received support from President George W. Bush who, after initially hesitating, came out in support of a federal constitutional amendment banning same-sex marriage.[146] This did not translate into policy change at the federal level, however. Congress has rejected the amendment with votes far short of the two-thirds requirement.[147] The House, however, symbolically passed a bill taking jurisdiction over the issue away from federal courts, but the Senate was unlikely to approve the measure.[148] The public is divided on the amendment and is far from the large majority needed for ultimate approval.[149] There is considerable more comfort with state, rather than federal, constitutional solutions with the U.S. public.

For the foreseeable future, then, it appears that some states, through litigation and progressive politics, will expand relationship recognition while others will continue their refusal to recognize same-sex couples. This should suit gay rights groups just fine, allowing them room to build judicial momentum at the state level with the safety of the lack of a genuine threat of a federal amendment. Many commentators have likened the situation to the patchwork of laws and legal opinions that characterized the status of interracial marriage from 1948 when the first state invalidated its anti-miscegenation law until 1967 and *Loving*.[150] Much will obviously depend on the U.S. Supreme Court, its personnel changes, and its willingness to build upon *Lawrence* and the evolving state jurisprudence (as it did in *Lawrence*) to find the federal Defense of Marriage Act and state same-sex marriage bans unconstitutional.

## WHAT CAN WE LEARN FROM SAME-SEX MARRIAGE LITIGATION?

A decade after the decision in Hawaii, policy change has occurred throughout the United States and the litigation continues. Liberal legal language has, in many cases, compelled political actors to protect the rights of same-sex couples. This process was substantially judicially driven. Although grassroots politics was combined with litigation, politics alone does not result in policy change. Same-sex marriage litigation was not, of course, as universally successful as sodomy litigation, given the parameters of U.S. political culture, but it did help to remind policy makers and citizens of political traditions other than libertarian liberalism.

On the question of legal mobilization, litigation has been highly consequential, especially when activists and lawyers became more coordinated and sophisticated. However, as Hawaii and Alaska demonstrate, even uncoordinated, local efforts can achieve short-term results. These results were, of course, overridden by the political process, but they inspired further waves of coordinated litigation. As more recent failures, like Arizona, illustrate, spontaneous litigation can be highly detrimental, but calls for justice by local litigants are hard to contain. This will be a challenge as the movement moves forward but points to the increasing convergence between rights claiming and democratic politics. Sexual minorities are increasingly unwilling to only live by majoritarian rules.

These developments also echo scholars who have argued that cause lawyers are becoming increasingly politically sophisticated in their approaches. Gay rights litigators are carefully selecting favorable judicial forums and combining grassroots political activism with litigation. However, as I noted with the Vermont litigation, they still privilege litigation over politics. In these instances, the political groundwork was laid mostly to affect post-decision politics, not to affect the judicial decisions themselves. In fact, recall that the Vermont lawyers discouraged legislative action before the litigation could run its course. With same-sex marriage litigation, then, it was legal norms and litigation tactics that resulted in judicial victories for the movement.

Consequently, this analysis provides perhaps a third way of viewing the role of cause lawyers and their litigation. The first is the critical view of lawyers as myopic, naive crusaders. The second reaction to this view asserts that cause lawyers are much more sophisticated and politically savvy. The view I am presenting expands upon the latter view. The savvy lawyer view perhaps overstates the extent to which political activity actually contributes to judicial outcomes. A more accurate view, derived from the case of same-sex marriage litigation, is that political considerations weigh heavily in forum shopping considerations, but law takes over once the decision to litigate is made. This is particularly important if we wish to tease out causal variables. It is not enough to simply assert that cause lawyers are, or have always been, politically sophisticated. We must also examine the relationship between their political activities and their litigation efforts.

Clearly, then, sexual minorities have been able to use litigation in ways that Galanter ascribes to the "haves."[151] Even some "one-shotters" achieved success in court. Gay rights groups have been able to mobilize, deploy financial and technical resources, and coordinate and focus their efforts. They also gave birth to an emerging legal consensus that banning same-sex marriage is unconstitutional, a little discussed issue prior to the 1990s. Litigation provided enormous leverage and helped to put the issue of same-sex marriage on the national agenda in the United States. Favorable decisions also legitimized arguments in favor of same-sex marriage. Even the ultimate failures of Hawaii and Alaska had tremendous "radiating" effects.

Although most state and federal courts face enormous constraints (like public opinion, place in the judicial system, conservative or restraintist ideology of the judges, etc.) to aggressive adjudication in favor of same-sex marriage claims, some courts, obviously, have overcome or ignored these constraints. Early decisions in Hawaii, Alaska, and Vermont certainly had public opinion working against them. And the sheer novelty of their approaches and the potential effects of their decisions certainly must have given them pause. The Massachusetts court ruled in favor of same-sex marriage and directly challenged the legislature, despite having recently endured a confrontation with legislators over a previous aggressive decision. Perhaps most remarkably, lower courts in Oregon and Washington, unlike their counterparts in all other states facing litigation, stepped out of the "norm enforcement" role and ruled in favor of same-sex marriage claims. On the question of judicial selection, most all of the decisions in favor of relationship equality came from states with merit selection.[152] The two exceptions are Oregon and Washington, which utilize nonpartisan elections. This might indicate, since these were trial court decisions, that legal norms can drive judicial decision making, not simply political considerations.

This coincides with another interesting development stemming from this litigation, which was also a large factor in sodomy litigation: state court cross-citation and the spread of policy innovation at the state court level. From Hawaii to Washington, there has been an accumulation of judicial innovation, and, at each stage of the process, courts have relied on previous decisions in other states to justify their outcomes. The Washington court, in fact, simply adopted jurisprudence and a significant precedent from Oregon rather than apply its own precedent. Judicial federalism has been a crucial element of gay rights litigation in the United States.

The method of judicial reasoning used by courts when confronted with same-sex marriage claims follows the framework outlined by Feeley and Rubin.[153] Where courts were unwilling to find in favor of same-sex marriage claims, their opinions were highly deferential to legislative positions and justifications, particularly on the procreation justification, and they saw little merit in constitutional arguments challenging opposite-sex-only marriage policies. In the 1990s and early 2000s, these courts adjudicated as did courts in the 1970s. More aggressive courts were not bound by prior jurisprudence and were much more willing to innovate at the expense of legislatures. In these decisions, one finds much more reference to moral, as opposed to strictly legal, norms and much more abstract discussions about justice, coupled with an innovative application of established jurisprudence to this new subject area of gay rights. Opponents of these decisions are obsessed with their separation of powers and counter-majoritarian implications, but this is not the paramount consideration for these judges. This was especially true after Vermont, when the Massachusetts court dispensed with the Vermont court's ambivalence about the use of its power.

This litigation also demonstrated the increasing power and resonance of richer liberal legal norms. Although there is no question that same-sex marriage litigation has challenged dominant policy norms in the United States to a much greater degree than sodomy litigation, the idea that same-sex couples deserve recognition in the law has spread through courts since the early 1990s. Most pro–same-sex marriage decisions discussed the requirements of equality or the need to move beyond libertarianism toward a fuller liberalism. This was much more difficult to do in the political arena, where pro–gay rights political actors mostly emphasized libertarian arguments rather than the richer liberalism advocated by litigants and judges, especially when they were not responding directly to judicial decisions. However, where the political process was driven by action of the judiciary, political actors articulated a richer liberalism. These judicially supported arguments were consequential in the legislative arena, directly in the cases of Hawaii and Vermont, and indirectly in the case of California. In situations lacking judicial action, equality arguments and arguments supporting a fuller view of liberalism gained little traction. Also, as developments in California and Oregon demonstrate, these legal norms affect not only judges but also mayors, county executives, and attorneys general. Recall the striking consensus that developed in Oregon on the unconstitutionality of that state's prohibition of same-sex marriage.

These findings support the claim, contrary to Gerald Rosenberg and others, that courts can effect social change. In short, litigation matters. This will be discussed further in Chapter 11, after we look at the Canadian case.

# 10   Canada: Rethinking Courts, Rights, and Liberalism

THE PAST HALF DECADE has seen remarkable developments in Canada concerning gay rights claims, particularly with same-sex marriage. Same-sex marriages have been legalized in a majority of provinces and the government will likely make this national policy. This chapter examines these developments and contrasts them to the United States. Most notably, I argue that the differences stem primarily from the combination of a richer liberalism in Canadian political culture and a judiciary emboldened by a relatively recent constitutional change that elevated its rights consciousness, as well as that of the citizenry. These developments also illustrate the ability of courts to achieve social change.

In a few short years, Canada has gone from a typically gay rights hesitant country to one in which it is increasingly clear that same-sex marriage, or a similar policy, may become a political and legal reality. Even some conservatives increasingly support this, like former Conservative Party leader Joe Clark, or at least see it as inevitable.[1] Carl Stychin attributes this kind of rapid change to the fact that Canada is a postmodern nation, in that it understands and values marginalized groups. These groups are not placed outside the polity but are incorporated. They are part of the national political dialogue and often change the parameters of political practice and discourse in fundamental ways. Therefore, according to this argument, the rapid change on same-sex marriage in Canada stems from the fact that queer "others" have transformed the society and legitimated same-sex marriage. According to Stychin, "there may be found in the fabric of Canadian life a greater willingness to incorporate new social movements and identities in terms of national citizenship. . . . The Canadian national imaginary displays an instability which leaves it particularly open to contestation."[2] In this view, change takes place outside of the formal legal and political processes; indeed, it is the authority of the state that preserves the status quo against which the outsiders rebel. However, this explanation falls into the "everything that changes is queer" category, often put forth by postmodern theorists. Since liberalism is their great foil, they cannot admit that fundamental change can be facilitated by liberalism. Liberalism is always an agent of oppression, never liberation. Recall Bakan's description of Canadian courts as conservative entities as cited in Chapter 1. This position also has trouble explaining the rapid about-face from Canada's political hostility to gay rights claims as recently as the mid-1990s. The actual explanation for Canada's rapid change, as mentioned above, is thoroughly liberal and rights based. The dynamic reflects not Foucault, but Mill and Hart. Canada certainly has a different, and often more progressive, political culture than the United States, but this stems from its liberal, not postmodern, tradition. This is particularly notable in this context, since the rapid change in the gay rights arena has come through courts utilizing liberal legal arguments, grounded in a liberalism that is richer than the dominant negative variety in the United States. Canadian courts, empowered by the Charter of Rights and Freedoms, are enforcing a rich liberalism that is pushing the polity forward on gay rights. Courts in Canada have recently become a powerful policy maker as the nation has turned toward a U.S.-style litigation-based approach to policy making. Indeed, in the past several decades, there has been a constitutional litigation explosion in Canada as politics has become "judicialized."[3]

## COURTS AND JUDICIAL REVIEW IN CANADA BEFORE THE CHARTER

These developments are particularly noteworthy, since, before the 1980s, courts in Canada were not policy makers, and the Supreme Court of Canada, unlike its counterpart in the United States, was weak and lacked legitimacy. According to one commentator, "For most of its 112-year history, the Supreme Court of Canada was the forgotten institution of Canadian politics."[4] From its creation after Canadian independence, the Supreme Court of Canada dealt with only minor legal matters, not substantive legal interpretation. Certainly, there was no *Marbury v. Madison* to propel the Court onto the stage of national policy making. Canadian political culture in the mid-1800s, when Canada gained independence, distrusted legal elites. Efforts by national leaders to create a strong, centralized legal system went nowhere in such a decentralized polity.[5] The Canadian political tradition, emphasizing parliamentary sovereignty, was also less supportive of judicial review than was the written, limited U.S. Constitution. The judges did nothing to help the situation, often handing down multiple, conflicting judgments.[6]

Thus, by the end of the nineteenth century, the Court was held in low esteem. It was common for politicians to attack the Court and call for revocations of its jurisdiction. Lawyers, as well, had little regard for the institution. The editor of the *Canadian Law Journal* asserted that the Court "is held in Contempt by the profession." Most of the appointments to the Court were explicitly political, and justices often acted as legal and political advisors to the prime minister, thereby further undermining legitimacy.[7] The Court was also in a difficult legal position, since it was not a court of last resort; its decisions could be appealed to the Privy Council in England, and decisions of provincial courts could bypass the Court entirely on their way to the Privy Council.[8] The Court lacked the finality upon which U.S. Supreme Court justices relied. In general, the Court was unable to transcend politics and impart an independent influence on the polity for most of its history. According to Peter McCormick, the Court "was reluctant to display initiative or judicial independence and to which it was frequently difficult to recruit the most able lawyers and judges."[9]

By the 1930s, the Court gained some legitimacy as new governments began to refer to the Court for review of large portions of the previous government's legislative program. This was certainly a political ploy, but it served to reestablish the

Court as a national player.[10] In the late 1940s, the Court was given a new, dignified home, and the Liberal government enacted legislation making the Supreme Court the nation's court of last resort.[11] The 1950s saw the Court assert itself a bit in the realm of civil liberties, for example, protecting Jehovah's Witnesses from discrimination by the Quebec government.[12] However, by the 1960s the Court retreated from any embryonic activism. Nowhere was this clearer than in the Court's own assessment of a newly adopted Bill of Rights in Canada. The Conservative government passed the Bill of Rights in 1960, but the Court soon limited its application by holding in a 1963 case that this legislative enactment did not include any fundamental rights outside of rights already established in Canadian political culture and practice—there was nothing new that courts could apply independently. One justice dissented, arguing for stronger protection for civil rights by the courts, but even he rethought his position and saw the possibility for too-aggressive courts. The Court, then, was still extremely deferential to the more political branches.[13] And, despite the proliferation of rights around the world, mid-century Canadian political elites were quite hostile to the idea of entrenched rights.[14] The 1970s saw some positive developments for the Court's role, as Parliament gave it even more control over its docket, and a strong chief justice, Bora Laskin, was appointed, who advocated for a stronger civil liberties agenda.[15]

## THE CHARTER'S RIGHTS REVOLUTION AND CANADIAN LIBERALISM

Everything changed after 1982. In that year, Canada adopted the Charter of Rights and Freedoms, a constitutional bill of rights. The Charter was adopted as a larger effort at constitutional reform, an effort that was largely driven by considerations of federalism and Quebecois nationalism. Many regions of Canada felt that they did not have a voice in the national government. According to Patrick Monahan, "By the late 1970s, political commentators began writing of a 'crisis of representation' in Canada's central institutions. Because regional interests had been so systematically suppressed within the institutions at the center, the federal government had lost the legitimacy required to reconcile competing regional interests."[16] As a result, the Trudeau government introduced Bill C-60 in 1978, which was a wide constitutional reform bill that attempted to assign more power to the provinces.[17] In particular, Pierre Trudeau was trying to head off Quebec nationalism. Indeed, he entered politics in reaction to secessionist politics and ultimately hoped to overcome them by advocating a policy of bilingualism, even enshrining such a policy constitutionally. This eventually led to the Charter, a general bill of rights, for reasons described by Michael Mandel:

> Trudeau saw the entrenchment of a general Bill of Rights, that is one not restricted to language rights, as an *expedient*, as a means to break the logjam of constitutional reform, which was itself just an expedient to his goal of entrenched bilingualism. Trudeau believed that the attachment of the popular, indeed increasingly irresistible, idea of a general constitutional Bill of Rights to any amending proposal would

immeasurably enhance its chances of success. And tucked away somewhere in the general Bill of Rights would be the key to the whole enterprise: entrenched minority language rights.[18]

Trudeau hoped that an attachment to rights would be a uniting force for Canadians in the face of a divided culture and polity.[19] This also merged with Canadian expectations about civil rights that had been increasing for decades. Much of this stemmed from developments south of the border. As Snell and Vaughan state, "In the 1960s Canadians were inundated with accounts of how the Supreme Court of the United States was applying the terms of the American Bill of Rights in dramatic ways."[20] Liberal legal norms do not adhere to national boundaries.

The full package of constitutional reforms failed because of the Liberal Party defeat in 1979 and unfavorable Supreme Court rulings, but the Charter was ultimately ratified after the Liberals soon resumed power. Antirights forces still made their arguments (but they lost many advocates in the legal profession),[21] but the Charter was politically quite popular: Two polls in 1981 showed public support at 82 percent and 72 percent, respectively.[22]

Some commentators contend that the adoption of the Charter was not that revolutionary. Brian Dickson, a former chief justice of the Supreme Court, claims that Canadian courts have always been concerned with individual rights, even creating an "implied Bill of Rights" from the 1930s to the 1950s. In fact, Dickson asserts that the advent of the Charter "is well rooted in the judiciary's heritage and recent events in the courts' history are but a manifestation of the political fabric of Canada's ongoing revolution."[23] This appears to be a bit of a political and legal "spin" by an activist chief justice. Certainly Canada, with its common law legal tradition, has maintained a certain respect for individual rights, but the norm of parliamentary sovereignty was a much larger pull on the system. After the Charter, however, this is no longer true. The Supreme Court of Canada is challenging parliamentary sovereignty. Much has been made by commentators of the "notwithstanding clause," which allows violations of individual rights or equality principles to be okayed by courts, if a compelling public interest reason can be made for the violation, thereby preserving parliamentary supremacy. But this has essentially become a dead letter in Canadian constitutional jurisprudence.[24]

Many Canadian legal commentators, like Dickson, go out of their way to stress the less-than-radical nature of the Charter, or they are highly critical of the turn toward litigious politics after 1982. The argument from the legal academy is either that this is no big deal or it is a monstrous aberration in Canadian politics. On one side of the monstrous aberration argument commentators, like Joel Bakan, view judicial policymaking under the Charter from the lens of critical legal studies. For them, the courts are thwarting progressive social change that has always been driven by Parliament from their conservative perch on the bench. The other side of the critique comes from those who are highly critical of developments in Canadian politics after the Charter. Their critiques are similar to those of Jean Elshtain and Andrew Sullivan, who make several similar claims: litigation under the Charter undermines the deliberative process in legislatures; the rights of the Charter are too positive and give too much responsibility to government and falsely raise citizen expectations (this view bemoans the abandonment of "limited" government and favors adjudication that is more procedural than substantive);[25] and the shift to litigation empowers legal elites, or what Knopff and Morton call the "Court Party."[26] It is at times difficult to find many commentators that approve of post-Charter trends, but these trends continue, especially in the realm of lesbian and gay rights, despite the criticisms. Given real judicial and political outcomes, these commentators of all political persuasions are looking increasingly irrelevant in an age where court enforcement of liberal legal norms is becoming a reality.

Charles Epp, however, argues that the Supreme Court of Canada was already coming into its own before the Charter, and Canada was seeing an overall trend toward the judicialization of politics. He asserts that the Court's ability after 1975 to control its own docket shifted the focus of its efforts away from private legal disputes to public law. Indeed, he argues that "the Charter itself may be understood as a product of changes in the Canadian support structure [for litigation] that transformed the Court's agenda."[27] He points to relaxed standing requirements, a proliferation of civil rights advocacy groups (many of whom directly contributed to the drafting of the Charter), and the decision by the Court to open up legal challenges to third party interveners, the Canadian equivalent of amicus parties.[28] Also noteworthy is the Court Challenges Program, which was established in 1978 and provided government funding for individual rights challenges. The program contributed to the rise in the number and diversity of lawyers in the 1970s and their new willingness to see courts as legitimate policy makers.[29] This demonstrates that the Charter was part of a moving stream, but its adoption was more like a waterfall than a gentle change in stream elevation. The Charter dramatically accelerated the trend toward the judicialization of politics in Canada.

The legitimacy of aggressive judicial policy making is still a political and scholarly (as noted above) point of contention. Since the mid-1980s, when adjudication under the Charter began in earnest (that is when the equality provision took effect), critics have vociferously criticized the Court for placing its judgment in place of elected officials. Like the criticism of Warren and Burger Courts' activism in the United States, this has come primarily from conservative political circles. It was a staple of criticism of the Reform/Alliance Party, which later merged into a larger conservative party with the Tories. According to Ted Morton, a political scientist and Reform Party leader, "The Supreme Court under Lamer has been an instrument of the federal Liberal party, advancing the interests of feminists, gays and lesbians, and aboriginals. Small-c conservatives are deeply disillusioned."[30] There is some indication that this criticism has stuck: After the real or perceived[31] period of activism of the Lamer Court in the 1990s, the current chief justice has explicitly made reining in the Court one of her goals. Indeed, Prime Minister Jean Chretien appointed Beverly McLachlin over perceived activists, particularly in the realm of the rights of the accused, in an attempt to rein in the Court.[32] And there is some evidence that the Court is adjudicating less aggressively than previous courts, for instance not striking down a single federal law in 2000.[33] Beyond the rights of the accused, the current chief justice appears to be concerned about the path of the

Court's jurisprudence in the realm of equality and Section 15(1). To a Toronto legal conference in April 2001 she expressed concerns that the Court had entered, in her words, an "uncertain sea of value judgments. Equality debates usually turn on the proponent's view of society and what it should be. This raises the question of whether the courts can capture the complexity of social life in a way that permits them to make the best decisions."[34] In fact, McLachlin had concerns about the Charter at the time of its adoption.[35] The Court is also increasingly thin-skinned about criticism and engages in public relations efforts to counter criticism, even revisiting a controversial decision concerning aboriginal rights in the face of hostile public reaction. The members of the Court have even undertaken road trips together to increase their visibility and connection to the public.[36]

The Court, however, may be responding to only elite sentiments and a small slice of public opinion. Public support for the Charter has always been high and is growing with time. A poll in 2002 placed approval of the Charter among respondents who had heard of it at 92 percent, a 10 percent increase over the previous decade. Seventy-one percent of respondents said that the Supreme Court, not Parliament, should have the final say over Charter controversies.[37] Perhaps Canadian politics is turning the counter-majoritarian question on its head. As legal and political elites question the capacity and wisdom of courts to adjudicate aggressively, large majorities of citizens are unconcerned about this, and, in fact, wish to see more of it. Scholar and commentator Christopher Manfredi has condemned the Court, arguing that is "is getting bolder all the time in its belief it can get away with more activism."[38] But it looks as if a strong majority of Canadian citizens are in favor of it too.

As was discussed in Chapter 1, Canadian political culture differs from the political culture of the United States. According to Lipset, Canada is Tory and the United States is Whig, in that Canada traditionally has valued deference to authority, emphasis on the collective good, and a stronger consideration for groups, whereas American think in more strictly individualistic and libertarian terms (as was demonstrated in Chapter 3).[39] Although this may be a bit oversimplified,[40] the broad contrast is valid, especially when it comes to liberal individualism. Both the Tory and socialist traditions in Canada, like continental Europe, deemphasized atomistic individualism. According to A. E. Bogart, "both these ideologies turn their face against the pervasive claims of individualism as the race for happiness so cherished by liberalism."[41] Or, to put it in Hartzian terms, Canada was more in touch with the European feudal past and relied on more than just Locke in framing its polity.

This had consequences for the Charter and the type of liberalism reflected in the document. Overall, the Charter reflects a mix of traditionally liberal individual negative rights elements, like provisions for freedom of speech and protection against illegal searches—very much like the U.S. Bill of Rights. But the Charter reflects other values, specifically a strong equality provision and explicit protection for groups. As evidence of these other values, high percentages of Canadian citizens, 85 percent according to one poll, approve of laws preventing the promotion of hatred toward groups (recall Sullivan's use of negative freedom to critique these laws), and high percentages (68 percent overall, 77 percent for women and 57 percent for men) of Canadians favor regulating obscene material because of its harmful effects on women.[42] In general, Canadians are much less libertarian in their approach to rights and public policy. In addition, language rights protections in the Charter are obviously aimed at minority French speakers. Thus, group rights are constitutionally enshrined in Canada—an idea that does not receive a favorable hearing in "one person, one vote" America.[43] In fact, the Charter states: "This Charter shall be interpreted in a manner consistent with the preservation and enhancement of the multicultural heritage of Canadians."[44] This would certainly put a different gloss on debates over multiculturalism in U.S. society and its universities, since opponents of, for example, diversity in education and speech codes argue cultural prejudice should be tolerated in the name of preserving freedom of thought and expression. In a nation like Canada, where assimilation is not necessarily the cultural norm, group differences are recognized and given constitutional protection. U.S. constitutional practice is to globalize and generalize these conflicts in universal, individualistic language.

Although the United States' approach may be noble, there is a potential downside to this difference, or at least a qualitative difference for legal claims of equality. For example, the Charter endorses affirmative action policies. Section 15(2) states that the equal protection provision of the Charter "does not preclude any law, program or activity that has as its object the amelioration of conditions of disadvantaged individuals or groups." The Charter thus views equality substantively: outcomes and end results are important. The Charter contemplates that surface appearances of equality may mask true inequality and that color-blindness is not enough to preserve equality.

U.S. constitutional jurisprudence, however, increasingly rejects this argument as a guiding principle, instead favoring a formal interpretation of equality. In this view, as long as a policy or practice is neutral in regard to race or some other protected factor, the policy passes constitutional muster. Conversely, policies that are facially discriminatory in the service of ameliorating deeper "conditions" of inequality are deemed unconstitutional. This is clearly demonstrated in *Adarand Constructors v. Pena*, one of the U.S. Supreme Court's most recent substantive statements on affirmative action. The Court took its most critical look to date at federal affirmative action policies and, for the first time, subjected the federal government's affirmative action programs to strict scrutiny review—the highest standard of review in U.S. constitutional jurisprudence. In doing so, the majority emphasized a highly formal interpretation of the demands of equality. As Justice Clarence Thomas stated, "Government cannot make us equal; it can only recognize, respect, and protect us as equal before the law."[45] Notice the strictly negative strain of liberalism valued here: Thomas asserts that the state should play no role in individual development and enforcing rich notions of personhood. The only role for government is that of a neutral arbiter. In dissent, Justice John Paul Stevens argued for a substantive approach to equal protection jurisprudence. He was critical of the majority's emphasis on consistency and neutrality: "The consistency that the Court espouses would disregard the difference between a 'No Trespassing' sign and a welcome mat.... An interest in 'consistency' does not justify treating differences as though they were similarities."[46] Mere consistency has been rejected by the U.S. Supreme Court in the no-so-distant past. For example, the Supreme Court struck down Virginia's anti-miscegenation statute, despite the fact that it treated whites and blacks equally, since neither could marry the other. The Court argued that the goal behind the law, the preservation of white racial purity, was outside the realm of legitimate state action.[47] Increasingly, however, in the United States this position is becoming marginalized in favor of Thomas's position. But in Canada, Stevens's approach is enshrined in the constitution and favored by the courts.

## THE CANADIAN COURTS MOVE AGGRESSIVELY ON GAY RIGHTS CLAIMS UNDER THE CHARTER

Judicial policy making on gay rights in Canada is interesting, because success in the political arena was not too far in advance of successes in the United States. This makes the courts' activity all the more relevant, in that they are not just affirming what other political branches have done. In fact, as in the United States, there have been significant political obstacles to the gay rights movement in addition to some successes.

In 1969, the Trudeau government eliminated sodomy laws in Canada as part of an effort to liberalize laws affecting marital and reproductive privacy, no doubt in response to the Wolfenden developments in England. But sexual orientation was rejected from a 1976 civil rights law for federal workers, and the committee considering the Charter in the early 1980s rejected the inclusion of sexual orientation in the equality provisions of the document. The provincial governments of Quebec and Ottawa added sexual orientation to their antidiscrimination laws in 1977 and 1986, respectively, but the federal government had not done so by the early 1990s. Courts began to force the issue by asserting that the federal antidiscrimination law was unconstitutional because of its lack of sexual orientation protection (this will be discussed in greater detail below), and the Conservative government began to respond, but a call for new elections in 1993 ended these efforts.[48]

The Liberals won decisively in 1993 and their record on gay rights has been mixed. A hate crime bill that included sexual orientation provisions was passed in 1994 but with significant dissent within the caucus. Activists, elements in the media, and the Human Rights Commission began putting pressure on the Liberals to add sexual orientation to the federal antidiscrimination law, the Human Rights Act. At a convention in 1996, Liberals voted overwhelmingly to add sexual orientation protection, but with a caveat that heterosexual marriage would not be affected by the policy change. The bill presented to Parliament contained such assurances. The bill ultimately passed nearly 3 to 1 on second reading, with some Liberals defying the party on a free vote and with strong support from the Bloc Quebecois and the New Democratic Party (NDP) (these two parties would prove more supportive of marriage rights, as discussed below). Unanimous opposition came from the conservative Reform Party.[49]

Obviously, this outcome is quite different from efforts in the United States, where attempts to pass a national antidiscrimination law have been rebuffed. David Rayside points to several factors that explain the Canadian success: an effective advocacy group, Egale Canada that was able to unify pro-gay advocacy in this very federal republic; positive media exposure; the power and discipline of Canadian political parties (once the Liberals decided on this as a course of action, it was almost a foregone conclusion), as well as the disarray of the main opposition party, Reform; supportive decisions from courts and civil rights commissions; and favorable public opinion.[50]

The government of Ontario directly addressed the same-sex marriage/equal relationship benefits issue in the mid-1990s. An NDP law that would have given same-sex couples the provincial legal rights and benefits of marriage was narrowly defeated on second reading. NDP members voted 59 to 12 in favor of the law, but Liberals and Conservatives voted overwhelmingly against it.[51] The NDP brought the issue forward as an attempt to energize their progressive constituency as its government was faltering, but party leaders were also fearful of negative backlash, thus allowing for a free vote.[52] Bottom line, there was (and still is) more political room for gay rights claims in Canada in the 1990s, but barriers to change in the realm of marriage rights still existed and would await court intervention to push things along.

Canadian courts have done so, since equality jurisprudence under the Charter is substantive rather than formal. Whereas American equal protection jurisprudence tends toward formal interpretations of the demands of constitutional equality provisions, the Supreme Court of Canada has created a jurisprudence that both extends the reach of constitutional protection against discrimination and demands a more substantive assessment of claims of discrimination, explicitly relying on a more contemporary, Dworkinian understanding of liberalism and the value it places on "equal concern and respect." Indeed, judges use precisely this language in their rulings. This has allowed Canadian courts to go beyond formal and tautological interpretations of marriage laws (recall the early U.S. court decisions) and increasingly assert that equality provisions of the Charter demand inclusion of same-sex couples in the benefits of marriage policy. In fact, the Supreme Court of Canada explicitly stated, soon after it began its Charter adjudication, that its mode of adjudication would be "purposive," in that they would find in Charter provisions principles to be used to limit legislation. In addition to rejecting formalism, original intent was given no standing, even though the intent of those who framed the Charter was not all that remote. The Court's embrace of an unabashed substantive reasoning/rights as trumps approach was clearly a more modern form of adjudication. As a result, according to Robert Sharpe, "Charter adjudication is anything but the mechanical application of pre-established rules. The judges are called upon to delve deeply into the very foundations of our legal system and political culture to answer questions of the most fundamental nature."[53]

The Supreme Court in *Andrews v. Law Society of British Columbia* articulated the parameters and trajectory of equality jurisprudence in 1989. In that case, the British Columbia Court of Appeal upheld a B.C. law that required Canadian citizenship for admission to the provincial bar. The Court upheld the law using a pre-Charter formal equality approach; thus, citizens and noncitizens could be treated differently under the law. The Supreme Court rejected this approach in favor of an explicitly substantive approach, one that takes a much richer view of the demands of equality. As Justice William McIntyre stated:

> The [formal] test as stated, however, is seriously deficient in that it excludes any consideration of the nature of the law. If it were to be applied literally, it could be used to justify the Nuremberg laws of Adolf Hitler. Similar treatment was contemplated for all Jews. The similarly situated test would have justified the formalistic separate but equal doctrine of Plessy v. Ferguson. . . . In our view, s. 15(1) [the equality provision of the Charter] read as a whole constitutes a compendious expression of a positive right to equality in both the substance and the administration of the law. It is an all-encompassing right governing all legislative action. Like the ideals of "equal justice" and "equal access to the law," the right to equal protection and equal benefit of the law now enshrined in the Charter rests on the moral and ethical principle fundamental to a truly free and democratic society that all persons should be treated by the law on a footing of equality with *equal concern and respect* [italics added].[54]

As clear as this statement appears, however, the Court in *Andrews* also attempted to limit the application of this principle to legislation. For instance, the Court declared that not all violations of equality were contrary to the Charter. The important legal question was that of discriminatory effects of a law, not simply facial discrimination. Once such discrimination is established, the question then becomes whether or not the discrimination is legislatively justified. This is the *Oakes* test formulated by the Court in 1986. The Charter states that the document "guarantees the rights and freedoms set out in it subject only to such reasonable limits prescribed by law as can be demonstrably justified in a free and democratic society."[55] Thus, the approach seen in U.S. equal protection jurisprudence, with its varying levels of review, is constitutionally mandated in Canada, but the Supreme Court of Canada applies a high level of scrutiny to more classifications, not just race, alienage, and illegitimacy. This is the case not only because categories protected from discrimination are listed in the Charter ("race, national or ethnic origin, colour, religion, sex, age, or mental or physical disability"), but because the Court in *Andrews* applied Charter protection to "analogous, non-enumerated" categories, thereby expanding the scope of Charter and Court protection.[56] However, after this approach was articulated, the Court was not unified on its application, especially as to which groups were analogous and how the stringency of the *Oakes* test applied.

Sexual orientation discrimination was an area that showed the Court's divisions. In *Egan v. Canada*, a same-sex couple applied for benefits under the Old Age Security Act, which provided for spousal allowances. A spouse was defined by the act as "a person of the opposite sex who is living with that person, having lived with that person for at least one year, if the persons have publicly represented themselves as husband and wife." As will be discussed in a later case, Canada provides extensive benefits for common law couples. The same-sex couple in question had lived together since 1948 and they sued under Section 15(1) of the Charter when the government denied their claim for an allowance. The Federal Court of Appeals affirmed the denial. A divided Supreme Court kept this trend going. The majority held that while sexual orientation may fall into the "analogous" category, since "sexual orientation is a deeply personal charactcristic that is either unchangeable or changeable only at unacceptable personal costs," the distinction made by the government between same-sex and opposite-sex couples was valid. The majority's reasoning was anchored on the procreation justification of marriage as a uniquely heterosexual institution: "It would be possible to legally define marriage to include homosexual couples, but this would not change the biological and social realities that underlie the traditional marriage." This reasoning would not hold sway on the Court for very long; however, in this case, deference to Parliament's policy judgments outweighed Charter requirements. The dissenters applied the modern liberalism of the Charter to majoritarian policy considerations. As Justice Peter deCarteret Cory stated: "In its attempt to prohibit discrimination, the Charter seeks to reinforce the concept that *all* human beings, however different they may appear to the majority, are *all* equally deserving of concern, respect and consideration." In a brief four years later, this would become the position of a near-unanimous majority.[57]

Solidifying the doctrine that sexual orientation is a category protected by Section 15(1) of the Charter, the Court required Alberta to include sexual orientation in its antidiscrimination law in 1998.[58] Recall that, contemporaneously, the U.S. Supreme Court was subjecting sexual orientation discrimination to minimal standards of review in *Romer v. Evans*. In must be emphasized, however, that the two courts diverged on this issue only recently. Canadian courts before the mid-1990s were not exactly gay-positive. Before this, formal equality interpretations were dominant, as evidenced by lower courts' (and the Supreme Court majority's) unwillingness in *Egan* to apply substantive equality interpretation. And it was not a given that courts would be appreciative of the legal and political problems faced by sexual minorities. In 1986, for example, some members of the Supreme Court found validity in the "homosexual panic" defense, and those who did not also did not dispute the reasoning of the defense.[59] This defense holds that violent acts that result from same-sex advances and the "panic" they cause in heterosexuals justify the act or should result in the lowest penalty for an act, say from murder to manslaughter. To reject this defense requires a sophisticated understanding of the oppression of sexual minorities. A formal, first-blush approach might take the defense seriously: As with self-defense, it might appear to make legal sense that this type of panic is a legitimate mitigating element, especially if the implications are not analyzed. Upon deeper consideration, however, one may uncover two compelling issues: (1) The level of fear and marginalization of sexual minorities present in society that would lead individuals to respond so violently to real or perceived sexual advances, and (2) the injustice of allowing this prejudice to be used against the victim of such a crime. Thus, sexual minorities are attacked and their attackers are treated leniently because of whom they attacked. This type of reasoning, however, was beyond the reach of even the Supreme Court of Canada until recently. Like the situation in the United States reflected in the *Bowers v. Hardwick* reasoning, sexual minorities had not achieved full "personhood" in Canadian legal doctrine in the 1980s.

However, by the late 1990s, the modern liberal logic of the Charter and the turn toward substantive reasoning in service of this logic began working in favor of gay rights claims. The landmark case of *M. v.H.* represents a significantly different jurisprudence of liberalism than anything seen south of the Canadian border and is grounded in an approach to equality adjudication based in the concept of human dignity. *Law v. Canada* paved the way for *M.v.H.* and cleared up some of the divisions on the Court concerning equality jurisprudence reflected in *Egan*. In that case the Court grounded its Section 15(1) analysis in the concept of human dignity and was not afraid of the vagueness of the term, instead embracing the purposive approach and its substantive analytical requirements and avoiding "the pitfalls of a formalistic or mechanical approach." Despite critics of Charter adjudication and political opposition to rising court power, the Court clearly was not retreating from embracing modern liberalism, declaring that "the purpose of s. 15(1) is to prevent the violation of essential human dignity and freedom through the imposition of disadvantage, stereotyping, or political or social prejudice"[60]

The development of substantive equality jurisprudence was tailor-made for same-sex marriage and relationship equality claims. Thus, when a lesbian applied for spousal support under Ontario's Family Law Act after her relationship ended, three levels of Canadian courts sided with her claim and declared that Ontario's limiting of post-relationship spousal support benefits to opposite sex couples contravened the Charter. This was not directly a same-sex marriage case, however, since the law in question dealt with benefits stemming from common law relationships. The law stated that two individuals of the opposite gender became "spouses" when they lived together for three years.[61] Canada has a well-developed system of common law marriage that brings with it most of the rights and benefits of solemnized marriage.

The particular question in this case was whether Section 29 of the law, which excluded same-sex couples from the definition of "spouse," violated the equality provision of the Charter. Interestingly, the NDP Ontario government originally stipulated to the provision's unconstitutionality, but the government changed its mind after the NDP lost control of the government and the Conservatives took over in 1995. The decision was also delayed to await the Supreme Court's decision in *Egan*. Eventually, the lower court judge, relying on *Egan's* "reading in" of sexual orientation to the Charter, found a violation under Section 15(1) and, rather radically, ordered the exclusive opposite-sex definition of spouse to be replaced by the words "two persons." Justice Gloria Epstein was unconcerned with the far-reaching implications of her decision. Using the failure of the legislative process to address the concerns of gay rights claimants, she stated: "It is difficult for the legislature to change the law in a particularly unpopular way, even if to do so would enhance a constitutionally protected right. It is precisely for this reason that an independent judiciary must take appropriate action."[62]

The Ontario Court of Appeals upheld this decision, although it was split 2 to 1. The majority, like Epstein, relied on the logic of purposive review, and found that the government could not overcome the requirements of the *Oakes* test. According to the majority, "The evidence is overwhelming that cohabitation between partners who have intimate relationships, regardless of sexual orientation, creates emotional and financial interdependencies."[63] This did not go over well with the judge in the minority, Finlayson, who considered the decision an overt example of judicial activism that would lead to a judicial mandate for same-sex marriage. Because the real issue was same-sex marriage and not a general equal benefits issue, according to Finlayson, *Egan* did not apply, since that case explicitly held that marriage laws were not invalidated by finding sexual orientation an analogous category. Ultimately, he argued that there is a legitimate policy reason for limiting marriage, even common law marriage, to opposite-sex couples: procreation. But he went further, asserting his own policy preference on the issue: "I reject the suggestion that same-sex couples can create a family unit that parallels the heterosexual family," Finlayson declared.[64] Despite his criticism that the reasoning of the majority resulted in the court's evaluation of policy alternatives, he was doing the same. Finlayson's reliance on formal, nonexpansive reasoning served his normative view, just as substantive reasoning supported the majority's normative agenda. There is nothing necessarily neutral about formal reasoning.

During oral arguments before the Supreme Court, Ontario's lawyer argued that, given the economic disadvantage of women in Canadian society, the law was intended to address issues of gender imbalance after relationship break-ups, thereby grounding the law in a progressive public policy position (Finlayson also emphasized this argument in his dissent). M.'s lawyer instead emphasized the need for the Charter to trump majoritarian considerations, stating rather frankly: "Gays and lesbians cannot trust this majoritarian legislature, they cannot trust their own elected politicians, and they cannot trust this government, who has argued this case from both sides of its mouth." The oral argument was also notable, since Justice William Binnie had recently apologized for referring to a law school fraternity party as a "faggoty dress-up affair."[65]

The Supreme Court was more receptive to the arguments of M.'s lawyer, and it upheld the view of Epstein and the Ontario Court of Appeals majority in an 8 to 1 decision. Reflecting the trajectory of cases like *Egan* and *Law v. Canada*, and their combination of Charter protection for sexual orientation and modern liberalism, the Court stated:

> The exclusion of same-sex partners from the benefits of s. 29 promotes the view that M., and individuals in same-sex relationships generally, are less worthy of recognition and protection. It implies that they are judged to be incapable of forming intimate relationships of economic interdependence as compared to opposite-sex couples, without regard to their actual circumstances. Such exclusion perpetuates the disadvantages suffered by individuals in same-sex relationships and contributes to the erasure of their existence.[66]

The Court ordered the government of Ontario to take appropriate action within six months to rectify the situation. The lone dissenter, Justice Charles Doherty Gonthier, adopted Finlayson's position, arguing that the decision would lead to a change in the institution of marriage, despite the majority's assertions to the contrary, and that the Ontario government ought to be allowed to make policy distinctions between same-sex and opposite-sex couples because of the procreation issue. A concern for equal consideration and respect did not require a transformation in the status of marriage, solemnized or common law, according to Gonthier.[67] But he was only one of nine to hold this view. Even Binnie sided with the gay rights claim. Perhaps the power of legal reasoning can overcome personal prejudice.

## THE POLITICAL RESPONSE: A REFLECTION OF A RICHER LIBERAL CULTURE

Remarkably, especially compared with the politics of same-sex marriage in the United States, the federal government and several provinces responded quickly to the decision, revising a wide array of laws dealing with common law relationships. An examination of this response, especially at the federal level, illustrates the fuller and richer liberalism that is at play in the Canadian polity.

Even before the decision of the Supreme Court, the *M.v.H.* litigation affected Canadian politics. The Liberal Party increasingly came to the conclusion that it would need to respond to the equality claims and change federal law to allow for same-sex couple benefits. This was a top issue at a Liberal convention in early 1998,[68] as oral arguments were about to be heard before the Supreme Court. The government also proposed allowing gays and lesbians to sponsor their foreign partners for immigration purposes in early 1999. Favorable public opinion was also facilitating the Liberal government's actions—the Justice Department's own poll in the fall of 1998 showed support for same-sex common law benefits at 67 percent.[69] Consequently, the government, realizing that it would likely lose the Court battle, began to lay the groundwork to address the issue legislatively. Consistent with contemporary political practice, the Justice Department used focus groups of moderate voters to develop "sellable" language. As a result, "fairness" was the overriding principle; "partner" was deemed better than "spouse"; the word "compassion" would be avoided because of its condescending nature; and benefits affecting children would be emphasized (recall the child-centered strategy in Massachusetts).[70]

The Reform Party, however, wished to throw a wrench in workings of the Liberal public relations campaign. Citing out-of-control courts, Eric Lowther presented a nonbinding resolution defining marriage as only between one man and one woman, a kind of symbolic Canadian Defense of Marriage Act. Liberals quickly declared support, Justice Minister Anne McLellan stating, "We on this side agree that the institution of marriage is a central and important institution in the lives of many Canadians." Several speakers from the NDP, Bloc Quebecois, and even the Conservatives called the motion a cheap political shot, aimed only at the demonization of sexual minorities. Most interesting was the rhetoric of negative freedom utilized by the Reform Party, Canada's most conservative political party and one that most mirrors U.S. perspectives on liberalism. Like conservatives in Hawaii and Vermont, Reform members wished to de-gay the issue of equal benefits, since the question of sexuality was not appropriate for public policy, only the bedroom. According to one Reform member, "If we take the concept of what people do in their bedrooms behind closed doors out of this issue, it will enable us to uphold the traditional concept marriage." A conservative member of the liberal caucus also echoed this sentiment. This linking of negative, minimal liberalism with gay rights claims exists in Canadian discourse, but it is by no means dominant, given that the Liberals were just trying to get past this episode with little political damage on their way to significant reform based on gay rights claims. This also shows that, despite a broader liberalism, same-sex marriage debates can be contentious in Canada. The final vote on the resolution was 216 to 55.[71]

Indeed, even when the Liberal government proposed legislation amending sixty-eight statutes in February 2000, in response to *M.v.H.*, it eventually included an opposite–sex-only definition of marriage in the preamble.[72] Liberals were more than willing, like Democrats in the United States, to pander to real or perceived majoritarianism. But in Canada, pandering was not the end result. Compared to the U.S. Congress, the Canadian Parliament found much more room to articulate and actuate rich gay rights claims. Indeed, the differences between congressional debates over DOMA and the parliamentary response to *M.v.H.* are striking. Whereas very few in Congress were willing to stand up for substantive equality for sexual minorities, the situation in the Canadian Parliament was exactly the opposite.

Anne McLellan opened the debate on Bill C-23, the Modernization of Benefits and Obligations Act. Citing the mandates of the Supreme Court, legislative developments in several provinces,[73] the federal government's own Bill C-78, which provided pension benefits to same-sex partners of federal employees, and favorable public opinion, McLellan declared that Bill C-23 "ensures that federal laws reflect the core values of Canadians, values that are enshrined in the Canadian Charter of Rights and Freedoms. The fundamental tenets of Canadian society—fairness, tolerance, respect and equality—are touchstones of our national identity and serve to enhance our international reputation."[74] Thus, a document that reflects modern liberalism was, for McLellan, at the core of Canadian national identity and serves as a model for the evolution of liberalism throughout the world. It took the Supreme Court to trigger this sentiment politically in regard to gay rights claims, but once triggered, it was wholeheartedly embraced.

Not just Liberals felt this way. Every party except for the Canadian Alliance (formerly Reform) seconded these sentiments.[75] Real Menard of the Bloc Quebecois congratulated the government "on finally taking action to respect human rights." Reflecting a Hartian take on intimacy and liberalism, he asserted that "There is no difference in the feeling of love [between same and opposite sex couples]" and stressed citizenship and full inclusion in the polity, arguing that "same sex partners must be recognized as full fledged members of society."[76] Although Conservatives were not thrilled, neither were they adamantly opposed to the legislation. Heartened by the reaffirmation of the exclusive definition of marriage, the Conservative position was one of resignation to political and legal reality, given the position of the Supreme Court. Their position was not to fall back on moral arguments but to approach the issue soberly and pragmatically. According to one member,

> this legislation is not, I would suggest, about governments making judgments or being intrusive into the bedrooms of the nation. This is about reflecting responsibilities and obligations upon individuals who have entered into a relationship upon which there is a degree of dependency.... We must go forward ... in a reasoned, moderate and tolerant approach.[77]

Members of the NDP, not surprisingly given their efforts in 1994, were also quite supportive of the Liberals' effort, led by openly gay member Svend Robinson.

Strong opposition came from the Canadian Alliance, and their rhetoric would have been quite at home in the halls of the U.S. Congress. They covered the main bases covered by advocates of DOMA: illegitimate court decisions and morality concerns, particularly about societal decline resulting from affirming same-sex relationships. Whereas a year before, the strategy was to emphasize negative freedom considerations and view gay rights claims in a "live and let live but do not endorse" fashion, now Alliance put all of its rhetorical cards on the table. Eric Lowther was again leading the charge, declaring that "Bill C-23 is a benefits for sex bill. It is crazy." Echoing the objections of conservatives to civil unions in Vermont, Lowther declared that the legislation was marriage in everything but name, and overlooked other dependent relationships.[78] Other Alliance members emphasized arguments about moral decline. Reflecting a common neoconservative theme, one member placed contemporary developments in the context of the sexual revolution and its aftermath, with a "gradual blurring of the sexes" leading to a "militant homosexuality," which resulted in "things that had been considered improper ... looking for a desperate legitimacy." Thus, after Trudeau abolished the sodomy laws, "our government started its assault on traditional family and marriage." This led, according to this member, to a perversion of the idea of privacy, since "the party that told us that government has no business in the bedrooms of the nation continues to invade them."[79]

The use of privacy as a tool of exclusion is thus not a uniquely U.S. phenomenon, but in Canada it is exercised not by arrogant majorities, but by arrogant minorities. The views of the Alliance Party are considerably more marginalized in the polity than those of U.S. conservatives.[80] Indeed, during the debate a Liberal member made the following statement: "Canadians have a great love for the charter. Why is that? Because the charter defines us as a people." Laughter erupted from Alliance Party members.[81] This should come as no surprise, since their moralism and negative, exclusive liberalism finds little space in a polity whose liberalism is reflected in the Charter. Ultimately, Bill C-23 passed on a vote of 174 to 72, with seventeen Liberals and four Conservatives joining the Alliance in opposition.[82]

## Common Law Marriage Isn't Enough for Activists: More Litigation and Future Political and Legal Prospects for Full Same-Sex Marriage in Canada

Given the Liberals' decision to define marriage as opposite-sex only in Bill C-23, attempts to fully equalize marriage policy for sexual minorities were at a standstill in the legislative arena. Svend Robinson, who did not vote on Bill C-23 to protest the marriage definition,[83] submitted a private member's bill that would change the federal definition of marriage to include same-sex couples. He knew that it would not pass but wished to spark renewed debate.[84] As a result of the political barriers, activists, emboldened by recent legal and legislative success, went back to court to push same-sex marriage claims further under the Charter.

Activists initiated litigation in three provinces: British Columbia, Ontario, and Quebec. Egale called this the "landmark trilogy," by which they hoped to push the Supreme Court of Canada to rule in favor of same-sex marriage.[85] In B.C., the Bureau of Vital Statistics rejected same-sex marriage applications, but the NDP provincial government was sympathetic to the cause and joined a lawsuit aimed at changing the federal marriage policy. When a Liberal government came to power, the provincial support for the challenge was ended, but the Supreme Court of British Columbia[86] heard the challenge with the couples and Egale as petitioners.[87] The decision by Justice Ian Pitfield rebuffing the plaintiffs was, consistent with opinions unfavorable to same-sex marriage challenges, narrowly argued, deferential to political decision making, and even utilized plain meaning and original intent interpretations, tools generally not embraced in modern Canadian jurisprudence. In many ways, it was more like a U.S. same-sex marriage decision of the 1970s than a Canadian case in 2001. Pitfield argued that marriage was defined by common law (there is no statutory definition of marriage in Canada), and this definition was opposite-sex only, adopting a dictionary definition of marriage from 1908 that had been utilized in the common law. The common law, he asserted, should only be changed incrementally, not radically, as was the request in this case.[88] And applying familiar tautological reasoning, combined with original intent, he argued that marriage under the Canadian Constitution could never be construed to include same-sex couples. In fact, not even Parliament could change the definition:

> There is nothing to suggest that "marriage," in ... [the Constitution Act of 1867] was used in any context other than its legal context ... namely, a monogamous, opposite-sex relationship. That being the case, if Parliament were to enact legislation saying that "marriage" means a relationship solemnized between two persons without reference to sex, it would be attempting to change the meaning of the head of power and thereby unilaterally amend the Constitution.[89]

This, of course, leaves little room, legally or politically, for policy change in the direction of same-sex marriage, and is a decision that a U.S. jurist like Antonin Scalia would certainly love.

Pitfield then turned to more modern Charter analysis, since, as he put it, the foregoing reasoning "may be incorrect." This was a remarkable shift in tone and focus and appeared to be a nod to the fact that his reasoning is outside the mainstream. Pitfield focused on the question of whether exclusion of same-sex couples from marriage violates the Charter, and he ultimately found that while constitutionally suspect discrimination is the result of the policy, exclusion is saved under the *Oakes* test. Because of procreation and the social entrenchment of marriage as an institution, Pitfield argued, "the salutary effect associated with the preservation of its opposite-sex core far outweighs the deleterious effect resulting from the refusal to provide legal status to same-sex relationships under the rubric of marriage."[90]

Other Canadian courts have thoroughly rejected Pitfield's approach. The Ontario Divisional Court dispensed with the common law definition and found that it contravened the equality provisions of the Charter, relying not on narrow and original intent interpretations but contemporary Charter adjudication methods. These judges and Pitfield were on different legal planets. As Justice Robert Blair stated:

> There is a short answer to the question posed by the Applicants in these two proceedings. It is this: the constitutional and Charter-inspired values which underlie Canadian society today dictate that the status and incidents inherent in the foundational institution of marriage must be open to same-sex couples who live long-term, committed, relationships—marriage-like in everything but name—just as it is to be heterosexual couples. Each is entitled to full and equal recognition, and the law must therefore be adapted accordingly.[91]

The court was divided over an appropriate remedy: One judge favored an immediate court redefinition of marriage, while the two others favored giving the federal government time, like the Vermont Supreme Court, to fashion a constitutionally adequate remedy. If not, the court would change the common law definition to include same-sex couples.[92] This decision was followed by a virtually identical decision by the Quebec Superior Court.[93]

These more activist decisions stand in stark contrast to earlier same-sex marriage adjudication in Canada. A Manitoba case from the 1970s was quite similar to U.S. cases from the same time. The court deferentially held that the statutory meaning of "any two persons" was the opposite-sex common law definition and, thus, the court was not willing to include same-sex couples in the definition.[94] Even as late as 1993, the Ontario Divisional Court rejected a Charter challenge to the marriage policy, relying on the common law definition, but a dissent did find a Section 15 violation.[95] The Ontario court thus overruled itself in 2002, reflecting the developments in Charter jurisprudence. For instance, the earlier decision was handed down before the Supreme Court read sexual orientation into the Charter.

In line with the evolving jurisprudence, in the summer of 2003, the Ontario Court of Appeals affirmed the lower court decision and the B.C. appeals court overturned Pitfield's decision and found in favor of same-sex marriage. The Ontario court ordered the Toronto city clerk to issue marriage licenses to same-sex couples.[96] It the wake of the decision, Ontario began granting licenses to same-sex couples throughout the province.[97] The Quebec Court of Appeals affirmed that province's lower court decision in favor of same-sex marriage in March 2004.[98]

Thus, it is clear that, the B.C. decision aside, Canadian courts have become considerably more receptive to full gay rights claims in recent years. When a Yukon court ruled in favor of same-sex marriage claims in 2004, the judge did not even delve into Charter analysis to justify his ruling; he merely asserted that the courts in the other provinces had clearly established that a ban on same-sex marriage contravened the Charter.[99] Soon after, a Manitoba court found in favor of same-sex marriage claims. As the judge stated, "The cumulative effect and the overwhelming effect of that judicial authority is to the effect that the traditional definition of marriage is no longer constitutionally valid in view of the provisions of the Charter of Rights and Freedoms."[100] This decision was itself soon followed by a similar decision by a Nova Scotia court.[101]

By 2004, then, a clear legal consensus had emerged in Canadian courts that same-sex marriage was required under the Charter. Even though the issue continued to cause minor political trouble for political actors, as will be discussed below, the government accepted the courts' position and halted challenges to same-sex marriage suits in other provinces.[102] Instead, the ruling Liberals asked for an advisory opinion from the Supreme Court of Canada as to whether their desire to enact nationwide same-sex marriage legislation was consistent with the Charter. In this reference, as it is called in Canadian law, the government completely accepted the finding of the courts of appeal.[103]

## THE POLITICAL RESPONSE TO MARRIAGE LITIGATION AND FUTURE PROSPECTS

The political response to this litigation has been predictably mixed, but with substantial room for gay rights claims. The decisions created a thorny political situation for the ruling Liberals, but, as was noted above, the decision was ultimately made not to challenge the court decisions in the Supreme Court. The government had previously defended the same-sex marriage ban in the courts, relying on the argument that the marriage/procreation link is valid and is enough to withstand Charter challenges.[104] Seeing the legal writing on the wall, along with relatively supportive poll numbers, the government pursued a legislative response. In late 2002, even before the appellate court decisions, Justice Minister Martin Cauchon, himself a supporter of same-sex marriage along with several Liberal ministers,[105] asked the House of Commons Justice Committee to examine four legislative paths: keeping the status quo; establishing something like civil unions; legalizing same-sex marriage; or eliminating the federal government's role in marriage and leaving it as a purely private matter (much like proposals from Hawaii governors).[106]

After the appeals court rulings, however, the government's hand was forced more directly. The government quickly decided not to appeal the decision and to draft same-sex marriage legislation for the entire country, over the objections of many in the Liberal Party, especially those from rural and western ridings.[107]

In the fall of 2003, in an attempt to derail the Liberals' move toward enacting same-sex marriage legislation, the Canadian Alliance forced a vote on a motion defining marriage as "the union of one man and woman, to the exclusion of all others." The motion narrowly failed, 137 to 132, with fifty Liberals voting in favor of the motion. Even though this vote again demonstrated the fairly complicated politics of same-sex marriage in Canada and shows that political actors were ambivalent, it was largely irrelevant, since the courts were continuing their assault on opposite-sex–only marriage by using the Charter. Indeed, many members of Parliament decided to vote against the amendment, fearing that it would lead to a confrontation with the courts and the invocation of the notwithstanding clause.[108]

The issue of same-sex marriage played a tangential role in the 2004 parliamentary elections. First, Prime Minister Paul Martin (the successor to Jean Chrétien) pushed back the Supreme Court reference until the fall of 2004, after the election. In an effort to unseat the Liberals as the ruling party, the two parties on the right, the Tories and the Alliance, merged. The issue of same-sex marriage was a sticking point in the merger negotiations, given that the Tories were generally much more supportive of relationship equality than were Alliance members.[109] Ultimately, the new party took a firm stand against same-sex marriages, especially under the leadership of Stephen Harper, who had campaigned on a culturally conservative agenda. During the campaign, Harper indicated that he would invoke the notwithstanding clause to overturn pro–same-sex marriage decisions but was rebuked by other Conservatives, including the deputy party leader, and reinforced the notion that his politics were too extreme for Canada.[110] Even though the Liberals lost seats, this was largely due to a poorly executed campaign and scandal.[111] There is little evidence that its push for same-sex marriage legislation was a large factor. In fact, Harper's strong stand against same-sex marriage and other culturally conservative positions may have actually slowed his momentum late in the campaign.[112] At any rate, given that the Bloc Quebecois and the NDP are firmly behind the new policy, the legislation will likely be enacted in the summer of 2005.[113]

There is also no apparent backlash against the courts. When given the opportunity to appoint judges to the Supreme Court, Prime Minister Martin did not select models of judicial self-restraint. In fact, one of the appointees was Rosalie Abella, author of the pro–gay rights *Rosenberg* decision in 1998.[114] And Canadian judges were clearly comfortable with their independence and rights activist role. Roy McMurtry, chief justice of Ontario, argued in a speech that judges should ignore public opinion and adjudicate solely on the basis of the requirements of the Charter, noting that "the judicial function may well be anti-majoritarian in the sense it is often charged with the responsibility of protecting the minority."[115] Indeed, during the reference hearings, the Supreme Court seemed highly skeptical of the arguments of opponents of same-sex marriage.[116] The legal consensus clearly has shifted in favor of same-sex marriage in Canada.

## LEGAL ELITES, LEGAL NORMS, AND PUBLIC OPINION: RETHINKING THE POWER OF THE COURTS

Critics of these developments rightly point out that their beginnings were rooted with lawyers and judges. Legal elites in Canada certainly favor same-sex marriage, as evidenced in recent court decisions. Additionally, in 2002 the Law Commission of Canada recommended the legal recognition of same-sex marriages.[117] Similar recommendations have been made by the British Columbia Law Institute and are linked to legislative developments in that province.[118] Cultural conservatives, parliamentary supremacists, republican revivalists, and legal realists all see the same dynamic taking place: counter-majoritarian forces (mostly legal elites) riding roughshod over the political process. But developments in Canada may provide a more nuanced view of these developments and allow us to gain a fuller perspective on the modern interaction among rights, politics, and the law.

For example, while Gerald Rosenberg argues that same-sex marriage litigation has not resulted in significant social change in the United States (this is, as I have argued, an incomplete analysis), the situation in Canada is much different. According to the Gallup poll, support for same-sex marriage in Canada in 1992, just before *Baehr v. Lewin* (a relevant consideration since U.S. news gets substantial attention in Canada), stood at 24 percent. By 1998 this had risen to 40 percent; in 1999 support dipped to 36 percent; by 2000, after *M. v. H.*, support rose to 43 percent; and in 2001 support stood at 46 percent.[119] The upward trend has continued. A poll conducted by the Liberal Party in late 2002 showed support for marriage rights at 48 percent, while 43 percent of respondents were opposed (in Quebec, 55 percent supported same-sex marriage).[120] When asked whether same-sex couples should receive the same legal benefits as opposite-sex couples, 61 percent of Canadian respondents said yes, up from 49 percent in 1994.[121] Thus, a plurality, and close to a majority, of Canadians supported same-sex marriage in 2002, and a large majority supported marriage-like rights. Overall, the numbers for marriage and civil unions are roughly 15 percent higher than in the United States.[122] Polls in 2003 and 2004 saw Canadians continue to strongly support relationship equality, with solid support of equality of benefits (68 percent of respondents in late 2003 favored marriage or civil unions),[123] and a divided or marriage rights–leaning public. The split on marriage in a 2003 poll was 46 percent in favor of same-sex marriage and 46 percent opposed,[124] while in 2004 a poll registered 57 percent support for same-sex marriage and 38 percent opposition.[125] Clearly, there has not been an opinion backlash in Canada similar to that in the United States. The legal and political discussion concerning same-sex marriage is resulting in a more supportive public.

Indeed, Alan Wolfe has noted that, for Americans, homosexuality continues to be a difficult issue to link with civil rights and equality arguments.[126] Given their more inclusive political tradition and richer liberalism, Canadians appear more willing to respond to legal and constitutional arguments favoring gay equality. They also have national courts willing to address the issue. Thus, Rosenberg's assertion that same-sex marriage litigation can only be disappointing and counterproductive for activists is, at best, nationally bounded.

Ultimately, then, we may need to rethink the binary distinction between rights-based litigation and majoritarianism, and Canada provides an especially interesting opportunity to do so. As was discussed earlier, the Charter has always enjoyed significant public support. Recall that in 2002 general support stood at 92 percent. This may be misleading, since a large majority of Americans might similarly support the Bill of Rights and the Constitution but not agree with its most expansive inter-pretations. But Canadians clearly support rights claims and judicial activism and supremacy. Only 11 percent think the Charter goes too far in protecting the rights of minorities (68 percent feel that sexual minorities should have Charter protec-tion), and, as previously indicated, 71 percent feel that the Supreme Court should be the final arbiter of Charter interpretation.[127] Perhaps counter-majoritarianism is an expectation of modern democratic citizens.

# 11   Courts, Social Change, and the Power of Legal Liberalism

THIS CHAPTER directly addresses Gerald Rosenberg's argument that courts are quite ineffective at achieving social change and that minority groups that look to the courts for change will be disappointed. In connection with same-sex marriage litigation, he has argued that litigation has had very little effect and has, in fact, led to a strong political reaction against it. Indeed, Rosenberg points out that nearly a decade after the litigation began, no right existed for same-sex couples to marry, and a significant majority of states and the federal government have specifically prohibited such marriages.[1] In this chapter, I present evidence that challenges Rosenberg's claims on U.S. public opinion (as I did with Canadian public opinion), and broadens the view of the actual effects of same-sex marriage litigation by relying on a more constitutive analysis.

## COURTS, PUBLIC OPINION, AND SOCIAL CHANGE

Central to Rosenberg's claim is the fact that public opinion has not substantially shifted since same-sex marriage litigation began, since, according to polls, in 1996, 27 percent of Americans supported same-sex marriage, and by 2000 this number was 34 percent.[2] Rosenberg claims that this change is insignificant, but this fails to account for the socially and culturally embedded nature of the institution of heterosexual marriage. Receptivity to changes in this institution is not as easily reflected in public opinion polls as other, more routine, public policy areas. Viewed from this perspective, an increase of seven percentage points in four years of same-sex marriage support can be seen as a significant shift.

And Rosenberg is not alone. Richard Posner has written that the U.S. public is staunchly opposed to same-sex marriage and even civil unions by citing one poll.[3] Indeed, he asserts that for federal courts to find in favor of same-sex marriage "in the face of adamantly opposed public opinion would be seriously undemocratic. . . . It would be moral vanguardism."[4]

The story is much more complex, however. First, public support for domestic partnerships and civil unions is higher than for marriage. A 1997 poll in Hawaii indicated that although 70 percent of respondents were opposed to same-sex marriage, only 55 percent were opposed to domestic partnerships.[5] The litigation in that state likely influenced public opinion in the direction of relationship equality just as it had influenced some legislators. A Gallup poll in 2001 indicated that 44 percent of respondents nationally favored a civil union–style approach. This was up from 42 percent in 2000.[6] In 2002 support rose to 46 percent, and was up to

49 percent by 2003.[7] An AP poll in 2000 also indicated that the public was split on the domestic partnership issue, with 41 percent in favor and 46 percent opposed. When the question is asked about specific benefits for same-sex partners, majority support emerges: 56 percent of respondents favored inheritance rights, 53 percent favored health insurance coverage, and 50 percent favored Social Security benefits for same-sex partners.[8]

Polling reflects a still fluid situation when it comes to same-sex marriage and civil unions but with emerging support for relationship equality. In a November 2003 national poll by the *Los Angeles Times*, 36 percent supported civil unions, 40 percent opposed them, and 24 percent did not know or had not heard enough. The U.S. public appeared to be divided on gay relationship equality, with a segment up for grabs in this poll. The same poll showed the following split on marriage for same-sex couples: 31 percent in support, 55 percent opposed, 14 percent no opinion.[9] Thus, opposition to marriage is no longer in the 60 to 70 percent range that existed in the mid-1990s. Indeed, opposition in a leading poll declined from 68 percent in 1996 to 55 percent in 2003.[10] Even a proposed federal constitutional amendment to ban same-sex marriage garners only 50 to 55 percent support—hardly the supermajority needed for a federal constitutional amendment.[11] And support has emerged for relationship equality nationally. In the 2004 national election exit poll, 24 percent of respondents supported same-sex marriage, 35 percent favored civil unions, and only 37 percent favored no legal recognintion for same-sex couples.[12]

Other polls tell an interesting story. A September 2003 poll asked the following question: "Just your best guess, do you think that allowing two people of the same sex to legally marry will change our society for the better, will it have no effect, or will it change our society for the worse?" Responses were respectively 10 percent, 40 percent, and 48 percent. Here we see more of a stalemate than overwhelming opposition: 50 percent (better and no effect) to 48 percent (worse). Responses to the question, "Do you think gay or lesbian couples should or should not be allowed all the same legal rights as married couples in every state, or does it not matter to you?" reflected more division than opposition, respectively, 32 percent, 35 percent, and 32 percent.[13] The diminished opposition to marriage equality policies is noteworthy and significant and was undoubtedly facilitated by continued litigation. Opinion is in flux, despite Posner's assessment, but it is no longer significantly against the notion of relationship equality. Perhaps it is a reflection of the split nation defined by the 2000 U.S. presidential election. In Canada, this shift was more pronounced and rapid with, as noted in Chapter 10, solid majorities in favor of civil unions or full marriage equality, with much smaller opposition than in the United States.

Regional and partisan divisions also tell a more complex story in the United States. According to a Pew poll in 2003, opposition in the United States to same-sex marriage is highest in the South (67 percent), followed by the West (58 percent), the Midwest (56 percent), and the East (50 percent).[14] Thus, the South's views on the issue are reflective of where the entire nation was in the mid-1990s, and the East is leading the way. Republicans are uniformly against same-sex marriage (75 percent) and civil unions (68 percent), while Democrats and independents are more divided, with a plurality of Democrats supporting civil unions (48 percent) and a slight majority of independents favoring that approach (52 percent).[15] Again, opposition is isolated by region and party, no doubt linked to traditional notions of cultural values. As was discussed in previous chapters, public opinion in some traditionally progressive states is more supportive of same-sex marriage and civil unions. A poll of states in New England showed 70 percent support for civil unions and 46 percent for same-sex marriage.[16] And, as was discussed, the Supreme Judicial Court's decision in Massachusetts was generally in line with opinion in that state. A very low percentage of the public, 17 percent in one poll, favor no recognition for same-sex couples.[17] And relationship equality has substantial support in Connecticut, New Hampshire, New Jersey, and New York as well.[18]

In California (representing 12 percent of the entire U.S. population), where a strong domestic partnership law was enacted, a poll in August 2003 found considerable support for that policy, and 42 percent of respondents were in favor of same-sex marriage and this increased to 44 percent in 2004.[19] Support for relationship equality is also emerging in Oregon and Washington. Support for marriage in Washington mirrors that of California at 44 percent with a much higher percentage in favor of an extension of rights.[20] Recall that in Oregon, about a third of respondents in a poll favored no relationship recognition, another third favored full marriage equality, and 29 percent favored a civil union solution.[21]

Even beyond the coasts, support for relationship equality is emerging. In Wisconsin, polls have shown majority support emerging for civil unions (48 percent), while support for same-sex marriage ranges from 27 percent to 32 percent.[22] Similar results were seen in Iowa where a poll registered 49 percent support for civil unions and 23 percent for same-sex marriage.[23] Even in conservative Indiana, a majority of respondents in a poll supported some form of recognition for same-sex couples (19 percent for marriage and 31 percent for civil unions) with 46 percent opposed to any recognition.[24] In Michigan, support for no recognition of relationships was lower (36 percent), with larger support for civil unions (43 percent).[25] The South is, not surprisingly, still strongly opposed to relationship equality. Polls in Alabama and Louisiana have shown weak support for marriage equality (around 20 percent and 24 percent, respectively).[26] Interestingly, Florida ranks with the upper Midwest, with support for marriage equality at 35 percent in one poll and support for civil unions at 53 percent.[27] Real change appears to be occurring on the coasts and in the upper Midwest. Support for civil unions is emerging in many of these states, and in the Northeast, majority support for full marriage equality is emerging. This is not noticeable in Rosenberg's sweeping analysis.

A significant generational difference exists in polling on this issue. Younger voters are much more likely to support the idea of same-sex marriage. In the California Field poll, 75 percent of respondents over the age of sixty-five opposed the idea, while only 45 percent of respondents between eighteen and thirty-nine did so.[28] In a Wisconsin poll, 52 percent of respondents under thirty supported same-sex marriage and 67 percent supported civil unions, while support from those sixty and over was only 12 percent and 37 percent respectively.[29] A national poll showed a similar dynamic: support for same-sex marriage stood at 61 percent for respondents from eighteen to twenty-nine, 40 percent for those thirty to forty-four, 38 percent for those forty-five to sixty-four, and 18 percent for those over the age of sixty-five.[30] This generational difference suggests that public support for same-sex marriage will substantially increase over time.

Additionally, intensity currently appears to be on the side of same-sex marriage opponents in the United States, anchored by traditional morality. As Mark DiCamillo of the Field poll noted, "Even though majorities of Democrats and Independents [in California], who really show you which way the wind blows, are on the side of allowing same-sex marriage, the overwhelming majority of Republicans who are opposed pulls it over to the other side."[31] Here, again, the combination of libertarianism and moralism in the Republican Party is a harmful combination for gay rights advocates. Democrats and independents are responding to the notions of positive freedom invoked by courts, like the Canadian citizenry, but Republicans are staunchly holding out, and their libertarian/moralistic outlook is a powerful force in U.S. politics, while it is at the fringe of Canadian discourse.

Interestingly, in the wake of the *Lawrence v. State of Texas* and Massachusetts same-sex marriage decisions in 2003, opposition to same-sex marriage appeared, in some polls, to strengthen. For example, in a CBS/*New York Times* poll, opposition grew to 61 percent in December 2003 from 55 percent in July.[32] A Gallup poll showed support for civil unions slipping from 49 percent to 40 percent after the *Lawrence* decision. However, an NPR poll after the Massachusetts decision registered pre-*Lawrence* opposition (56 percent) to same-sex marriage and a split on civil unions similar to that noted above (42 versus 49 percent in the context of a general question on civil unions and 45 versus 45 percent when specific rights were listed).[33] Given that intensity is on the side of opponents to same-sex marriage, this slight bump is understandable, but the NPR poll indicates that the overall trend is of increased, though not yet overwhelming, support for relationship equality. The dynamics of the NPR poll are confirmed by a return in a Gallup poll to pre-*Lawrence* and *Goodridge* opposition of 56 percent by May 2005 (it previously hit a low of 55 percent in June 2003).[34]

Additionally, candidates for national and state political offices, such as Bill Bradley and Al Gore in 2000, have advocated relationship equality. As an example of the salience of relationship equality on the state level, all three Democratic candidates for governor of Wisconsin supported domestic partnership legislation in 2002, as was the case in Massachusetts.[35] In New York, both Democratic candidates for governor also supported such legislation. Before dropping out of the race Andrew Cuomo stated about civil unions: "New York should have been first. When I am governor, New York will be the second."[36] Most of the Democrats in the 2004 presidential primary race supported civil unions or same-sex marriage. Certainly, these candidates were talking to their liberal bases, but this is still a significant political development. In the general election, President George W. Bush supported the proposed constitutional amendment to ban same-sex marriages, while John Kerry opposed the amendment, opposed same-sex marriage, but supported civil unions or some form of relationship equality.[37]

Thus, in the United States, talking about same-sex marriage is politically danger-ous, advocating civil unions is not. One can certainly argue that this is "marriage-lite" and therefore understandably less controversial (and less satisfying for same-sex marriage advocates), but one can also argue that the ideas of equality and inclusion are strongly, though not perfectly, reflected in domestic partnerships ar-rangements, especially if all of the benefits of legal marriage are granted. Clearly, courts, through same-sex marriage litigation, have helped to define these argu-ments. In addition, a 2001 *Wall Street Journal* poll indicated that two-thirds of Americans felt that same-sex marriage would become legal in the next century—perhaps a telling indication of the power of legal discourse.[38] And, interestingly, a *Boston Globe* poll in May 2005 found that 46 percent of respondents thought that their state should recognize Massachusetts same-sex marriages, with 50 per-cent opposed to the idea.[39] This further undercuts the "overwhelming opposition" argument and indicates that citizens take legally driven arguments seriously. By only accepting a profound shift in public opinion concerning a deeply traditional institution like marriage as evidence of social change, Rosenberg fails to see the actual impact of same-sex marriage litigation on society and its politics.

An interesting piece of evidence concerning the *Bowers v. Hardwick* decision also challenges the notion that courts cannot affect public opinion. According to the Gallup poll, a year before *Bowers* was decided, 47 percent of the public thought that consenting, same-sex relations should be legal, while 43 percent thought they should not. Since 1977, these numbers had always been close to each other. But when the question was asked in the immediate wake of the decision, and for several years thereafter, approval sank to 32 percent and disapproval rose to 57 percent.[40] Opinion went from parity to a twenty-five-point spread—a remarkable and nearly overnight shift. Certainly, the decision and the publicity surrounding it played a role in this. It is not unthinkable, then, that courts could also have the opposite effect.

## THE DEFICIENCIES OF THE ROSENBERG PERSPECTIVE

Ultimately, then, Rosenberg presents a thin account of the relationship between law and political culture and neglects the nuance and subtlety of the interaction between legal language and public opinion and social change. His high threshold for proof of social change and unwillingness to dig beneath the surface of opinion data inhibit the fullest understanding of the relationship between litigation and public opinion.

Rosenberg's constrained court analysis is certainly not without merit. Courts, especially in the United States, operate under real constraints. However, the "con-strained court" view is incomplete. As the case of gay rights litigation suggests, when one looks beyond the U.S. Supreme Court, the ability of courts to achieve change by setting new agendas and marshalling legal language that resonated in the political arena with shifts in public opinion and concrete policy change. Re-liance on a top-down approach in the context of gay rights litigation leads to an emphasis on the backlash and fails to capture the developments on the other side of the equation.

Gay rights litigation also furthers the reconsideration of cause lawyers, who are largely dismissed in the Rosenberg framework. This dismissal fits with other critiques of judicial decision making discussed in Chapter 1. Gay rights litigation demonstrates, however, that movement lawyers are much more sophisticated than some scholars have suggested, blending political with legal considerations. When litigation is carefully planned and targeted, positive outcomes have resulted for gay rights claims—results that would have been nearly unthinkable from a legislature. Rather than institutionally ill-equipped, courts have brought their unique institutional norms and values to bear in this relatively new policy area.

Indeed, courts have the ability to present arguments about civil rights that are not politically popular. In this instance, what started out as a perhaps naive attempt to legalize same-sex marriage has resulted in serious attempts to grant same-sex couples the same legal rights that come with traditional marriage. The litigation in Hawaii and Vermont did not lead to a same-sex marriage law, but it did lead to a reciprocal benefits law and a civil unions law. And the litigation in Massachusetts appears to have, for the time being, resulted in same-sex marriage equality like the litigation in Canada. Undoubtedly, these policies would not have been enacted if not for the litigation. In the case of Vermont, the courts directly forced the hand of the political branches, and a more thorough law resulted. But what is also remarkable about this litigation is the perhaps more intangible effect it had on political actors. In Hawaii, Vermont, and Canada, litigation resulted in a discussion of lesbian and gay civil rights that demanded a consideration of equality. Over and over again, one sees evidence that the intention of many political actors was to recognize same-sex relationships on a level similar to heterosexual marriage. Without the legal arguments and decisions to frame this debate, it can be argued that only arguments based on tradition and the desire to preserve the institution of marriage would have had any salience. By looking outside of politics and its largely majoritarian considerations, courts can compel the political process to move beyond where it might normally go.

A close look at some of the statements and actions by politicians in Vermont sheds light on this point. Consider a member of the House Kenneth Atkins who agonized over the decision and first voted for civil unions to keep debate alive, but ultimately voted against the bill. A newspaper account effectively summed up his decision-making process and gives some insight to what judicial language and expectation adds to political decision making:

> In the moments before the final vote, as his colleagues buzzed through the noisy chamber, Atkins sat quietly at his desk with his hands folded in front of his face. He appeared to be in almost physical pain. It was, he said later, literally one of the most difficult decisions in his entire life. "It's one I will second-guess many, many times in the future," he said later. "Some of my friends on the floor, who I respect and have learned to love, I let down." Atkins taught school for 34 years before winning a House seat in 1998. One of the subjects he taught his fifth-graders was history.

And, he said, the judgment of history always falls on the side of those who choose to expand rights for their fellow men and women. "When you look in retrospect," Atkins said, "10, 15, 20 years later, you say, what was wrong with those people? Didn't they realize what they were doing?"[41]

Kenneth Atkin's town of Winooski, Vermont voted 785 to 445 against civil unions,[42] and this ultimately led him to oppose the civil unions bill—but not without intense consideration of the right thing to do for "history." By looking outside of mere politics and its consideration of what the community desires, courts can compel the political process to move beyond where it might normally go.

The story of gay rights litigation, then, is one of how courts interact with other, more political branches of government and the way in which litigation interacts with public opinion. Sodomy litigation ultimately was a good "fit" with U.S. polity norms, but it also challenged the political process to move beyond where it had settled on the issue. Early same-sex marriage litigation was torpedoed largely because the political climate had not sufficiently progressed on lesbian and gay rights, but later litigation worked against public opinion. Lawyers and judges, using creative and substantive reasoning, started to step out of their purely deferential role to legislatures on the definition of marriage and began to incorporate arguments of equality that would justify the extension of legal benefits to same-sex couples. Political actors then utilized these arguments once they had been articulated. Courts can add an important element to the discourse and the political process, and legal arguments can directly affect and shape the making of public policy. In this case, the language of rights and equality strongly affected legislative outcomes. Scheingold's assertion that rights and litigation can be powerful, but limited, tools in achieving social change is still valid.[43] Courts cannot do everything. However, Rosenberg's unwillingness to look beyond the broad parameters of his theory ignores important aspects of same-sex marriage litigation. We need to fully explore both sides of the effects of rights claims.

Indeed, these changes occurred because of the introduction of liberal legal norms that reminded the U.S. polity of one of its core values (libertarianism) but also went beyond the dominant strain of U.S. liberalism (positive freedom). For example, in Vermont, political and legal change was achieved though the judicial articulation of liberal legal norms richer than America's dominant strain of liberalism. William Eskridge claims, however, that the outcome in Vermont was influenced by communitarian considerations. In particular, he asserts that the deliberative process in the Vermont legislature and the public led to an appreciation of same-sex marriage as a public good. The *Baker v. State* decision, itself, was communitarian in its lack of a direct remedy, thereby allowing for democratic deliberation. In this version of events, the general will was achieved by moderates forging a solution. The decision, according to Eskridge, "required the political process to listen to lesbian and gay couples, who realized in turn that their voices would be marginalized if they were not responsive to normative concerns of legislative moderates."[44]

This mistakenly treats the legislative activity as routine and not defined by legal norms. Absent the court, this outcome would not have been possible. Communitarian deliberation was not the driving force here. Except for those conservatives who viewed the decision in *Baker* as completely illegitimate, most legislators knew they were acting within the boundaries of legal constraints, as well as political ones. Eskridge describes the House Judiciary Committee members as relative blank slates, save for openly gay William Lippert, on the same-sex marriage issue: "Probably most of them did not understand how a woman could romantically and sexually love another woman, but they came away from the experience . . . with an appreciation of lesbian and gay humanity."[45] In Eskridge's view, this happened because testimony about the public good of same-sex marriage swayed the members. Although testimony emphasizing the humanity of lesbians and gay men no doubt influenced the outcome, the members were, as I have indicated, by no means blank slates. They reflected the liberal tenets of sympathy with outsiders and a belief in legally enforceable rights. This, not communitarian concerns, led them to their unanimity in favor of same-sex rights. It was communitarian values of tradition and preservation of the status quo that led to political conflict on the floor of the legislature. To call a ringing endorsement of liberal rights communitarian ignores important differences between the two approaches. Rights are more powerful tools for this policy area than communitarian considerations.

The perspectives of Posner, Rosenberg, and, to some extent, Eskridge share a certain normative resistance to court-driven change. They wish to privilege the political process by downplaying the independent and unique contributions of courts. However, the changes brought about by gay rights litigation should not be overlooked. As I have demonstrated, significant change has indeed been driven by courts and legal norms.[46]

# 12   Conclusion

THE PAST FEW YEARS have brought some remarkable developments on the gay rights front in the United States and Canada. Canadian courts mandated same-sex marriage in nearly the entire country and some U.S. courts have ruled in a similar fashion, adding momentum for the legal attainment of marriage equality in the United States. Additionally, the U.S. Supreme Court, long an outlier on gay rights, handed down the dramatic *Lawrence v. Texas* decision, which could have been handed down by a Canadian court, given its reliance on rich notions of liberalism. In this final chapter, I discuss the implications of these developments and refocus the main themes of the book: the ability of courts to achieve social change, especially in the context of rights claiming; the differences in outcomes in the two nations that stem from differences in their liberal traditions; and the need to, especially in the United States, refocus on courts as vital institutions for the promotion and preservation of social justice.

## REASSESSING COURTS AND SOCIAL CHANGE

Recent developments concerning the political and legal status of sexual minorities provide us with an opportunity to challenge the assumptions of the realist/political jurisprudence assumptions that have so dominated public law in recent decades. Although many of the tenets of this perspective were reflected in gay rights litigation (the role of public opinion as a constraint on courts, institutional deficiencies of courts for broad policymaking, etc.), constitutive insights help explain other developments. The ability of courts to set new agendas, frame political conflicts in liberal legal language that empowered sexual minorities, the leverage that litigation provided this minority, and the radiating effects of these arguments all have led to significant, thought not complete, social change. Certainly, the backlash in the United States is real, given ideological parameters, but, over the course of ten years, public attitudes and policies have changed markedly. These changes are difficult to imagine in the absence of litigation. Recall the resistance to policy change in the United States on both sodomy law reform and relationship equality absent the cover of litigation. In addition, this litigation also allows us to continue the reconsideration of the role played by cause lawyers. The lawyers examined here were politically astute and chose their forums carefully (perhaps being too hesitant initially on the issue of relationship equality), but legal considerations were paramount once litigation commenced. And it was the legal arguments that most directly propelled the successful outcomes.

This change occurred not because of communitarian, feminist, or queer arguments. Rather, a rich, rights-based liberalism was the primary philosophical driving force. Certainly, arguments from these other perspectives have created an environment that facilitated the success of liberal arguments in court, particularly by drawing attention toward those at the margins of society and by illuminating the influence of a wide variety of power structures. However, since courts respond most to liberal rights claiming, the liberal framing of gay politics most directly led to positive outcomes. Additionally, the criticism of liberalism from these perspectives is challenged by the developments outlined in this book. Rights are not simply hollow tools usable only for status quo reinforcing or oppression. They instead serve as tools of liberation.

## *LAWRENCE V. TEXAS* AND THE POSSIBLE "CANADIANIZATION" OF U.S. GAY RIGHTS JURISPRUDENCE

Differences in political culture explain much of the difference between the United States and Canada on the question of gay rights. The dominant libertarian ethic in the United States, combined with a powerful moralistic politics, has clearly inhibited the polity's ability to move strongly in the direction of relationship equality. The nation known for its embrace of rights does not always embrace the fullest range of rights. Canada, with its new constitution and tradition of embracing a broader liberalism, provided a more accommodating atmosphere for arguments in favor of relationship equality for same-sex couples. Increasingly, the United States is the outlier among Western liberal democracies on this issue.

However, *Lawrence* reflects a significant shift in U.S. jurisprudence. The historically gay rights–hesitant Supreme Court looked more like its northern counterpart. Indeed, one of the striking elements of the *Lawrence* decision was the Court's citation of international gay rights jurisprudence. Although Antonin Scalia cited Canadian same-sex marriage precedents disapprovingly, the majority was clearly influenced by them, applying a richer liberalism to U.S. gay rights jurisprudence. This is not to say that the U.S. Supreme Court will automatically rule in favor of same-sex marriage anytime in the near future. Certainly, political considerations may limit this, but the jurisprudence appears to be pointing in that direction. It may take longer for the United States to achieve Canadian outcomes, given the differences in political culture, among other factors, but U.S. courts are currently laying the foundation for change. The jurisprudence is converging more rapidly than convergence on political and cultural issues.[1]

Although it is true that a fuller range of gay rights claims have been more salient in Canada, the trajectory of U.S. legal norms appear to be headed in the Canadian direction, if we consider as evidence the rhetoric of *Lawrence* and developments at the state court level. However, in order for U.S. polity to more fully embrace relationship equality, the barrier of the libertarian moralism will need to be diminished. The dominant negative take on freedom will need to be augmented by a richer liberalism. The challenge is evidenced by columnist William Safire's thoughts on U.S. legal developments of 2003. Describing himself as a libertarian conservative, or "libcon," who applauded the *Lawrence* decision, Safire also expressed some discomfort with same-sex marriage. On that issue, he preferred that judges not enforce rights, but that communities extend their sanction to same-sex couples:

> Civil union connotes toleration of homosexuality, with its attendant recognition of and individual's civil rights; but marriage connotes society's full approval of homosexuality, with previous moral judgment reversed. The pace of profound cultural change is too important to be left to activist judges. As moral-political issues go, this big one deserves examination in communities with minds that can deal with internal contradictions—which is the libcon way.[2]

Safire ignores the fact that, for many, the *Lawrence* decision was activist. Furthermore, the problem is that libertarianism will not allow these communities to embrace full relationship equality. Freedom to be left alone does not automatically translate into public affirmation. This is the U.S. dilemma. "Activist judges" may need to remind the polity of the richness of its political traditions and to remind policy makers and citizens of the importance of rights in a liberal, not purely majoritarian, democracy. Some judges have already begun to do so, but they, so far, are the exceptions.

## A New Role for Courts?

One of the striking aspects of this study is the willingness of judges in both nations to reject the political and legal status quo on sexual minorities. Judicial activism, of course, is nothing new. But the consistent and transnational tendency for courts to seriously challenge majoritarian assumptions and assertions on such a "traditional" institution and policy and assert an alternative view grounded in a fuller conception of liberalism points to a potential transformation in the politics of modern liberal democracies. This also challenges court power-hesitant commentators especially on the political left. Progressives should not abandon the courts simply because they are populated by a certain ideology at a given time. Nor should those on the left view courts simply as tools of the powerful. Instead, courts need to be viewed as vital players in national political and philosophical conversations, given their capacity to enrich the debate by reminding majorities that a polity has more than one tradition that might apply to a particular problem.

As previously noted, this is not a call for "government by judiciary." It simply represents a desire for politics in liberal democracies to be about more than the power (and resulting arrogance) of majorities. And, as the case of Canada demonstrates, this may reflect the desire of modern democratic citizens: the willingness to embrace liberal constitutionalism enforced by courts. It also reflects the contemporary reality of the way that judges view their jobs in the United States and Canada. They are increasingly less hesitant across the board (especially at the state court level in the United States and all levels in Canada) to reason substantively rather than deferentially. Judicial activism has become increasingly normalized. And these judges are viewing themselves as part of a larger community of interpreters. Although there is potential danger lurking in these developments, excessive judicial power is potentially curbed by grounded interpretation in established polity traditions. As Lowi and McConnell noted,[3] calling for a larger court role does not diminish politics but expands it by asking a larger number of questions and considering a larger number of perspectives.

# Notes

CHAPTER 1

1. 2 S.C.R. 3 (1999).

2. "Quebec Oks Civil Unions, Adoption Rights," PlanetOut.com, June 7, 2002; "Controversial Same Sex Bill Passes Commons," *Canadian Press Newswire*, April 11, 2000.

3. Clifford Krauss, "Canadian Leaders Agree to Propose Gay Marriage Law," *New York Times*, June 18, 2003; "Gay marriage presented to Canadian court," *Associated Press Canada*, October 6, 2004.

4. 49 U.S. 186 (1986). The Supreme Court has, however, recently overruled this decision in *Lawrence v. Texas* using language that might signal a change in outlook toward same-sex marriage.

5. Abram Chayes, "The Role of the Judge in Public Law Litigation," *Harvard Law Review* (1976), 1308.

6. Patrick Atiyah and Robert Sommers, *Form and Substance in Anglo-American Law* (New York: Oxford University Press, 1987), 377.

7. Ibid., 391.

8. See Nancy Maveety and Anke Grosskopf, " 'Constrained' Constitutional Courts as Conduits for Democratic Consolidation," *Law and Society Review* 38:3 (2004), 463–88; Rachael A. Cichowski, "Women's Rights, the European Court, and Supranational Constitutionalism," *Law and Society Review* 38:3 (2004), 489–513; Neal C. Tate and Torbjorn Vallinder, eds., *The Global Expansion of Judicial Power* (New York: NYU Press, 1995).

9. Charles Epp, *The Rights Revolution: Lawyers, Activists, and Supreme Courts in Comparative Perspective* (Chicago: University of Chicago Press, 1998); Ran Hirschl, *Towards Jurisdocracy: The Origins and Consequences of the New Constitutionalism* (Cambridge: Harvard University Press, 2004).

10. R. Shep Melnick, *Between the Lines: Interpreting Welfare Rights* (Washington, D.C.: Brookings, 1994), 16.

11. Ibid., 274.

12. Ibid., 280.

13. Elizabeth Bussiere, *(Dis)Entitling the Poor: The Warren Court, Welfare Rights, and the American Political Tradition* (University Park, Penn.: Penn State University Press, 1997).

14. See Mary Ann Glendon, *Rights Talk: The Impoverishment of Political Discourse* (Free Press, 1993), and Stuart Scheingold, *The Politics of Rights: Lawyers, Public Policy and Political Change*, 2nd ed. (Ann Arbor: University of Michigan Press, 2004).

15. See Robert Dahl, "Decision-Making in a Democracy: The Supreme Court as a National Policymaker," *Journal of Public Law* 6 (1957), 279–295; Martin Shapiro, "Political Jurisprudence, *Kentucky Law Journal* 52 (1964), 294; Gerald Rosenberg, *The Hollow Hope: Can Courts Bring About Social Change?* (Chicago: University of Chicago Press, 1991).

16. David A. J. Richards. *Toleration and the Constitution* (New York: Oxford University Press, 1986), 12.

17. Scheingold, *The Politics of Rights*, 107.

18. Ibid., 123.

19. Ibid., 214.

20. Rosenberg, *The Hollow Hope*, 12.

21. Ibid., 338.

22. Ibid., 167–69, 178–80.

23. Ibid., 341–42.

24. Jonathan Goldberg-Hiller, *The Limits to Union: Same-Sex Marriage and the Politics of Civil Rights* (Ann Arbor: University of Michigan Press, 2002), 223–24.

25. Rosenberg, *The Hollow Hope*, 339.

26. Donald Horowitz, *The Courts and Social Policy* (Washington, D.C.: Brookings Institution Press, 1977).

27. Ibid., 41.

28. See, for example, William Lasser, *The Limits of Judicial Power* (Chapel Hill: University of North Carolina Press, 1988); Alexander M. Bickel, *The Least Dangerous Branch: The Supreme Court at the Bar of Politics* (New Haven, Conn.: Yale University Press, 1986).

29. See Herbert Jacob, *Justice in America: Courts, Lawyers, and the Judicial Process*, 4th ed. (Boston: Little, Brown & Co., 1984), 16–19.

30. See Bickel, *The Least Dangerous Branch*.

31. Lee Epstein and Joseph F. Kobylka, *The Supreme Court and Legal Change: Abortion and the Death Penalty* (Chapel Hill: University of North Carolina Press, 1992), 21–22. Epstein and Kobylka cite David Barnum, "The Supreme Court and Public Opinion: Judicial Decision Making in the Post-New Deal Period," *Journal of Politics* 47 (1985), 652–66; Gregory Caldiera, "Courts and Public Opinion," in *The American Courts: A Critical Assessment*, John B. Gates and Charles A. Johnson, eds. (Washington, D.C.: CQ Press, 1991); Thomas Marshall, *Public Opinion and the Supreme Court* (Boston: Unwin Hyman, 1989).

32. Herbert Jacob, "Decision Making in Trial Courts," in *The American Courts: A Critical Assessment*, John B. Gates and Charles A. Johnson, eds. (Washington, D.C.: CQ Press, 1991), 219.

33. Michael McCann, "How the Supreme Court Matters in American Politics," in *The Supreme Court in American Politics: New Institutionalist Interpretations*, Howard Gillman and Cornell Clayton, eds. (Lawrence, Kans.: University Press of Kansas, 1999), 64.

34. Michael McCann, *Rights at Work: Pay Equity Reform and the Politics of Legal Mobilization* (Chicago: University of Chicago Press, 1994), 282. See also John Brigham, *The Constitution of Interests: Beyond the Politics of Rights* (New York: NYU Press, 2000).

35. McCann, "How the Supreme Court Matters," 81.

36. Ibid., 67.

37. Gerald N. Rosenberg and Christopher M. Rohrbacher, "Same-Sex Marriage, Gay Rights and the (Counter?) Mobilization of the Law," paper prepared for presentation at the 2000 Annual Meeting of the American Political Science Association, August 31–September 3, 2000, Washington, D.C.

38. Lynn Mather, "Theorizing about Trial Courts," *Law and Social Inquiry* 23 (1998), 897–940.

39. McCann, "How the Supreme Court Matters," 73–75.

40. Troy Q. Ridell, "The Impact of Legal Mobilization and Judicial Decisions: The Case of Official Minority-Language Education Policy in Canada for Francophones Outside Quebec," *Law & Society Review* 38:3 (2004), 583–610; McCann, *Rights at Work*, 291.

41. Rosenberg and Rohrbacher, "Same-Sex Marriage, Gay Rights and the (Counter?) Mobilization of the Law."

42. Michael Kammen, *Sovereignty and Liberty: Constitutional Discourse in American Culture* (Madison: University of Wisconsin Press, 1988), 155.

43. Melnick, *Between the Lines*, 237; see also Susan Olson, *Clients and Lawyers: Securing the Rights of Disabled Persons* (Westport, Conn.: Greenwood, 1984). McCann states: "There is simply little evidence that reform activists are routinely duped either by myopic lawyers or the liberal myth of rights." *Rights at Work*, 296. See also, Michael McCann and Helena Silverstein, "Rethinking Law's 'Allurements': A Relational Analysis of Social Movement Lawyers in the United States," in Austin Sarat and Stuart Scheingold, eds., *Cause Lawyering: Political Commitments and Professional Responsibilities* (New York: Oxford University Press, 1998), 261–92.

44. Malcolm M. Feeley and Edward L. Rubin, *Judicial Policy Making and the Modern State: How the Courts Reformed America's Prisons* (New York: Cambridge University Press, 1988), 338.

45. Rogers Smith, "Political Jurisprudence, the 'New Institutionalism,' and the Future of Public Law," *American Political Science Review* 82 (1988), 90–102.

46. Ibid., 91.

47. Howard Gillman, "The Court as an Idea, Not a Building (or a Game): Interpretative Institutionalism and the Analysis of Supreme Court Decision-Making," in *The Supreme Court in American Politics: New Institutionalist Interpretations*, Howard Gillman and Cornell Clayton, eds. (Lawrence: University Press of Kansas, 1999), 78.

48. Interestingly, many prominent contemporary commentators on the left argue for a reduction in the role of courts. See Cass R. Sunstein, *One Case at a Time: Judicial Minimalism and the Supreme Court* (Cambridge: Harvard University Press, 1999), and Mark Tushnet, *Taking the Constitution Away from Courts* (Princeton, N.J.: Princeton University Press, 1999).

49. Miriam Smith, "The Politics of Same-Sex Marriage in Canada and the United States," in *PS: Political Science and Politics*, 37:2 (April 2005), 226. See also Paul Pierson and Theda Skocpol, "Historical Institutionalism in Contemporary Political Science," in *Political Science: The State of the Discipline,* Ira Katznelson and Helen Milner, eds. (New York: W. W. Norton, 2002), 693–721.

50. Ellen Ann Andersen, *Out of the Closets and into the Courts: Legal Opportunity Structure and Gay Rights Litigation* (Ann Arbor: University of Michigan Press, 2005), 3–16.

51. Smith, "The Politics of Same-Sex Marriage," 227.

52. H. N. Hirsch, *A Theory of Liberty: The Constitution and Minorities* (New York: Routledge, 1992), 7–8.

53. See Bickel, *The Least Dangerous Branch*.

54. Epp, *The Rights Revolution*, 5.

55. Jennifer L. Hochschild, *The New American Dilemma: Liberal Democracy and School Desegregation* (New Haven, Conn.: Yale University Press, 1984), 204.

56. Epp, *The Rights Revolution*, 5.

57. Feeley and Rubin, *Judicial Policy Making and the Modern State*, 358.

58. Such critiques of rights come from the critical legal studies movement (Tushnet), republican revival advocates, who prefer deliberation to adjudication (Sunstein), and the conservative legal academy (Glendon). See notes 14 and 43 in this chapter. See also McCann, *Rights at Work*, 296–97.

59. Joel Bakan, *Just Words: Constitutional Rights and Social Wrongs* (Toronto: University of Toronto Press, 1997), 103.

60. J. David Greenstone, *The Lincoln Persuasion: Remaking American Liberalism* (Princeton, N.J.: Princeton University Press, 1993), 60. For another discussion of negative and positive rights in the U.S. political tradition, see Sotirios A. Barber, *Welfare and the Constitution* (Princeton: Princeton University Press, 2003).

61. Ronald Dworkin, *Freedom's Law: The Moral Reading of the American Constitution* (Cambridge: Harvard University Press, 1996), 17.

62. Martha Minow, *Making All the Difference: Inclusion, Exclusion, and American Law* (Ithaca, N.Y.: Cornell University Press, 1990), 310.

63. Jeffrey A. Segal and Harold J. Spaeth, *The Supreme Court and the Attitudinal Model* (New York: Cambridge University Press, 1993), 65.

64. Daniel Pinello, *Gay Rights and American Law* (New York: Cambridge University Press, 2003), 84, 87–91, 151–52.

65. Ibid., 147–48.

66. Ibid., 148.

67. Ibid., 79, 86, 91–92.

68. Ibid., 144–45.

69. Ronald Kahn, "Liberalism, Political Culture, and the Rights of Subordinated Groups: Constitutional Theory and Practice at the Crossroads," in *The Liberal Tradition in American Politics: Reassessing the Legacy of American Liberalism*, David F. Ericson and Louisa Bertch Green, eds. (New York: Routledge, 1999), 178–79. Indeed, Kahn notes the domination of this view in the public law field. "We see instrumental liberalism not only in the scholarship of modern-day legal realists, such as critical legal, attitudinal, and rational-choice scholars. We also see it among originalists, and even in the more complex pluralist formulations of Supreme Court decision making by Robert Dahl, Gerald Rosenberg, and Mark Graber."

70. Ronald Kahn, *The Supreme Court and Constitutional Theory: 1953–1993* (Lawrence: University Press of Kansas, 1994), 206.

71. Ibid., 20–22.

72. Ibid., 29.

73. Michael Perry, *The Constitution, the Courts, and Human Rights* (New Haven, Conn.: Yale University Press, 1982), 102.

74. For a discussion of judges as rational policy makers, see Evan Gerstmann, "Litigating Same-Sex Marriage: Might the Courts Actually Be Bastions of Rationality?" in *PS: Political Science and Politics*, 37:2 (April 2005), 217–220.

75. See Kahn, *The Supreme Court and Constitutional Theory*, 182–85. Kahn notes that "critical pluralist scholars argue that localism, federalism, grass-roots politics, and free enterprise tend to narrow the scope of conflict and make political change and political equality more difficult." Ibid., 182.

76. Grant McConnell, *Private Power and American Democracy* (New York: Knopf, 1966), 114.

77. Ibid., 8.

78. Alexander Hamilton et al., *The Federalist* (New York: Modern Library), 341.

79. Theodore J. Lowi, *The End of Liberalism: The Second Republic of the United States*, 2nd ed. (New York: W. W. Norton, 1979), 63.

80. Theodore J. Lowi, *The End of Liberalism: The Second Republic of the United States*, 1st ed. (New York: W. W. Norton, 1969), 311.

81. See the second edition of Lowi, *The End of Liberalism*, 298.

82. Kahn, *The Supreme Court and Constitutional Theory*, 185.

83. Marc Galanter, "Why the 'Haves' Come Out Ahead: Speculations of the Limits of Legal Change," *Law & Society Review* 9 (1974), 95–160.

84. Charles Epp, "The Two Motifs of 'Why the "Haves" Come Out Ahead' and Its Heirs," *Law & Society Review* 33 (1999), 1089–98, quotes on 1090–91, 1094 (emphasis in the original).

85. See Ian Brodie and F.L. Morton, "Do the 'Haves' Still Come Out Ahead in Canada?" http://publish.uwo.ca/~irbrodie/newman.pdf (last accessed July 1, 2004).

86. Epp, *The Rights Revolution*, 19.

87. Lee Epstein and Joseph F. Kobylka, *The Supreme Court and Legal Change: Abortion and the Death Penalty* (Chapel Hill: University of North Carolina Press, 1992).

88. McCann, *Rights at Work*, 285. Also see Marc Galanter, "The Radiating Effects of Courts," in *Empirical Theories about Courts*, Keith D. Boyum and Lynn Mather, eds. (New York: Longman, 1983).

89. Frances Kahn Zemans, "The Neglected Role of the Law in the Political System," *American Political Science Review* 77 (September 1983), 690–703; McCann, *Rights at Work*.

90. Yoav Dotan, "Do the 'Haves' Still Come Out Ahead? Resource Inequalities in Ideological Courts: The Case of the Israeli High Court of Justice," *Law & Society Review* 33 (1999), 1059–80.

91. Scheingold, *The Politics of Rights*, xli.

92. Carl F. Stychin, *A Nation by Rights: National Cultures, Sexual Identity Politics, and the Discourse of Rights* (Philadelphia: Temple University Press, 1998), 17.

93. For a summary of these critiques, see Michael Thompson, Richard Ellis, and Aaron Wildavsky, *Cultural Theory* (San Francisco: Westview Press, 1990), 215–21. See also Sven Steinmo, "American Exceptionalism Reconsidered: Culture or Institutions?" in Lawrence C. Dodd and Calvin Jillson, eds., *The Dymanics of American Politics* (San Francisco: Westview Press, 1994), 106–31.

94. Thompson et al., *Cultural Theory*, 220.

95. Seymour Martin Lipset, *Continental Divide: The Values and Institutions of the United States and Canada* (Toronto: C. D. Howe Institute, 1989), 3.

96. Gerald A. Beaudoin and Errol Mendes, *The Canadian Charter of Rights and Freedoms*, 3rd ed. (Toronto: Carswell, 1996), 1–6.

97. F. L. Morton, "The Politics of Rights: What Canadians Should Know about the American Bill of Rights," in *The Canadian and American Constitutions in Comparative Perspective*, Marian C. McKenna, ed. (Calgary: University of Calgary Press, 1993), 117.

98. Wintemute, 151, 222. Robert Wintemute, *Sexual Orientation and Human Rights: The United States Constitution, the European Convention, and the Canadian Charter* (Oxford: Oxford University Press, 1996).

99. *M. v. H.*, 2 S.C.R. (1999).

100. For the nature and limits of American liberalism, see Louis Hartz, *The Liberal Tradition in America* (New York: Harcourt Brace & Co., 1991); Rogers Smith, *Civic Ideals: Conflicting Visions of Citizenship in U.S. History* (New Haven, Conn.: Yale University Press, 1997); Michael Sandel, *Democracy's Discontent: America in Search of a Public Philosophy* (Cambridge: Harvard University Press, 1996); Greenstone, *The Lincoln Persuasion*.

101. See *Bowers*, and *Romer v. Evans* 517 U.S. 620 (1996). A significant shift in Supreme Court jurisprudence occurred in the summer of 2003 in the case of *Lawrence v. Texas*. This case is discussed in Chapter 9.

102. For an excellent discussion of the emerging differences between the two countries, see Michael Adams, *Fire and Ice: The United States, Canada and the Myth of Converging Values* (Toronto: Penguin Canada, 2003).

## CHAPTER 2

1. For an elaboration of this point, see Joyce Murdoch and Deb Price, *Courting Justice: Gay Men and Lesbians v. The Supreme Court* (New York: Basic Books, 2001). Much of the discussion to follow in the beginning of this chapter relies heavily on their excellent original research on the Court and gay rights.

2. Murdock and Price, *Courting Justice*, 31.

3. *ONE v. Olesen*, 241 F.2d 772 (1958), 777.

4. Ibid.

5. This is discussed in more detail in Chapter 5.

6. 354 U.S. 476 (1957).

7. *ONE v. Olesen*, 355 U.S. 772 (1958). The decision read: "The petition for writ of certiorari is granted and the judgment of the United States Court of Appeals for the Ninth Circuit is reversed. *Roth v. United States*, 354 U.S. 476."

8. Murdock and Price, *Courting Justice*, 45.

9. 370 U.S. 478 (1962).

10. Ibid.

11. Ibid., 490.

12. Ibid., 481.

13. See Chapter 5.

14. Murdoch and Price point out that these decisions contributed to the gay rights movement by encouraging the gay publishing industry. Murdock and Price, *Courting Justice*, 82–83.

15. *Kameny v. Bruckner*, cert. denied, March 20, 1961.

16. *Schlegel v. U.S.*, cert. denied, April 20, 1970, *Adams v. Laird*, 397 U.S. 1039, cert. denied, April 20, 1970. These cases are described in Murdoch and Price, *Courting Justice*, 150–58.

17. *Boutilier v. INS*, 387 U.S. 118 (1967), 121.

18. Ibid, 125.

19. Murdoch and Price, *Courting Justice*, 134.

20. *Hardwick v. Bowers*, 760 F.2d 1202 (11th Cir.), 1212.

21. *Bowers v. Hardwick*, 478 U.S. 186 (1986), 190.

22. Ibid., 192.

23. Ibid., 197.

24. Murdoch and Price, *Courting Justice*, 338. Powell even changed his mind, originally voting to strike down the law, but, as a memo published by Murdoch and Price indicates, Powell could not imagine same-sex relationships on par with heterosexual relationships like his own. Ibid., 294–95, 313–14.

25. *Bowers v. Hardwick*, 201. Blackmun's argument is a descendant of H. L. A. Hart's position, which is discussed in Chapter 5.

26. Ibid., 204–5.

27. See Kenneth L. Karst, "The Freedom of Intimate Association," *Yale Law Journal* 89 (1980), 624.

28. Murdoch and Price, *Courting Justice*, 283–84.

29. Ibid., 284–308.

30. Ibid., 311–14.

31. *Irish-American Gay, Lesbian and Bisexual Group of Boston v. City of Boston et al.,* Mass. Super. LEXIS 320, December 15, 1993, Decided.

32. *Irish-American Gay, Lesbian and Bisexual Group of Boston v. City of Boston et al.,* 636 N.E.2d 1293 (Mass. 1994).

33. *Irish-American Gay,* Mass. Superior Court, 43–44.

34. *Irish-American Gay,* Supreme Court, 1305.

35. *Hurley v. Irish-American Gay, Lesbian, and Bisexual Group of Boston* 515 U.S. 557 (1995), 574–75.

36. Ibid., 578.

37. 308 N.J. Super. 516, 70 A.2d 270 (1998).

38. 734 A.2d 1196 (1999).

39. Ibid., 1227.

40. Ibid., 1229.

41. *Boy Scouts of America v. Dale,* 530 U.S. 640 (2000).

42. Ibid., 679.

43. Ibid., 700.

44. Ibid., 694–95

45. 517 U.S. 620 (1996).

46. See Evan Gerstmann, *The Constitutional Underclass: Gays, Lesbians, and the Failure of Class-Based Equal Protection* (Chicago: University of Chicago Press, 1999).

47. *Evans v. Romer,* 854 P.2d 1270 (Colorado 1993), 1282.

48. *Romer v. Evans,* 517 U.S. 620 (1996), 633.

49. Ibid., 635.

50. Ibid., 652–53.

51. Gerstmann, *The Constitutional Underclass,* 37.

52. Murdoch and Price, *Courting Justice,* 432–36, 494–96.

53. *Lawrence v. Texas,* 123 S. Ct. 2472 (2003), 2484.

54. *Dean v. D.C.,* 653 A.2d 307 (D.C. App. 1995).

55. *High Tech Gays v. Defense Industry Security Clearance Office,* 895 F.2d 563 (9th Cir. 1990).

56. *Ben-Shalom v. Marsh,* 881F.2d 454 (7th Cir. 1989), cert. denied sub nom. *Ben-Shalom v. Stone,* 494 U.S. 1004 (1990); *Watkins v. United States Army,* 847 F.2d 1329 (9th Cir. 1989), vacated; 875 F.2d 699 (9th Cir. 1989) (en banc), cert. denied, 111 S. Ct. 384 (1990); *Pruitt v. Cheney,* 943 F.2d 989 (9th Cir. 1991), amended, 963 F.2d 1160 (9th Cir. 1992), cert. denied sub. com. *Cheney v. Pruitt,* 113 S. Ct. 655 (1992).

57. *Watkins v. U.S. Army,* ibid.

58. *Adams v. Howerton,* 673 F.2d 1036 (9th Cir. 1982); *Dean v. District of Columbia,* 653 A.2d 307 (D.C. Cir. 1995). In the *Dean* case, however, one judge was willing to entertain a constitutional challenge to the ban on same-sex marriages.

59. *Adams v. Howerton,* 486 F. Supp. 1119 (Cent. Dist. CA 1980), 1123.

60. *Lofton v. Secretary of the Dept. of Children and Family Services,* 377 F.3d 1275 (11th Cir. 2004). President George W. Bush's conservative recess appointment, William Pryor—a profound opponent of gay rights—was a crucial part of the outcome in the case. See the weblog, "How Appealing," July 21, 2004, http://www.legalaffairs.org/howappealing/2004_07_01_appellateblog_archive.html#109046560984045887 (last accessed July 25, 2004).

61. Henry R. Glick, "Policy Making and State Supreme Courts," in *The American Courts: A Critical Assessment,* John B. Gates and Charles A. Johnson, eds. (Washington, D.C.: CQ Press, 1991), 102.

62. G. Alan Tarr and Mary Cornelia Aldis Porter, *State Supreme Courts in State and Nation* (New Haven, Conn.: Yale University Press, 1988), 1.

63. Ibid., 2.

64. Lawrence Baum and Bradley C. Canon, "State Supreme Courts as Activists: New Doctrines in the Law of Torts," in *State Supreme Courts: Policy Makers in the Federal System*, Mary Cornelia Porter and G. Alan Tarr, eds. (Westport, Conn.: Greenwood Press, 1982), 102.

65. Ibid., 97–98.

66. Porter and Tarr, *State Supreme Courts in State and Nation*, 27.

67. Ibid., 47–48.

68. Ibid., 40.

69. Glick, "Policy Making and State Supreme Courts," 106–13.

70. Ibid., 94.

71. Porter and Tarr, *State Supreme Courts in State and Nation*, 67.

72. Ibid., 51.

73. Glick, "Policy Making and State Supreme Courts," 94–96.

74. G. Alan Tarr. "The New Judicial Federalism in Perspective," *Notre Dame Law Review* 72:1097 (1997), 1102.

75. See William J. Brennan, Jr., "State Constitutions and the Protection of Individual Rights," *Harvard Law Review* 90 (1977), 459.

76. For good summaries of the scholarship and the issues involved in the "new judicial federalism," see James A. Gardner, "The Failed Discourse of State Constitutionalism," *Michigan Law Review* 90 (1992), 761, and Michael D. Weiss and Mark W. Bennett, "New Federalism and State Court Activism," *Memphis State University Law Review* 24 (1994), 229.

77. For a recent discussion of judicial federalism see chapter 4 of Daniel Pinello, *Gay Rights and American Law* (New York: Cambridge University Press, 2003).

78. Ibid., 2.

79. Ibid., 110.

80. Ibid., 144–45.

81. Ibid., 146.

CHAPTER 3

1. Canadian liberalism will be discussed in Chapter 10.

2. Louis Hartz, *The Liberal Tradition in America* (New York: Harcourt Brace & Co., 1991).

3. See James T. Koppenberg, *The Virtues of Liberalism* (New York: Oxford University Press, 1998).

4. Carlos Ball elaborates this point in "Moral Foundations for a Discourse on Same-Sex Marriage: Looking Beyond Political Liberalism," *Georgetown Law Journal* 85 (June 1997), 1871–1943 and more recently in *The Morality of Gay Rights: An Exploration in Political Philosophy* (New York: Routledge, 2003). My arguments are compatible with Ball's. What he refers to as "moral liberalism" is the richer liberalism I advocate. Where we differ, perhaps, is that I reject the communitarian influences that Ball sees an informing moral liberalism.

5. Isaiah Berlin, "Two Concepts of Liberty," in *Four Essays on Liberty* (Oxford: Oxford University Press, 1969), 157.

6. Benjamin Constant, *Political Writings*, Biancamaria Fontana, ed. (New York: Cambridge University Press, 1988), 86.

7. Ibid., 311.

8. Ibid., 327.

9. Ibid., 207.

10. William A. Galston, *Liberal Purposes: Goods, Virtues and Diversity in the Liberal State* (New York: Cambridge University Press, 1991), 227.

11. Jean Bethke Elshtain, "The Displacement of Politics," in *Public and Private in Thought and Practice*, Jeff Weintraub and Krishnan Kumar, eds. (Chicago: University of Chicago Press, 1987), 178.

12. Ibid., 177.

13. Nancy F. Cott, *Public Vows: A History of Marriage and the Nation* (Cambridge: Harvard University Press, 2000), 1–2.

14. Ibid., 5.

15. David A. J. Richards, *Sex, Drugs, Death, and the Law* (Totowa, N.J.: Rowman and Littlefield, 1982), 10.

16. For an excellent discussion of Rawls in this context, see Carlos Ball, above at note 4.

17. Richards, *Sex, Drugs, Death, and the Law*, 54.

18. Steven Seidman, *Difference Troubles: Queering Social Theory and Sexual Politics* (New York: Cambridge University Press, 1997), 111.

19. In fact, even the category of gay and lesbian would give way to the more inclusive description of gay, lesbian, bisexual, and transgendered to reflect this diversity.

20. Seidman, *Difference Troubles*, 116.

21. Jonathan Ned Katz, *The Invention of Heterosexuality* (New York: Dutton, 1995), 172.

22. Michel Foucault, *The History of Sexuality,* Volume I: *An Introduction*, Robert Hurley, trans. (New York: Random House, 1978), 49.

23. David M. Halperin, *Saint Foucault: Towards a Gay Hagiography* (New York: Oxford University Press, 1995).

24. Foucault, *The History of Sexuality*, 93.

25. Ibid., 26.

26. Halperin, *Saint Foucault*, 79.

27. Mark Blasius, *Gay and Lesbian Politics: Sexuality and the Emergence of a New Ethic* (Philadelphia: Temple University Press, 1994), 1.

28. Ibid., 27.

29. Ibid., 129.

30. Ibid., 86.

31. Ibid., 133, 137.

32. John Stuart Mill, *On Liberty* (New York: W. W. Norton, 1975), 54. Carlos Ball also notes the liberal nature of the political solutions advocated by postmodernists. See Ball, *The Morality of Gay Rights*, 16.

33. Blasius, *Gay and Lesbian Politics*, xi.

34. Mill, *On Liberty*, 54.

35. Morris B. Kaplan, "Liberte! Egalite! Sexualite!: Theorizing Lesbian and Gay Politics," *Political Theory* 25:3 (June 1997), 418–19.

36. Michael Warner, *The Trouble with Normal: Sex, Politics, and the Ethics of Queer Life* (New York: Free Press, 1999), 66.

37. Ibid., 36.

38. Seidman, *Difference Troubles*, 193.

39. Martha Nussbaum, "Experiments in Living," *New Republic*, January 3, 2000.

40. Shane Phelan, *Getting Specific: Postmodern Lesbian Politics* (Minneapolis: University of Minnesota Press, 1994), 114.

41. Shane Phelan, *Sexual Strangers: Gays, Lesbians, and Dilemmas of Citizenship* (Philadelphia: Temple University Press, 2001), 141.

42. Ibid., 6.

43. Ibid., 161.

44. Ibid., 87.

45. Ibid., 73.

46. See William N. Eskridge, Jr., "Comparative Law and the Same-Sex Marriage Debate: A Step-by-Step Approach Toward State Recognition," *McGeorge Law Review* 31 (2000), 641–672.

47. Phelan, *Getting Specific*, 126.

48. Rhonda Copelon, "Beyond the Liberal Idea of Privacy: Toward a Positive Right of Autonomy," in *Judging the Constitution: Critical Essays on Judicial Lawmaking*, Michael McCann and Gerald Houseman, eds. (Glenview, Ill.: Scott, Foresman & Co., 1989), 304.

49. Judith A. Baer, *Our Lives Before the Law: Constructing a Feminist Jurisprudence* (Princeton: Princeton University Press, 1998), 189.

50. Michael Sandel, *Democracy's Discontent: America in Search of a Public Philosophy* (Cambridge: Harvard University Press, 1996), 6.

51. Ibid., 25.

52. Ibid., 107.

53. Phelan, *Sexual Strangers*, 61.

54. H. N. Hirsch, *A Theory of Liberty: The Constitution and Minorities* (New York: Routledge, 1992), 257.

55. Ball, *The Morality of Gay Rights*, 75.

56. See Carlos Ball, "Communitarianism and Gay Rights," *Cornell Law Review* 85 (2000), 443–517. In fairness, Ball does not wish to abandon liberalism in this essay but improve it on the basis of communitarian critiques. My point is that, given the pitfalls of communitarianism for sexual minorities, a better approach is to find a solution within the liberal tradition. He appears to walk away from liberalism more in *The Morality of Gay Rights*.

57. Ball, *The Morality of Gay Rights*, 76.

58. Robert George, *Making Men Moral: Civil Liberties and Public Morality* (New York: Oxford University Press, 1993), 5.

59. Ibid., 97.

60. Stephen Macedo, "Sexuality and Liberty: Making Room for Nature and Tradition?" in *Sex, Preference, and Family: Essays on Law and Nature*, David M. Estlund and Martha C. Nussbaum, eds. (New York: Oxford University Press, 1997), 91.

61. Michael Walzer, *Spheres of Justice: A Defense of Pluralsms and Equality* (New York: Basic Books, 1984), 50; Hirsch, *A Theory of Liberty*, 257–58.

62. Ronald Dworkin, "Liberalism," in *Liberalism and Its Critics*, Michael Sandel, ed. (New York: New York University Press, 1984), 71.

63. Mark Tushnet, "An Essay on Rights," *Texas Law Review* 62 (May 1984), 1371.

64. See Gerald Rosenberg, *The Hollow Hope: Can Courts Bring About Social Change?* (Chicago: University of Chicago Press, 1991).

65. See Tushnet, "An Essay on Rights," 1387–87.

66. Mary Ann Glendon, *Rights Talk: The Impoverishment of Political Discourse* (New York: Free Press, 1991), 14.

CHAPTER 4

1. J. David Greenstone, *The Lincoln Persuasion: Remaking American Liberalism* (Princeton, N.J.: Princeton University Press, 1993), 54.

2. Ibid., 59.

3. Ibid., 100–101.

4. Ibid., 223.

5. Ibid., 227.

6. Ibid., 236.

7. See George Fitzhugh, *Cannibals All*, C. Vann Woodward, ed. (Cambridge: Harvard University Press, 1960, 1988).

8. Woodrow Wilson, *The New Freedom* (New York: Doubleday, 1913), 284.

9. See Sidney Milkis, *The President and the Parties: The Transformation of the American Party System since the New Deal* (New York: Oxford University Press, 1993); Elizabeth Bussiere, *(Dis)Entitling the Poor: The Warren Court, Welfare Rights, and the American Political Tradition* (University Park: Penn State University Press, 1997). Bussiere chronicles that a richer liberalism was rejected by the Warren Court's refusal to fully constitutionalize welfare rights.

10. Bussiere, *(Dis)Entitling the Poor*.

11. See Richard Hofstadter, *The American Political Tradition* (New York: Vintage Books, 1989).

12. Daniel Walker Howe, *The American Whigs: An Anthology* (New York: John Wiley & Sons), 66.

13. Roy P. Basler, *Abraham Lincoln: His Speeches and Writings* (New York: Da Capo Press, 1946), 361.

14. William N. Eskridge, Jr., "Equality Practice: Liberal Reflections of the Jurisprudence of Civil Union," *Albany Law Review* 64 (2001), 871.

15. The use of this term is problematic, since liberationism is associated more with the tradition of gay politics and thought of the 1970s that was grounded in the neo-Marxist analysis of Herbert Marcuse. These liberationists sought to free sexual minorities from imposed heterosexuality. But queer theory rejects these categories altogether. By this view, there is no such thing as heterosexuality or homosexuality. Indeed, postmodern critiques often view the liberation movement as only reinforcing masculine norms and privileged gay male sexuality at the expense of other sexualities that are nearly infinite.

16. Andrew Sullivan, *Virtually Normal: An Argument About Homosexuality* (New York: Knopf, 1995), 159.

17. Ibid., 151.

18. Ibid., 153.

19. Andrew Sullivan, "What's So Bad about Hate? The Illogic and Illiberalism behind Hate-Crime Laws," andrewsullivan.com, last visited September 17, 2001.

20. Ibid.

21. Alexander Hamilton et al., *The Federalist* (New York: Modern Library), 55.

22. Sullivan, *Virtually Normal*, 163.

23. John Locke, *A Letter Concerning Toleration* (Indianapolis: Bobbs-Merrill, 1976), 48.

24. Ibid., 49.

25. As he states, "The truth is, leaving private discrimination aside, liberalism has not yet succeeded in achieving even the most basic *public* equality to homosexuals." Sullivan, *Virtually Normal*, 153.

26. Andrew Sullivan, *Love Undetectable: Notes on Friendship, Sex, Survival* (New York: Knopf, 1998), 67.

27. Ibid., 73.

28. Although Sullivan claims liberalism as an intellectual influence, his position in contemporary politics is aligned with the conservative movement. He was a supporter of Margaret Thatcher and Ronald Reagan and is an outspoken supporter of George W. Bush.

29. Sullivan is a devout Catholic.

30. See Gertrude Himmelfarb, *The De-moralization of Society* (New York: A. A. Knopf, 1995). For an account of the merging of Straussian and neoconservative thought, see Robert Devigne, *Recasting Conservatism: Oakeshott, Strauss, and the Response to Postmodernism* (New Haven, Conn.: Yale University Press, 1994), 64–65.

31. See Stephen Holmes, *The Anatomy of Antiliberalism* (Cambridge: Harvard University Press, 1993), 63–66.

32. See Saul Bellow, *Ravelstein* (New York: Viking Press, 2000).

33. Sullivan, *Love Undetectable*, 177.

34. Ibid., 187–88.

35. Ibid., 198–99

36. Andrew Sullivan, "Intimations Pursued: The Voice of Practice in the Conversation of Michael Oakeshott," Doctoral dissertation, Harvard University 1990, 12.

37. Ibid., 272–73

38. Ibid., 276.

39. Ibid., 5.

40. Ibid., 212.

41. Ibid., 213.

42. Ibid., 215

43. Ibid., 260.

44. Ibid., 285.

45. Ibid., 286.

46. Ibid., 330.

47. Sullivan, "What's So Bad about Hate?"

48. See Louis Hartz, *The Liberal Tradition in America* (New York: Harcourt Brace & Co., 1991).

49. J. David Greenstone, "Against Simplicity: The Cultural Dimensions of the Constitution," *University of Chicago Law Review* 55 (1988), 428.

50. See Catherine MacKinnon, *Feminism Unmodified: Discourses on Life and Law* (Cambridge: Harvard University Press, 1987).

## CHAPTER 5

1. Richard D. Mohr, *Gays/Justice* (New York: Columbia University Press, 1988), 59–60 (emphasis in the original).

2. Four states, Oklahoma, Missouri, Texas, and Kansas, singled out homosexual sodomy. See http://sodomy laws.org (last accessed December 7, 2002).

3. John D'Emilio, *Sexual Politics, Sexual Communities: The Making of a Homosexual Minority in the United States, 1940–1970* (Chicago: University of Chicago Press, 1983), 14.

4. Ibid.

5. Byrne Fone, *Homophobia: A History* (New York: Metropolitan Books, 2000), 216.

6. William N. Eskridge, Jr., *Gaylaw: Challenging the Apartheid of the Closet* (Cambridge: Harvard University Press, 1999), 157.

7. Ibid.

8. Ibid., 158.

9. Ibid., 164.

10. *State v. Guerin*, 152 P. 747 (Montana 1915).

11. Eskridge, *Gaylaw*, 19.

12. See George Chauncey, *Gay New York: Gender, Urban Culture, and the Making of the Gay World, 1890–1940* (New York: Basic Books, 1994).

13. Eskridge, *Gaylaw*, 26–34.

14. Ibid., 25.

15. D'Emilio, *Sexual Politics, Sexual Communities*, 24.

16. Ibid., 37.

17. William N. Eskridge, Jr., "Privacy Jurisprudence and the Apartheid of the Closet, 1946–1961," *Florida State Law Review* 24 (1997), 703, 708.

18. Ibid., 710–13.

19. Ibid., 714.

20. Mohr, *Gays/Justice*, 51–54.

21. Gregory B. Lewis, "Public Opinion and State Sodomy Laws," paper prepared for presentation at the American Political Science Association annual meeting, Atlanta, Georgia, September 1999, 5.

22. See N.E.H. Hull, "Restatement and Reform: A New Perspective on the Origins of the American Law Institute," *Law and History Review* 8 (1990), 55–96; and G. Edward White, "The American Law Institute and the Triumph of Modernist Jurisprudence," *Law and History Review* 15 (1997), 1–47.

23. American Law Institute, *Model Penal Code and Commentaries (Official Draft and Revised Comments) with Text of the Model Penal Code as Adopted at the 1962 Annual Meeting of the American Law Institute at Washington, D.C., May 24, 1962* (Philadelphia, Pa.: ALI, 1980), 13.

24. Letter from Herbert F. Goodrich to Learned Hand, December 30, 1954. ALI archives, University of Pennsylvania Law School, Philadelphia, Pa. (copy on file with author).

25. Letter from Learned Hand to Herbert F. Goodrich, January 3, 1955 (copy on file with author).

26. "The Law: Sin and Criminality," *Time*, May 30, 1955, 13.

27. "Article 201—Sexual Offenses," Submitted to the Criminal Law Advisory Group of the American Law Institute for discussion at the meeting on January 13–15, 1955, January 7, 1955.

28. Unpublished proceedings of the American Law Institute, May 19, 1955, 129.

29. Ibid.

30. Ibid., 128.

31. *Model Penal Code and Commentaries*, 363.

32. Ibid.

33. Ibid., 370.

34. Ibid., 371.

35. *The Wolfenden Report: Report of the Committee on Homosexual Offenses and Prostitution* (New York: Stein and Day, 1963), 48.

36. Ibid., 5.

37. Ibid.

38. Ibid., 120.

39. See generally David J. Garrow, *Liberty and Sexuality: The Right to Privacy and the Making of* Roe v. Wade (New York: Macmillan, 1994).

40. Quoted in Garrow, *Liberty and Sexuality*, 195.

41. H. L. A. Hart, *Law, Liberty, and Morality* (Stanford, Calif.: Stanford University Press, 1963), 12.

42. Ibid., 15.

43. For a summary of the Hart-Devlin debate, see Ronald Dworkin, *Taking Rights Seriously* (Cambridge: Harvard University Press, 1978), 240–58.

44. Ibid., 22.

45. Hart, *Law, Liberty, and Morality*, 70–71.

46. See Nicola Lacey, *A Life of H.L.A. Hart: The Nightmare and the Noble Dream* (New York: Oxford University Press), 2004.

47. Larry Cata Backer, "Exposing the Perversions of Toleration: The Decriminalization of Private Sexual Conduct, the Model Penal Code, and the Oxymoron of Liberal Toleration," *Florida Law Review* 45 (1993), 755, 770.

48. Ibid., 774.

49. Ibid., 787.

50. Although, to be fair, Backer's assessment was given in 1993, before many of the landmark sodomy cases.

51. Backer, "Exposing the Perversions of Toleration," 795.

52. George Painter, "The Sense of Our Forefathers: The History of Sodomy Laws in the United States," www.sosomylaws.org (last accessed November 23, 2001).

53. Richard Mohr argues that Illinois was not progressive, since the sodomy law reform was accepted as part of a larger package of reform and legislators did not know that they were explicitly passing it. See Mohr, *Gays/Justice*, 53–54.

54. ACLU website, "Lesbian and Gay Rights: State Sodomy Statutes," http://www.aclu.org/issues/gay/sodomy.html (last accessed November 19, 2001). The following are states that repealed sodomy laws in the 1970s and 1980s: Connecticut (1971), Colorado (1972), Oregon (1972), Delaware (1973), Hawaii (1973), Ohio (1974), North Dakota (1975), New Hampshire (1975), New Mexico (1975), California (1976), Maine (1976), Washington (1976), West Virginia (1976), Indiana (1977), South Dakota (1977), Vermont (1977), Wyoming (1977), Nebraska (1978), New Jersey (1979), Alaska (1980), Wisconsin (1983).

55. Painter, "The Sense of Our Forefathers," 69. Painter cites Levitt and Klassen, "Public Attitudes Toward Homosexuality," *Journal of Homosexuality* 1 (1974), 29–45.

56. Alan Yang, "From Wrongs to Rights, 1973–1999: Public Opinion on Gay and Lesbian Americans Moves Toward Equality," a publication of the Policy Institute of the National Gay and Lesbian Task Force. When the question, asked by the Gallup poll, was framed in the following way, "Should homosexuality be legal?" the results point to a striking development in the public opinion on this issue. From 1977 through 1985, public opinion was generally divided on the question, with those answering in the affirmative mirroring the percentage of respondents who favored legalization. For instance in 1977, the split was 43–43; in 1982, 45–39; and in 1985, 44–47.

57. Donald Haider-Markel and Kenneth Meier, "The Politics of Gay and Lesbian Rights: Expanding the Scope of the Conflict," *Journal of Politics* 58:2 (1996), 332–49.

58. Dorothy Toth Beasley, "Federalism and the Protection of Individual Rights: The American State Constitutional Perspective," in *Federalism and Rights*, Ellis Katz and G. Alan Tarr, eds. (Lanham, Md.: Rowman & Littlefield, 1996), 112.

59. See *Bowers v. Hardwick*, 49 U.S. 186 (1986).

60. For a description of the Court's reasoning, see Anne B. Goldstein, "History, Homosexuality, and Political Values: Searching for the Hidden Determinants of *Bowers v. Hardwick,*" *Yale Law Journal* 97 (1988), 1073.

61. *Doe v. Commonwealth's Attorney*, 425 U.S. 901 (1976).

62. Patricia A. Cain, "Litigating for Lesbian and Gay Rights: A Legal History," *Virginia Law Review* 79 (1993), 1583.

63. Ibid., 1584.

64. Ibid., 1586–87. The New York case was *People v. Onofre*, 415 N.E.2d 936 (N.Y. 1980), *cert* denied, 451 U.S. 987 (1981).

65. Randy Shilts, *Conduct Unbecoming: Lesbians and Gays in the U.S. Military: Vietnam to the Persian Gulf* (New York: St. Martin's, 1993), 283.

66. Ibid., 284.

67. *Doe v. Commonwealth's Attorney*, 403 F. Supp. 1199 (E.D. Va. 1975), 1201.

68. Ibid., 1202.

69. Ibid., 1203.

70. Bob Woodward and Scott Armstrong, *The Brethren: Inside the Supreme Court* (New York: Avon Books, 1979), 505.

71. *Doe,* 425 U.S. 901 (1976).

72. Shilts, *Conduct Unbecoming*, 284. The story is also told in Woodward and Armstrong, *The Brethren*, 505–6.

73. Woodward and Armstrong, *The Brethren*, 505.

74. Andrew Wolfson, "Court Asked to Reconsider Sodomy Ruling," *Louisville Courier-Journal*, October 15, 1992, 1C.

75. Beverly Bartlett, "High Court Hears Debate on Legality of Sodomy Law," *Louisville Courier-Journal*, April 3, 1992, 1B.

76. *Commonwealth v. Wasson,* 842 S.W. 2d 487 (Ky. 1992).

77. Ibid., 493.

78. Ibid., 497.

79. Ibid., 498.

80. Ibid., 507.

81. Ibid., 500.

82. Ibid., 502.

83. Ibid., 509.

84. Andrew Wolfson, "A Force for Change; Leibson Wields Great Influence on Court," *Louisville Courier-Journal*, October 25, 1992, 1A.

85. Deborah Yetter, "Supreme Question . . . Will the State Court Tilt Right?" *Louisville Courier-Journal*, March 25, 1996, 1A.

86. Wolfson, "A Force for Change," 1A.

87. Andrew Wolfson, "Sodomy Case Reflects Move to Seek Rights at State Level," *Louisville Courier-Journal*, September 26, 1992, 1A.

88. Ibid.

89. Yetter, "Supreme Question."

90. Daniel Pinello sees this decision more driven by attitudinal factors. He found that religion is a significant variable for determining the outcome of gay rights cases. In *Wasson*, the majority was made up of a Jew, a moderate Protestant, and two liberal Protestants, while in the minority were a fundamentalist Protestant and two Catholics. See Pinello, *Gay Rights and American Law*, 90–91.

91. Bill Wolfe, "Presbyterians File Brief Challenging Sodomy Law," *Louisville Courier-Journal*, July 24, 1991, 1B.

92. Wolfson, "Court Asked to Reconsider Sodomy Ruling."

93. Ibid.

94. Al Cross, "House Panel Passes Two Proposed Amendments," *Louisville Courier-Journal*, March 24, 1994, 4B.

95. Patrick Crowley, "Sodomy Ban Considered," *Cincinnati Enquirer*, January 16, 1996, archived at http://www.sodomylaws.org (last accessed October 6, 2001).

96. William H. Koch, Jr., "Reopening Tennessee's Open Courts Clause: A Historical Reconsideration of Article I, Section 17 of the Tennessee Constitution," *Memphis State University Law Review* 27 (Winter 1997), 339.

97. Sabine Koji, "*Campbell v. Sundquist*: Tennessee's Homosexual Practices Act Violates the Right to Privacy," *University of Memphis Law Review* 28 (1997), 311.

98. *Tennessee Public Acts, 1989,* Chapter 591; Rebecca Ferrar, "State High Court Chooses Not to Hear Sodomy Case," *Knoxville News-Sentinel*, June 12, 1996, A1.

99. "Judge Weighs Sodomy Ban," *Memphis Commercial Appeal*, November 24, 1994, 17A.

100. Ferrar, "State High Court Chooses."

101. Paula Wade, "Right to Privacy Shields Gays, Judge Rules," *Memphis Commercial Appeal*, December 9, 1994, 1B.

102. Ibid.

103. "Tennessee High Court May Clarify Sodomy Law," *Memphis Commercial Appeal*, November 22, 1995, 2B.

104. *Campbell v. Sundquist*, 926 S.W. 2d 250 (Tenn. 1996), 259.

105. Ibid., 260.

106. 842 S.W. 2d 588 (Tenn. 1992).

107. *Campbell* 926 S.W. 2d 250, 260.

108. *Young v. State*, 531 S.W.2d 560 (Tenn. 1975), 563.

## CHAPTER 6

1. The original law read: "Whoever commits with mankind or beast the abominable and detestable crime against nature shall be confined in the penitentiary for not less than five nor more than fifteen years." *Pruett v. State* 463 S.W. 2d 191 (Tex. Crim. App. 1970), 195.

2. Ibid. The 1943 revision read: "Whoever has carnal copulation with a beast, or in an opening of the body, except sexual [presumably non-anal] of another human being, or whoever shall use his mouth on the sexual parts of another human being for the purpose of having carnal copulation, or who shall voluntarily permit the use of his own sexual parts in a lewd or lascivious manner by any minor, shall be guilty of sodomy."

3. See *Furstonburg v. State*, 190 S.W. 2d 362 and *Slusser v. State*, 232 S.W. 2d 727. These cases were decided before the U.S. Supreme Court began to carve out areas of marital privacy.

4. *Buchanan v. Batchelor*, 308 F. Supp. 729 (N.D. Texas 1970), 730.

5. Ibid., 733.

6. Ibid.

7. *Pruett*, 463 S.W. 2d 191, 195.

8. Ellena Fortner, "State Sodomy Law Unconstitutional," *Forth Worth Star-Telegram*, June 9, 2000, 1.

9. Randy Von Beitel, "The Criminalization of Private Homosexual Acts: A Jurisprudential Case Study of a Decision by the Texas Bar Penal Code Revision Committee," *Human Rights* 6:23 (1977), 24–30.

10. Ibid., 31–32.

11. Ibid., 46–53.

12. Ibid., 61.

13. *State v. Morales*, 826 S.W. 2d 201 (Tex. App. 1992), 202.

14. Ibid., 204.

15. Ibid., 205.

16. Angela Ward, "Gay Rights Group Will Challenge State Anti-Sodomy Law," *Texas Lawyer*, November 30, 1998, 4.

17. Clay Robison and R. A. Dyer, "Morales Says State's High Court Should Rule on Anti-Sodomy Law," *Houston Chronicle*, March 12, 1992, 1A.

18. *Morales*, 826 S.W. 2d 201, 204. See also *Texas State Employees Union v. Texas Department of Mental Health and Retardation*, 746 S.W. 2d 203 (Tex. 1987).

19. Ibid., 205.

20. Ibid., 204. *Passel v. Ft. Worth Independent School District,* 440 S.W.2d 61 (Tex. 1969).

21. *City of Dallas v. England*, 846 S.W. 2d 957 (Tex. App. 1993).

22. Ross Ramsey, "State Sodomy Law Taken to Task," *Houston Chronicle*, January 6, 1993, A15.

23. Ibid.

24. Janet Elliott, "Sodomy Case Arguments Delve into Psychiatry," *Texas Lawyer*, January 11, 1993, 5.

25. Ibid.

26. Clay Robison, "The 73rd Legislature: Senate, House at an Impasse over Sodomy Laws," *Houston Chronicle*, May 24, 1993, A9.

27. Clay Robison, "Sodomy Law Fuss a Low Point for House," *Houston Chronicle*, May 9, 1993, Op. 2.

28. Robison, "Impasse over Sodomy Laws."

29. Ross Ramsey, "Committee Compromises on State's Sodomy Law," *Houston Chronicle*, May 25, 1993, A1.

30. Ross Ramsey, "State High Court Sidesteps Ruling on Sodomy Statute," *Houston Chronicle*, January 13, 1994, A1.

31. David Elloit, "Bush Promises to Veto Attempts to Remove Sodomy Law," *Austin American-Statesman*, January 22, 1994, B3.

32. Ibid.

33. *Gryczan v. State of Montana,* 942 P. 2d 112 (Mont. 1997).

34. Ron Selden, "After a Winter of Fear and Defeat, Advocates Renew Their Fight to Same-Sex Rights," *Missoula Independent*, May 31, 2001, archived at http://www.sodomylaws.org (last accessed October 6, 2001).

35. "Judge Strikes Down State's Gay Sex Law," *Billings Gazette*, February 18, 1996, archived at http://www.sodomylaws.org (last accessed October 6, 2001).

36. William C. Rava, "Toward a Historical Understanding of Montana's Privacy Provision," *Albany Law Review* 61:1681 (1998), 1683.

37. Ibid., 1699.

38. George Painter, "The Sense of Our Forefathers: The History of Sodomy Laws in the United States (Montana)," at http://www.sodomylaws.org (last accessed October 6, 2001).

39. *Gryczan*, 942 P. 2d 112, 121.

40. Ibid. at 126

41. Ibid. at 125.

42. See the dissent by Chief Justice J. A. Turnage in *Gryczan*, 942 P. 2d 112, 126.

43. Bob Anez, "Montana Votes to Register Homosexuals," Associated Press, March 22, 1995.

44. Painter, "The Sense of Our Forefathers."

45. Kathleen McLaughlin, "Panel Refused to Erase Unconstitutional Law," *Billings Gazette,* February 16, 2001, archived at http://www.sodomylaws.org (last accessed October 6, 2001).

46. Plaintiff's Brief in *Gryczan v. State of Montana*, http://www.lawlibrary.state. mt.us/dscgi/ds.py/Get/File-8273/96-202_(11-29-96)_Respondent_Brief.pdf (last accessed November 17, 2001).

47. Amicus Curiae Brief of the Women's Law Caucus of the University of Montana Law School, http://www.lawlibrary.state.mt.us/dscgi/ds.py/Get/File-8275/96-202_ (11-26-96)_Amicus_Curiae_ Brief.pdf (last accessed November 19, 2001).

48. *Gryczan*, 942 P. 2d 112, 122.

49. *Powell v. Georgia*, 270 Ga. 327 (Ga. 1998), 330.

50. Ibid., 332.

51. 468 S.E. 2d 188.

52. Ibid., 190.

53. Andrew M. Jacobs, "*Romer* Wasn't Built in a Day: The Subtle Transformation on Judicial Argument over Gay Rights," *Wisconsin Law Review* 893 (1996), 928.

54. Bill Rankin, "Georgia Supreme Court: A Shift in Philosophy," *Atlanta Journal and Constitution*, December 20, 1998, 1H.

55. "Georgia Overturns Anti-Sodomy Law," Associated Press, November 24, 1998.

56. Bill Rankin and Kathey Pruitt, "Sodomy Ruling May Stand," *Atlanta Journal and Constitution*, November 24, 1998, 1D.

57. See *State v. Lindsey*, 310 So. 2d 89 (La. 1975) and *State v. Bluain*, 315 So. 2d 749 (La. 1975).

58. Rawls was not on his own, however. Numerous amicus briefs were submitted in favor of overturning the law, including briefs from Lambda, the ACLU, and many progressive social and religious groups. See *State v. Baxley*, 633 So. 2d 142 (La. 1994).

59. *State v. Baxley*, 633 So. 2d 142, 146 (emphasis in the original).

60. Ibid., 147.

61. *State v. Baxley*, 656 So. 2d 973 (La. 1995), 981–82.

62. *Louisiana Electorate of Gay and Lesbians, Inc. (LEGAL) v. Louisiana*, cert denied, 640 So. 2d 1319 (La. 1994). The lower court ruling is described in Evan Wolfson and Robert Mower, "When the Police Are in Our Bedrooms, Shouldn't the Courts Go in After Them? An Update on the Fight against 'Sodomy' Laws," *Fordham Urban Law Journal* 21 (1994), 997–1055, 1009.

63. George Painter, "The Sense of Our Forefathers: The History of Sodomy Laws in the United States (Louisiana)," at http://www.sodomylaws.org (last accessed October 6, 2001).

64. *State of Louisiana v. Smith*, No. 99-KA-0606 (2000); Pamela Coyle, "Sodomy Ban Upheld by Louisiana's Highest Court," *Times Picayune*, July, 8, 2000, A1.

65. Pamela Coyle, "Court Strikes Down Sodomy Law," *Times Picayune*, February 13, 1999, A3.

66. *State v. Smith*, No. 99-KA-0606, 13.

67. Ibid., 10.

68. Ibid.

69. Ibid., 13.

70. Ibid., footnote 11.

71. Anne Rochell Konigsmark, "Louisiana Law against Sodomy Goes on Trial," *Atlanta Journal Constitution*, October 27, 1998, 3A; Pamela Coyle, "Second State Court Overturns Sodomy Law," *Times-Picayune*, March 18, 1999, A1.

72. Cain Burdeau, "Judge Rules Anti-Sodomy Laws Unconstitutional," Associated Press, March 19, 2001.

73. Susan Finch, "State's Sodomy Law Called Discriminatory: Appeals Court to Weigh Gay-Rights Argument," *Times-Picayune*, January 9, 2001, 2.

74. "Louisiana Sodomy Law Challenged," *Planet Out News*, January 8, 2001.

75. Tara Young, "Court Upholds 197-Year-Old Sodomy Law: Privacy Rights Aren't Violated, Justices Say," *Times-Picayune*, March 29, 2002.

76. Susan Finch, "Appeals Court Upholds Sodomy Law: Gay Discrimination Claim Rejected 2-1," *Times-Picayune*, November 23, 2002, 4.

77. "Supreme Mistake on Sodomy," *Times-Picayune*, July 10, 2000, B6.

78. Coyle, "Sodomy Ban Upheld."

79. Kevin McGill, "Bill Would Do Away with Louisiana Sodomy Law," Associated Press, May 15, 2001.

80. Scott Dyer, "Bill to Change Sodomy Law Fails in House," *Baton Rouge Advocate*, May 15, 2001, A1.

81. "House Doesn't Agree to Get Rid of Anti-Sodomy Law," Associated Press, May 17, 2001.

82. Marsha Shuler and Randy McClain, "Senate Revives Proposal to Change Sodomy Law," *Baton Rouge Advocate*, June 14, 2001, A12. The Senate vote came a month after Arizona repealed its sodomy law, which is discussed below.

83. Scott Dyer, "House Rejects Proposal to Revamp Sodomy Law," *Baton Rouge Advocate*, June 15, 2001, A14.

84. Alan Glendenning, "Gay Rights Bills Uncertain in Legislature," Associated Press, April 4, 1999.

85. Mike Fleming, "Louisiana Sodomy Law Survives Repeal Effort," *Southern Voice* (Atlanta), June 21, 2001. Archived at www.sodomylaws.org (last accessed December 10, 2001).

86. Fortner, "State Sodomy Law Unconstitutional," 1.

87. Angela Ward, "Gay Rights Group Will Challenge State Anti-Sodomy Law," *Texas Lawyer*, November 30, 2000, 4.

88. See *Lawrence v. State*, 2000 Tex. App. LEXIS 3760.

89. Ibid., 2.

90. See *Henry v. City of Sherman*, 928 S.W. 2d 464 (1996).

91. *Lawrence*, 2000 Tex. App., 5.

92. Ibid., 14.

93. Ibid., 20 (emphasis in the original).

94. Ibid., 14.

95. Ibid., 34.

96. Fortner, "State Sodomy Law Unconstitutional," 1.

97. Alan Bernstein, "Republicans Target One of Their Own," *Houston Chronicle*, July 4, 2000, A1.

98. Brenda Sapino Jeffreys, "Criminal Investigation Sought Because of Alleged Pressure Tactics," *Texas Lawyer*, July 17, 2000, 6.

99. Bernstein, "Republicans Target One of Their Own."

100. Ibid.

101. Alan Bernstein, "Local GOP Heads Defend Tactics," *Houston Chronicle*, September 28, 2000, A21.

102. Jeffreys, "Criminal Investigation Sought," 6.

103. *Lawrence v. State*, affirmed on rehearing en banc March 15, 2001, Justice Yates concurring, http://www.14thcoa.courts.state.tx.us/Opinions/031501/990109cf.PDF (last accessed December 12, 2001).

104. Mary Flood, "Appeals Court Upholds State Sodomy Ban," *Houston Chronicle*, March 16, 2001, A1.

105. See the majority opinion, http://www.14thcoa.courts.state.tx.us/Opinions/031501/990109f.PDF (last accessed December 12, 2001).

106. "Time for Texas to Let Go of Archaic Anti-Sodomy Law," *Houston Chronicle*, March 20, 2001, A22.

107. Steve Brewer, "Delay Could Help Gay-Rights Forces Fight Sodomy Law," *Houston Chronicle*, June 10, 2000, A35.

108. Brewer, "Delay Could Help Gay-Rights Forces"; Alan Bernstein, "Court Upholds Sodomy Ban in Refusing to Hear Appeal," *Houston Chronicle*, April 19, 2002.

109. "Lambda, Arkansas Activists to Announce Challenge to State Sodomy Ban," Lambda Legal Defense and Education Fund press release, January 28, 1998.

110. *Bryant v. Picado*, 996 S.W. 2d 17 (Ark. Sup. Ct. 1999), 18.

111. "Arkansas Court to Hear Argument against Anti-Gay Sodomy Law," Lambda Legal Defense and Education Fund press release, January 23, 2001.

112. The quote and background information are taken from George Painter, "The Sense of Our Forefathers: Arkansas," http://sodomylaws.org/sensibilities/arkansas.htm#fn63 (last assessed, May 16, 2005).

113. Tracey Shurley, "Time Short to Appeal Overturned Sodomy Law," *Arkansas Democrat-Gazette*, April 12, 2001, B1.

114. *Bryant*, 996 S.W. 2d 17, 19.

115. Pierce Presley, "Both Sides Present Arguments on State Sodomy Law," Associated Press, January 29, 2001.

116. Ibid.

117. *Picado v. Jegley*, http://www.lambdalegal.org/sections/library/decisions/picado decision.pdf (last accessed December 10, 2001).

118. *Jegley v. Picado*, http://courts.state.ar.us/opinions/2002a/20020705/01-815.html (last accessed September 5, 2002).

119. "Former Watergate Lawyer Sets Sights on State's 'Crazy' Sodomy Law," Associated Press, June 13, 1999.

120. Pamela Stallsmith, "Sodomy Bill Endorsed," *Richmond Times Dispatch*, February 15, 2000, A10.

121. C.S. Murphy, "Bill to Lessen Sodomy Law Gets Quashed," *Roanoke Times & World News, February 24, 2000, B1.*

122. Stephan Dinan, "Panel Rejects Less-Strict Sodomy Laws," *Washington Times*, January 20, 2001, C7.

123. *DePriest v. Virginia*, 537 S.E. 2d 1 (Va. App. 2000), 2.

124. Ibid., 5.

125. Ibid., 5–6.

126. "Lawyer Expands VA Sodomy-Law Challenge with Straight Couple," Associated Press, March 2, 2001.

127. Rhonda Smith, "Virginia Sodomy Case Loses Final Appeal," *Washington Blade*, August 17, 2001.

128. *Schochet v. State*, 580 A. 2d 176 (Md. 1990).

129. Peter S. Goodman, "Anti-Gay Bias Alleged in Maryland Sex Law," *Washington Post,* February 6, 1998, D5.

130. *Williams v. Glendening*, No. 98036031/CL-1059 (Baltimore City Cir. Ct., October 15, 1998). The court did not find the law unconstitutional but interpreted the statute to exclude private, consensual relations for persons of the same sex, as the *Schochet* court did for heterosexuals.

131. "Maryland Officials Agree to Limit Application of Sodomy Laws," *Lesbian/Gay Law Notes,* February 1999.

132. "Attorney General Will Not Appeal Sodomy Ruling," *Minneapolis Star Tribune*, September 1, 2001.

133. *Michigan Organization for Human Rights v. Kelley*, No. 88-815820 C2 (Mich. Cir. Ct. July 9, 1990).

134. *People v. Brashier*, 496 N.W. 2d 385 (Mich. Ct. App. 1992).

135. John Ellement, "SJC Limits Prosecution for Sodomy," *Boston Globe*, February 22, 2002, archived at http://sodomylaws.org/usa/massachusetts/manews13.htm (last accessed October 11, 2004).

136. Andrew M. Jacobs, "*Romer* Wasn't Built in a Day: The Subtle Transformation on Judicial Argument over Gay Rights," *Wisconsin Law Review* 893 (1996), 926. Courts in Missouri issued somewhat conflicting rulings, but the law was not invalidated until *Lawrence.*

137. Jerry Fink, "Bill Takes Gay Rights to New Level in Nevada," *Las Vegas Sun*, April 4, 1999, archived at www.sodomylaws.org (last accessed November 23, 2001).

138. *State v. Lopes*, 660 A. 2d 707 (Rhode Island 1995), 710.

139. Katherine Gregg, "Legislature Drafts Bill to Repeal Oral-Sex Law," *Providence Journal-Bulletin*, February 24, 1998, 1B.

140. Ibid.

141. Jonathan Saltzman, "State Senate Repeals 1896 Sodomy Law," *Providence Journal-Bulletin*, June 3, 1998, 1B.

142. Thomas J. Morgan, "East Side Candidates Denounce Sodomy Law," *Providence Journal-Bulletin*, August 19, 1994, 1C.

143. Gregg, "Legislature Drafts Bill to Repeal Oral-Sex Law."

144. Donald P. Haider-Markel, "Lesbian and Gay Politics in the States: Interest Groups, Electoral Politics, and Policy," in *The Politics of Gay Rights*, Craig Rimmerman et al., eds. (Chicago: University of Chicago Press, 2000), 313.

145. Saltzman, "State Senate Repeals 1896 Sodomy Law."

146. Ibid., 1B.

147. Editorial, "Repeal This Sex Law," *Providence Journal-Bulletin*, March 23, 1998, 4B.

148. Scott McKay, "Move to Repeal Sex Law Sparks Contentious Debate," *Providence Journal-Bulletin*, March 12, 1998, 1B.

149. Beth DeFalco, "Repeal of Sex Laws Advances," *Arizona Republic*, April 27, 2001, B8.

150. Scott Thomsen and Paul Davenport, "House Voted to Repeal Archaic Sex Laws," Associated Press, March 20, 2001.

151. Ibid.; Scott Thomsen, "Senate Votes to End Archaic Sex Laws," Associated Press, April 26, 2001.

152. Beth DeFalco, "Opposition to Repeal of Sex Laws; Flood of Emails Urges Governor to Veto Bill," *Arizona Republic*, May 5, 2001, B5.

153. Scott Thomsen, "Governor Signs Archaic Sex Law Repeal," Associated Press, May 8, 2001.

154. Thomsen, "Senate Votes."

155. Gary D. Robertson, "Gay-Rights Activists Prepared for Session Campaign to Change Laws," *Raleigh News & Observer*, March 4, 2001.

156. *Lawrence v. Texas*, 123 S. Ct. 2472 (2003), 2484.

157. Ibid., 2478.

158. Ibid., 2481.

159. Ibid., 2498.

160. Ibid., 2486–88.

161. See Gerald Rosenberg, *The Hollow Hope: Can Courts Bring About Social Change?* (Chicago: University of Chicago Press, 1991); Stuart Scheingold, *The Politics of Rights: Lawyers, Public Policy and Political Change*, 2nd ed. (Ann Arbor: University of Michigan Press, 2004); Mary Ann Glendon, *Rights Talk: The Impoverishment of Political Discourse* (New York: Free Press, 1993), as discussed in Chapter 1.

162. Ellen Ann Andersen, *Out of the Closets and into the Courts: Legal Opportunity Structure and Gay Rights litigation* (Ann Arbor: University of Michigan Press, 2005), 42, 103–104.

163. "Georgia Overturns Anti-Sodomy Law," Associated Press, November 24, 1998.

164. "Gallup Topics: A-Z—Homosexual Relations," Gallup Organization, Princeton, N.J., http://www.gallup.com/poll/indicators/indhomosexual.asp (last accessed June 21, 2001). The *Bowers* effect is discussed further in Chapter 11.

165. "Sexual Prejudice: Prevalence," http://psychology.ucdavis.edu/rainbow/html/prej_prev.html (last accessed October 11, 2004).

166. "Poll: "80 Percent of Alabamians Oppose Gay Marriage," Associated Press, March 15, 2004.

167. See *Campbell v. Sundquist,* 926 S.W. 2d 250 (Tenn. 1996).

168. "Judicial Selection in the States: Appellate and General Jurisdiction Courts," American Judicature Society, January 2004, http://www.ajs.org/js/JudicialSelectionCharts_old.pdf (last accessed September 20, 2004). Although the type of election may be significant, those states with courts ruling against sodomy laws either chose judges through merit (Tennessee and Maryland) or nonpartisan election (Kentucky, Georgia, Montana, Arkansas, Minnesota). The states where courts were resistant to striking down sodomy laws, or where court decisions were mixed, selected judges through partisan elections (Louisiana, Michigan, and Texas) or legislative appointment (Virginia). One exception is Rhode Island. Recall that the court there upheld the state's law. Rhode Island has a system of merit selection. Another, Oklahoma, where courts repelled challenges, appoints thorough a merit commission, but hold a retention election with a year.

169. Daniel Pinello, *Gay Rights and American Law* (New York: Cambridge University Press, 2003), 91–92.

170. Andersen, *Out of the Closets*, 140.

171. John J. Dinan, *Keeping the People's Liberties: Legislators, Citizens, and Judges as Guardians of Rights* (Lawrence: University of Kansas Press, 1998).

172. Ibid., 162–63.

## CHAPTER 7

1. Arthur S. Leonard, *Homosexuality and the Constitution*, vol. 4 (New York: Garland, 1997), viii.

2. *Loving v. Virginia*, 388 U.S. 1 (1967).

3. David L. Chambers, "Couples: Marriage, Civil Union, and Domestic Partnership," in *Creating Change: Sexuality, Public Policy, and Civil Rights*, John D'Emilio et al., eds. (New York: St. Martin's Press, 2000), 283–84.

4. *Baker v. Nelson* 191 N.W. 2d 185.

5. *Baker*, 191 N.W. 2d 185, 185–86.

6. *Baker*, 191 N.W. 2d 185, 186.

7. *Baker*, 191 N.W. 2d 185.

8. *Baker*, 191 N.W. 2d 185.

9. *Jones v. Hallahan*, 501 S.W. 2d 588.

10. *Jones*, 501 S.W. 2d 588, 590.

11. *Singer v. Hara*, 522 P. 2d 1187, 1188.

12. *Singer*, 522 P. 2d 1187, footnote 1.

13. The article cited was "The Legality of Homosexual Marriage," *Yale Law Journal* 82 (1973), 573, as cited in *Singer*, 522 P. 2d 1187, at 1193.

14. *Singer*, 522 P. 2d 1187, 1195.

15. Leonard, *Homosexuality and the Constitution*, ix–x.

16. Chambers, "Couples," 288–90.

17. Ibid., 293.

18. Ibid., 293.

19. Barbara J. Cox, "Same-Sex Marriage and Choice-of-Law: If We Marry in Hawaii, Are We Still Married When We Return Home?" *Wisconsin Law Review* 1994 (1994), 1033, 1038–39.

20. Leonard, *Homosexuality and the Constitution*, x.

21. *Dean v. District of Columbia*, 653 A. 2d 301 (D.C. Ct. App. 1995).

22. Humphries cited in Walter Wright, "Same-Sex Marriage Ban May Be Tested: Gay, Lesbian Couples Want to Overcome Legal Obstacles," *Honolulu Advertiser*, November 25, 1990, A1; Woods cited in Linda Hosek, "3 Unwed Gay Couples to Sue State," *Honolulu Star-Bulletin*, February 22, 1991, A3.

23. Walter Wright, "Couples Challenge Ban on Same-Sex Marriage: Licenses Await Ruling from AG," *Honolulu Advertiser*, December 18, 1990, A1.

24. Letter from Warren Price III to John Lewin, December 27, 1990. Appendix A of defendant's answering brief, *Baehr v. Lewin*, docket no. 15689, 126–63 at 167–68 (on file at the Hawaii Supreme Court clerk's office).

25. Walter Wright, "First Gay Marriage Here Ruled Illegal," *Honolulu Advertiser*, December 18, 1990, A4.

26. Linda Hosek, "ACLU Probes Taboo on Gay Marriage," *Honolulu Star-Bulletin*, December 29, 1990, A4.

27. Hosek, "3 Unwed Couples"; "ACLU Probes Taboo."

28. Linda Hosek, "Isles May Be First for Gay Marriages: Hawaii's Privacy Law Will Be the Springboard for Test Cases," *Honolulu Star-Bulletin*, April 24, 1991, A1.

29. *Baehr v. Lewin*, Circuit Court of the First Circuit, State of Hawaii, Civil No. 91-1394-05, October 1, 1991.

30. *Baehr v. Lewin*, 852 P. 2d 44 (Haw. 1993).

31. *Baehr*, 852 P. 2d 44, 57.

32. *Baehr*, 852 P. 2d 44, 63.

33. *Baehr*, 852 P. 2d 44, 82.

34. As quoted in *Baehr*, 852 P. 2d 44, 72.

35. *Baehr*, 852 P. 2d 44, 74.

36. *Baehr*, 852 P. 2d 44.

37. *Baehr*, 852 P. 2d 44, 48.

38. Linda Hosek, "Homosexuals Ask Court for Right to Marry," *Honolulu Star-Bulletin*, October 14, 1992, A1.

39. Quote from Ken Kobayashi, "Gay Marriage Case Gets Hearing: State Questioned Sharply in High Court," *Honolulu Advertiser*, October 14, 1992, A3.

40. Andrew Koppelman, "The Miscegenation Analogy: Sodomy Law as Sex Discrimination," *Yale Law Journal* 98:145 (1988), 160–61.

41. Ibid., 162.

42. Andrew Koppelman, "Why Discrimination against Lesbians and Gay Men Is Sex Discrimination," *N.Y.U. Law Review* 69:197 (1994), 286.

43. *Baehr*, 852 P. 2d 44, 87.

44. Cox, "Same-Sex Marriage and Choice-of-Law."

45. Jeffrey Schmalz, "In Hawaii, Step toward Legalized Gay Marriage," *New York Times*, May 17, 1993, 14A.

46. Kobayashi, "Gay Marriage Case Gets a Hearing."

47. See "Defendant's Motion for Reconsideration or Clarification," May 27, 1993, *Baehr v. Lewin*, Supreme Court clerk docket no. 15689, 585–86. See also Linda Hosek, "Attorney General Seeks Reversal on Gay Marriage," *Honolulu Star-Bulletin*, May 18, 1993, A1.

48. Ken Kobayashi, "Supreme Court Denies State Gay-Marriage Plea," *Honolulu Advertiser*, May 28, 1993, A1.

49. "Gay Marriage: Some Smoke Is Clearing," *Honolulu Advertiser*, May 30, 1993, B2.

50. Ken Kobayashi, " 'New Generation' Court Makes Waves Nationwide," *Honolulu Advertiser*, May 7, 1993, A7.

51. Ibid.

52. Jane Gross, "After Ruling, Hawaii Weighs Gay Marriages," *New York Times*, April 25, 1994, 1A.

53. *Journal of the House of Representatives of the Seventeenth Legislature, State of Hawaii*. Regular Session of 1994, 858.

54. *Journal of the Senate of the Seventeenth Legislature of the State of Hawaii*. Regular Session of 1994, 1101.

55. *House Journal*, 1994, 135–36.

56. Ibid., 129.

57. Ibid., 130.

58. Quoted in Ibid., 655.

59. Quoted in Ibid., 653.

60. Ibid., 655.

61. *Senate Journal*, 1994, 393–94.

62. Ibid., 447–49.

63. Ibid., 450.

64. Ibid.

65. Ibid., 452.

66. Ibid.

67. Act 217, Session Laws of Hawaii, 1994, Section 1. See also Andrew Koppelman, "No Fantasy Island," *New Republic*, August 7, 1995, 23.

68. Koppleman, ibid.

69. Koppelman, "No Fantasy Island," 22.

70. Gross, "After Ruling."

71. For a discussion of the politics involved, see Gross, "After Ruling."

72. See Andrew Koppelman, "Same-Sex Marriage, Choice of Law, and Public Policy," *Texas Law Review* 76 (1998), 921.

73. National Gay and Lesbian Task Force, "Specific Anti-Same-Sex Marriage Laws in the U.S.—January 2001," http://www.ngltf.org/downloads/marriagemap0201.pdf (last accessed April 23, 2001).

74. H.R. 3396, 104 Cong., 2d Sess. (1996).

75. *Report on the Defense of Marriage Act [H.R. 3396]*, Report 104-664. Committee on the Judiciary, U.S. House of Representatives, 104th Congress, 2nd Session, July 9, 1996, 2–4.

76. Journal of the House of Representatives of the United States, July 11, 1996, H7441.

77. Ibid., H7442.

78. Journal of the House of Representatives of the United States, July 12, 1996, H7483.

79. House Journal, July 11, 1996, H7444.

80. Ibid., H7448.

81. *Journal of the Senate of the United States*, September 10, 1996, S10105.

82. Ibid., S10122.

83. Ibid., S10124.

84. Act 217, Session Laws of Hawaii, 1994, Section 6.

85. Ibid.

86. Koppelman, "No Fantasy Island," 23.

87. See *McGivern v. Waihee* (Civil no. 94-00843 HMF). Interestingly, the case was brought by Christian evangelicals who resented the fact that only Mormons and Catholics were represented.

88. See Minutes of the Commission of Sexual Orientation and the Law, January 5, 1995.

89. Session Laws of Hawaii, Act 5, 1995, Section 3.

90. *Journal of the House of Representatives of the Eighteenth Legislature of the State of Hawaii*, Regular Session of 1995, 491–92.

91. *Baehr*, 852 P. 2d 44, at 48.

92. Tom Ramsey, "Hawaii, Aug. 17," http://abacus.oxy.edu/pub/marriage/digests/v01.n057 (last accessed April 23, 2001). Press release, the Hawaii Equal Marriage Project, September 1995.

93. Tom Ramsey, "Hawaii, Oct. 3," http://abacus.oxy.edu/pub/marriage/digests/v01.n075 (last accessed April 23, 2001).

94. In January of 1994, a poll taken by the *Honolulu Star-Bulletin*, indicated that 58 percent of respondents opposed same-sex marriage. Susan Essoyan, "Social Issues: Hawaii Tries to Take a Stand against Same-Sex Marriages," *Los Angeles Times*, April 24, 1994, A5.

95. Tom Ramsey, "Hawaii, May 24," http://abacus.oxy.edu/pub/marriage/digests/v01.n017 (last accessed April 23, 2001).

96. Minutes of the Commission on Sexual Orientation and the Law, State of Hawaii, September 13, 1995.

97. See "Testimony Received at October 11th and 12th Meetings," Commission on Sexual Orientation and the Law, State of Hawaii.

98. See generally, Minutes of the Commission on Sexual Orientation and the Law, State of Hawaii, September–November 1995.

99. E-mail from Morgan Britt to same-sex marriage discussion group, December 9, 1995. Copy on file with the author.

100. Letter from Speaker Joseph M. Souki, Hawaii House of Representatives, to Thomas Gill, Chair, Commission of Sexual Orientation and the Law, December 7, 1995. Copy on file with the author.

101. Draft Minutes of the Meeting Majority Subcommittee of the Commission on Sexual Orientation and the Law, November 13, 1995.

102. Report of the Commission on Sexual Orientation and the Law, December 8, 1995, 40–41.

103. See Majority and Minority Subcommittee Minutes of the Commission on Sexual Orientation and the Law, November 1995. On file at the Hawaii State Archives.

104. Britt e-mail.

105. Report of the Commission on Sexual Orientation and the Law, December 8, 1995, 9, 23–33.

106. Quoted in David W. Dunlap, "Panel in Hawaii Suggests Legalizing Same Sex Marriages," *New York Times*, December 11, 1995.

107. Tom Ramsey, "House Judiciary Committee Kills DP and All Friendly Bills, 'Defers' Votes on Constitutional Amendments to Ban Same-Sex Marriage," http://abacus.oxy.edu/pub/marriage/digests/v01.n127 (last accessed April 23, 2001).

108. Tom Ramsey, "Hawaii, Jan. 25," http://abacus.oxy.edu/pub/marriage/digests/v01.n132 (last accessed April 23, 2001).

109. Tom Ramsey, "Senate Judiciary Committee Votes on Three Bills," http://abacus.oxy.edu/pub/marriage/digests/v01.n188 (last accessed April 23, 2001).

110. Tom Ramsey, "Hawaii House and Senate Bills Cross Over," http://abacus.oxy.edu/pub/marriage/digests/v01.n205 (last accessed April 23, 2001).

111. Tom Ramsey, "Holt Forces Constitutional Amendment to the Senate Floor," http://abacus.oxy.edu/pub/marriage/digests/v01.n267 (last accessed April 23, 2001).

112. Ibid.

113. Mike Yuen, "'96 Legislature: Dud," http://www.starbulletin.com/96/04/30/news/story1.html (last accessed April 8, 2001).

114. Leonard, *Homosexuality and the Constitution*, xi.

115. "Trial on Same-Sex Marriages Postponed," *Phoenix Gazette*, May 15, 1995, A4.

116. Susan Essoyan and Bettina Boxall, "Gay Marriages on Hold while Ruling Is Appealed," *Los Angeles Times*, December 5, 1996, A3.

117. See the State of Hawaii's pretrial brief, http://www.hawaiilawyer.com/same_sex/briefs/statbref.txt (last accessed April 7, 2001).

118. Ibid.

119. See plaintiff's pretrial brief, http://www.hawaiilawyer.com/same_sex/briefs/prbrief1.txt (last accessed April 7, 2001).

120. *Baehr v. Miike*, Circuit Court of Hawaii, First Circuit, Civil No. 91-1394, http://www.hawaiilawyer.com/same_sex/briefs/opinion.txt (last accessed April 7, 2001).

121. Essoyan and Boxall, "Gay Marriages on Hold."

122. Quoted in Linda Hosek, "Judge Approves Same-Sex Marriage," *Honolulu Star-Bulletin*, http://starbulletin.com/96/12/03/index.htm (last accessed April 24, 2001).

123. Ibid.

124. Alan Matsuoka, "Gay Unions Score Low in *Star-Bulletin Poll*," *Honolulu Star-Bulletin*, http://starbulletin.com/96/03/29/news/story1.html (last accessed April 24, 2001).

125. "House Rejects Senate Proposal on Same-Sex Marriage," *Honolulu Star-Bulletin*, http://starbulletin.com/97/04/09/news/story2.html (last accessed April 24, 2001).

126. "Governor Set to OK Same-Sex Benefits," *Honolulu Star-Bulletin*, http://starbulletin.com/97/06/04/business/story1.html (last accessed April 24, 2001).

127. *Journal of the House of Representatives of the Nineteenth Legislature State of Hawaii* Regular Session of 1997, 117–18.

128. Ibid., 120.

129. Chief Justice Ronald T. Y. Moon, Supreme Court of Hawaii, State of the Judiciary Address, January 22, 1997, http://www.state.hi.us/jud/ADRS.HTM (last accessed April 11, 2001).

130. For instance, see the remarks by Representative Moses on January 23, 1997. *House Journal*, 1997, 118.

131. Ramsey, "Senate Judiciary Committee Reports out Two Bills," http://abacus.oxy.edu/pub/marriage/digests/v01.n650 (last visited April 23, 2001).

132. "Bills Give Gay Couples Tax, Insurance Benefits," *Honolulu Star-Bulletin*, February 4, 1997.

133. "Senate OKs Benefits for Gay Partnerships," *Honolulu Star-Bulletin*, http://www.starbulletin.com/97/02/07/news/story3.html (last accessed April 24, 2001).

134. William Kresnak, "Same-Sex Marriage Strategy Shifting," *Honolulu Advertiser*, April 8, 1997.

135. William Kresnak, "House Softens Terms on Same-Sex," *Honolulu Advertiser*, April 15, 1997.

136. "Gay Marriage Ban in Voters' Hands," *Honolulu Star-Bulletin*, http://starbulletin.com/97/4/17/news/story1.html (last accessed April 9, 2001).

137. Mike Yuen, "Legislators Showed They Listened to Voters," http://www.starbulletin.com/97/04/30/news/story1.html (last accessed April 9, 2001).

138. Linda Hosek, "A Peek Inside Hawaii's 'Pandora's Box,'" *Honolulu Star Bulletin*, http://www.star bulletin.com/97/07/03/news/storys.html (last accessed April 9, 2001).

139. Mike Yuen, "'Yes' Won with Focus, Clear Message," http://starbulletin.com/98/11/05/news/story4.html (last accessed April 9, 2001).

140. Mike Yuen, "Gay Rights Group Tries to Keep Dream Alive," http://starbulletin.com/98/10/29/news/story1.html (last accessed April 9, 2001).

141. Yuen, "'Yes' Won."

142. Yuen, "Gay Rights Group Tried to Keep Dream Alive.

143. Jonathan Goldberg-Hiller, *The Limits to Union: Same-Sex Marriage and the Politics of Civil Rights* (Ann Arbor: University of Michigan Press, 2002), 161–62. Goldberg-Hiller notes the irony (or at least the complicated nature) of this, given that traditional Hawaiian culture permitted same-sex relationships. See pp. 147–60.

144. *Baehr v. Miike*, http://www.hawaii.gov/jud/20371.htm (last accessed April 24, 2001).

145. *Brause v. Bureau of Vital Statistics*, 1998 WL 88743.

146. Liz Rushkin, "Judge Backs Gay Marriage; Superior Court Ruling Puts Burden on State to Justify Ban," *Anchorage Daily News*, February 29, 1998, 1A.

147. "Knowles Weighs Veto of Ban on Same-Sex Marriages," *Anchorage Daily News*, May 3, 1996, 2B.

148. Steve Rinehart, "Same-Sex Marriages Outlawed; Knowles Won't Veto or Sign Bill," *Anchorage Daily News*, May 7, 1996, 1B.

149. "Knowles Weighs Veto."

150. Rinehart, Same-Sex Marriages Outlawed."

151. 501 P.2d 159 (Alaska 1972).

152. *Brause*, 1998 WL 88743.

153. *Alaska Gay Coalition v. Sullivan*, 578 P. 2d 951 (Alaska 1978).

154. *S.N.E. v. R.L.B.*, 699 P. 2d 875 (Alaska 1985). The court stated: "Simply put, it is impermissible to rely on any real or imagined social stigma attaching to Mother's status as a lesbian."

155. *Faipeas, et al. v. Municipality of Anchorage*, 860 P. 2d 1214 (Alaska 1993). The city of Anchorage passed an ordinance adding sexual orientation to the city's antidiscrimination provisions. A citizens group collected signatures for a referendum titled, "A Special Homosexual Ordinance." The court held that the title was inflammatory and misleading and therefore prohibited under Alaska law. This was a case like *Romer v. Evans*, an attempt to police the parameters of democratic politics, but the Alaska court ruled without the lead of the U.S. Supreme Court. They refused to sanction the argument that adding sexual orientation to antidiscrimination laws amounts to "special rights" for gays.

156. Liz Ruskin, "Same-Sex Marriage Ban Fills Hearing; Amendment Clears Hurdle," *Anchorage Daily News*, March 10, 1998, 1A.

157. Liz Ruskin, "Limits on Marriage Passes in Landslide," *Anchorage Daily News*, November 4, 1998, 1A.

158. Steve Reinhart, "Gay Marriage Haunts Campaign," *Anchorage Daily News*, September 13, 1998, 1A.

159. Paul Queary, "Gay Marriage Advocates Slam Mormon Contribution," Associated Press, October 2, 1998.

160. Ruskin, "Limits on Marriage Passes."

161. Quoted in Rushkin, "Judge Backs Gay Marriage."

162. Rushkin, "Same-Sex Marriage Ban Fills Hearing."

163. Liz Ruskin, "Same Sex Marriage Measure Argued," *Anchorage Daily News*, September 19, 1998, 1D.

164. *Bess, et al., v. Ulmer*, 985 P. 2d 979 (Alaska 1999).

165. Jim Clarke, "Supreme Court Strikes Prisoner's Rights Question, Modifies Same-Sex Question," Associated Press, September 23, 1998.

## CHAPTER 8

1. *Baker v. State of Vermont*, 744 A.2d 864 (Vt. 1999).

2. David Moats, *Civil Wars: A Battle for Gay Marriage* (New York: Harcourt, 2004), 65–66. Moats is an editor at the *Rutland Herald* and had a front seat to the unfolding development in Vermont.

3. Ibid., 66–77. A Democratic legislator, John Murphy, reacted to hate crimes legislation by stating, "You're doing all this for the lezzies and the queers. This bill puts homosexual people on a golden pedestal." Ibid, 67.

4. Ibid., 97–98.

5. Ibid., 80–81.

6. Quoted in Rhonda Smith, "Vermont Lawyers Leave Their Mark," *Washington Blade*, May 19, 2000.

7. Abbey Duke, "How Did Spotlight Turn to Vt.?" *Burlington Free Press*, December 21, 1999, 3A.

8. Transcript of the Vermont Senate Government Operations Committee, April 4, 1997, 5.

9. Nancy Remsen and Abby Duke, "Landmark Case Touched Many Lives," *Burlington Free Press*, December 22, 1999, 1A.

10. Moats, *Civil Wars*, 35.

11. Ibid., 105.

12. "Plaintiff's Press Release of July 22, 1997," http://vtfreetomarry.org/pressre 1072297.htm (last accessed April 24, 2001).

13. *Baker v. State, Chittenden* (Vt.) Superior Court S1009-97CnC (1997).

14. Groups represented included: the Vermont Human Rights Commission (pro); Lambda (pro); the ACLU and PFLAG (pro); Unitarians and Quakers (pro); NOW and the National Center for Lesbian Rights (pro); the Vermont Psychiatric Association and the National Association of Social Workers (pro); a group of academics, including William Eskridge, Walter Dellinger, Daniel Farber, Jane Schacter (pro); Take It to the People (con); the Family Research Council (con); the American Center for Law and Justice (con); the states of Nebraska, Hawaii, Pennsylvania, Illinois, Arizona, Mississippi, Alabama, Michigan, South Dakota, Virginia (con), a group of academics, including Gerald Bradley, William Duncan, John Finnis, Robert George, and Douglas Kmiec (con); Concerned Women for America and the Free Congress Foundation (con); the Catholic and Mormon churches (con); Agudath Israel of America (con); Christian Legal Society (con); and a group of Vermont legislators (con). See amicus curiae briefs submitted in the *Baker* litigation, on file at the Vermont State Law Library.

15. Videotape of oral arguments in *Baker v. State*, November 18, 1999, provided by the Vermont Freedom to Marry Taskforce.

16. Moats, *Civil Wars*, 139.

17. *Baker v. State*, 170 Vt. 194, 229.

18. *Baker*, 170 Vt. 194, 200–201.

19. Chapter I, Article 7 of the Vermont Constitution states: "government is, or ought to be, instituted for the common benefit, protection, and security of the people, nation, or community, and not for the particular emolument or advantage of any single person, family, or set of persons, who are a part only of that community."

20. *Baker*, 170 Vt. 194, 207.

21. *Baker*, 170 Vt. 194, 208.

22. *Baker*, 170 Vt. 194, 211.

23. *Baker*, 170 Vt. 194, 206.

24. *Baker*, 170 Vt. 194, 217.

25. See Appellant's brief in *Baker v. State*, archived at http://www.vtfreetomarry.org/ fs_lawsuit_appealbriefs_plaintiff.html (last accessed August 1, 2002) and brief of Professors of Legislation and Statutory Interpretation, http://www.vtfreetomarry.org/ fs_lawsuit_amicusbriefs_professors.html (last accessed August 1, 2002).

26. *Baker*, 170 Vt. 194, 224–25.

27. Baker, 170 Vt. 194, 44. "When a democracy is in moral flux . . . courts do best by proceeding in a way that is catalytic rather than preclusive and that is closely attuned to the fact that courts are participants in the system of democratic deliberation." The quote is taken from Cass Sunstein's article, "Foreword: Leaving Things Undecided," *Harvard Law Review* 110:6 (1996), 101.

28. See Gil Kujovich, "An Essay on the Passive Virtue of *Baker v. State*," *Vermont Law Review* 25 (2000), 93–112.

29. *Baker*, 170 Vt. 194, 241–42.

30. See Carey Goldberg, "How Vermont's Top Judge Shaped Law on Civil Unions," *New York Times*, April 28, 2000, A14.

31. Baker, 170 Vt. 194, 241.

32. *Baker*, 170 Vt. 194, 261.

33. Moats, *Civil Wars*, 140.

34. Ibid., 144–45.

35. Diane Derby, "Political Climate Was Right for Court's Ruling on Gay Rights," *Rutland Herald*, 26 December 1999, http://www.rutlandherald.com/vtruling/story13.html (last accessed April 25, 2001).

36. "Ghost of Brigham Hides within Ruling," unsigned editorial, *Burlington Free Press*, December 26, 1999, 4E.

37. "Current Methods of Judicial Selection in Vermont," American Judicature Society, http://www.ajs.org/js/VT_methods.htm (last accessed September 20, 2004).

38. Adam Lisberg and Nancy Remsen, "Legislators Embrace Idea of 'Domestic Partnership,'" *Burlington Free Press*, December 21, 1999, 1A.

39. Bensen quoted in Abbey Duke, "Opponents Gather Forces for Messy Battle with Legislature," Burlington Free Press, December 22, 1999.

40. "Poll: Most Disapprove of Benefits," http://www.burlingtonfreepress.com, Special Report: Civil Unions, January 2000 (last accessed April 25, 2001).

41. Memorandum from Thomas A. Little to the House Judiciary Committee Members, January 4, 2000, http://www.leg.state.vt.us/baker/intro.htm (last accessed April 25, 2001).

42. Quoted in Jack Hoffman, "House Votes 79-68 for Civil Unions Bill," *Rutland Herald,* March 16, 2001, http://www.rutlandherald.com/vtruling/housevotes.html (last accessed April 25, 2001).

43. Audio recording of the Vermont House Judiciary Committee, February 9, 2000 (copy on file with the author).

44. "Summary: Work of the House Judiciary Committee for the Week of January 11–14, 2000," http://www.leg.state.vt.us/baker.Jan11/htm (last accessed April 24, 2001).

45. "Summary: Work of the House Judiciary Committee for the Week of January 24–28, 2000," http://www.leg.state.vt.us/baker.Jan24/htm, "Summary: Work of the House Judiciary Committee for the week of February 1–4, 2000," http://www.leg.state.vt.us/baker.Feb01/htm (last accessed April 25, 2001).

46. Moats, *Civil Wars*, 152. Edwards preferred to do nothing, but the court's decision and the willingness of legislative leaders to craft a response forced him to take a position.

47. Committee members' statements and positions taken from the audio recording of the Vermont House Judiciary Committee, February 9, 2000 (copy on file with the author).

48. Quoted in Adam Lisberg, "Panel Backs Gay Partnerships," *Burlington Free Press*, February 10, 2000, 1A.

49. Quoted in ibid.

50. "Summary: Work of the House Judiciary Committee for the Week of February 8–11, 2000," http://leg.state.vt.us/baker.Feb08/htm (last accessed April 25, 2001).

51. Audio recording of the Vermont House Judiciary Committee, February 21, 2000 (copy on file with the author).

52. Quoted in Adam Lisberg, "Eleven Lives, One Mission," *Burlington Free Press*, http://www.burlingtonfreepress.com/samesex/newstory27.htm (last accessed April 25, 2001).

53. Audio recording of the Vermont House Judiciary Committee, February 23, 2000 (copy on file with the author).

54. Audio recording of the Vermont House Judiciary Committee, February 29, 2000 (copy on file with the author).

55. Quoted in Frederick Bever, "Domestic Partnership Act May Be Course of Action," *Rutland Herald*, December 21, 1999, http://www.rutlandherald.com/vtruling/story2.html (last accessed April 25, 2001).

56. Quoted in ibid.

57. Jack Hoffman, "Panel Backs Domestic Partnership," *Rutland Herald*, February 10, 2000, http://www.rutlandherald.com/apps/pbcs.dll/article?AID=/20000210/NEWS/2100330&SearchID=73208479287491 (last accessed May 18, 2005).

58. Diane Derby, "Well-Oiled Machine Was Decisive Factor," *Rutland Herald*, March 17, 2000, http://www.rutlandherald.com/vtruling/machine.html (last accessed April 25, 2001).

59. Ross Sneyd, "Twelve Legislators Join Effort to Impeach Court," *Rutland Herald*, February 11, 2000, http://www.rutland herald.com/vtruling/legjoineffort.html (last accessed April 25, 2001); Hoffman, "House Votes 79-68 for Civil Unions Bill."

60. Diane Derby, "Same-Sex Marriage Backers Hire Lobbying Firm," *Rutland Herald*, January 5, 2000, http://www.rutlandherald.com/vtruling/story15.html (last accessed April 25, 2001); Hoffman, "House Votes 79-68 for Civil Unions Bill."

61. Jack Hoffman, "Towns Vote No to Same-Sex Marriage," *Rutland Herald*, March 7, 2000, http://www.rut landherald.com/vtruling/swsamesex.html (last accessed August 14, 2002).

62. Jack Hoffman, "Reactions Vary to Marriage Votes," *Rutland Herald*, March 9, 2000, http://www.rutland herald.com/vtruling/reactions.html (last accessed August 14, 2002).

63. David Gram, "Exit Polls Show Division," *Rutland Herald*, March 17, 2000, http://www.rutlandherald.com/vtruling/exitpoll.html (last accessed August 14, 2002).

64. Nancy Remsen, "Partnership Bill to See Second Life," *Burlington Free Press*, February 25, 2000, 1A.

65. Adam Lisberg, "House Agonized over Civil Unions," http://www.burlington freepress.com/samesex/newstory58.htm (last accessed April 25, 2001).

66. *Journal of the House of the State of Vermont*, Adjourned Session, 2000, vol. 1, 648–49.

67. Lisberg, "House Agonized."

68. Quotes in this paragraph from audio recording of the debates of the Vermont House of Representatives, March 15, 2000 (copy on file with the author).

69. Derby, "Well-Oiled Machine"; Frederick Bever, "Women Provided Key Votes for Bill," *Rutland Herald*, March 18, 2000, http://www.rutlandherald.com/vtruling/womenvotes.html (last accessed April 25, 2001).

70. Jack Hoffman, "Senate Approves Civil Unions Bill," *Rutland Herald*, April 19, 2000, http://www.rutlandherald.com/vtruling/approval.html (last accessed August 14, 2002).

71. Audio recording of the Vermont Senate, April 18, 2000 (copy on file with the author).

72. Quoted in Adam Lisberg, "Civil-Union Bill in Stretch Run," *Burlington Free Press*, April 20, 2000, 1A.

73. Diane Derby, "Dean Signs Civil-Unions Bill into Law," *Rutland Herald*, April 27, 2000, http://www.rutlandherald.com/vtruling/deansigns.html (last accessed April 25, 2001).

74. Quoted in Tracy Schmaler, "On Road, Dean Touts Civil Unions," *Rutland Herald*, January 27, 2002, http://www. rutlandherald.nybor.com/News/Story/41453.html (last accessed May 5, 2002).

75. Jack Hoffman, "Poll Suggests Limited Fallout from Gay Bill," *Rutland Herald*, May 1, 2000, http://www.rutlandherald.com/vtruling/limitedfallout.html; "Voters Show Anger over Civil Unions Law," *Rutland Herald*, September 13, 2000, http://www.rutlandherald.com/vtruling/cuvoters.html (both accessed April 25, 2001).

76. "Vermont Civil Union Election Results," Gay and Lesbian Advocates and Defenders website, www.glad.org (last accessed April 25, 2002).

77. Quoted in Ross Sneyd, "Vermont Vote Will Keep Law Intact," *Rutland Herald*, November 9, 2000, http://www.rut landherald.com/vtruling/lawintact.html (last accessed April 25, 2001).

78. Tracey Schmaller, "Bill in Works to Challenge Dismantling of Civil Unions," *Rutland Herald*, April 11, 2001, http://www.rutlandherald.com/vtruling/aprilbill.html (last accessed April 25, 2001).

79. Tracey Schmaller, "House Votes 84-55 for Law Barring Gay Marriage," *Rutland Herald*, March 16, 2001, http://www.rutlandherald.com/vtruling/hvlaw.html (last accessed April 25, 2001).

80. Ross Syned, "House Passes Reciprocal Partnership Bill," Associated Press, May 24, 2001.

81. "Lawmakers Criticize Pastor's Letter on Civil Unions," Associated Press, April 5, 2002.

82. Moats, *Civil Wars*, 262.

83. Pamela Ferdinand, "With Vermont in the Lead, Controversy Progresses," *Washington Post*, September 4, 2001, A3.

84. "Civil Unions: More States to Follow?" *Rutland Herald*, July 15, 2000, http://www.rutlandherald.com/vtruling/5weekjul.html (last accessed April 25, 2001).

85. Jonathan Ringel, "Ga. High Court May Be Pulled into Dispute on Civil Unions," *Fulton County Daily Report*, January 29, 2002; Carlos Frias, "Ga. Court Rejects Same-Sex Bond," *Atlanta Journal-Constitution*, January 26, 2002, 1A.

86. Press release, Indiana Civil Liberties Union, August 22, 2002, http://www.aclu.org/civil%20union.htm (last accessed September 8, 2002).

## CHAPTER 9

1. Beth Barlo, "Marriage Lawsuit Filed on Behalf of Seven Couples," *Bay Windows*, April 12, 2001, http://www.baywindows.com/media/paper328/news/2001/04/12/LocalNews/Marriage.Lawsuit.Filed.On.Behalf.Of.Seven.Couples-67317.shtm (last accessed May 20, 2005).

2. *Goodridge, et al. v. Dept. of Public Health, Massachusetts Superior Court* (Suffolk County), No. 2001-1647-A, 3–8.

3. *Goodridge*, No. 2001-1647, 25

4. *Goodridge*, No. 2001-1647, 21.

5. "Background on *Goodridge v. Dept. of Public Health*," GLAD website, http://www.glad.org (last accessed December 15, 2002).

6. Kathleen Burge, "A New Order in the Court," *Boston Globe*, October 21, 2001, B1. Also recall the pro–gay rights decision of the Court in *Hurley*.

7. The proposed amendment read: "It being the public policy of this Commonwealth to protect the unique relationship of marriage in order to promote among other goals, the stability and welfare of society and the best interests of children, only the union of one man and one woman shall be valid or recognized as a marriage in Massachusetts. Any other relationship shall not be recognized as marriage or its legal equivalent nor shall it receive the benefits or incidents exclusive to marriage from the Commonwealth, its agencies, departments, authorities, commissions, offices, officials, and political subdivisions. Nothing herein shall be construed to effect an impairment of a contract in existence as of the effective date of this amendment." Supporters of the amendment claimed that it would not disallow civil unions or domestic partnerships, but the language "or its legal equivalent" appears to state otherwise. Steven LeBlanc, "Gay Marriage Debate Heats Up on Beacon Hill,"

http://boston.com/news/daily/10/gay_marriage.htm, April 10, 2002 (last accessed July 2, 2002).

8. Yvonne Abraham, "Same-Sex Marriage Ban Dealt a Setback," *Boston Globe*, April 25, 2002, B1.

9. Conversation with Lauree Hayden, a student of mine at Brandeis University and an activist involved in the opposition efforts.

10. Rick Klein, "Birmingham Pressured to Block Same-Sex Marriage Ban," *Boston Globe*, May 2, 2002, B8.

11. Chris Tangney, "Birmingham Looking to Block Gay Marriage Ban," *Boston Globe*, July 16, 2002, B1.

12. Quoted in Abraham, "Same-Sex Marriage Ban."

13. Jennifer Peter, "Legislature Kills Proposed Amendment to Ban Gay Marriage," Associated Press, July 17, 2002, http://www.boston.com/news/daily/17/gay_marriage_ban.htm (last accessed July 17, 2002).

14. Quoted in "Governor Hopeful Supports Gay Marriage," PlanetOut.com, June 24, 2002, http://www.planetout.com/pno/news/article.html?2002/06/24/1 (last accessed July 2, 2002).

15. Quoted in Kathleen Burge, "Judge Dismisses Same-Sex Marriage Suit," *Boston Globe*, May 9, 2002, B1.

16. Quoted in Yvonne Abraham, "10 Years' Work Led to Historic Win in Court," *Boston Globe*, November 23, 2003, A1.

17. Ibid.

18. Quoted in Abraham, "10 Years' Work."

19. Emily Bazelon, "A Bold Stroke," *Legal Affairs*, May/June 2004, http://www.legal affairs.org/issues/May-June-2004/feature_bazclon_mayjun04.html (last accessed October 16, 2004).

20. Abraham, "10 Years' Work."

21. *Goodridge v. Massachusetts Dept. of Public Health*, slip opinion, Mass. Supreme Judicial Court, SJC-08860, November 18, 2003, 20–21.

22. *Goodridge*, Mass. Supreme Judicial Court, SJC-08860, 14.

23. *Goodridge*, Mass. Supreme Judicial Court, SJC-08860, 23–25.

24. *Goodridge*, Mass. Supreme Judicial Court, SJC-08860, 3.

25. *Goodridge*, Mass. Supreme Judicial Court, SJC-08860, 36.

26. Thanassis Cambanis, "Ruling Extends 20 Years of Cases," *Boston Globe*, November 19, 2003.

27. *Goodridge*, Mass. Supreme Judicial Court, SJC-08860, 19.

28. *Goodridge*, Mass. Supreme Judicial Court, SJC-08860, 38.

29. Bazelon, "A Bold Stroke."

30. Ibid., 41.

31. *Goodridge*, Mass. Supreme Judicial Court, SJC-08860, 42.

32. See the dissent by Spina, *Goodridge*, Mass. Supreme Judicial Court, SJC-08860, 43–44.

33. *Goodridge*, Mass. Supreme Judicial Court, SJC-08860, 77. The case citation is 7 Mass. 48 (1810).

34. *Goodridge*, Mass. Supreme Judicial Court, SJC-08860, 2.

35. Bazelon, "A Bold Stroke."

36. Bazelon ("A Bold Stroke") quotes Martha Minow's reaction to Marshall's opinion regarding the connection to South Africa: "It is like a South African decision. Beginning with

the use of the word 'scar' there's a directedness about injury and the emotional dimensions of injury.... And there is her attention to dignity, which comes right from the South African constitution."

37. Ibid.

38. Kathleen Burge, "sjc Peppers Lawyers on Same-Sex Marriage," *Boston Globe*, March 5, 2003, A1.

39. Bazelon, "A Bold Stroke."

40. Frank Phillips and Raphael Lewis, "Civil Union Law Sought: Romney Says Move Would Satisfy the sjc," *Boston Globe*, November 20, 2003, A1; Frank Phillips and Raphael Lewis, "AG Suggests Bill: Same-Sex Benefits Without Marriage," *Boston Globe*, November 21, 2003, A1.

41. Raphael Lewis, "sjc Affirms Gay Marriage, *Boston Globe*, February 5, 2004, http://www.boston.com/news/local/massachusetts/articles/2004/02/05/sjc_affirms_gay_marriage/ (last accessed September 27, 2004).

42. Rick Klein, "Vote Ties Civil Unions to Gay Marriage Ban," *Boston Globe*, March 30, 2004, http://www.boston.com/news/specials/gay_marriage/articles/2004/03/30/vote_ties_civil_unions_to_gay_marriage_ban/ (last accessed September 27, 2004).

43. See E. J. Graff, "False Analogy," New Republic Online, May 17, 2004, http://www.tnr.com/doc.mhtml?i=express&s=graff051704 (last accessed August 30, 2004).

44. Margo Williams, "Mass. Court Rejects Immediate Relief to Out-of-State Gay Couples," 365Gay.com, August 18, 2004, http://www.365gay.com/newscon04/08/081804mass Ruling.htm (last accessed October 16, 2004).

45. Frank Phillips and Rick Klein, "50% in Poll Back Ruling on Gay Marriage," *Boston Globe,* November 23, 2003, A1.

46. Michael Meade, "Mass Voters Support Gay Marriage," 365Gay.com, http://www.365gay.com/news content/1120403massPoll.htm (last accessed December 19, 2003). The numbers are from a *Boston Herald* poll released on November 23, 2003.

47. "New Survey Shows Massachusetts Residents Approve of Same-Sex Marriages," Associated Press, April 8, 2003.

48. Phillips and Klein, "50% in Poll Back Ruling."

49. "Poll Shows Public Split on Question Of Gay Marriage," Associated Press, February 23, 2004. The poll cited was a Suffolk University-WHDH-TV poll.

50. "University of Massachusetts Survey Finds Split Among State Residents over Gay Marriage," Associated Press, April 6, 2004.

51. Jeffrey Gold, "N.J. High Court Has Record of Support For Gay Rights," Associated Press, June 27, 2002.

52. Elizabeth Kennedy, "Gay Couples File Suit over Denial of Marriage Licenses," Associated Press, June 26, 2002.

53. *Lewis, et al. v. Harris et al.*, complaint filed with the Superior Court of New Jersey, Chancery Division: Hudson County on June 26, 2002, http://www.lambdalegal.org/binary-data/lambda_pdf/pdf/135.pdf (last accessed July 15, 2002).

54. From a compilation of quotes associated with the New Jersey litigation, Associated Press, June 26, 2002.

55. Herb Jackson, "Stem Cell Studies and Gay Marriage Lead GOP Debate," *Bergen County Record*, May 25, 2002, A3.

56. Michael Booth, "Gay Marriage Suit May Derail Push for 'Civil Union' Status," *New Jersey Law Journal*, June 28, 2002.

57. Jeff Linkous, "McGreevey Opposes Same-Sex Marriage Recognition," Associated Press, June 28, 2002.

58. *Lewis v. Harris*, Docket #15-03, Mercer County Super. Ct. (N.J.), November 5, 2003.

59. Tom Bell, "Suit to Legalize Gay Marriage Tossed," Associated Press, November 5, 2003.

60. Paul Davenport, "State Court Upholds Arizona's Ban on Same-Sex Marriage," Associated Press, October 8, 2003; "Judge Dismisses Same-Sex Marriage Lawsuit," Associated Press, May 8, 2003.

61. Josh Gohlke and Ruth Padawer, "Gay Couples to Get New Rights In N.J.," *Bergen County Record*, January 9, 2004, A1. The governor signed the legislation before his coming out as a gay man.

62. Julie Goodman, "Vermont Marriage Case Could Hurl Rhode Island into Same Battle," Associated Press, November 20, 1999.

63. Quoted in "Rhode Island Lawmaker Says State Not Ready for Gay Marriages," Associated Press, March 18, 2000.

64. Dan Harr and Daniela Altimari, "The Same-Sex Marriage Debate: Efforts for Legislation Quietly Beginning in Connecticut," *Hartford Courant*, January 30, 2001, A1.

65. Ron Zapata, "Legislative Committee Hears Arguments on Same-Sex Marriages," Associated Press, March 16, 2001.

66. Masha Herbst, "Gay Rights Advocates Won't Push for Vote," Associated Press, March 30, 2001.

67. Kathryn Masterson, "Poll: Majority of Residents Support Expanding Rights for Gay Couples," Associated Press, April 23, 2002.

68. Kathryn Masterson, "Senate Gives Final Approval to Expanded Rights for Gay Couples," Associated Press, May 7, 2002.

69. GLAD Press Release, August 24, 2004, http://www.glad.org/News_Room/press80-8-25-04.html (last accessed October 16, 2004).

70. "Connecticut Civil Unions Bill Becomes Law," 365gay.com, http://www.365gay.com/newscon05/04/042005connUnions.htm (last accessed May 21, 2005).

71. James C. McKinley, Jr., "Gay Marriages Are Still Far from Approval in Albany," *New York Times* online, September 24, 2003, http://www.nytimes.com/2003/09/25/nyregion/25GAY.html (last accessed September 25, 2003).

72. "NY Recognizes Gay Partners as Next of Kin," 365Gay.com, August 12, 2004, http://www.365gay.com/newscon04/08/081204nyHosp.htm (last accessed August 18, 2004).

73. "Second New York Mayor to Marry Gay Couples," 365Gay.com, March 3, 2004, http://www.365gay.com/newscon04/03/030304nyakWed.htm (last accessed October 16, 2004).

74. McKinley, "Gay Marriages Are Still Far from Approval."

75. Beth Shapiro, "25 Couples Sue NY to Marry," 365Gay.com, June 3, 2004, http://www.365gay.com/newscon04/06/060304ithSuit.htm (last accessed June 3, 2004).

76. Allen Drexel, "Another Trial Judge Finds New York Marriage Law Unconstitutional," *Lesbian/Gay Law Notes*, September 2004, 163–64; Beth Shapiro, "New York Court Rules Gays Must Be Allowed to Marry," 365gay.com, February 4, 2005, http://www.365gay.com/newscon05/02/020405nyMarr.htm (last accessed May 23, 2005).

77. William Wan and Lee Romney, "Marriage Debate in a New Arena,"*Los Angeles Times* online, August 14, 2004, http://www.latimes.com/news/local/la-me-marry14aug14,1,6651306.story (last accessed August 17, 2004).

78. Carl Ingram, "Senate OKs Bill on Rights for Unwed Couples," *Los Angeles Times*, August 24, 1994, A21.

79. Ibid.

80. Jerry Gillam, "Bill Would Recognize Rights of Unmarried Domestic Partners," *Los Angeles Times*, February 17, 1994.

81. Jerry Gillam, "Assembly OKs Rights Bill for Unwed Couples," *Los Angeles Times*, June 1, 1994, A3.

82. Ibid.; Ingram, "Senate OKs Bill."

83. Jerry Gillam, "Wilson Signs Bill Ending No-Pants Rule for Women," *Los Angeles Times*, September 12, 1994, A1.

84. Robert Gunnison, "Setback for Opponents of Gay Marriage," *San Francisco Chronicle*, August 20, 1996, A13.

85. Bettina Boxall, "A New Era Set to Begin in Benefits for Gay Couples," *Los Angeles Times*, July 17, 1997, A3.

86. Quoted in Robert Gunnison, "Assembly OKs New Stab at Same-Sex Marriage Recognition Bill," *San Francisco Chronicle*, August 21, 1996, A15.

87. Robert Salladay, "Governor Forces Weaker Bill on Domestic Partners," *San Francisco Chronicle*, July 8, 1999, A6.

88. Quoted in Mark Gladstone, "Davis Likely to Sign Domestic Partners Bill," *Los Angeles Times*, September 3, 1999, A3.

89. Jennifer Warren, "Bill Expanding Domestic Partner Benefits Signed," *Los Angeles Times*, October 5, 2001, 6.

90. "Lawmaker Drops Gay Rights Bill," *Ventura County Star*, January 17, 2002, A4.

91. Cheryl Wetzstein, "Gray Warms to Same-Sex Unions," *Washington Times*, April 4, 2002, A4.

92. A.B. No. 2116, State of California, 2002.

93. Gregg Jones and Nancy Vogel, "Domestic Partners Law Expands Gay Rights," *Los Angeles Times*, September 20, 2003, 1.

94. Lee Romney, "State's High Court Voids S.F. Same-Sex Marriages," *Los Angeles Times*, August 13, 2004, A1.

95. Doug Windsor, "Gay Marriage Comes to New York," 365Gay.com, February 26, 2004, http://www.365gay.com/newscon04/02/022604nyWed.htm (last accessed October 16, 2004).

96. Robert Salladay, "Gay, Lesbian Marriage Bill Advances,"*Los Angeles Times* online, April 20, 2004, http://www.latimes.com/news/local/la-042004gaywed_lat,1,7012341.story (last accessed April 20, 2004).

97. Wan and Romney, "Marriage Debate in a New Arena."

98. Mark DiCamillo and Mervin Field, "California Voters Disapprove of Same-Sex Marriage," Field Poll Press Release #2109, February 26, 2004, http://www.field.com/fieldpollonline/subscribers/RLS2109.pdf (last accessed October 15, 2004).

99. Ibid. See also *Lockyer v. City and County of San Francisco*, slip opinion S122923, Supreme Court of California, August 12, 2004, http://www.courtinfo.ca.gov/opinions/documents/S122923.DOC (last accessed August 18, 2004).

100. David Austin and Laura Gunderson, "First Two Gay Couple Wed in Multnomah County," March 3, 2004, OregonLive.com (*The Oregonian*), http://www.oregonlive.com/special/gaymarriage/index.ssf?/special/oregonian/gay marriage/040303.html (last accessed August 23, 2004).

101. Agnes Sowle, Memorandum to the Multnomah County Commission, March 2, 2004, http://www.aclu-or.org/litigation/Gay%20Marriage%20Filing/Link%201.pdf (last accessed August 23, 2004); Tanner v. OHSU, 971 P.2d 435 (1998).

102. David Austin and Laura Gunderson, "County Will License Gay Nuptuals," *The Oregonian*, March 3, 2004, A1.

103. "Editorial: Secrecy Distorts the Message," OregonLive.com (*The Oregonian*), March 4, 2004, http://www.oregonlive.com/special/gaymarriage/index.ssf?/special/oregonian/gaymarriage/040304_ed.html (last accessed August 23, 2004). "What arrogance. What self-indulgence. What breathtaking gall," the editorial declared.

104. Ibid.

105. Patrick O'Neill, "Public Process; Same Result," OregonLive.com (*The Oregonian*), April 2, 2004, http://www.oregonlive.com/special/gaymarriage/index.ssf?/special/oregonian/gaymarriage/040402_vote.html (last accessed August 24, 2004).

106. David Austin, "Group Abandons Recall Campaign," OregonLive.com (*The Oregonian*), June 8, 2004, http://www.oregonlive.com/special/gaymarriage/index.ssf?/special/oregonian/gaymarriage/040608_recall.html (last accessed August 24, 2004); David Austin, "Linn Makes Apology for Mistakes as County Chief," OregonLive.com (*The Oregonian*), May 6, 2004, http://www.oregonlive.com/special/gaymarriage/index.ssf?/special/ oregonian/gaymarriage/040506_linn.html (last accessed August 24, 2004).

107. Henry Stern, "Portland Candidates Support County," OregonLive.com (*The Oregonian*), March 4, 2004, http://www.oregonlive.com/special/gaymarriage/index.ssf?/special/oregonian/gaymarriage/040304_support.html (last accessed August 23, 2004).

108. Bill Graves, "Gay Marriage Critics Step Up Fight," OregonLive.com (*The Oregonian*), March 6, 2004, http://www.oregonlive.com/special/gaymarriage/index.ssf?/special/oregonian/gaymarriage/040306_process.html (last accessed August 23, 2004).

109. Mark Larabee and Jeff Mapes, "Benton Stops All Marriage Licensing," OregonLive.com (*The Oregonian*), March 23, 2004, http://www.oregonlive.com/special/gaymarriage/index.ssf?/special/oregonian/gaymarriage/040323_benton.html (last accessed August 24, 2004). The county was later ordered by a judge to begin granting licenses to opposite-sex couples; "Oregon County Ordered to Resume Issuing Marriage Licenses Halted in Gay Flap," Associated Press, August 26, 2004.

110. Letter from Hardy Myers, Attorney General of Oregon to Governor Ted Kulongoski, March 12, 2004, http://www.oregonlive.com/news/AG_samesexopinion.pdf (last accessed August 24, 2004).

111. Jeff Mapes, "Legislators' Top Lawyer Backs Gay Marriage," OregonLive.com (*The Oregonian*), March 10, 2004, http://www.oregonlive.com/special/gaymarriage/index.ssf?/special/oregonian/gaymarriage/040310_lawyer.html (last accessed August 24, 2004).

112. Ashbel S. Green, "High Court History Favors Gay Marriage," OregonLive.com (*The Oregonian*), March 14, 2004, http://www.oregonlive.com/special/gaymarriage/index.ssf?/special/oregonian/gaymarriage/040314_history.html (last accessed August 24, 2004).

113. Ashbel Green, "Gay Debate Challenges Marriage Laws," OregonLive.com (*The Oregonian*), April 17, 2004, http://www.oregonlive.com/special/gaymarriage/index.ssf?/special/oregonian/gaymarriage/040417_judge.html (last accessed August 24, 2004).

114. Ashbel S. Green, "Deal Sets Up Marriage Ruling," OregonLive.com (*The Oregonian*), March 20, 2004, http://www.oregonlive.com/special/gaymarriage/index.ssf?/special/oregonian/gaymarriage/040320_deal.html (last accessed August 24, 2004).

115. Ashbel Green, David Austin, and Laura Gunderson, "Judge Declines to Halt Licenses to Gay Couples," OregonLive.com (*The Oregonian*), March 9, 2004, http://www.oregonlive.com/special/gaymarriage/index.ssf?/special/oregonian/gaymarriage/040309_judge.html (last accessed October 16, 2004); *Li v. Oregon*, slip opinion, Multnomah Circuit Court, no. 0403-03057, April 20, 2004.

116. *Li*, Multnomah Circuit Court, no. 0403-03057, 10–11.

117. *Li*, Multnomah Circuit Court, no. 0403-03057, 13.

118. *Li*, Multnomah Circuit Court, no. 0403-03057, 15–16.

119. Noelle Crombie, "Oregon Records Gay Marriages," OregonLive.com (*The Oregonian*), July 10, 2004, http://www.oregonlive.com/special/gaymarriage/index.ssf?/special/oregonian/gaymarriage/040710_records.html (last accessed August 25, 2004). The marriages were recorded but not recognized by the state.

120. Ashbel S. Green, "New Ruling, but No Resolution," OregonLive.com (*The Oregonian*), March 13, 2004, http://www.oregonlive.com/special/gaymarriage/index.ssf?/special/oregonian/gaymarriage/040313_ruling.html (last accessed August 25, 2004); Bill Graves and Dan Hortsch, "Measure Banning Same-Sex Marriages Makes Ballot," OregonLive.com (*The Oregonian*), July 27, 2004, http://www.oregonlive.com/special/gaymarriage/index.ssf?/special/oregonian/gaymarriage/040727_ballot.html (last accessed August 25, 2004).

121. Bill Graves, "Voters Vote against Land Rules, Gay Marriage," OregonLive.com (*The Oregonian*), http://www.oregonlive.com/special/gaymarriage/index.ssf?/special/oregonian/gaymarriage/041103.html (last accessed May 21, 2005).

122. Green, "High Court History Favors Gay Marriage."

123. Ashbel Green and Michelle Cole, "Court Annuls Gay Marriages," OregonLive.com (*The Oregonian*), April 15, 2005, http://www.oregonlive.com/news/oregonian/index.ssf?/base/front_page/111355919461341.xml&coll=7 (last accessed May 21, 2005).

124. The quote is from Green, "Deal Sets Up Marriage Ruling." A poll right after Multnomah County began to issue licenses showed a substantial majority of respondents in Oregon supported same-sex marriage (about one-third) or civil unions (29 percent). Only about a third who responded favored no legal recognition of same-sex relationships. Jeff Mapes, "54 Percent in Oregon Oppose Same-Sex Marriage, Poll Says," OregonLive.com (*The Oregonian*), March 7, 2004, http://www.oregonlive.com/special/gaymarriage/index.ssf?/special/oregonian/gaymarriage/040307_poll.html (last accessed August 25, 2004).

125. Green, "Deal Sets Up Marriage Ruling."

126. See, for example, Dahlia Lithwick, "Chipping Away at the Wall," *New York Times*, August 22, 2004, 4:9.

127. Ashbel S. Green and Brent Walth, "Tenacity, Timing Prove Pivotal in Push for Same-Sex Marriage," OregonLive.com (*The Oregonian*), March 11, 2004, http://www.oregonlive.com/special/gaymarriage/index.ssf?/special/oregonian/gaymarriage/040311_pivotal.html (last accessed August 30, 2004).

128. *Anderson v. Sims*, slip opinion, King County Superior Court, No. 04-2-04964-4 SEA, August 4, 2004; Lynn Marshall and Elizabeth Mehren, "Judge Backs Same-Sex Marriage," *Los Angeles Times* online, August 5, 2004, http://www.latimes.com/news/nationworld/nation/la-na-gaymarry5aug05,1,7752024.story?coll=la-headlines-nation (last accessed August 25, 2004).

129. Ibid., 5.

130. Ibid., 14. Downing rejected the plaintiffs equal protection claims since that route had been rejected by another Washington court, the court of appeals, in *Singer v. Hara* (discussed in Chapter 7). Ibid., 23.

131. Ibid., 18–22.

132. Ibid., 3.

133. Ibid., 4, 26.

134. Ibid., 24.

135. *Castle v. Washington*, slip opinion of the Thurston County (WA) Superior Court, no. 04-2-00614-4, September 7, 2004, 4.

136. *Castle*, Thurston County (WA) Superior Court, no. 04-2-00614-4, 30–35.

137. *Castle*, Thurston County (WA) Superior Court, no. 04-2-00614-4, 30.

138. Lornet Thurnbull and Sanjay Bhatt, "Gay Marriage Fight Heats Up after Ruling," *Seattle Times*, August 8, 2004, A1.

139. Kavan Peterson, "50-State Rundown on Gay Marriage Laws," Stateline.org, August 26, 2004, http://www.stateline.org/stateline/?pa=story&sa=showStoryInfo&id=353058 (last accessed August 30, 2004).

140. Kavan Peterson, "Florida Lawyer Seeking Gay Marriage Limelight," State-line.org, http://www.state line.org/stateline/?pa=story&sa=showStoryInfo&id=392857 (last accessed August 30, 2004).

141. Michael Kiefer, "Arizona Men Take Same-Sex Marriage Issue to High Court," *Arizona Republic*, May 17, 2004.

142. *Standhardt v. Arizona*, 77 P. 3d 251 (Ariz. Ct. App. 2003).

143. Scott Thomsen, "Committee Endorses Proposal to Recognize Domestic Partners," Associated Press, January 29, 2002; "Arizona DP Measures Put on Hold," advocate.com, February 7, 2002, http://www.advocate.com/new_news.asp?id=2995&sd=02/07/02 (last accessed April 11, 2002); Paul Davenport, "Domestic Partner Bills on Hold as Supporters Avoid Showdown," Associated Press, February 5, 2002.

144. "Missouri Approves Same-Sex Marriage Ban," CNN.com, August 4, 2004, http://www.cnn.com/2004/ALLPOLITICS/08/04/samesex.marriage.ap/ (last accessed October 16, 2004).

145. Michael Kranish, "Gay Marriage Bans Passed," *Boston Globe*, November 3, 2004, A22.

146. "Bush Calls for Ban on Same-Sex Marriages," CNN.com, February 24, 2004, http://www.cnn.com/2004/ ALLPOLITICS/02/24/elec04.prez.bush.marriage/ (last accessed October 17, 2004).

147. "Same-Sex Marriage Senate Battle Is Over, War Is Not," CNN.com, July 15, 2004, http://www.cnn.com/2004/ALLPOLITICS/07/14/samesex.marriage/ (last accessed October 17, 2004); Helen Dewar, "House Rejects Same-Sex Marriage Ban," *Washington Post*, October 1, 2004, A27. Supporters of the amendment could only get forty-eight votes in the Senate. The House vote was forty-nine votes, short of the necessary two-thirds for passage.

148. Mary Fitzgerald and Alan Cooperman, "Marriage Protection Act Passes," *Washington Post*, July 23, 2004, A4.

149. This is discussed in greater detail in Chapter 11.

150. See Jeffrey Rosen, "The Gay Marriage Anti-Climax," *New Republic Online*, May 3, 2004, http://www.tnr.com/doc.mhtml?i=20040503&s=rosen050304 (last accessed May 17, 2005.

151. See the discussion of Galanter in Chapter 1.

152. American Judicature Society, "Judicial Selection in the States," http://www.ajs.org/js/ (last accessed May 17, 2005).

153. See the discussion of Feeley and Rubin in Chapter 1.

## Chapter 10

1. Sheldon Alberts, "Clark Backs Same-Sex Marriage 'in Principle,'" *National Post*, September 19, 2002, A13.

2. Carl F. Stychin, *Law's Desire: Sexuality and the Limits of Justice* (New York: Routledge, 1995), 106–7.

3. See Christopher Manfredi, "The Judicialization of Politics: Rights and Public Policy in Canada and the United States," in *Degrees of Freedom: Canada and the United States in a Changing World*, Keith Banting et al., eds. (Montreal: McGill-Queen's University Press, 1997).

4. Patrick Monahan, *Politics and the Constitution: The Charter, Federalism and the Supreme Court of Canada* (Toronto: Carswell, 1987), 245.

5. James C. Snell and Frederick Vaughan, *The Supreme Court of Canada: A History of the Institution* (Toronto: University of Toronto Press, 1985), 21–23.

6. Ibid., 35.

7. Quoted in Ibid., 79–82, 134. Quotation appears on page 79.

8. Ibid., 102, 178.

9. Peter McCormick, *Canada's Courts* (Toronto: Lorimer, 1994), 75.

10. Snell and Vaughan, *The Supreme Court of Canada*, 165–69.

11. Ibid., 190.

12. Ibid., 207.

13. Ibid., 314–21.

14. Frederick Vaughan, "Judicial Politics in Canada: Patterns and Trends," in *Judicial Power and Canadian Democracy*, Paul Howe and Peter Russell, eds. (Montreal: McGill-Queen's University Press, 2001), 10–11.

15. McCormick, *Canada's Courts*, 77–78.

16. Monahan, *Politics and the Constitution*, 172.

17. Ibid., 174. For a discussion of Trudeau's influence on the Charter, see H. D. Forbes, "Trudeau's Moral Vision," in *Rethinking the Constitution: Perspectives on Canadian Constitutional Reform, Interpretation, and Theory*, Anthony A. Peacock, ed. (New York: Oxford University Press, 1996).

18. Michael Mandel, *The Charter of Rights and Freedoms and the Legalization of Politics in Canada* (Toronto: Thompson Educational Publishing, 1994), 21.

19. Charles Epp, "Do Bills of Rights Matter? The Canadian Charter of Rights and Freedoms," *American Political Science Review* 90:4 (December 1996), 765–79, 768; Rainer Knopff and F. L. Morton, "Nation Building and the Charter," in *Constitutionalism, Citizenship and Society in Canada*, Alan Cairns and Cynthis Williams, eds. (Toronto: University of Toronto Press, 1985).

20. Snell and Vaughan, *The Supreme Court of Canada*, 226.

21. Vaughan, "Judicial Politics in Canada," 13.

22. Mandel, *The Charter of Rights and Freedoms*, 27.

23. Brian Dickson, "The Canadian Charter of Rights and Freedoms: Context and Evolution," in *The Canadian Charter of Rights and Freedoms*, 3rd ed., Gerald A. Beaudoin and Errol Mendes, eds. (Toronto: Carswell, 1996), chaps. 1, 2.

24. See Howard Leeson, "Section 33, The Notwithstanding Clause: A Paper Tiger?" in *Judicial Power and Canadian Democracy*, Paul Howe and Peter Russell, eds. (Montreal: McGill-Queen's University Press, 2001).

25. See Christopher Manfredi, "On the Virtues of a Limited Constitution: Why Canadians Were Right to Reject the Charlottetown Accord," in *Rethinking the Constitution: Perspectives on Canadian Constitutional Reform, Interpretation, and Theory*, Anthony A. Peacock, ed. (New York: Oxford University Press, 1996); Karen Selick, "Rights and Wrongs in the Canadian Charter," in *Rethinking the Constitution: Perspectives on Canadian Constitutional Reform, Interpretation, and Theory*, Anthony A. Peacock, ed. (New York: Oxford University Press, 1996).

26. See Rainer Knopff and F. L. Morton, "Canada's Court Party," in *Rethinking the Constitution: Perspectives on Canadian Constitutional Reform, Interpretation, and Theory*, Anthony A. Peacock, ed. (New York: Oxford University Press, 1996).

27. Epp, "Do Bills of Rights Matter?" 776.

28. Ibid.

29. Ibid., 770–71.

30. Quoted in Bruce Wallace, "Activists in Black Robes," *Maclean's*, September 6, 1999, 14. Commentators on the right in the United States are also taking notice of the Court's trend, and their criticism may even be stronger. The following comes from David Frum in the *Wall Street Journal*: "Since 1982, when Pierre Trudeau grafted a justiciable Charter of Rights onto Canada's 1867 Constitution, Canada's courts have become for the legal left what Spain was for the Wehrmacht in the 1930s: a place to test the tanks and dive-bombers with which it intended to even greater damage elsewhere." David Frum, "Rule of Law," *Wall Street Journal*, November 15, 1999, A51:3.

31. Even at the height of activism, the Court was sustaining the government's position in two-thirds of Charter claims. Janice Tibbits, "Top-Court Charter Rulings Tend to Back Politicians," *Montreal Gazette*, April 17, 1999, A13.

32. Janice Tibbits, "Top Court No Longer Prisoner's Friend: Expert Expects McLachlin-Led Bench to Halt Pro-Accused Trend," *Ottawa Citizen*, May 8, 2000, A1. Some also see Chretien's appointments as a reflection of his desire to appear independent from the pressure of legal elites to pick certain justices. See John Geddes, "The Legal Eagles," *Maclean's* 113:2 (January 10, 2000), 30.

33. Janice Tibbets, "Top Court Shows New Restraint: Justices Stopped Making Law in 2002, Analyst Suggests," *Montreal Gazette*, April 6, 2002, A1.

34. Quoted in Brian Kappler, "Slippery Slope of Equality," *Montreal Gazette*, April 10, 2001, A8.

35. Julian Beltrame, "Judging Beverly," *Maclean's* 115:20 (May 20, 2002), 28–31.

36. Ibid.; Janice Tibbits, "Supreme Court Judges Hit the Road for First Time; Historic Trip Seen as Smart PR," *Ottawa Citizen*, April 29, 1999, A3.

37. "The Charter: Dividing or Uniting Canadians?" Center for Research and Information on Canada (CRIC), April 2002.

38. Quoted in Wallace, "Activists in Black Robes."

39. Seymour Martin Lipset, *Continental Divide: The Values and Institutions of the United States and Canada* (New York: Routledge, 1990), 8.

40. See William Mishler, "Review of Continental Divide, by Seymour Martin Lipset," *Journal of Politics* 53 (1991), 272–74.

41. W. A. Bogart, *Courts and Country: The Limits of Litigation and the Social and Political Life of Canada* (New York: Oxford University Press, 1994), 7.

42. Both sets of poll numbers come from the CRIC report.

43. For arguments in favor of U.S. group rights, see Lani Guinier, *The Tyranny of the Majority* (New York: Free Press, 1994).

44. Canadian Charter of Rights and Freedoms, Section 27.

45. *Adarand Constructors v. Pena*, 515 U.S. 200 (1995), 240.

46. *Adarand*, 515 U.S. 200, 244.

47. *Loving v. Virginia*, 388 U.S. 1 (1967).

48. This historical policy summary is taken from David Rayside, *On the Fringe: Gays and Lesbians in Politics* (Ithaca: Cornell University Press, 1998), 108–11.

49. Ibid., 111–17.

50. Ibid., 118–32.

51. Ibid., 142–49.

52. Ian Urquhart, "Same-Sex Legislation Gets Smoother Ride This Time Around," *Toronto Star*, October 27, 1999.

53. Robert J. Sharpe, "The Impact of a Bill of Rights on the Role of the Judiciary: A Canadian Perspective," in *Promoting Human Rights Through Bills of Rights: Comparative Perspectives*, Philip Alston, ed. (New York: Oxford University Press, 1999), 438.

54. *Andrews v. Law Society of British Columbia* (1989) 1 S.C.R. 143.

55. Canadian Charter of Rights and Freedoms (1982), Section 1. Chief Justice Robert Dickson defined this test as follows: "Two central criteria must be satisfied to establish that a limit is reasonable and demonstrably justified in a free and democratic society. First, the objective to be served by the measures limiting a *Charter* right must be sufficiently important to warrant overriding a constitutionally protected right or freedom. The standard must be high to ensure that trivial objectives or those discordant with the principles of a free and democratic society do not gain protection. At a minimum, an objective must relate to societal concerns which are pressing and substantial in a free and democratic society before it can be characterized as sufficiently important. Second, the party invoking s. 1 must show the means to be reasonable and demonstrably justified. This involves a form of proportionality test involving three important components. To begin, the measures must be fair and not arbitrary, carefully designed to achieve the objective in question and rationally connected to that objective. In addition, the means should impair the right in question as little as possible. Lastly, there must be a proportionality between the effects of the limiting measure and the objective—the more severe the deleterious effects of a measure, the more important the objective must be." *R. v. Oakes*, (1986) 1 S.C.R. 103.

56. *Andrews*, 1 S.C.R. 143.

57. *Egan v. Canada*, (1995) 2 S.C.R. 513.

58. See *Vriend v. Alberta* (1998) 1 S.C.R. 493.

59. See *R. v. Hill* (1986) 1 S.C.R. 313.

60. *Law v. Canada (Minister of Employment and Immigration)* (1999) 1 S.C.R. 497, para. 4.

61. Family Law Act, R.S.O. 1990, c. F.3.

62. *M. v. H.* (1996), 132 D.L.R. (4th) 538, 563.

63. *M. v. H.* (1996), 142 D.L.R. (4th) 1, para. 124.

64. *M.*, 142 D.L.R. (4th) 1, para. 42.

65. Allan Thompson, "Same-Sex Dispute Before Top Court," *Toronto Star*, March 19, 1998, A1.

66. *M. v. H.* (1999) 2 S.C.R. 3.

67. *M.*, 2 S.C.R. 3, para. 250.

68. Nahlah Ayed, "Liberals Peg Same-Sex Benefits as a Priority," Canadian Press Newswire, March 20, 1998.

69. "Ottawa Warms to Same-Sex Partners' Rights: The Government Is Looking for Ways to Redress Inequality of Gays," *Vancouver Sun*, January 8, 1999, A12.

70. Janice Tibbets, "Soft Sell Urged on Same-Sex Rights," *Montreal Gazette*, February 1, 1999, A8.

71. Tonda MacCharles, "MPS Tie the Knot on Marriage," *Toronto Star*, June 9, 1999; summary of debate and quotes taken from the Edited Hansard of the Federal Parliament of Canada, June 8, 1999.

72. The party leadership was clearly trying to placate backbenchers, especially those

from rural ridings, who were a bit queasier on the issue. See Valerie Lawton, "Same-Sex Bill to Exclude Gay Marriage," *Toronto Star*, March 23, 2000.

73. Nova Scotia, British Columbia, Ontario, Alberta, Saskatchewan, and Quebec have amended laws in accordance with *M. v. H.* "Quebec OKs Civil Unions, Adoption Rights," Gay.com, June 7, 2002, http://www.planetout.com/pno/news/article.html?2002/06/07/2 (last accessed May 22, 2005).

74. Edited Hansard of the 36th Parliament of Canada, 2nd session, No. 49, February 15, 2000, 1005.

75. After the 1997 elections, each party had the following parliamentary seats: Liberals—155, Conservatives—20, NDP—21, Bloc Quebecois—44, Reform/Alliance—60. These numbers are taken from Rayside, *On the Fringe*, 111.

76. Hansard No. 49, 1150–205.

77. Ibid, 1315–25.

78. Ibid, 1135–40.

79. Edited Hansard of the 36th Parliament of Canada, 2nd session, No. 82, April 10, 2000, 1325–30.

80. Rayside notes that outside of some western provinces and parts of rural Ontario, the religious right has little effect on Canadian politics. See Rayside, *On the Fringe*, 106, 111.

81. Hansard, No. 82, 1310.

82. Tim Naumetz, "Liberal Backbenchers Break Ranks over Same-Sex Spousal Benefits," *Ottawa Citizen*, April 12, 2000, A3.

83. "Controversial Same Sex Bill Passes Commons," Canadian Press Newswire, April 11, 2000.

84. James Baxter, "Robinson Tables Same-Sex Marriage Bill," *Vancouver Sun*, February 15, 2001, A4.

85. EGALE press release, "B.C. Court Releases Decision in Same-Sex Marriage Case," October 3, 2001, www.egale.ca/pressrel/011003.htm (last accessed November 30, 2002).

86. The Canadian judicial system does not have parallel state and federal court structures, as is the case in the United States. Judges are appointed by the federal government but lower courts are organized on a provincial basis, usually with a trial court (similar to U.S. District Courts) and an intermediate appellate court, the decisions of which may be appealed to the Supreme Court of Canada. See "Canada's Court System," Canada Department of Justice website, http://canada.justice.gc.ca/en/dept/pub/trib/index.html (last accessed December 5, 2002).

87. EGALE press release, "B.C. Supreme Court to Hear Landmark Same-Sex Marriage Challenge," July 2001, www.egale.ca/documents/bc-marriage-case.htm (last accessed November 30, 2002); Kim Pemberton, "Same-Sex Unions Won't Cause Upheaval, Court Told," *Vancouver Sun*, July 26, 2001, A7.

88. *EGALE, et al. v. Attorney General*, 2001 B.S.C. 1365, para. 86–92.

89. *EGALE, et al.*, 2001 B.S.C. 1365, para. 102.

90. *EGALE, et al.*, 2001 B.S.C. 1365, para. 214.

91. *Halpern v. Canada*, Ontario Divisional Court, July 12, 2002, 20–21.

92. *Halpern*, 6. See also, Shannon Kari, "Gays Win: Ban on Same-Sex Marriage Violates Rights," *Montreal Gazette*, July 13, 2002, A1.

93. John MacFarland and Sidhartha Banerjee, "Same-Sex Marriage One Step Closer," *Montreal Gazette*, September 7, 2002, A1.

94. *In Re North and Matheson* (1974) 52 D.L.R. (3rd) 280 (Man. Co. Ct.).

95. *Layland v. Ontario* (1993) 14 O.R. (3rd) 658 (Ont. Div. Ct.).

96. Amy Carmichael, "B.C. Court Backs Same-Sex Marriage,"Canadian Press, May 1, 2003; Tom Cohen, "Canadian Gay Marriage Ban Loses in Court," Associated Press, June 10, 2003.

97. "Ontario Will Register Same-Sex Marriages: Attorney General," CBC News, June 13, 2003, http://www.cbc.ca/stories/2003/06/11/samesex_030611 (last accessed May 22, 2005).

98. Jean-Pierre O'Brien, "Quebec Court Rules Gays Can Marry," 365Gay.com, March 19, 2004, http://www.365gay.com/newscon04/03/031904queMarry.htm (last accessed October 22, 2004).

99. *Dunbar & Edge v. Yukon*, 2004 YKSC 54 (1994).

100. Rich Peters, "4th Canadian Province oks Gay Marriage," 365gay.com, September 16, 2004, http://www.365gay.com/newscon04/09/091604manMarry.htm (last accessed September 17, 2004).

101. Derwin Parsons, "Gay Marriage Sweeps into Canada's Maritimes," 365gay.com, September 24, 2004, http://www.365gay.com/newscon04/09/092404nsMarry.htm (last accessed September 24, 2004).

102. Steve Lambert, "Manitoba Likely to Become Next Canadian Province to Legalize Gay Marriage," 365gay.com, August 26, 2004, http://www.365gay.com/newscon04/08/082604manMarr.htm (last accessed August 26, 2004).

103. Factum of the Attorney General of Canada, October 24, 2003, archived at http://www.egale.ca/index.asp?lang=E&menu=54&item=832 (last accessed September 13, 2004). In December 2004, the Supreme Court of Canada ruled that same-sex marriage legislation would be constitutional and is supported by the Charter. See "Decision of the Supreme Court of Canada on the Marriage Reference," Canada Department of Justice news release, http://canada.justice.gc.ca/en/news/fs/2004/doc_31342.html (last accessed May 22, 2005).

104. Janice Tibbits, "Feds Spell Out Gay Marriage Stance," *Montreal Gazette*, September 16, 2002.

105. Campbell Clark, "Cabinet Takes Aim at Casting Same-Sex Policy." *Toronto Globe and Mail,* August 1, 2002, A1.

106. Randall Palmer, "Canada to Consider Same-Sex Marriage," *Boston Globe*, November 8, 2002, A16. A Liberal Party poll showed support for same-sex marriage at 48 percent to 43 percent. Campbell Clark, "Ottawa to Appeal Same-Sex Ruling," *Toronto Globe and Mail*, July 30, 2002, A1.

107. Bill Curry and Robert Benzie, "Liberal MP Warns against Gay Marriages," *National Post*, July 18, 2002, A4; Campbell Clark, "Government Steers Vote on Accepting Same-Sex Ruling," *Toronto Globe and Mail*, June 13, 2003, A5.

108. Kim Lunman and Drew Fagan, "Marriage Divides the House," *Toronto Globe and Mail*, September 17, 2003, A1.

109. Brian Laghi and Simon Tuck, "Alliance-Tory Merger Hit Roadblock on Gays," *Toronto Globe and Mail*, November 28, 2003, A1.

110. Isbel Teotonio, "Clause a 'Bomb': MacKay Breaks Ranks," *Montreal Gazette*, June 15, 2004, A14.

111. L. Ian McDonald, "The Liberals Are Losing, Thanks to a Lousy Campaign," *Montreal Gazette*, June 10, 2004, A12.

112. Rich Peters, "You Do Your Job, Let Us Do Ours, Marriage Judge Tells Lawmakers," 365Gay.com, February 8, 2004, http://www.365gay.com/newscon04/02/020804mcmurtry Marr.htm (last accessed October 22, 2004).

113. Clifford Krauss, "Canadian Leaders Agree to Propose Gay Marriage Law," *New York Times*, June 18, 2003; Ben Thompson, "Gay Marriage Bill On Track As Canada's

Government Survives Crucial Vote," 365gay.com, May 19, 2005, http://www.365gay.com/newscon05/05/051905canVote.htm (last accessed May 22, 2005).

114. John Geddes, "Passing Judgment," *Maclean's* (September 6, 2004), 27.

115. Quoted in Peters, "You Do Your Job, Let Us Do Ours."

116. Janice Tibbets, "Same-Sex Marriage Foes Get Tough Ride," *Montreal Gazette*, October 8, 2004, A10.

117. See "Beyond Conjugality: Recognizing and Supporting Close Personal Adult Relationships," Report of the Law Commission of Canada, January 29, 2002.

118. Petti Fong, "B.C. Extends Legal Rights for Same-Sex Couples," *Vancouver Sun*, February 5, 1998, B7; "Report of Recognition of Spousal and Family Status," British Columbia Law Institute, November 30, 1998.

119. Gary Edwards and Josephine Mazzuca, "About Four-in-Ten Canadians Accepting of Same Sex Marriages, Adoption," Gallup Canada, Inc., March 7, 2000. The 2001 number is taken from Janice Tibbits, "Seven Cabinet Ministers Back Marriage Right: Gays," *Montreal Gazette*, August 2, 2002, A10.

120. Palmer, "Canada to Consider Same-Sex Marriage"; William Johnson, "Can Charter Trump Religion?" *Toronto Globe and Mail*, August 1, 2002, A19.

121. Edwards and Mazzuca, "About Four-in-Ten Canadians Accepting of Same Sex Marriages."

122. In 2000, Gallup found U.S. support for same-sex marriage at 34 percent and 46 percent support for civil unions in 2002. Frank Newport, "Homosexuality," Gallup In-Depth Analyses, September 2002, http://www.gallup.com/poll/analysis/ia020911v.asp (last accessed December 10, 2002); "Homosexual Relations," Gallup Poll Topics A-Z, http://www.gallup.com/poll/indicators/indhomosexual.asp (last accessed June 21, 2001).

123. Jan Prout, "Divided on Marriage," 365Gay.com, December 3, 2003, http://www.365gay.com/newscontent/120303canMarriagePoll.htm (last accessed December 19, 2004).

124. "Canadians Split over Same-Sex Marriage: Poll," CBC News, September 5, 2003, http://www.cbc.ca/stories/2003/09/04/samesexpoll030904 (last accessed May 22, 2005).

125. Michael Valpy, "Canadians Tolerant—Well, Mostly," *Toronto Globe and Mail*, July 1, 2004. .

126. Alan Wolfe, "The Homosexual Exception," *New York Times Magazine*, February 8, 1998, http://www.nytimes.com/books/98/03/08/home/wolfe.html (last accessed May 22, 2005).

127. "The Charter: Dividing or Uniting Canadians?"

CHAPTER 11

1. Gerald N. Rosenberg and Christopher M. Rohrbacher, "Same-Sex Marriage, Gay Rights and the (Counter?) Mobilization of the Law," paper prepared for presentation at the 2000 Annual Meeting of the American Political Science Association, August 31—September 3, 2000, Washington, D.C.

2. Rosenberg and Rohrbacher, "Same-Sex Marriage," 8.

3. Richard Posner, "Wedding Bell Blues," *New Republic*, December 22, 2003, 35. Posner cites a *Washington Post* poll taken in the wake of the *Lawrence* decision, a period of time that saw a slight anti–gay rights backlash, which I discuss below and largely discount.

4. Ibid., 36.

5. "Voters Strongly Oppose Gay Unions," *Hawaii Star-Bulletin*, http://starbulletin.com/97/02/24/news/story2.html (last accessed April 24, 2001).

6. Frank Newport, "American Attitudes toward Homosexuality Continue to Become More Tolerant," Press Release, Gallup News Service, June 4, 2001, http://www.gallup.com/poll/releases/pr010604.asp (last accessed October 29, 2001).

7. Christopher Lisotta, "6 in 10 Americans OK Gay Unions," planetout.com, May 15, 2003, http://www.planetout.com/pno/news/article.html?2003/05/15/2 (last accessed May 23, 2005). The article is based on Gallup poll data.

8. Associated Press poll results found at http:/pollingreport.com/civil.htm (last accessed July 17, 2002). A 2002 poll found similar results: 71 percent of respondents favored hospital visitation rights, 60 percent supported joint property rights, 59 percent supported inheritance laws, and 48 percent supported same-sex Social Security survivor benefits. See "National Survey Shows Growing Support for Same-Sex Partner Rights," *PR Newswire*, July 11, 2002.

9. *Los Angeles Times* poll, November 15–18, 2003, http://pollingreport.com/civil.htm (last accessed November 20, 2003).

10. CNN/*USA Today*/Gallup poll. June 27–29, 2003. Archived at PollingReport.com, http://pollingreport.com/civil (last accessed July 15, 2003).

11. Shawn Hubler, "Acceptance of Gays Is Now Widespread—but Same-Sex Marriage Could Be the Biggest Battle," *Los Angeles Times*, August 31, 2003, A1; Will Lester, "Poll: Majority Wants Gay Marriage Ban," *Associated Press*, August 18, 2003; "Strong Support Is Found for Ban on Same-Sex Marriage," *New York Times*, December 21, 2003, A1.

12. Exit poll data archived at CNN.com Election 2004 Election Results, http://www.cnn.com/ELECTION/2004/pages/results/states/US/P/00/epolls.0.html (last accessed May 23, 2005).

13. CNN/USA *Today*/Gallup poll. September 19–21, 2003. Archived at PollingReport.com, http://pollingreport.com/civil2htm (last accessed May 23, 2005).

14. Pew Research Center for the People and the Press and Pew Forum on Religion and Public Life survey, October 15–19, 2003. Archived at PollingReport.com, http://pollingreport.com/civil.htm (last accessed November 20, 2003).

15. Ibid.

16. University of Connecticut Press Release, "New England Poll," May 20, 2004, http://www.news.uconn.edu/2004/may2004/rel04062.htm (last accessed August 17, 2004).

17. Frank Phillips, "Poll Finds Split Over Marriage Amendment," *Boston Globe*, April 6, 2004.

18. University of New Hampshire polls showed 54 percent support for "civil marriage licenses" in 2003 and 55 percent support in 2004. "UNH poll shows support for gay marriage," Associated Press, February 25, 2004. A Zogby poll found 55 percent support for same-sex marriage in New Jersey. Tom Bell, "Advocates Say Poll Shows New Jersey Voters Back Gay Marriage," Associated Press, July 28, 2003. In Connecticut, support for civil unions is high, 74 percent, and opinion on same-sex marriage is more split with 46 percent in favor and 49 percent opposed (this is very similar to opinion in Massachusetts). University of Connecticut Press Release, "Uconn Poll: Same-Sex Marriage and Civil Unions," April 5, 2004, http://www.news.uconn.edu/2004/aor2004/rel04039.htm (last accessed August 12, 2004). A Quinnipiac University poll showed 52 percent support for civil unions and 37 percent support for same-sex marriage in New York. "Poll: Most New Yorkers Oppose Gay Marriage Ban, Back Helping Poor Schools," Associated Press, April 15, 2004.

19. Lisa Leff, "Poll: Californians Split on Subject of Same-Sex Marriage," Associated Press, August 29, 2003; Mark DiCamillo and Mervin Field, "California Voters Disapprove of Same-Sex Marriage," Field Poll Press Release #2109, February 26, 2004,

http://www.field.com/fieldpollonline/subscribers/ RLS2109.pdf (last accessed October 15, 2004)

20. "Poll: Most Favor Legal Benefits for Gays, but Not Marriage," Associated Press, March 29, 2004.

21. Jeff Mapes, "54 Percent in Oregon Oppose Same-Sex Marriage, Poll Says," OregonLive.com (*The Oregonian*), March 7, 2004, http://www.oregonlive.com/special/gaymarriage/index.ssf?/special/oregonian/gaymarriage/040307_poll.html (last accessed August 25, 2004).

22. Tom Held, "Most Oppose Same-Sex Marriage," *Milwaukee Journal Sentinel*, JSOnline, September 18, 2003, http://www.jsonline.com/news/state/sep03/170817.asp (last accessed December 18, 2003); Stacy Forster, "Majority Favor Marriage Restriction," *Milwaukee Journal Sentinel*, JSOnline, April 11, 2004, http://www.jsonline.com/news/state/apr04/221662.asp (last accessed April 14, 2004).

23. Jonathan Roos, "Most Iowans Oppose Same-Sex Marriage," DesMoines Register.com, October 17, 2003, http://desmoinesregister.com/news/stories/c44788998/22523914.html (last accessed August 12, 2004).

24. Ken Kusmer, "Gay Activists Encouraged by Poll Numbers," Associated Press, May 24, 2004.

25. Kathleen Gray, "Poll Shows Solid Support for Gay Marriage Ban," *Detroit Free Press*, July 12, 2004.

26. "Poll: "80 Percent of Alabamians Oppose Gay Marriage," Associated Press, March 15, 2004; Mike Dunne, "Poll: La. Voters Oppose Gay Marriage," 2theadvocate.com, August 12, 2004, http://www.2the advocate.com/news/poll2003/stories/new_0105gay001.shtml (last accessed October 15, 2004). The support in Louisiana may have also included those who favor civil unions, since the question asked about "legal status for same sex couples similar to that provided married couples."

27. Tamara Lush, "Floridians Oppose Gay Marriage," *St. Petersburg Times* online, March 8, 2004, http://www.sptimes.com/2004/03/08/State/Floridians_oppose_gay.shtml (last accessed October 16, 2004).

28. Leff, "Poll: Californians Split on Subject of Same-Sex Marriage."

29. Held, "Most Oppose Same-Sex Marriage." This is purely anecdotal, but the students in my classes at St. Norbert College, a Catholic college in Wisconsin, are generally quite supportive of the idea of same-sex marriage.

30. CBS News/*New York Times* poll, July 13–27, 2003. Archived at PollingReport.com, http://pollingreport.com/civil (last accessed December 30, 2003).

31. Leff, "Poll: Californians Split on Subject of Same-Sex Marriage."

32. CBS News/*New York Times* poll, December 10–13, 2003. Archived at PollingReport.com, http://pollingreport.com/civil (last accessed December 30, 2003).

33. National Public Radio Poll, December 10–15, 2003, Archived at PollingReport.com, http://pollingreport.com/civil (last accessed December 30, 2003).

34. CNN/*USA Today*/Gallup poll, April 29-May 1, 2005. Archived at PollingReport.com, http://pollingreport.com/civil.htm (last accessed May 23, 2005).

35. Action Wisconsin Primary Survey 2002, http://www.actionwisconsin.org/primarysurvey02.html (last accessed September 8, 2002).

36. Joel Siegel, "Dems Back N.Y. Law on Gay Unions," *New York Daily News*, July 20, 2002, 22.

37. Carla Marinucci, "Kerry Backs Full Rights for Same-Sex Couples," *San Francisco Chronicle*, SFGate.com, March 4, 2004, http://www.sfgate.com/cgi-bin/article.cgi?f=/c/a/2004/03/04/MNG8H5E0RC1.DTL (last accessed October 20, 2004).

38. Christy Harvey, "Optimism Out Duels Pessimism," *Wall Street Journal*, September 16, 2001, A10.

39. *Boston Globe* poll, May 4–9, 2005. Archived at PollingReport.com, http://pollingreport.com/civil.htm (last accessed May 23, 2005).

40. Frank Newport, "American Attitudes toward Homosexuality Continue to Become More Tolerant," Gallup News Service, June 4, 2001.

41. Quoted in Adam Lisberg, "House Agonized over Civil Unions," http://www.burlingtonfreepress.com/samesex/newstory58.htm (last visited April 25, 2001).

42. Ibid.

43. See Stuart Scheingold, *The Politics of Rights: Lawyers, Public Policy, and Political Change*, 2nd. ed. (Ann Arbor: University of Michigan Press), 212–18.

44. William N. Eskridge, Jr., *Equality Practice: Civil Unions and the Future of Gay Rights* (New York: Routledge, 2001), 164.

45. Quote in ibid., 146.

46. For another discussion and critique of the Rosenberg framework similar to mine, see Evan Gerstmann, *Same-Sex Marriage and the Constitution* (New York: Cambridge University Press, 2004), especially chapters eight and nine. Gerstmann also defends a rights-based approach to same-sex marriage that relies, to a significant degree, on litigation. He critiques equal protection approaches, preferring to use a fundamental rights approach. Both, in my view, are supportive of a richer liberalism.

## CHAPTER 12

1. For a discussion of the cultural differences between the two nations, see Michael Adams, *Fire and Ice: The United States, Canada and the Myth of Converging Values* (Toronto: Penguin Canada, 2003).

2. William Safire, "On Same-Sex Marriage," *New York Times*, December 1, 2003, http://www.nytimes.com/2003/12/01/opinion/01SAFI.html (last accessed December 1, 2003).

3. See the discussion of Lowi and McConnell in Chapter 1.

# Index

Abella, Roaslie, 184
abortion, 79–80, 90
Adams, John, 49
*Adarand Constuctors v. Pena* (1995), 171
adoption rights, 30, 130, 135
adultery, 65
affirmative action, 61, 171
AIDS/HIV, 40, 57, 81, 102, 107, 141
Ajello, Edith, 96
Alaska, 125–29, 162
Allen, Diane, 150
Alliance for Marriage, 150
Alliance Party (Canada), 169, 179–80, 183, 184
American Civil Liberties Union (ACLU), 21, 71,
    75, 101, 128; and same-sex marriage, 107,
    108, 112, 160; and sodomy laws, 95
American Law Institute (ALI), 67–68, 75,
    93–94, 98, 103; and Model Penal Code, 22,
    64, 66, 68–69, 70, 78
Amestoy, Jeffrey, 132–35, 138
Andersen, Ellen, 10, 102
Anderson, John S., 91–92
*Andrews v. Law Society of British Columbia*
    (1989), 173–74
antidiscrimination laws, 52–53, 55–56, 58, 60,
    90, 116; in Canada, 172–73, 175; and gay
    rights litigation, 105; in Hawaii, 109, 113; in
    New York, 152; in Oregon, 158; in Vermont,
    130. *See also* discrimination
antimiscegenation laws, 111, 161, 172. *See also*
    interracial marriage; race
Arizona, 96, 97, 160–62
Arkansas, 93–94
arrogance, 128, 137, 180; liberalism and, 35–36,
    46–47, 138
Atiyah, Patricia, 2
Atkins, Kenneth, 192–93

Backer, Larry Cata, 68–69
Baehr, Nina, 107
*Baehr v. Lewin* (1993), 90, 107–15, 135, 147,
    153, 155; litigation of, 107–12, 118, 121–22;
    political reaction to, 112–15. *See also* Hawaii;
    same-sex marriage
Baer, Judith, 44

Bakan, Joel, 12, 48, 165, 168
*Baker v. Nelson* (1971), 105
*Baker v. State of Vermont* (1998), 130–43, 147,
    157, 160, 193–94; litigation of, 130–35;
    political reaction to, 135–43, 152. *See also*
    same-sex marriage
Ball, Carlos, 45
Basic Rights Oregon (BRO), 156, 158
Baum, Lawrence, 30
Bearden, Frank, 157, 159
Beasley, Dorothy Toth, 70
Bellow, Saul, 57
Benson, Craig, 135, 142
Bentham, Jeremy, 3
Berlin, Isaiah, 34–35, 36
Bickel, Alexander, 11
Bill C-23 (Modernization of Benefits and
    Obligations Act), 179–81
Bill of Rights (Canada), 167–68
Bill of Rights (U.S.), 50, 170, 186
Binnie, William, 177
Birmingham, Thomas, 145
Blackmun, Harry, 23–25, 44
Blackstone, William, 91
Blair, Robert, 182
Blasius, Mark, 39–42
Bloc Quebecois (Canada), 172, 178, 179, 184
blood relatives, 138, 142. *See also* same-sex
    marriage laws
Bloom, Allan, 58
Bogard, David, 93
Bogart, A. E., 170
Bonauto, Mary, 131, 146
*Boutilier v. INS* (1967), 22–23, 24
*Bowers v. Hardwick* (1986), 1, 28–29, 83, 102,
    176; and *Campbell* case, 75; and *Lawrence*
    case, 98, 99; and *Powell* case, 85; and privacy,
    23, 24–25, 44, 67, 71; and public opinion,
    100, 191; and *State v. Lopes,* 96
Boxer, Barbara, 116
Bradley, Bill, 190
Brandeis, Louis, 23, 84
Brause, Jay, 125–27
*Breese v. Smith* (1972), 126
Brennan, William, 24, 31, 72

British Columbia Law Institute, 185
Britt, Morgan, 119–20
*Brown v. Board of Education* (1954), 5
Bryant, Anita, 93
buggery, 62–63. *See also* sodomy laws
Burger, Warren, 23, 24, 72
Burns, Walter, 111–12
Bush, George W., 82, 161, 190
Bussiere, Elizabeth, 3

California, 147, 153–56, 160, 189; and Oregon, 158; San Francisco, 64, 153, 155
Calogero, Pascal, 87
*Campbell v. Sundquist* (1996), 75–76, 88, 89, 94, 101
Canada, 1–2, 165–86; and affirmation action, 61; and *Andrews* case, 174; and Canadian Alliance, 183, 184; civil rights in, 168, 169, 172, 173, 192; civil unions in, 1, 180, 183, 185; conservatism in, 18, 169, 179–80, 183, 184; and *Egan* case, 174–77; and equality, 168, 170–72, 173–76, 178–79; and gay rights litigation, 17; group politics, 10–11, 171; and *Law* case, 176–77; liberalism of, 34, 165–66; Liberal Party, 168, 169, 179–81, 183–85; and *M. v. H.* case, 176–79; marriage policy of, 18; and Massachusetts, 147; and negative liberty, 37–38; New Democratic Party, 172–73, 176, 178, 180, 184; and policy change, 166, 195–98; Reform/Alliance Party, 169, 179–80; rights revolution of, 167–72; and Rosenberg, 8; same-sex marriage in, 7, 9, 20, 173, 185; Tories in, 169, 170, 184; *vs.* U.S. political culture, 10, 170. *See also* Charter of Rights and Freedoms; Parliament (Canada); Supreme Court, Canada
Canady, Charles, 115
Canns, Julius, 135, 141
Canon, Bradley, 30
Carmolli, Diane, 137
Carroll, Jimmy, 79
Cauchon, Martin, 183
cause lawyers, 99, 131, 159, 162, 192, 195
Cayetano, Benjamin, 118, 122, 126
Chandler, Harriette, 145
Chang, Kevin, 121–22
Charter of Rights and Freedoms (Canada), 12, 19, 34, 48, 179–86; adoption of, 167; and Canadian Supreme Court, 169; and *M. v. H.*, 1; and minority protection, 11
Chayes, Abram, 2, 5, 8
children, 64, 145–46, 150; adoption rights, 30, 130, 135

Chisum, Warren, 81
Chretien, Jean, 169
*Christenson v. State* (1991), 85
Christianity, 46. *See also* conservatism; morality; religion
Chumbly, Avery, 123
*City of Dallas v. England* (1993), 80, 82
civil rights, 40, 125, 136, 148, 185; in Canada, 168, 169, 172, 173, 192; and civil rights movement, 3, 5, 116; and lesbian politics, 42; and sodomy laws, 62; and state courts, 28, 31–32
civil unions, 51, 137, 139–43, 197; in California, 154–55; in Canada, 1, 180, 183, 185; in Connecticut, 151–52; in Massachusetts, 146–46; in Oregon, 157; U.S. public opinion of, 187–93; in Vermont, 132, 151
Clark, Joe, 165
Coles, Matt, 107
Commission on Sexual Orientation and the Law (Hawaii), 117–21
common benefits clause, 133, 135, 144
common law marriage, 174, 176–78, 181, 182
*Commonwealth v. Bonadio* (Pennsylvania, 1980), 94
*Commonwealth v. Wasson* (Kentucky, 1992), 74, 94
communitarianism, 44–47, 47–48, 194
community, 42; and liberalism, 34–35
Congress, U.S., 2–3, 64, 180; and DOMA, 115–17
Connecticut, 151–52, 160, 189. *See also Griswold v. Connecticut* (1965)
Connolly, Thomas, 144–45
conservatism, 4, 12, 52, 148, 178; in Canada, 18, 169, 179–80, 183, 184; and Republican Party, 44, 188, 190; and Sullivan, 56, 58
Conservative Party (Canada), 18, 169, 180
Constant, Benjamin, 34–35, 44
Constitution, U.S., 1, 14, 27, 31, 74; Bill of Rights, 50, 170, 186; and feminism, 43; First Amendment, 21, 25–26, 71; and morality, 91
Copelon, Rhonda, 43
Cordy, Robert, 148
Cornyn, John, 81–82
Cott, Nancy, 37
counter-majoritarianism, 186. *See also* majoritarianism
counter-mobilization, 5. *See also* legal mobilization
courts: Canadian, 32; Canadian *vs.* U.S., 17–20; constraints on, 5–6, 162–63, 191; as policymakers, 2–4, 7, 8, 10–11, 30–32, 114,

134, 151; Rosenberg's view of, 4–5; and
social change, 187–94, 195–98; and state
cross-citation, 163; U.S., 4–5. *See also* federal
courts; state courts; policy making in courts;
Supreme Court
Cowin, Judith, 148
Cox, Barbara, 107
crimes against nature, 87–88, 94, 97
Criminal Law Advisory Group, 65
cruel and unusual punishment, 87, 88, 95
culture: gay, 63; political, 9–10, 18, 102, 150,
170
Cummings, Michele, 139, 142
Cuomo, Andrew, 190

Dahl, Robert, 5, 6
*Dale v. Boy Scouts of America* (2000), 26, 150
Dancel, Genora, 107
Daniels, Matt, 150
date rape, 87
Davis, Gray, 154
*Davis v. Davis* (1992), 76
Dean, Howard, 135, 139, 141–42
deCarteret Cory, Peter, 175
Declaration of Independence, 50–51
Defense of Marriage Act (DOMA), 12, 115–17,
121, 161; in Canada, 178–80; mini state
DOMAs, 125, 143, 144, 152, 159, 160
Delvin, Patrick, 46, 68, 88
D'Emilio, John, 63
democracies, 11, 43, 51, 53–54, 55, 197
Democrats, 188–90
DiCamillo, Mark, 190
Dickson, Brian, 168
Dinan, John, 102
discrimination, 19, 25–27, 88, 99, 125; and
gender, 106, 109, 123, 127, 133, 135; against
homosexuals, 26–27, 29, 90, 117, 174–75;
laws on, 25–27; racial, 116; and sexual
minorities, 117, 120–21, 132–33, 145, 157,
174–75. *See also* antidiscrimination law
diversity, 38, 68, 171; of judges, 13
*Doe v. Commonwealth's Attorney* (Virginia,
1976), 71
DOMA. *See* Defense of Marriage Act
domestic partnerships, 51, 110, 115, 117–20,
139–41; in Alaska, 127; in Arizona, 161; in
California, 153–56; Democratic support of,
190; in Hawaii, 112; in Massachusetts, 145; in
New Jersey, 150–51; in New York, 152; in
Oregon, 157–58; and sodomy laws, 43; U.S.
public opinion of, 187–88, 191; in Vermont,
132, 134, 135–37

Dooley, John, 132, 134
Douglas, Stephen A., 13, 49–50, 54, 61
Douglas, William O., 23, 71–72, 79
Downing, William, 159
Dugan, Gene, 125–27
Dworkin, Ronald, 13, 37 38, 45, 47

Edwards, John, 137
EGALE/Egale Canada (advocacy group), 173,
181
*Egan v. Canada* (1995), 174–77
election of judges, 101, 163
Elshtain, Jean Bethke, 36, 53–54, 59, 168
Ely, John Hart, 27
Employment Nondiscrimination Act, 116
Enoch, Craig, 81–82
Epp, Charles, 2, 11, 169
Epstein, Gloria, 176–77
equality, 9, 12–13, 40, 116, 135; in Canada, 168,
173–76, 178–79; and equal concern and
respect, 174–75; and equality practice, 45; in
federal courts, 26–28; language of, 193; and
liberalism, 33–34; and litigation, 192–93;
litigation and, 159; and marriage, 163; and
positive freedom, 50; for racial minorities, 51;
for sexual minorities, 54; and sodomy laws,
79, 101; in U.S. Constitution, 31–32; in
Vermont, 130
equal protection, 87, 92, 104, 116, 120, 147; in
Alaska, 126–28; in Arkansas, 93; in
California, 155; in Canada, 170–72; federal,
90; in Hawaii, 109–11, 119–21, 123–25; in
Massachusetts, 144–45, 149–50; in New
Jersey, 150–51; in Oregon, 156; and sodomy
laws, 102; by state, 90; in Vermont, 133,
135–38
Equal Rights Amendment (Texas), 90
Equal Rights Amendment (Washington), 106
Eskridge, William, 45, 51, 63, 64, 193–94
Ettelbrick, Paula, 107

federal courts (U.S.), 1, 3, 6, 15, 21–32;
conservatism of, 29–30, 32; and gay rights, 19
federalism, 30, 32, 163
Feeley, Malcolm, 8, 11, 101, 163
feminism, 45–46, 61, 107
Finlayson, George, 177–78
Finnis, John, 46–47
First Amendment, 21, 25–26, 71
Fisher, Jeff, 82
Florida, 30, 160, 189
Flory, Peg, 138–39, 142
Foley, Daniel, 108–9, 114, 122, 124

Forrester, Douglas, 150
Foster, Mike, 90
Foucault, Michel, 38–39, 40–41, 42
*Foundations of the Metaphysics of Morals*
   (Kant), 85
Frank, Barney, 116
free choice, 153
freedom, 13, 17, 52, 54, 66. *See also* negative
   freedom; positive freedom
freedom to marry, 130, 139, 141
friendship, 57–58
"full faith and credit clause," 111, 115

Galanter, Marc, 16–17, 162
Galston, William, 36
Gammage, Robert, 81–82
Gardner, Tryon, 90, 92
Garrison, Sam, 95
Gay and Lesbian Advocates and Defenders
   (GLAD), 96, 131, 144–46, 149, 152, 160
*Gay and Lesbian Politics* (Blasius), 40
gay culture, 63
gay liberation, 38–39, 52, 55, 105
gay magazines, obscenity law and, 21–22
gay politics, 33–48; and Blasius and Warner,
   39–42; and communitarianism, 44–47; and
   lesbians, 42–44; and majoritarianism, 35–36;
   and negative freedom, 37–38; and positve
   freedom, 34–35; and queer critiques, 38–39;
   and rights rejection, 47–48
gay rights, 7, 21–32, 195–98; activists for, 99,
   106; and arrogance, 36; and *Boutilier* case,
   22–23, 24; Canadian *vs.* U.S., 10, 17–20, 48;
   and communitarianism, 45–46; and *Dale* case,
   26–27; and federal courts (U.S.), 1, 6, 15–16,
   19, 21–32; and *Hurley* case, 25–26; and
   judges, 13–14, 102; and *Lawrence* case, 29,
   78; and legislation, 70; and liberalism, 12–13,
   49, 59–61; and litigation, 8–9, 10, 17, 105,
   192–94; and negative liberty, 38, 52–55; and
   *ONE* case, 21–22; and *Romer* case, 27–28;
   and state courts, 30–32; and Stonewall Riots,
   104; Sullivan on, 52–59. *See also* privacy;
   same-sex marriage; sodomy laws
gay rights groups, 115; litigation strategies of,
   8–9, 17, 62, 71, 105, 130–31
Geertz, Clifford, 7
gender, 63; and discrimination, 109–11, 123,
   127, 133, 135
George, Robert, 46, 47, 50
Georgia, 23, 25, 71, 90, 99; and DOMA, 143;
   and *Powell* case, 85–86, 88, 100
Gerstmann, Evan, 28
*Getting Specific* (Phelan), 42

Gill, Thomas, 118–19
Gill-Jefferson, Carolyn, 88–89
Gillman, Howard, 9
Glendon, Mary Ann, 3, 9, 48
Glick, Henry, 30–31
Goldberg, Susanne, 90
Goldberg-Hiller, Jonathan, 5
Golden, Mike, 91
Gonthier, Charles Doherty, 178
Goodrich, Herbert, 64–65
*Goodridge v. Dept. of Public Health* (2003),
   148, 157, 159, 160, 190
Gore, Al, 190
Gorman, Chris, 74
Graulty, Rey, 120–21, 124
Greany, John, 147, 148
Greenstone, J. David, 19, 49–50, 60–61; and
   Kahn, 14; and liberalism, 12–13, 24, 33, 45
*Griswold* v. *Connecticut* (1965), 71, 77–79, 109;
   and privacy, 23, 69, 72, 98, 105; and *Roe v.
   Wade,* 23, 67, 98
group rights, 10–11, 171
*Gryczan* v. *Montana* (1993), 83, 84
Gunther, Gerald, 72

Haider-Markel, Donald, 70
Halcomb, Charles, 93
Halperin, David, 39
Hand, Learned, 64–65
Hardwick, Michael, 24–25
Harlan, John M., 22, 67
Harper, Stephen, 184
Hart, H. L. A., 67–69, 88–89, 98
Hartz, Louis, 34
hate crime laws, 52–53, 56, 58, 60, 81; in
   Canada, 172; in Vermont, 130
Hawaii, 5, 90, 107–25, 138, 146, 161; and
   Alaska, 126; and *Baehr* litigation, 107–12,
   118, 121–22; and *Baehr* political reaction,
   112–15; and California, 153; and civil unions,
   155; and Commission on Sexual Orientation
   and the Law, 117–21; and DOMA, 115–17;
   and legislation, 112–15, 122–25, 162; public
   opinion in, 187; and Washington, 106
Hayashi, Yoshimi, 110, 112
Heen, Walter, 110, 112
Hervey, Barbara Parker, 93
Hicks, Richard, 159–60
Hilliard, Marie, 152
Himmelfarb, Gertrude, 57
Hingtgen, Steve, 137
Hirsch, Harry, 10, 45
Hirschl, Ran, 2
HIV/AIDS, 40, 57, 81, 102, 107, 141

Hochschild, Jennifer, 11
Hofstadter, Richard, 28
*Holdman v. Olim* (1978), 110
*Hollow Hope, The* (Rosenberg), 4
Holmes, Oliver Wendell, 23–24
homosexuality, 23, 63, 66, 78, 81, 128;
   lesbian-feminism, 38; lesbian politics, 42–44.
   *See also* gay rights; sexual minorities
Homosexual Practices Act (Tennessee), 75–76,
   101
Horowitz, Donald, 5, 6
hospital visitation rights, 152, 154
Hudson, Harvey, 91–92
Hull, Jane, 97
human rights, 18, 172
Human Rights Act (Canada), 172
Humphries, Tom, 108
Hunter, Nan, 107
*Hurley v. Irish-American Gay, Lesbian, and*
   *Bisexual Group of Boston* (GLIB) (1995),
   25–26, 27, 29

individualism, 24, 33–35, 46, 48, 170; and Hart,
   68; and liberty, 52–55; and Lincoln, 50; in
   Montana, 83; and same-sex marriage, 55–56,
   60
inequality, 44. *See also* equality
institutionalism, 9–10, 14, 56, 147
interracial marriage, 104, 149. *See also*
   antimiscegenation law; race
Ireland, Roderick, 148
Iwase, Randy, 113

Jackson-Lee, Sheila, 116
Jacobs, Andrew, 86
Jefferson, Thomas, 49
Johnson, Denise, 134–35
*Jones v. Hallahan,* 106
judges, 2–3, 5–6, 13–16
judicial activism, 10, 74–75, 92, 112, 113, 197;
   in Canada, 167, 177, 184, 186
judicial decision making, 13–14
judicial policy making, 7–9, 11, 168; in Canada,
   169, 172. *See also* policy making in courts
judicial review, 1, 18
jurisprudence, 10, 11, 12, 80, 102, 195; Canadian
   constitutional, 168; equal protection, 15, 28;
   evolving, 147, 150; gay rights, 20, 196;
   liberal, 132; Oregon, 156–57, 163; privacy,
   24, 84–85; U.S. Constitutional, 23, 27, 171

Kahn, Ronald, 14, 16
Kainen, Michael, 137
Kammen, Michael, 8

Kant, Immanuel, 45, 85
Kaplan, Morris, 41
Karen, David, 75
Katz, Jonathan Ned, 39
Kennard, Joyce, 155
Kennedy, Anthony, 27–28, 29, 98–99
Kennedy, Patrick, 115
Kennedy, Ted, 116
Kentucky, 72–75, 99, 102, 106
Kerry, John, 190
Kinsey Report, 65
Klein, Robert, 109, 112
Knopff, Rainer, 169
Knowles, Tony, 126
Kobayashi, Ann, 113
Koch, Dale, 157
Koki, Stan, 114
Koppelman, Andrew, 111, 114
Kulongoski, Ted, 158

Lambda Legal and Empire State Pride, 152, 160
Lambda Legal Defense and Education Fund, 71,
   90, 93–94, 99, 107, 150; and Homosexual
   Practices Act, 101; in Washington, 159
Lamer, Antonio, 169
language rights, 167–68, 171
Laskin, Bora, 167
Law Commission of Canada, 184–85
*Lawrence v. Texas* (2003), 1, 62, 78, 90–94,
   160–61; and *Bowers* case, 29, 100, 102, 103;
   and gay rights opposition, 7, 190; and
   Massachusetts, 147; and Michigan, 96; and
   privacy, 29, 98–99; and social change, 195,
   196–97; and Virginia, 95
*Law v. Canada* (1999), 176–77
lawyers. *See* cause lawyers
legal elites, 22, 184–86
legal language, 161, 191
legal liberalism, 187–94
legal mobilization, 5, 16–17, 162
legal norms, 6, 7, 184–86, 194
legal racism, 11
legal realism, 6, 12, 37, 65
*LEGAL v. State* (1998), 87
legislation, 2, 15, 112–15, 114; in Alaska,
   125–28; in Arizona, 161; in California, 153; in
   Canada, 174, 183; and domestic partnerships,
   153–56; and gay rights litigation, 192; for *M.*
   *v. H.,* 178; and marriage definition, 147–48; in
   Massachusetts, 163; in Oregon, 157; and
   policy change, 144–45; problems with,
   151–52; and sodomy laws, 96; in Texas,
   92–93; *vs.* courts as policymakers, 151
Leonard, Arthur, 104, 106

lesbian-feminism, 38
lesbian politics, 42–44
*Letter Concerning Toleration, A* (Locke), 54
Levi, Jennifer, 145
Levinson, Steven, 111–12
Levitt, Linda, 132
Lewin, John, 108, 116
liberalism, 3, 14, 33–48, 49–61, 98; and
    arrogance, 35–36, 46–47, 138; and Blackmun,
    24–25; in Canada, 173, 178, 185; Canadian
    *vs.* U.S., 17–20, 34, 37–38; and civil unions
    *vs.* marriage, 143; and communitarianism,
    44–47; and gay rights, 33–35, 59–61; in
    Hawaii, 123; humanist, 49; and *Lawrence*
    case, 195; legal, 187–94; and lesbian politics,
    42–44; and libertarianism, 34, 44, 50, 99, 117,
    134, 161, 164; and Lincoln, 49–51; and *M. v.
    H.* case, 176–79; and majoritarian politics,
    35–36; queer critique of, 38–39; reform, 49;
    and rights, 12–13, 47–48, 195–98; and
    sodomy laws, 67–69; and Sullivan, 52–59; in
    U.S., 8, 37, 179, 193; in Vermont, 133–34,
    137, 140; *vs.* majoritarianism, 10–11
Liberal Party (Canada), 168, 169, 183–85; and
    Bill C-23, 179–81
liberals, modern, 52–53, 148
liberationists, 38–39, 52, 55, 105
libertarianism, 33, 74, 99–100, 170, 193; and
    *Bowers* case, 102; in Canada, 171; concepts of
    freedom, 17, 66, 117; and conservatism, 56,
    100, 135, 196; liberalism and, 34, 44, 50, 99,
    117, 134, 161, 164; and morality, 129, 190;
    and Texas, 78, 97
Liebson, Charles, 73–74
Lincoln, Abraham, 13, 49–51
Linn, Diane, 156, 158
Lippert, William, 137, 138, 140, 194
Lipset, Seymour Martin, 19, 170
Little, Thomas, 136–37, 138, 142
Livingston, Judith, 137
Locke, John, 54–55
Louisiana, 86–90
*Love Undetectable* (Sullivan), 57
*Loving v. Virginia* (1940), 90, 120, 121, 147,
    161
Lowi, Theodore, 5–16, 198
Lowther, Eric, 178, 180
Lum, Herman, 112

*M. v. H.* (1999), 19, 176–79
McCann, Michael, 6–7, 17
McConnell, Grant, 15–16, 198
McConnell, Michael, 105

McCormick, Michael, 93, 141
McCormick, Peter, 166
Macedo, Stephen, 46
McGreevy, James, 150–51
McIntyre, William, 174
Mackinnon, Bill, 137
McLachlin, Beverly, 169–70
McLellan, Anne, 178–79
McMurtry, Roy, 184
Madison, James, 53–54, 55
majoritarianism, 10–11, 35–36, 101–2, 117, 162;
    and Alliance for Marriage, 150; in California,
    155; in Canada, 170, 177–78, 179; and civil
    unions, 141; counter-majoritarianism, 186;
    and Massachusetts, 150; and policy change,
    192–93; *vs.* rights-based litigation, 185
Mandel, Michael, 167–68
Manfredi, Christopher, 170
Mansfield, Harvey, 57
Mansfield, Steve, 93
*Manual Enterprises Inc. v. Day* (1962), 22
*Marbury v. Madison* (1803), 113
marijuana, 81
marriage, 23–24, 36, 77, 104, 157; benefits of,
    12, 119, 185, 191; in Canada, 174, 183–84;
    common law, 1, 174, 176–78, 181, 182;
    definition of, 29, 105–6, 131, 146, 180–84,
    193; and individualism, 55–56; licenses
    denied same-sex couples, 160; licenses
    granted same-sex couples, 144, 149, 153, 155,
    156–57, 182; and marriage laws, 99; right to,
    127, 144, 159; tautology of, 109. *See also*
    civil unions; domestic partnerships; same-sex
    marriage
Marshall, Margaret, 148
Marshall, Thurgood, 24, 72
Martin, Jim, 86
Martin, Paul, 184
Marxism, 38
Maryland, 95, 160
Massachusetts, 25–26, 96, 151, 160; and
    California, 155; and Oregon, 156; and public
    opinion, 149, 189, 190–92; same-sex
    marriage in, 144–50; and Vermont, 144,
    147, 163
Massachusetts Citizens for Marriage, 144–45.
    *See also* Defense of Marriage Act
    (DOMA)
Mather, Lynn, 7
Matheussen, John, 150
Matsunga, Richard, 114, 124
May, Steve, 97
Meier, Kenneth, 70

Melnick, Shep, 2–3, 8
Menard, Real, 179–80
Michalski, Peter, 126–28
Michigan, 95–96
Midgen, Carole, 154
*Milford v. Worcester* (1810), 148
Mill, John Stuart, 67, 88, 102
Miller, Zell, 86
Miller Act, 64
Minnesota, 95, 105
Minow, Martha, 13
Missouri, 96, 161
Moats, David, 130–31
Modernization of Benefits and Obligations Act
    (Bill C-23), 179–81
Mohr, Richard, 62
Monahan, Patrick, 167
Montana, 83–85
Montesquieu, Baron de, 91
Moon, Ronald, 112, 123
Moore, Roy, 158
Morales, Dan, 80
morality, 20, 68, 89–90, 91, 98; in Arkansas, 93;
    and *Baker* case, 141; and *Bowers* case, 29; in
    Canada, 180; and homosexuality, 101, 132;
    and liberalism, 45–46, 137; and Lincoln, 50;
    in Louisiana, 87; politics of, 98, 100, 123, 129,
    139; and privacy, 74; and Republicans, 190;
    and same-sex marriage, 117, 119–20; and
    sodomy laws, 65–66, 79; Straussian, 56–58;
    and Sullivan, 52–59; in United States, 8,
    125
Morse, James, 132
Morton, Ted, 169
Moseley-Braun, Carol, 116
Murdoch, Joyce, 23, 25, 29
Murphy, Paul, 91–92
Murray, Susan, 130–31

Nakayama, Paula, 112
natural law, 11, 46–47
negative freedom, 20, 21–22, 29, 154, 156, 196;
    and *Bowers* case, 48; and Canada, 170, 179,
    180; and DOMA, 117; and gay rights, 52–55;
    insufficiency of, 37–38; and privacy, 27, 36; in
    U.S., 49, 50, 125. *See also* positive
    freedom
Nevada, 96
New Democratic Party (NDP, Canada), 172–73,
    176, 178, 180, 184
new institutionalism, 9–10
New Jersey, 150–51, 160, 189
New Left, 38–39

Newsom, Gavin, 153, 155, 156, 158
New York, 152, 160, 189
Nitka, Alice, 137–38
Nolan, Joseph, 25–26
Northwest Women's Law Center, 159
"notwithstanding clause" (Canada), 168,
    184
Nussbaum, Martha, 41–42, 45
Nystrom, Peter, 151–52

Oakeshott, Michael, 52, 56–59, 58
*Oakes* test, 174, 177, 182
O'Connor, Sandra Day, 99
*ONE* v. *Olesen,* 21–22
oppression, 43–44, 68
Oregon, 156–60, 189
Ortique, Revius, 87
Ostrander, Kent, 74

Parker, Judge, 65
Parliament (Canada), 168, 170, 172, 175, 179;
    and marriage definition, 181, 184; sovereignty
    of, 19
*Passel v. Fort Worth Independent School District*
    (1969), 80
Perry, Michael, 15
Phelan, Shane, 42–43, 45
Pincllo, Daniel, 13–14, 32, 101
Pisaturo, Michael, 151
Pitfield, Ian, 181–82
*Planned Parenthood v. Casey* (1992), 98
pluralism, 15–16
*Poe v. Ullman* (1961), 67
policy making in courts, 1–11, 30–32, 114, 134,
    151; and constitutive change, 6–9; constraints
    on, 5–6; legitimacy of, 10–11; and new
    institutionalism, 9–10; and social change,
    4–5, 195–98. *See also* public policy
Polikoff, Nancy, 107
political culture, 9–10, 102, 150; Canadian *vs.*
    U.S., 10, 170, 196
*Politics of Rights, The* (Scheingold), 4
Polland, Gary, 91
polling, 7, 188–90. *See also* public opinion
pornography, 108. *See also* obscenity
Porter, Mary, 30–31
positive freedom, 125, 158, 159, 193; and
    equality, 50; and liberalism, 34–35, 45,
    49
Posner, Richard, 187, 194
Potter, Harry III, 80–81
Powell, Lewis, 23, 24–25
*Powell v. Georgia* (1998), 85–86, 88, 100

power, 6, 39, 40–41, 42, 44, 163
Price, Deb, 23, 25, 29
Price, Warren III, 108
privacy, 23, 37, 40, 92, 100, 111; in Alaska,
    126–28; in California, 154; in Canada, 172,
    180; in Constitution, 31–32; and *Dale* case,
    26–27; in Hawaii, 108–9; in Massachusetts,
    145; and morality, 77–81; provisions, 90;
    sexual, 40, 66–67, 71–76, 72, 88, 95; and
    sexual minorities, 19, 83, 98, 102; and
    sodomy laws, 62, 93–94, 95–98; in U.S., 153,
    180; and Virginia, 94–95
privacy, right to, 19, 29, 43, 70–71, 105; in
    Alaska, 126–28; and *Davis* case, 76; in
    Georgia, 85–86; and *Lawrence* case, 98–99; in
    Louisiana, 86–90; in New Jersey, 150; and sex
    acts, 1, 40, 72, 88, 95; and sodomy laws, 62,
    95–98, 102; and *State* v. *Morales* (Texas),
    79–80. *See also* public *vs.* private domain
Privy Council (England), 166
procreation justification, 35–36, 113–14,
    120–21, 163; in Arizona, 160; in Canada, 175,
    177–78, 182, 183; in Hawaii, 110; in
    Massachusetts, 144, 148; in Montana, 63; and
    natural law, 46–47; in Vermont, 132; in
    Washington state, 106, 159
prostitution, 89, 109
public accommodation law (Massachusetts),
    25–26
public interest litigation, 30–31
public opinion, 6, 18, 184–91; on *Baker* case,
    136; in Canada, 184–86; in Massachusetts,
    149; and Rosenberg, 7, 187–91
public policy, 110, 113, 117–21; in Canada, 171;
    in Hawaii, 125; in Massachusetts, 148; and
    Rosenberg, 187. *See also* policy making in
    courts
public *vs.* private domain, 36, 43, 44, 52–58,
    69

queerness, 38–44. *See also* gay rights

race, 81, 111, 116, 121, 149; racial
    minorities, 51, 53, 54, 60–61; and racism,
    11, 38
Racicot, Marc, 84
*Ravelstein* (Bellow), 57
Rawls, John, 4, 13, 34, 37–38, 45, 86–89
Rayside, David, 173
Reed, Jack, 114
Reform/Alliance Party (Canada), 169, 183, 184;
    and Bill C-23, 179–80
Rehnquist, William, 24, 28, 72

Reich, Robert, 145
relationship equality, 154, 159, 184–85,
    188–90. *See also* equality; equal protection
    rights
religion, 46, 54, 57, 59, 81, 124; in Alaska, 127;
    and *Baker* case, 141; and civil unions, 137; in
    Virginia, 95. *See also* conservatism; morality;
    traditionalism
Republicans, 44, 188, 190
Rhode Island, 96–97, 151
Richards, Ann, 82
Richards, David A. J., 4, 37–38
Ridell, Troy, 7
rights, 2–3, 9–13, 20, 33–48, 196; and
    communitarianism, 44–47; and federal courts,
    15–16; for groups, 10–11, 171; human, 18,
    172; and individualism, 33–35, 83; language
    of, 3, 9–10, 193; and liberalism, 12–13,
    195–98; and litigation, 103, 185, 193; and
    majoritarianism, 35–37; and negative
    freedom, 37–38; politics of, 4, 17, 39–44, 99;
    queer critique of, 38–39; rejection of, 47–48;
    and rights revolution, 2–4, 3, 11; and
    Wolfenden Report, 69. *See also* gay rights;
    same-sex marriage; sodomy laws
rights-based litigation, 103, 185
Robb, Chuck, 116–17
Robinson, Beth, 130–31
Robinson, Svend, 180, 181
*Roe* v. *Wade* (1973), 5, 23, 67, 71, 98
*Romer* v. *Evans* (1996), 27–28, 99, 102,
    175
Romney, Mitt, 145, 149
Roosevelt, Franklin, 50
Rosehill, Linda, 125
Rosenberg, Gerald, 4–5, 6, 48, 164, 185,
    187–94; perspective of, 7, 191–94; and public
    opinion, 187–91
*Rosenberg* v. *Canada* (1986), 184
*Roth* v. *United States* (1957), 21–22
Rubenfeld, Abby, 75
Rubenstein, William, 112
Rubin, Edward, 8, 11, 101, 163
Rutherford Foundation, 118
*R.* v. *Oakes* (1986), 174, 177, 182

Safire, William, 196–97
same-sex marriage, 18, 98–100, 103, 195–98; in
    Alaska, 125–29; and *Baker*, 105; bans on,
    157, 160–61, 162; in California, 153–56; in
    Canada, 7, 9, 20, 173, 185; in Connecticut,
    151–52; and federal laws, 104; in Indiana,
    151; and individualism, 24, 34, 60; and *Jones*

case, 106; and liberalism, 33–35, 45; litigation
of, 20, 161–64, 181, 193; and *Loving* case,
104–5; in Massachusetts, 144–50; in New
Jersey, 150–51; in New York, 152; in Ontario,
173; opponents of, 35; in Oregon, 156–60;
and procreation, 35  36; in Rhode Island, 151;
and sodomy laws, 43, 100, 161; in state
courts, 12–13, 31–32, 150–52; and Sullivan,
52, 55–56, 59; in Texas, 90–91; U.S. public
opinion of, 187–94; in Washington state,
106–7, 159–60. *See also Baehr v. Lewin;
Lawrence v. Texas;* sodomy laws
Sandel, Michael, 44, 47
San Francisco, 64, 153, 155
Scalia, Antonin, 28, 99, 181, 196
Scheingold, Stuart, 3, 4, 5, 9, 17, 193
Schwarzenegger, Arnold, 155
Segal, Jeffrey, 13
segregation, 54, 111. *See also* race
Seidman, Steven, 38
sex acts, 23, 62–63, 77, 83; in Georgia, 85–86;
in Louisiana, 87; and privacy, 40, 72, 88, 95;
in Texas, 91. *See also* sodomy laws
sex crimes, 64, 68, 97
sexism, 111. *See also* discrimination;
gender
sexually transmitted diseases, 81; AIDS/HIV, 40,
57, 81, 102, 107
sexual minorities, 17, 21, 38, 64, 65, 99;
discrimination against, 117, 120–21, 132–33,
145, 157, 174–75; freedom of, 23;
homosexuality, 23, 63, 66, 78, 81, 128; legal
status of, 1, 22, 27–29, 62, 65, 68; and
liberalism, 42–43, 54; and Lincoln, 50–51;
and morality, 75–76; politics of, 10–11, 40;
and privacy, 19, 98, 102; protection for, 70,
83, 89; rights claims of, 3, 11–13, 19; and
Wolfenden Report, 66–69. *See also* gay rights;
gender
sexual orientation, 39; discrimination against,
26–27, 29, 90, 174–75; homosexuality, 23, 63,
66, 78, 81, 128. *See also* gay rights
Sharpe, Robert, 174
Sheldon, Marie, 118–19
Sheltra, Nancy, 141
Sherlock, Jeffrey, 83
Shon, James, 113
Shumlin, Peter, 139
*Singer v. Hara* (1974), 109, 159
Skoglund, Marilyn, 132, 135
slavery, 50, 54, 60–61
Smith, David, 124–25
Smith, Michael, 87

Smith, Miriam, 10
Smith, Rogers, 9
Snell, James, 168
Socarides, Charles, 119
social change, 20, 48, 76, 168; and litigation,
6–9, 193; and policy making in courts, 4–5, 7,
165, 195–98; and Rosenberg, 187–91
socialism, 170
sodomy laws, 20, 62–103, 193; in Arkansas,
93–94; and *Campbell* case, 75–76, 88, 89, 94,
101; in Canada, 172, 180; and discrimination,
111; in Georgia, 23, 25, 71, 85–86, 90, 99;
history of, 62–67; and individualism, 9, 34; in
Kentucky, 72–75, 99; and lesbian-feminism,
42–43; and liberalism, 67–69; and litigation,
71–72, 107; in Louisiana, 86–90; in Montana,
83–85; nonjudicial repeal of, 96–97; and
*Powell* case, 85–86, 88, 100; and privacy, 62,
95–98; reform of, 69–71; and state courts, 1,
12–13, 24, 31–32, 99–103, 163; in Tennessee,
75–76, 83, 84, 101; in Texas, 29, 62, 77–83,
90–93, 98–99; in Vermont, 141; in Virginia,
72, 94–95, 98; *vs.* same-sex marriage laws,
43, 100, 161
Sommers, Robert, 2
Souki, Joe, 118, 119–20, 123
Souter, David, 25–26
Sowle, Agnes, 156–57
Spaeth, Harold, 13
Spina, Francis, 147
Spitzer, Eliot, 152
state courts, 4–5, 30–32; and same-sex marriage,
12–13, 31–32, 150–52; and sodomy laws, 1,
12–13, 24, 31–32, 99–103, 163. *See also
specific state*
*State v. Baxley* (Louisiana, 1989), 87
*State v. Kam* (Hawaii, 1988), 108–9
*State v. Lopes* (Rhode Island, 1995), 96
*State v. Morales* (Texas, 1992), 79–80, 90
*State v. Smith* (Louisiana), 89
Stauffer, Robert, 120
Stephens, Robert, 73
Stevens, John Paul, 27, 72, 171
Stoddard, Tom, 107
Stonewall Riots, 104
Strauss, Leo, 46, 52, 56–59
Stychin, Carl, 18, 165
Sullivan, Andrew, 49, 52–59, 60, 168; and
same-sex marriage, 55–56
Sunstein, Cass, 134
Supreme Court, Canada, 1, 48, 166–67, 169–70,
174–80, 183–84; Canada, 1, 48, 166–67,
169–70, 174–80, 183–84

Supreme Court, U.S., 1, 3, 21–29, 62, 67, 102; and Bill of Rights, 168; and *Bowers* case, 85–86, 98; conservatism in, 32; and constitutional protection, 111; and discrimination laws, 109, 171–72; and DOMA, 161; and equality, 26–28, 150; and *Lawrence* case, 77, 195, 196; and *Loving* case, 104–5, 147; and Massachusetts, 189; obscenity cases, 21–22; and policy change, 191; and public opinion, 6; and right to marry, 127; and right to privacy, 23–24, 71–72; and *Romer* case, 175; Rosenberg on, 7; and sodomy laws, 23–24, 29, 83, 94; state courts and, 31. *See also individual justices*

Take It to the People, 135, 139, 141
*Tanner v. OHSU* (1998), 156–57, 159
Tarr, G. Alan, 30–31
Taylor, Mark, 86
Tennessee, 75–76, 83, 84, 101
Texas, 29, 62, 77–83, 90–93, 98–99. *See also Lawrence v. Texas*
*Texas State Employees Union v. Texas Dept. of Mental Health and Retardation* (1987), 79
*Theory of Justice, A* (Rawls), 4
Thielen, Cynthia, 113
Thomas, Clarence, 28, 171
Thorpe, Rochella, 158
Tom, Terrance, 113, 118, 120, 122–24
Toqueville, Alexis de, 2
Tories (Canada), 169, 170, 184
totalitarianism, 34–35
traditionalism, 82, 91, 114, 124, 147, 192; and liberalism, 20, 40, 44–47; in Vermont, 140
Tribe, Lawrence, 24, 73
Trudeau, Pierre, 167, 180
Tushnet, Mark, 48

United States, 1–2, 9, 176; and equal protection, 27, 31–32; and gay rights litigation, 17; group politics in, 10–11; judicial activism in, 169; liberalism in, 33–35; morality in, 52–55, 125; and negative freedom, 37–38, 49; partisan divisions within, 188; pluralism in, 15–16; and policy change, 195–98; and privacy, 153, 180; and Sullivan, 52–59, 60; *vs.* Canadian

political culture, 10, 170. *See also* Congress, U.S.; Constitution, U.S.; Supreme Court, U.S.

Varady, Carl, 108
Vaughan, Frederick, 168
Ventura, Jessie, 95
Vermont, 130–43, 144, 146, 157, 160; and *Baker* litigation, 130–35; and *Baker* political reaction, 135–43, 152; and California, 153, 154, 155; and civil unions law, 51; and legislature, 132–40, 142; and litigation, 192–93; lower courts in, 151; and Massachusetts, 144, 147, 163
Vinton, Michael, 137
violence, 60. *See also* hate crime laws
Virginia, 72, 94–95, 98, 101, 104, 172
*Virtually Normal* (Sullivan), 52, 58
Voeller, Bruce, 71
Von Beitel, Randy, 79
Voyer, Cathy, 137

Waihee, John David, 112, 126
Wakatsuki, James, 112
Walzer, Michael, 47
Warner, Michael, 39–42
Washington, D.C., 107
Washington state, 106–7, 156, 159–60, 160, 189
Wasson, Jeffrey, 72
Webster, Daniel, 51
Wechsler, Herbert, 64
Weld, William, 148
welfare, 8
Whig Party, 51, 170
White, Byron, 24
Whitmire, John, 81
Wilson, Pete, 153–54
Wilson, Woodrow, 50
Wisconsin, 189, 190
Wiseman, Patrick, 80–81
Wolfe, Alan, 185
Wolfenden Report, 66–67, 98, 172
Wolfson, Evan, 107
women, 43, 61, 141. *See also* gender; lesbian
Woods, Bill, 107–8
Wyden, Ron, 117

Yates, Leslie Brock, 92